The Trip That Took Itself

An American Zen Buddhist woman's
solo pilgrimage through SE Asia

Ellen Warburton

The Trip That Took Itself

Edited by Reba Fournier and Marie Simirenko
Photos by Michael Warburton

ISBN: 978-1-61170-221-7

Published by:

 **Robertson Publishing**™
www.RobertsonPublishing.com

Printed in the USA and UK on acid-free paper.
To purchase additional copies of this book go to:

amazon.com
barnesandnoble.com

"To all the people who helped me on my way and especially my granddaughter Katie, who will undoubtedly find her own magical path through this beautiful world."

—Ellen Warburton

Table of Contents

Chapter 1 - Starting Out

As I was leaving the safe cushion of a tour group, softened by a month's submission to the China Travel Service, which provided all our needs, meals, accommodations, where to go, what to look at, a tour companion asked, "Ellen, what are you going to do when you arrive in a new place late in the evening? Where are you going to stay without reservations?"

I replied vaguely, "I don't know". It wasn't as if I had been a world traveler before or knew how to travel. I'd only spent three weeks in Mexico seven years ago—no other time spent on my own away from the U.S. Yet I'd started out on a year's travel around the world with only an airline ticket to get me from country to country. I was fifty-two years old, and I'd decided to travel alone.

Scary? A little, but some strange readiness and excitement propelled me beyond the usual panic of facing unknown experiences. I wanted the adventure. I'd dreamed of it for years. Now was the time, and the urgency of the trip didn't even give me a chance to stock up on available guidebooks or historical information.

I dashed headlong into Asia with an open mind and a budget consciousness that prompted three vows: I would follow where the way seemed to lead; I would take the cheapest accommodations I could find; and I would travel in the way most people in the country traveled as much as I could—no taxis unless absolutely necessary.

I had already gotten confirmation of my last vow. On first arriving in Japan in September 1981, prior to my trip to China, I had been traveling with my friend, Chris, for several days. The sounds of an unfamiliar language surrounded us. We had asked a taxi driver what the fare was to reach an historical school where Japanese ceremonial tea service originated. We could hardly believe the answer of $40! With the help of many compassionate English-speaking Japanese, we figured out the bus route. The cost by bus was only 200 Yen or $1.00

That was to set the style of my travel—trusting that I would have help when I needed it, and believing in the friendliness of people everywhere. It had all happened so fast I didn't have time to think—which was perhaps the greatest gift of the whole trip.

I had gone to Maine for 2 months and suddenly returned one month early. The filmy vision of a trip around the world had already been gliding in and out of my thoughts ever since I'd come into some unexpected money. I often woke up with the gnawing questions: "What do you want to do when you travel? Why are you going? What do you want to learn?" I hadn't come up with any satisfactory answers, but the trust that I'd find one led to a series of events that clarified the direction of the trip.

One day, a friend showed me a brochure on a Buddhist and Christian Meditation Conference to be held the next week in Boulder, Colorado. A Zen master, a Quaker leader, and a Benedictine monk were to help participants of differing religious practices to share the common experience of meditation. It was scheduled for the following week. I immediately signed up.

Though I don't usually attend conferences, this one sounded interesting. It proved to be a marvelous integration of all my experiences of various religions. It confirmed the idea that words and dogma so often stymie communication between people, and block the understanding that comes with a deeper level of being together in silence.

Still there was no further impetus to action. I went home full of the euphoria I always get when people of "different views" have been together in an understanding way and have experienced their commonality. But I didn't know how to relate this to my travel plans. Then an old newsletter of three months' vintage fell into my hands. I seldom read newsletters, but my eye caught the fact that Eido Roshi, the Zen Master I'd enjoyed in Colorado, was leading a pilgrimage to China to visit historical spots where the Zen practice that I'd begun seven years before had originated.

With surprising alacrity I wrote to see if there were still room. Before the reply came, I learned that my friend, Chris, was going to bicycle through China on a tour, and the cost seemed exorbitant. So when I learned that my tour would last a week longer for the same price and that there was still space for me, I leaped at the chance. I felt as if I'd found a real bargain.

I had only three days to obtain a passport and express mail it to the group in New York. I tied up my affairs hurriedly; no time to study Chinese history; no time to decide where else I'd go. I drew up a "mileage ticket" with a cost-conscious travel agent, including as many stops along a continuous line around the world as I could think of. I could cancel any stops later if I wished but could only add others for an additional fee.

I knew only that the center of the trip would be to look at Asia from the roots of the religions that rested there—a tour of "the mind of the East", I thought then. Little did I realize it would also be a tour of my own mind.

There could not have been a more ignorant traveler! I had good intentions but was totally unschooled when it came to Asian history. Yet I began with a hopeful confidence that I could learn as I progressed.

I first began to realize that my trip would not go as planned, even the scheduled airline flights, when I discovered I could sit zazen, the Zen meditation practice, for a week at Eiheiji Betsuin, a monastery in Tokyo. I postponed my leaving Japan for a week and instead settled into the quiet routine of a Japanese temple.

Both Japanese and American Zen groups set aside several weeks a year for a more concentrated retreat than the daily sitting practice provides. These periods occur in April, December, and February. The sitting period in December draws many people who are not monks but who want to sit in the quiet atmosphere of a monastery for a short time.

Some students from the University of Tokyo, some business-men and women, a friend who was a nun, and I sat and lived in the monastery for the whole week.

The seven women slept in one room walled by sliding shoji screens, the eight men in another. By night the unfolded mats stretched wall to wall on the floor. We slept till the 5:30 morning bell signaled a rapid folding of mats. We quickly changed into the gray sitting skirts and tops that had been issued to us. Then working in teams we lifted the heavy bedding onto storage shelves hidden behind the sliding doors along the wall. In fifteen minutes the room was clear.

From my diary:

Eight men, seven women march silently in rows down across the Giant Buddha hall to the tiny sitting place where in the early morning young monks crowd the larger Zendo while lay practitioners sit in the long hallway outside.

Booming voices of the monks chanting leads our thinner chant. Then Silence. In the dim light we sit in a long line facing the wall. The hours pass amid sitting for 40 minute intervals, walking slowly for ten minutes, sitting again for several more periods, and then eating in silence.

Each day at work period, we form cleaning crews to polish already polished and dusted wood of shoji screens and to sweep some fallen leaves from walkways with brooms of tied twigs. We take short walks along the garden paths through the quiet, mossy graveyard where monuments rise, each with a fresh offering of flowers blowing in the chilly air.

How deep the sitting goes, into the core of me. After breakfast, when the monks leave to pursue their studies, we move into the larger Zendo, where rows of black round cushions rest on raised wood platforms which provide the beds where the monks sleep at night. The chants still ring in the stillness of my mind. We sit on and on.

Perhaps it was in that deep emptiness that my travels really began—taken from the silence inside. Out of what appeared at the time to be nothing—only sitting—came a host of adventures I could not have imagined.

Only smiles and eye contact, sometimes only walking together without words. It cemented the conviction that language is not the only way to reach across the differences in culture. There's a silent river of closeness we can all float on together.

It was in this quiet that I received the most powerful jolt into independence—one that I would use all through my trip. It happened during the most profound quiet after five days of sitting. It felt so still that all the world around me seemed to sink into a deep purple quiet of serenity. There was no need to talk, only to be.

Suddenly I was called to the telephone. It was Kobun, my teacher of Zazen in California. He was in Japan and wanted to know how I was getting along. He told me he was leaving from the airport. All my usual busy mind leaped at the thought that I could see him off. I hastily pulled away from the quiet of the sitting, hoping to catch a minute with my teacher even though the best of our conversation had already taken place on the telephone.

I hurried out into a jangling Tokyo world to catch buses, to stand impatiently in ticket lines, locate trains, and change twice to get to the airport. I arrived one and a half hours later, full of anticipation and urgency, frustrated by the delays in modern city rush hour.

Kobun had already slipped irrevocably into the passport control section beyond which no visitor can penetrate. All that rush, all that confusion, anticipation, desperation dissolved into a burst of laughter at myself for running after some word of wisdom from outside myself. I had already tapped my own inner wisdom which I refused to acknowledge before as I dashed off in my futile chase to the airport.

It was a wonderful lesson. Listen to what's inside—don't go chasing off after wisdom from others, even a teacher, when you already know what to do next. This was the best preparation for the adventures ahead!

I spent another week visiting friends and seeing older parts of Tokyo and other points of interest. Then it was time to leave Japan, which had become so familiar and seemed like home. It was time to move on to stranger spots.

Chapter 2 - Philippine Surprise

My ticket scheduled me to leave one morning, stop overnight in Manila, and leave the next morning for Bali. I'd planned to spend a month on the beach recuperating and collecting my thoughts about the recent trip to Japan and China before setting out for more travel.

After a week of getting up for sitting at 5:30 am, I was looking forward to sleeping in for a few days. The plane landed ahead of time in the tawdry airport in Manila, and I carried my pack out past the first barrage of taxi drivers who refused to give me information about buses. I wandered along the roads packed with jeepneys. These are large jeeps the size of a station wagon, painted all over with garish colors, flashing metal horses across the hood, fringe on the windshield. Each jeepney sports a name, often as outlandish as the slogans found on T-shirts, expressing the individuality of the driver. Fifty or sixty jeepneys clogged the streets while I looked for a bus.

As I wandered through the clanging chaos, I was besieged by an onslaught of street vendors. Amid the waving banana leaves on the few trees that shaded the jeep-encircled central square were crowds of vendors selling chewing gum and cigarettes from small bags or improvised trays hung around their necks. Women dressed in hand-me-down dresses sold oranges and bananas. Children, obviously not attending school, were smiling hopefully at me, thrusting popcorn and chewing gum in my face. Everywhere, peanuts in grubby paper bags appeared in shoving hands held in front of hopeful dark faces.

The push to obtain my business prompted several jostling and elbowing incidents, until it became clear I was not a good prospect. The crowd dispersed, leaving one small shy girl carrying five bags of peanuts silently following me. She stood by me as I waited for the bus. I finally bought one bag of unwanted peanuts from the girl, whose hopeful face lit into a gleam of surprised delight. I was just lucky the bus came by at that moment, or I'd have been stampeded by a second attack of reinforced vendors.

So Manila hit me with a jolt. It took two and a half hours to get to the youth hostel. Every intersection became a chaos of jeepney drivers blocking the crossing. Ignoring the rest of traffic, they engaged in a vigorous verbal contest of insults. The individuality so whimsically expressed on the flower-and-sunset-painted cars found its outlet in a more aggressive way in these debates over right-of-way. Meanwhile our bus driver passively watched the show with no particular impatience, as if it were a regular traffic stop, a matter of course, an event to be enjoyed.

On the bus, I met a woman doctor who traveled daily between three clinics in different parts of the city. She took the long interludes in stride by getting to know the people she traveled with. For her it was an opportunity to meet people, not a frustration. I remembered my hasty impatience as I rushed to the airport to see Kobun off in Japan. Now I suddenly acknowledged that I was going to meet teachers all along the way. This lesson set the pace for my traveling—to be open to whatever happened without a feeling of haste.

This attitude of "Asian patience" made all the difference in my seeing what I saw. I was really grateful for having had the foresight to allow plenty of time for my journey. I also began to appreciate the benefits of not using taxis.

I wonder now if it was my surrender to this Asian sense of Time which brought about so much of the magic to follow. If I had dwelt on the frustrations of the wasted time, would my difficulties have continued?

I made it to the youth hostel. I had to chuckle at a girl who ingenuously asked: "I beg your pardon, but this is a youth hostel, can you stay here?" As I climbed contentedly into the top bunk of the bed in an eight person dormitory, I mumbled something about feeling young.

The hostel was full of young Western travelers, all writing in their diaries, or talking about what restaurants they'd visited. I wanted to be further away from my own culture, and walked down to watch the sunset on Manila Bay.

There on a stone wall I sat dreamily gazing at the red sun sliding into the water, thinking of all the pictures of Manila Bay I'd seen during the Second World War. How serene it looked now. Ships out on the dark water were outlined by ropes dotted with bright electric lights. Waves slapped the palm tree lined shore.

I felt a delicate touch to my elbow, which loosely rested on my purse. Looking around, in the dim light I caught the face of an old woman. She obviously had been trying to nudge the purse out of my hand, but quickly offered a begging palm. I looked at her dignified old wrinkled face, beautiful and full of pride. That instant in the dark, I knew I'd met another teacher. I pulled out a peso for tuition. She beamed surprise and disappeared. From then on I clutched my purse more carefully even when in reverie!

Next day, amazingly bouncy after dozing around the edges of shouts from a rollicking party in the next room, I set off for the airport with plenty of time to catch the flight to Indonesia.

I'd been a bit irked at my travel agent for slipping in this overnight stop in Manila on my way to Bali. But I was glad to catch a glimpse of this strange city. The streets seemed littered with banana leaves and trash, lined with little restaurants, beer halls and stereo tape stores blaring out American jazz. Or at least that's what I saw.

At the airport, I was already a seasoned traveler used to the barrage of cigarette salesmen, and somehow, I found them less overwhelming than the day before. Had I changed? Did my attitude of imperviousness penetrate the beggars? It seemed less fierce somehow. I still couldn't be fully clear about the children selling peanuts. But I knew I could spend my whole travel budget on all the demanding hands, and somehow it was easier to hold off till I felt pressed by a particularly appealing expression on some child that caught my eye.

After the shiny affluence of Japan's steel and plastic waiting rooms with padded seats, Manila Airport looked like a tired bus station with its dusty benches, plywood dividers between counters, and bare cement garage-type floors.

When I finally got to the counter and presented my passport and ticket, I was advised that my visa to Indonesia had lapsed! The visa was supposed to be used within three months. I had gotten it in San Francisco before my trip to China. My spontaneous change of plans in order to sit in the monastery in Tokyo had exceeded the time limit during which I could activate my visa. I must get it renewed at the Indonesian Embassy here in Manila. I couldn't take the flight out, and the next flight available at my price was a week away.

This was the first unexpected clobber of my trip. No time to dash over to the Indonesian Embassy; traffic was too slow. Stunned, I turned towards the benches and sat down—next to a Catholic nun in a gray habit. Surprisingly I was feeling no frustration, only puzzlement as to what to do next. A whole week in the Philippines? I was sort of laughing at my predicament, and sharing my surprise with the nun beside me, when the thought occurred that I might try to visit schools in Manila.

In Mountain View, before I left, I'd been working in a public school attended by many Philippine children. I might give all my small international friends in Mountain View a taste of home. "We have a school", the nun offered, "Why don't you come see that?" With no other plans, and a week to pass, I accepted the offer. So began my Philippine adventure.

A group of nuns, of the order of the Sisters of St. Francis of the Immaculate Conception, surrounded me. They had come to see one of their members off on the plane I had missed. With smiling peaceful faces, they escorted me to their beautiful blue jeepney, helped me hoist my pack up, and we all drove in splendor through the streets of Manila. This time, there was not so much traffic. I felt already a warm friendship with these nuns, and the time passed quickly. They drove me directly to the Indonesian Embassy.

The Embassy was located in the modern part of Manila, with shining cement skyscrapers. The airlines and banks all had sparkling glass and steel buildings, the streets were clean and wide. I saw a different, spacious order in comparison to the jumbled tangled streets I'd just come from. There were few jeepneys here. It was a different world.

Oh, the wonderful convenience of a car that goes where you want it to! How I appreciated that luxury! And so many people there in Manila will never feel that experience. I was made very conscious of the privilege of being an American, where a car is almost like an appendage.

After leaving my passport to be processed, we all went to the St. Joseph's College. Sister Stephanie, with whom I felt an immediate connection, and I talked all the way. She had a degree in psychology, and told me all the sisters were well trained teachers, social workers, public health nurses, and psychologists.

When we arrived at the college, I saw their elementary school, with 1500 pupils, situated in the same compound. The students were enthusiastically preparing for Christmas. It was their last day. How at home I felt. I was so engrossed I never noticed the time pass till I was invited to dinner.

By that time I also had an invitation to spend the night, and had been shown to a beautiful guest room with fifteen foot high ceilings. I wanted to throw open the windows, but Sister Stephanie gently let me know about the mosquitoes. In fact, the bed had a big mosquito net hanging from a point on the ceiling and spreading over the bed like a white gauzy tent canopy. I had time to shower before prayers.

Then I joined with the whole group of seventy or so nuns, all in gray habit, who gathered in the chapel for a short time of quiet prayer. I joined in the singing of hymns I'd known since childhood, feeling a little like a novice in my brown suit next to all the sisters in gray.

Afterwards, as everyone filed out, Sister Stephanie guided me to one of the seven community dining areas. The convent was divided into groups of six to ten sisters who always work and eat together. At this dinner with such lively sisters, curious and interested in everything, I learned that they had all sat zazen as a part of a group therapy experience. I wondered if I were dreaming. Here I was at dinner, surrounded by delightful old friends!

The stillness from my sitting in Tokyo remained with me, creating a feeling that I was watching myself from another time when I might have been a nun with all these sisters.

As we finished dessert, a sister came breezing in to leave Christmas gifts. She had spent a few days with her brother in another part of Manila and was returning to her outpost in Zambales the next day. They all exclaimed: "Ellen, there's where you should go. Go with Sister to Zambales!" Well! With no place else to go, such a warm feeling of belonging — no map — no idea of where Zambales was, I felt the suggestion sounded great!

It is the custom throughout all the Philippines to hold Morning Mass at 4:30 am for the nine days before Christmas, and I planned to join the sisters, but I couldn't sleep well. All night I was aware of a strange clicking. It had the sound of two blocks of wood being clapped together, something I'd heard daily at the Zendo in Japan while I sat zazen. With the low chants of the monks still reverberating in my ears, I wondered if this were some dreamlike recurrence. Then finally towards morning I fell asleep — missing the 4:30 Mass. I woke at 6:00, too late.

During a hasty breakfast, while Sister Fe was preparing to leave, I learned what the clicking noise was. It came from little lizards that I'd seen crawling on the walls. They hunted insects at night, waiting till an insect flew by so they could snap at it. I later found these little creatures everywhere in Asia, like diminutive house pets working a lot more effectively than fly paper and providing a sort of reptilian companionship.

Chapter 3 - Zambales

Sister Fe came for me shortly after breakfast, driven by her nephew who helped us catch up with an air-conditioned bus headed for Zambales. In December, even though it was the coolest season of the year, I was already sweltering, and an air-conditioned bus was welcome.

It was an all-day ride, past small villages of bamboo huts with people plowing nearby rice paddies next to the road. The great black water buffaloes were everywhere, sloshing through the muddy fields, pulling wooden plows with a pole fixed in such a way that someone standing on it could push it deeper into the soil. As we got further away from Manila, the buffaloes became more scarce. People pulled the plows themselves, over land stubbled with the remains of a rice crop just harvested. The pointed coolie hat I'd seen in Japan was visible everywhere, sheltering people from the sun as they leaned over nearly double, preparing the earth for another crop. Sister Fe explained to me that wherever farmers can irrigate, they plant three rice crops a year.

The overall impression was one of tawdry survival. Rice paddies alternated with untended land of shrubs and reeds and mingled in one stretch of haphazard, disheveled desolation for miles. Unlike the uniformly tended prosperous fields of China, this land displayed its poverty in threadbare paddies where the depletion of the soil could be seen in the uneven height and color of the crops. By the side of the road, banana trees shook in the wind, and coconut palm trees swayed their unlikely looking pin heads.

Without a map or any idea of where we were going, I trusted all to Sister Fe.

A licensed social worker, she'd been in Botolan, in Zambales, for years. She was presently helping a group of Negritos who had been living in the forests. Unable to survive there any longer, they had begun to come out of the hills, naked, malnourished and diseased. They had no money, and no skills to earn any. With the help of some skilled carpenters, she'd taught them how to build bamboo houses and arranged for a farmer to lend them a water buffalo to carry the bamboo out of the jungle.

Sister Fe was also helping these people to build a school and a health clinic, but the building was going very slowly. They had taken a year to build the three cement walls so far. They traded charcoal with Sister Fe for occasional bags of cement. In their eyes, the labor of day's work collecting wood and burning it made an equal exchange, though it cost Sister Fe much more.

She spoke to me knowledgeably of the poor people all over the Philippines and their efforts to improve their standard of living, efforts strongly discouraged by the existing political structure, which favors the rich. She illustrated the difficulties in helping by telling the story of a nun. She had been working in a hospital and had discovered the janitor was stealing. As she tried to report this, she discovered the corruption went all the way to the director. She had gotten very upset by this and worked very hard to uncover the cheating, but she was found stabbed to death. The official announcements stated she'd died of a heart attack. When I asked if there had been any change in conditions as a result of her efforts, Sister Fe just said "No."

Sister Fe preferred to direct her energies towards building a loving, cooperative community of people.

We arrived in Botolan, where the white Mission church faced a small square. It was constructed of blocks cut out oaf a coral reef. Three ancient deciduous trees stood along the roadside, giving a different appearance from the bamboo and banana trees everywhere else.

The architecture of the church and square in front of it was like Spanish Mission squares in Mexico and the Southwest United States. I had a sort of "*déjà vu*" feeling of the similarity of religious compounds all over the world, as if a model of Catholic Missions floated like a dream in the universe and could appear in any country with the same feeling of peace predominating, only there were people of different complexion and speaking a different language walking in the squares.

I found myself thinking of other small worlds that seem equally transferable to any part of the globe. Now that I'm back, I'm aware of such similarities shared by the 7-11 stores, McDonalds, Holiday Inns, and Safeway stores, for example. The atmosphere is identical no matter where you go in the country and even the world. But more of that strange perception later.

We walked past the great Mission to the small, modest compound where Sister Fe, five other nuns, and two novices lived, a small house with inner garden. Small rooms for each sister and a common bath and shower provided the basic necessities with no extra decoration. There was a modest kitchen where all the nuns shared the duties of cooking and dishwashing. A space to wash clothes outside with pump and pans, a cement drain, and a few pens for animals in the back yard completed the compound. I helped Sister Mercy feed the pigs while Sister Fe was settling in. Sister Mercy was a cheerful, loving woman with whom I felt instantly at home.

Sister Fe then shared with me some of her projects in Botolan, the name of the village. She met with a group of mothers of young men for whom she'd helped find jobs in Saudi Arabia. It was hoped they could send their income back to their families. She showed me another project — a demonstration farm to teach people how to grow their own vegetables and avoid the exorbitant market prices. She'd also shared the information she collected when she traveled to Manila, where she saw merchants selling, at enormous markups, the rice purchased from her farm families. She had encouraged them to raise their own prices a bit higher so some of the income could benefit the growers.

Then it was time for prayers. Quietly, we entered a small room in the inner courtyard. A plain cross hung on a wall; some wicker chairs and kneeling pillows served as furnishings. Here all six sisters gathered every morning and evening for Bible-reading, chanting "Hail Mary's", prayer and meditation. Always there was some time devoted to individual thanksgiving, prayers for self-knowledge, self-discipline, understanding and patience, drawn from fresh experiences of the day.

How real this daily recognition of the greater Energy that works in us all! There was no difference, only a continuation of the spirit I felt while sitting zazen in Tokyo. The deep sonorous chants of the young monks in Japanese blended in with the higher voices of the sisters' "Hail Mary's", and my pilgrimage continued.

That first evening we had gone to the shore (where, I still did not know) facing out across the China Sea, and watched the sun glow in a golden path across the water to its setting. Two sisters who loved the peace of nature and I, together, felt the calm of nighttime settle on a shore of sand by the quiet sea. It could have been anywhere in the world. It could have been California. It was home.

I was already aware that it was a Philippine custom to have the 4:30 am Mass each morning for the nine days before Christmas, and I felt it would be good to get up with them, but I was not prepared for the startling wake-up at 3:00 am! Over loud-speakers which felt as if they were set up right outside my room, came a jolly male voice singing "Rudolph, The Red Nosed Reindeer" — the same recording familiar to all shoppers who have ever trod the department stores at Christmas time. Then without a pause, while I was struggling to remember where I was, in the dark little room on the cot, sleeping, the sentimental chimes and Bing Crosby's voice crooned out "I'm dreaming of a white Christmas". Then all was silent for a while — just long enough to doze off again. Next the jolly jolt of 1950's memories came blasting "Winter Wonderland" into the air, which had not cooled off in the night from the tropical heat of the day before, and where snow must have been only a legend.

By this time I was fully awake, so I got up, washed in the outside room with a basin of hot water, used the Asian toilet (with all the experience in Japan), and followed the sisters into the dark under the stars.

Already the air was full of excited children's voices, as we came out of our little driveway onto the main square in front of the gigantic Mission. People were gathering dressed in their best, little boys in white suits, their hair combed, faces as shiny as their excited eyes, men in suits, women in frills. A few fire crackers burst in front of the Mission door — reflections even here of young teenagers' delight in open rebellion against the old traditions.

The enormous church, which looked to be a block long inside, was already full when we entered. People were standing twenty deep at the back. We cut through the crowd, as everyone fell back respectfully to let the sisters pass. They motioned to me to follow. Down the center aisle we walked — longer than any procession I'd ever marched — to the front row where the sisters showed me a seat. They vanished, and I was left up there in front, towering over everyone who seemed only four feet high around me. I was the only Western face in this vast sea of Filipinos, so I stood out. There was no way to hide. So there was nothing to do but carry the sincere good will of all Western people — authors of those cheery Christmas carols — from the world of mysterious snows, and participate with them as best I could.

There must have many who only attended church during this time all year, because the native Tagalog responses and prayers were flashed on a giant board from an opaque projector. Still the familiar letters of the Arabic alphabet helped me sound out the phrases of the slower hymns. These strains joined phonetically with the Japanese chants still ringing in my system. We chimed our voices together in that same united choral flow of affirmation that all generations and all cultures find to celebrate the spirit in us all.

There must have been 500 people gathered in the church that morning. They approached the altar and took Communion while I sat quietly and watched the neatly dressed families line up and one by one receive the wafer and wine from the Irish priest and the sisters. Above, in the high arches of that old Mission, sparrows flew in and out, chirping and settling familiarly on the shoulders of St. Francis, Jesus, and Mary, then flying to other perches celebrating with the rest of the congregation.

An old loved dog belonging to one of the nuns sauntered comfortably down the aisle and curled up at her feet while she administered the Sacrament.

Then, at around 6:00 am, we filed out into the courtyard with everyone as dawn pulled all the families toward their work world. Time for more quiet "Hail Mary's" in the tiny chapel in the nuns' compound, and a hearty breakfast.

This first day I went with one of the novices to see the Negrito community school. She had started a small class of 20 children who could not even speak Tagalog, but a tribal language none of the nuns could speak. As I watched some of the girls sweep out the classroom (an open thatched shelter), some mischievous boys gathered and played till school began.

When the energetic young novice clapped her hands, they lined up, wearing hand-me-down clothes, too big for them, and sang some Christmas carols they'd learned in English. Then it was exercise time. Children of parents who had run naked in the woods, independent and free, were learning the behavior of "civilized" living — action in unison.

The great dignity and pride of a free people shone in the eyes of a 12-year-old boy, son of the chief, who later danced a monkey dance for me. Alertness, grace, and joy swept across his face as he danced. The humor and spark of the woodlands came through his agile motions, and I almost felt I could have stayed forever, perhaps to help him learn the civilized world without losing all that magic aliveness in him.

I felt so close to these black faced people. I loved the dark sparkle in their proud eyes. The exchange I had with a cousin of the chief, who let me use his bow and arrow, I will never forget. I could feel the skilled way it was crafted, feel the strength of the string and the sharpness of the arrow — which looked like the old American Indian arrowheads. He shot the arrow into the trunk of a tree, retrieved it and handed it to me. I stepped a bit closer, grinning at him, in acceptance of my lesser marksmanship, and shot the arrow into the tree also, luckily. A bond shot between us. No language needed — only the love of a bow and arrow. He showed me his house — of beautiful bamboo, woven from dark and light reeds in herringbone designs with zigzag patterns for the walls. His baby was hanging in a swinging basket cradle in one small room, and his wife smiled as I saw the kitchen, where a square charcoal hearth provided fuel for cooking.

I recognized immediately the proportions of the rooms. They were identical to the layout of the rooms of my friend, Midori, in Japan. There was the same place for storage of supplies, room to use the same space in many different ways. The Philippine house was dictated by the length of the bamboo. The other city structure was more remotely determined by traditional structure; they were the same! Only the materials mirrored a different stage of civilization, cement, plaster, wood or bamboo.

We returned from this outpost in the hills driving in a jeep back through unkempt fields, past barefoot rice farmers lined in rows, pushing the green slips of rice into the mud.

Next day, the same repertoire of songs greeted the 3 am dark. In the church, as the rhythms of the Mass quickly became familiar, I sang along more confidently.

The second day, Sister Fe met with a young Peace Corps worker, eager to help her in her project of trying to find ways the Negritos could earn some income. She hoped they could harvest the cashew nuts in the forests, but she needed a market for the nuts. I watched as she spent a whole morning erecting a chart system on a little easel, full of requirements and forms. No wonder Sister Fe preferred to believe help would come from other sources, since she could have spent all her time in writing proposals. She preferred to trust help would come. She wanted me to stay for a year, showed me a small house and their retreat places where the nuns periodically went for meditation. But I was aware that this was the "cool season", and I was sweating uncomfortably.

Chapter 4 - Baguio

I was sweltering in the heat, and it was only December. To cool off a bit, I set off for a two day trip to Baguio, carrying Christmas gifts and messages from the sisters in Zambales to the sisters there.

Riding on the dilapidated bus, I was fascinated by a tooth-less, good natured woman in a bright orange flowered dress who was sitting with a great basket of frogs in her lap. When I indicated my wonder that they didn't hop out, she grinned and lifted twenty frogs tied in a bouquet by their legs, all dangling upside down. Then she indifferently dropped them down on their heads, where they squirmed to right themselves.

I stayed at the youth hostel in Baguio; it had been a summer hilltop retreat for the wealthy. Sister Fe had assured me it would be cold there, so I'd brought my winter gear, a down vest and sweaters, only to find that "cold" meant cool enough so I didn't sweat.

Because I met only the traveling Westerners, this was the last youth hostel I stayed in for the rest of the trip. However, I did catch a glimpse of some American Peace Corps workers on vacation from "the provinces". They were all in their twenties, working on developing handicrafts and trying to create a market for them, in hopes they could provide income for the "up country" people. Brooms, woven placemats, and rattan baskets were for sale everywhere.

The whole of Baguio's marketplace was littered with tiny shops looking like fragmented Cost Plus stores. The sale of food and hand crafts appeared to be the only money-making occupations other than a few drugstores and motorcycle shops. There were also the tape stores, from which American jazz and rock music hammered out rhythms in a noisy frenzy.

My memory of the Philippines is virtually littered with garbage. At Olongpo, a bus terminal near an American Army base, the streets were ankle deep in litter. Slimy, half rotted banana leaf wrappings from around "fast foods", such as rice cakes and fish, were casually draped everywhere and mingled with dark brown fibrous coconut husks and plastic. Inside the houses, there must have been a cleaner standard, because the coconut husks were the residue of floor polishing. I had watched a janitor display a clever skill of skating across the waxed floor with the brown "brushes" of the coconut husks under each bare foot. When finished, he just tossed them out the door on to the street.

This was my first introduction to a bamboo society emerging into modern urban living. The custom of tossing banana leaves anywhere must not have created a problem when the population was small and storms could wash the litter away down the stream. Everything disintegrated in time. But with increasing population, the use of plastic, and the same habit patterns, the streets and rivers were paved with junk, not disintegrating fast enough. It piled up along curbs, and in the eddies of the river. Children were swimming in and around floating beer cans, plastic wrappings, and garbage.

In Baguio, I was also able to witness the reverse prejudice of Asia. A pretty blond Peace Corps worker complained that she was tired of being carried from one party to another by a native "friend" who was showing her off. She found people attracted to her not for who she was, but because she was light skinned. I had also wondered at the extreme eagerness of people to talk with me, but I found it a convenient opportunity to get to know people. Everywhere people approached me wanting to have conversations with an American; it didn't seem to matter what about. To be seen talking with a Westerner seemed to give prestige.

There was another odd experience I had while walking through the streets. Before I left the States, a friend had sewn me some travel clothes. Knowing I would be in the Orient much of the time, she'd crafted two very Japanese slack suits fashioned after the sitting clothes many Zen students wear to practice zazen in America. They felt a bit ostentatious in the beginning, but they fit me well, were loose enough to be cool and sturdy enough to last a year. They packed easily and were easy to hand wash. I had one brown suit on when I went out. I could see the change in expression, mostly on the faces of older Filipino men and women as they came toward me. First a frown and hostile look, then, as they came closer and realized I was not Japanese, a puzzled expression would cross their eyes, and finally as they came close enough to see I was a woman, open laughter full of relief and curiosity would break out.

At first I didn't understand, but as the greeting was repeated, I realized these people were responding with a conditioned fear of my Japanese outfit, born of their suffering in World War II. This realization was a big relief to me. I must have been deprogramming long ingrained, fearful reactions in a funny unintentional way, but I began to wear my blue jersey T-shirt after that, not wishing to evoke such uncomfortable emotions.

I finally found the Convent where the Sisters of St. Francis were located. There were many convents, many missionaries, Baptist, Methodist, and others, and I walked through a good part of the hilly city before I found the right convent. In fact, I went to a different order of Sisters first, and a lovely young woman whose name was also Ellen guided me to the right place, where I delivered the Christmas gifts and was cordially invited to dinner. We ate in a large hall with a cluster of nuns and a group of young Seminary students, who were on retreat at the convent and were very interested in Zen.

Then a sister, a music teacher at the High School, took me to an evening of Christmas carols at the gymnasium of Baguio University. Thousands of high school students lined the balconies, girls in white, boys in dark suits. From all those fresh Filipino faces came a whole evening of Christmas carols sung in English, with a few beautiful ones in their native Tagalog.

This was Christmas 1981, and I recalled with much tingling awareness the winters of 1944 and 1945, when I was at the National Cathedral School for Girls in Washington D.C. The combined chorus of voices of the boys' and girls' schools had broadcast a program of Christmas carols to our armed forces in the Philippines.

All the Christian missionaries and churches heard those voices singing Peace and Good Will towards men. Here, nearly 40 years later, the same strains of faith and hope echoed back from hundreds of finely trained Filipino throats.

To make the harmonies of music takes much practice and good intentioned working together. There in Baguio, full of the uplift of trust in the goodness of men, I felt the hope that the people of the world can still work together. We still keep reaching out beyond nationalities and races for peace and understanding brotherhood among ordinary people, while energies for conflict and suspicion seem to mingle in the more impersonal politics of nations.

I spent the night in one of the small cubicles used by sisters, and enjoyed a congenial breakfast. I had cooled off a bit, and it was time for the long trip back to Botolan.

The winding mountain road paralleled a gorge where waterfalls plummeted pure white water into the torrent, soon to become sluggish with the strewn trash of the cities downhill.

The woman beside me on the bus had grown up all her life in the hills where Igorote tribes ran free in the surrounding forests. She told of occasional Igorete attacks on their village, where five of her closest friends had been stabbed to death. Her mother had raised her whole family of six children after her husband had been killed.

I lamented the change in the landscape. Many houses now are made of cement blocks, and the beautiful bamboo houses are becoming worn and frayed. She said her mother had kept a bamboo house for many years, but after a full day's work, she had had to come home to repair the destruction left by the typhoons which often swept away walls and roof. She finally had switched to a cement block house and was delighted with its sturdiness. Beauty was not so important.

Sister Fe greeted me in Botolan. Since all the other sisters had gone to see their families for Christmas, we were left to feed the pigs and water the plants. I had time to read while Sister Fe finished some work.

I picked up a book on the life of St. Francis, nestled into a shady spot near a banana tree, and began to read. I couldn't tear myself away from the story of this young nobleman who felt so keenly the call to a totally simple life, fully carrying out the teachings of Jesus in a time of great affluence and poverty in Italy. The similarity of his life to that of Buddha, who was also a prince and left all his possessions to go in poverty teaching compassion and brotherly love, struck me profoundly.

The Sisters were carrying out this simple life honestly, holding no possessions, going in small groups, examining always their motivations and preparing themselves through training and conferences to serve and strengthen those who needed help.

I felt the flow of all the religions that have touched my life: Episcopal, Christian Science, Lutheran, Roman Catholic, Presbyterian, Unitarian, Quaker, and Buddhist. I feel fortunate to have been able to bring them all together in my zazen, where everything melts in wordless, dogma-less silence without discord. I knew also that I could not stay in Zambales, much as I was pulled to do so. I had to go on moving, hoping to pick up the wisdom shared by all religions, and to feel the commonality of them all.

I went back to Manila with Sister Fe and attended a wonderful family dinner at her brother's house. He runs an organization that helps young Philippine men find jobs in foreign lands, assisting with transportation costs so they can bring much needed income to their own families. I stayed in several of the other "communities" in St. Joseph's Convent, becoming even closer to many loving sisters, as if they were all my family.

I had spent two whole weeks in the Philippines. My flight was again due. I sadly said goodbye to the sisters and climbed into the blue jeep that had brought me at the beginning of my stay.

On the way to the airport, the old driver, who had been helped as a homeless child by the sisters, drove me to the slum section of Manila where hovels of corrugated cardboard crushed each other upon the other. There were many thousands, of Muslims mostly, living on the old World War II landing strip. They had to buy their water, so they skimped in using it for washing or bathing. Disease was commonplace, and the Sisters were busy here administering medicine. The houses were demolished every time a typhoon came, and they had to scrounge for more cardboard.

Then we drove past a park where my driver showed me a big building. It had been built in 45 days just to house the Miss Universe Pageant at a cost of 2 million dollars. Now it is unused and empty. Contrasts! It brought home the meaning of the Sister's comment that Mrs. Marcos' rosary was made of diamonds!

Chapter 5 - Dini

In the airplane headed for Jakarta, Indonesia, I wondered whether the magic which had transformed an overnight stay in Manila into two weeks with the sisters in Zambales would continue.

Soon, I began a conversation with a beautiful young airline hostess who charmingly asked if I had any sons who were single. She didn't seem to consider personality as anything important, just that she marry a Westerner. She admitted that her father was concerned about her indiscriminate searching, and I also suggested she might find herself in a very unhappy situation if she didn't realize that not everything "Western" was admirable, that people were disagreeable or pleasant everywhere.

The one hour flight was nearing its end. The hostess had to prepare for landing, but quickly asked where I was going to stay that night. I still didn't know, and was sort of curious as to what I could find at 8:00 pm that was within my budget. She said, "Why don't you come with me to my house?" Another adventure had begun. Dini, the hostess, usually went home by taxi, so I paid the fare. We rode through the streets of Jakarta, which seemed lined with many small shops.

Most of the men I saw on the streets were wearing a funny combination of traditional and modern dress. They wore the typical Western short sleeved shirts, so from the waist up they appeared well dressed in the modern world. From the waist down they wore the traditional Asian wraparound skirts.

It had poured rain before we arrived, and the street where Dini lived was still calf deep in water. We stepped out of the taxi barefoot. I carried my sandals, and Dini held her high heels, as we waded cheerfully up the narrow street to the house where Dini lived. All the neighbors watched and laughed with us as they stood dry at their doors.

Dini's father, who impressed me as a big, sturdy, tall man, was a Muslim. Since most Indonesians were shorter than I was, perhaps his "size" was my perception of his presence. He was open to new ideas and spoke English easily. His diminutive wife smiled a friendly welcome.

We were then surrounded by three other giggling and enthusiastic daughters. The father took great pride in explaining that he was seeing that all of them were being educated fully so they could speak English, prepare for careers, and travel widely.

I was invited to dinner, but they put the meal before me and waited. No one else had any food in front of them. Only I was to eat, it seemed. I ate, as the family looked on, since it is the custom not to eat until the guest has finished.

The father talked of his Muslim way and his responsibilities in society. I think he rather enjoyed expounding his beliefs to uninformed foreigners. He earned substantially more than his neighbors since he worked for the airlines, but he still maintained his home in a very simple way. It was comfortable, with a 10 by 12 foot dining room where plaster board was finished with lath. The rooms on the second floor had to be reached by a steep stair. There were only the bare necessities—a bed, and dresser. There was a TV in the living room, the only one in the neighborhood, around which clustered a group of neighbor children. He (and it was obviously a patriarchal system where his views predominated) preferred to put his earnings into the education of his daughters and into helping his neighbors when they needed it rather than into beautifying his house, which he felt was comfortable as it was.

I found myself toying with the ideas of American decoration. Perhaps a few more additions. A set of curtains would dress up the wood framed windows, perhaps some smooth wall covering would cover up the lath, and maybe some easily cleaned formica would make the wooden counter in the kitchen appear more easily cleaned. Just a few improvements for easier housekeeping, nothing much really. But where does one stop? After the necessities what else does one really need? I could feel the American desire for something just a "bit prettier" never finds satiation once you get started. He had the contentment and restraint to know when he had sufficient material comfort.

The whole family helped me learn to eat the Indonesian way with my hands. Rice is the staple food. Unlike the American way of using the rice to hold the sauce, the sauce was a small flavoring to the side. So I also scooped up the rice, drawing it through the sauce with my right hand with much friendly laughter. One only eats with the right hand. Getting it into my mouth produced a few dribbles as I learned to shove the rice forward with my thumb as my hand poured the rice in. The whole family delighted in watching. I must have been a sight, with my elbows out, my mouth ready to catch a fly ball. A baby could have been more graceful. But as I laughed with them at my clumsiness we all relaxed together.

I was afraid to eat much, since I wondered if there would be enough for the rest of the family, so I ate what was for me a scanty portion. Since many situations like this arose later in my trip, I got used to "scanty" portions and learned I didn't need anywhere near what I was used to eating. I also learned to leave a small portion on my plate, since a new portion was added each time I emptied it. Only when there was some food left uneaten could my hosts feel I was satisfied. How different from the American custom of cleaning the plate.

After my dinner, the father asked if I would greet the neighbors in the back courtyard. The family sat down to a hearty feast while I "conversed" with the curious neighbors. Out the back door was a small courtyard where I found myself surrounded by many teenaged boys wearing the black velvet hat indicating that they were Muslims. Nearly all male adults I'd seen in Jakarta wore this hat. Beyond the ring of boys were women, each circled by a cluster of small children. They stared at me shyly, crowding the small stone courtyard.

Dini had taught me the word for hello (salamet bagi), and I

mumbled it uncertainly. They laughed, corrected me, and began to teach me words.

All their clothes looked like hand-me-downs — either too large or too small, and somewhat ragged at the seams. But it didn't matter. Friendliness gleamed in their eyes along with a wistful curiosity. I showed them a picture of the third grade class from Monta Loma School in California. They carefully studied the mixture of oriental, black, and Caucasian faces, which they pointed out with surprise. A plump blond girl of Dutch descent was singled out as pretty.

One woman touched my arm, indicating she liked my white skin, and didn't look so fondly on her own darker complexion. This attitude, I guessed later, must have developed from the long time of occupation by the Dutch, whose blond hair, blue eyes, and clear white skin symbolized success, domination and superiority. Indonesians are "independent" now, but still seem to hold the weight of psychological inferiority from those long years.

Dini had also said she wished she had my skin. It's all wrinkled and freckled with 53 years of living, while her fresh radiance of life bloomed in healthy beauty, but she refused to see it. This was only the first time I would see this wistful longing, which seemed to be a prevailing feeling. I could only express my surprise at this unwarranted admiration and show appreciation for all the fine faces before me, not as possessors of a particular skin color but as friends and equals.

Here in the courtyard, I again experienced my "recognition" of a face which I would see repeatedly during my travels. One woman with whom I felt immediate closeness, who without words extended friendship with her eyes, looked exactly like a friend of mine, Patricia, back in California. She had the same dark eyes, high cheek bones, and a slender build. It was like a shock to see "her" here surrounded by children gesturing to me their ages.

I had to catch myself and realize that I wasn't in a play where my old friends were all dressed up in different costumes in a different setting, that this was a different country and I truly didn't know the woman. But the friendship I felt for Patricia crossed the boundary between me and that Indonesian woman and we enjoyed a wonderful time of closeness — like sisters meeting after eons of time. This time I was only surprised. As "Patricia" and other friends popped up in different "costumes" again and again in my travels, I could only reach more deeply into the nature of the reality I was treading. Was it all a dream?

We bowed to each other. The custom of the "gassho", the greeting with palms pressed together before the face accompanying a gentle bow, seemed so natural to me. All over China and Japan, without words, people acknowledged their common friendship with this gesture.

Dini, who had finished her dinner, came from the dining room to translate. She told me, "She loves you." I returned the love — which we could both understand without words. There was a strange recognition of each other's spirit across cultural worlds, a commonality of motherhood, human-hood. Such a sweeping feeling, and so unexpected.

It was already dark and time for bed. We bowed a "goodnight", and I was ushered inside, through the small kitchen. Dini's sisters were washing dishes but they refused to let me help. I negotiated the Asian toilet on the first floor, with the now familiar cement drain, the faucet and tin can for flushing, which the Sisters in the Philippines had taught me how to use. No toilet paper. I thought how Dini must be experiencing the differences in life styles as she worked for the airlines. Then Dini and I climbed the steep stairs which felt almost like a ladder to share the comfortable double bed in the tiny bedroom.

Next morning, I was awakened at 4:30 by the Muslim call to prayer blasting from loudspeakers over the dark streets of Jakarta. Soon thereafter came the busy sounds of households coming to life. I could hear many people sweeping. Even at that early hour it seemed everyone was awake and busy with the day's activities. The family didn't rise till 7:00 a.m., though.

The father again lectured me on the Muslim responsibility

towards one's neighbors while I ate breakfast. This time the family ate with me. He felt he was there to help any of his neighbors when they got sick and to share what he could with them, including his TV for instance, and of course food if it were needed.

He began each morning by drinking a very bitter tasting brew, similar to tea, made up of many herbs. He mixed a small quantity for me, which I drank without making too wry a face, as he laughed. It was a part of his daily practice, which began with the Muslim prayers, then meditation, then this bitter drink — a whole 10 ounces.

I downed one small quarter cup and couldn't imagine forcing myself to keep drinking it on a regular basis. It tasted a bit like leather soaked in creosote and smelled as powerful. He felt it was a healthful concoction, and very good "discipline" to sample such a bitter drink daily. So far from the pleasure-filled way of Americans, who cover the least bad tasting pill with candy coating!

That morning, Dini and I wandered through some of the back streets of Jakarta visiting some of her cousins, friends, and an aunt. All had comfortable homes with heavily stuffed furniture, reminiscent of furniture from the 1950's. Two chairs and a sofa seemed to be the uniform of all Asian middle class homes. The women were very style conscious, with high heels and fashionable knit dresses. I must have seemed a bit archaic to them with my sandals and plain slacks.

I wondered for a moment if Dini was not showing off a Western friend. Her whole family was greatly interested in "America". They always referred to the United States as America, as did most Asians I met. They all expressed a desire "to go there some day". But here I was drinking tea with women in a living room looking much like any I had known thirty years ago. If I hadn't known where I actually was, I could have been having tea with any of my friends in the United States.

The architectural floor plan of the rooms in these houses was almost identical to the Philippine bamboo village houses that I'd visited with Sister Fe. Even though these were cement, the architects still continue to think within the limitations of bamboo.

By afternoon it was time to go to the airport. Dini accompanied me. I needed to change my ticket. My travel agent had suggested that I spend a month living on a beach in Bali to recuperate from the strenuous month long tour of China. But the direction of my trip had already taken a less self-indulgent turn as I stayed with Sister Fe and saw her consciousness of the suffering of people around her. Then I had decided to skip going to Bali and donate the money I would have spent there to Sister Fe.

I went to the ticket office to change my ticket to omit the stop in Bali and instead go straight on to Jogjakarta. I met with some of the frustrations that accompany travel as a single person. The airline ticket window was oddly constructed. Glass or plastic walled me off from the ticket agent except for a small hole at the bottom where money and tickets could pass through. There was no provision for vocal communication unless the person buying the ticket bent over nearly double and talked through the little opening at elbow level. Even Asians who had shorter stature had to bend over as well in order to be heard.

The ticket agent, a young woman whose makeup looked like a mask of rouge and eye shadow, gave me a disgusted look when I requested to eliminate my trip to Bali. I wanted to go to Jogjakarta and back. She impatiently grabbed my ticket and with a superior sigh, rerouted my trip reversing my original ticket plan without omitting the stop in Bali. I didn't notice this change till later.

The superiority of this woman, perhaps because she felt the importance of her job, was a taste I was to experience often while going as a single traveler rather than with a tour group. Was this a result of the behavior modeled by Dutch occupying officials who might have shown a lack of respect for common people? How many times had Indonesians been subject to the same superior attitude? Funny, though to be on the other side. I was not represented by an agent. I was in the odd position of being one of the "privileged" Westerners who were free to travel to other lands, but was not one of the wealthier Westerners. They followed a whole different set of paths through the same lands and cities I visited. There is a polite prescribed behavior towards those "tourists", for which I was apparently not eligible.

Parting with Dini was hard. She felt like a daughter, and I was touched when she burst into tears at my leaving. Still, I wasn't sure if this was the way people part in Indonesia, or if it was a real feeling of closeness which again had made my stay feel like home.

Chapter 6 - The Rama Hotel

The plane landed in Jogjakarta after an hour's flight, and I was glad that there were two young women, Australian teachers on vacation, who were looking for cheap lodgings. They had addresses of more reasonably priced hotels they found in a book, "Southeast Asia on a Shoestring". Understandably, this book was impossible to buy in Indonesia, so I appreciated looking at it. We shared the cost of a jeep from the airport, and got off in a section of town where cheap hotels abounded.

The first night, we shared a room in a hotel which was mostly for Indonesian travelers, but a few young German guests were also there.

The proprietor said this was all he had except for one single room, but that he thought I wouldn't be interested in it. When I asked to see it anyway, he showed me a tiny room more like a closet with no windows at all. It felt stuffy and was already too hot to sleep in. Even though I was, in my view, very adjustable, I could not imagine sleeping in it. Indonesians preferred the rooms with no windows, even though the temperature was boiling hot. I gratefully moved in with the other two women who were happy to share the cost of the larger room with me. Our room had three metal cots, two windows, two chairs, one standing closet. That's all.

When the 4:30 a.m. wailing call to prayers blasted me to wakefulness, I was resigned to the fact that I would not be permitted a vacation from my meditation schedule. After waking at 5:30 a.m. in China, 4:30 a.m. in Japan, then 3:30 am in the Philippines, merely rising at 4:30 a.m. in Indonesia felt almost like sleeping in. Perhaps I was internally wishing to continue my early morning zazen, and so noticed these "alarms". Whether this early rising was impelled by outside customs or was inwardly invited, it felt good to keep on sitting zazen. About this time I recognized that the whole trip was to be a pilgrimage.

The teachers moved to a more "Western" hotel the next day. I decided to stay where I was. I liked the proprietor and I'd gotten used to the Asian toilets. The open cement drains gave me the feeling that I was really living the way other Indonesians lived.

That first day I came down the stairs through the open inner courtyard where the cement floor and plants were all damp from the night's rain. Some of the Indonesian guests, all young men whom I later learned were students on vacation, were washing clothes near an enormous well. A bucket was supported on the end of a long bamboo pole, and they brought up water enough to wet their clothes. They rubbed soap on the wet garments, deftly scrubbed them with a kneading motion on the cement floor, and dumped the rest of the water on to rinse, letting the waste soapy water flow in a rivulet along the open gully which carried the water to the street. Clothes were already draped on every horizontal surface and railing. It was obvious they expected a good day.

I found the small dining room, with just two tables. Apparently there were so many restaurants in the area that guests preferred to eat out, but the proprietor's wife occasionally served meals of rice with sauce or eggs for the Westerners.

The proprietor, a kindly quiet man, spoke English well. His build was slim, and he wore the traditional wrap-around skirt with obvious comfort. He told me he had nine children, and seemed proud of each one. (A grandchild was crawling around the entry room making delightedly happy sounds.) He seemed genuinely interested in recommending places to visit, helping each guest find what he wanted.

We got to talking as I ate. He had ordered me a spoon, but was pleased by my attempts to eat the rice with my hands. I was glad for the chance to practice eating in an inconspicuous place.

Apparently he had looked through the flimsy curtain into my room and had noticed me sitting zazen that morning. (I promised myself to remember that lack of privacy after that.) He showed interest in my meditation posture, telling me that he too meditated in the small open room at the head of the stairs. I had seen a rug laid out for daily prayers. This was where he practiced Muslim Yoga.

He said Muslim Yoga originated not from the Hindu but from Arabic tradition, and proceeded to demonstrate to me his sitting posture. He sat on one heel with only the tips of his toes resting on the ground. The other knee rested on the ground with the foot sole up. From the front it looked like the Japanese Sesa posture, where they sit on both heels. His hands were resting on his knees in a gently closed fist.

He commented that if you practice this way long enough with the help and guidance of a teacher, you become sensitized and have the ability to project your astral body and to see auras. But, he said, these powers were not to be considered important. He commented that there was a danger in that many people in Indonesia seemed to get stopped with these powers and not develop the spiritual attitude which they could enhance. These people chose to practice black magic.

If someone had a resentment towards another, he could go to a magician. He would put out a plate full of water. Then he would concentrate and chant till the face of the "enemy" would appear in the water. He then pierced the water with a needle, and across the town, the enemy would have a heart attack or get very sick. He'd seen it happen. He said that the police had a way of controlling this, though. They employed their own magician, to whom the victim's family would go. The face of the offending magician and his employer would appear in a similar plate of water and they would be arrested.

He warned me that I should be very careful how I held my purse because many young men knew how to "cloud your mind" and take anything they wanted.

He had been teaching his sons how to practice Yoga as they matured. He was proud of each, but a younger one was worrying him. He knew that if he abused the powers he had gained, they would fade, and already noticed that the spiritual aura was gone from this son. He was very concerned because of the influence of his son's friends, who rode motorcycles and wanted nothing but easy money. Even a good and conscientious father couldn't keep all his children in line.

Chapter 7 - Prambanan

During our morning conversation, the proprietor suggested that I go see Prambanan, an ancient Hindu temple ruin nearby. It was a beautiful sunny day, and I was ready to explore. He told me how to find the bus "station". I had to walk several blocks. When I got there, one of the young men I'd seen at the hotel came running to catch up with me. He'd been listening to my conversation with the proprietor and asked if he could join me.

During our half hour bus ride I learned about this young man. He was a student at Jogjakarta University and had studied to be a teacher but had given up after one year of rambunctious 9th graders. Apparently Junior High School students are challenging everywhere. He had then decided to study to be a newspaper reporter, but was struggling greatly with his honest desire to report the truth about corruption in government, and he spoke of his fear of being put in prison. Some of his friends were already in prison for speaking openly.

Since he head heard I meditated, he asked me about zazen. He wanted to know if I wasn't afraid to travel alone, giving me a chance to think out loud what I felt was the result of the stillness of meditation on fear.

The state of my mind that had developed from all this sitting seemed to be one of "watching" what I was doing and what was happening. I had a strange trust that things were going as they should without feeling the need to do any particular thing to bring the happening about. I'm not sure whether this is the mind of every traveler, but certainly the opportunity to be away from a job, demanding schedules, and friends produced an objectivity and restful calm much harder to achieve in everyday life. Zazen is a way of doing this for the time you sit. All turmoil of demanding life existence drifts away while you're in that stillness. The process of watching your thoughts becomes like a floating through time and space on some great river where the current propels and you drift along not trying to guide at all.

Sometimes during my travels, I'd felt as if I, myself, was a thought, as I wandered through strange cities as if through some strange reality. It seemed just the way my mind often wandered in zazen when I wasn't watching. When accompanied by that dreamlike state, I wondered if maybe I wasn't really travelling at all but only sitting zazen at home.

I told him about a strange experience I'd had in the Philippines. I was in Baguio during the week before Christmas. There were many "Salvation Army" type missionaries on every street. They were effectively helping distribute clothes and food to those who needed them, with no profit to themselves. I'd given donations wherever I could. However, I discovered I'd given away all my money, and had gone to a bank to cash a Traveler's Check.

At the clerk's desk, ready to sign my check, I reached for my identification. It was then that I remembered I'd left my passport in Manila at the Indonesian Embassy when I had applied for my visa. All I had were my U.S. driver's license and Youth Hostel card. I fumbled through my purse, my wallet, my back pack. I couldn't find them anywhere. Finally, I called the youth hostel where I'd spent the night, but I hadn't left them there. So I was stuck in Baguio alone and without money and apparently with no way of identifying myself. In the search, I found my airline ticket was missing also.

The young bank clerk who'd taken my application had kindly let me use the phone to call the hostel, but he insisted I should have some type of identification before he would let me cash a check. I began to feel panic creep over me as I looked more frantically a second time through my purse.

Then my "watching mind" took over as I recognized the same frantic actions of a woman I'd seen just minutes before. She had only a short time in which to catch an airplane in Manila, and her bus was already dangerously late. As the time dwindled between the departure time of the plane and the arrival of the bus, she became frantic. In her agitated state, she paced, fumed, and lamented out loud about the inefficiency of the transportation in Asia, her fear of the airplane leaving without her, and just general irritation about her travels.

People were staring at her. I finally observed that no matter what the buses did, her feeling was all she could control. She was getting herself very upset, and her frantic state would not change the bus schedule. She could either get desperate or she could laugh, the bus would not be affected either way. The situation would be the same no matter how she looked at it. This somehow struck her funny and just as she smiled, the long awaited bus arrived!

In the bank, my words echoed. I must have been talking to myself. So I took a deep breath, leaned back and just asked, "Now what?" I was ready to accept what came, regaining my resignation and patience.

I sat only a few moments before I got an idea. I went back to the clerk, who seemed a friendly and sympathetic young man. "There must be some way I can prove I'm me. I can sign my signature dozens of times and they'll all look like the one on this traveler's check."

He looked at me. They had to keep the rules. He hesitated, but since it was only for $20.00, he'd take the risk as his own and authorize the slip for me. I thanked him for his trust. I shared with him my feeling that sometimes we meet tests where we can't rely only on rules. I was glad he had the courage not to stick blindly to the regulations.

As I lined up at the cashier's counter to pick up my money, my hand brushed the zippered sandwich bag I wore against my back around my waist. I had forgotten it. Now I looked in and there was my driver's license and youth hostel card. It seemed to have been out of my sight or memory to see how I would behave, and when I passed the test, it appeared. I jubilantly ran back to the clerk and waved the driver's license, verifying his trust in me. "We both passed our tests in Trust today", I laughed.

As I said this, a nun who had been watching the whole episode caught my eye and smiled a recognition of that awareness.

I shared this whole story with the young Indonesian. He commented that somehow something had brought us together, because I'd helped him decide what he wanted to do. He knew if he honestly wanted to make known what should be known, then he could face what came more easily than if he'd dodged out of fear. It seemed to me he was having to show a lot more courage than I'd ever been provoked to muster, but to him it seemed I was courageous! Funny how we each look at the problems others face as harder than our own!

By the way, I lived for two weeks with the uncertainty of whether I had left my airline ticket at the Embassy along with my passport. I found that I was leaving it to circumstances. Maybe I was going to spend a year in the Philippines. However, to my relief, it was safe along with my passport at the Embassy.

We arrived at Prambanan, an ancient Hindu temple spread out in ruins among green rice paddies. Although it had been shaken by many earthquakes, quite a few buildings of black carved stone were still standing. My friend served as my guide as we walked and stumbled among the stones. He pointed out the large bas relief panels, telling the Ramayana story, that wrapped all around one temple building. This story figures prominently in Hindu lore and Indonesian puppet and dance presentations, and I later recognized references to it in Nepal and India.

The story centers about the adventures of the Hindu god, Shiva, who has to rescue his consort. She was kidnapped by the Monkey King, a powerful and clever adversary.

We climbed the crumbling stairs together, stood in the sanctuaries, and I had a strange feeling that we two had wandered together in this place some other time. Is it the predominance of Asian thought that brings such feelings to mind? I only mention the sensation and a question rising as to what is this illusion of Time? Over and over as I stood at sites in China and later in Burma, Nepal, and India, I had a sensation of the "nowness" including all Time: Past and Future — a vague response to the harmonies in myself that vibrated to a tune played in a different frequency of Time.

My "guide" had to leave at noon, and I chose to explore the area a little longer by myself. We parted with an acknowledgment that the morning we'd spent together felt like an entire lifetime.

I was getting dizzy in the noonday sun, and as there were many shops under canopies at the outskirts of the temple site, I wandered through them looking for a hat. I saw many Western type "cowboy" hats with big brims, but I didn't want this kind. Ever since I had been in Japan, I had wanted a farmer or "coolie" type hat. I described it with pantomime and pointing, yet none of the old smiling merchants seemed to have any. Then as I was about to give up, I spotted a salesman without a stall. He stood over a few hats spread out on a bench. There was a fine woven bamboo hat with a tiny inner crown to hold it away from a sweltering head. It even had a chin strap, and it fit me perfectly!

I put it on gleefully while all the old merchants and wives cooking strange fishy meals laughed in delight with me. Everyone gave me the "thumbs up" gesture of great approval. It didn't appear that many foreign tourists wanted to identify with the farmers.

I felt totally at ease as I wandered along the outlying rice paddies towards some even bigger ruins about a quarter of a mile away. Two boys were out "grazing" their ducks. A whole cluster of ducks waddled through the muddy water, which was all prickly where green tips of rice poked up. They were sifting the dark water for snails and bugs They moved slowly in a group across the glistening marshy square. If one duck was too slow, a boy would throw mud at it till it scuttled along and caught up with the rest.

I'd seen the good behavior of many domesticated animals in Asia before. The goats, left to graze, walked only along the raised earth paths and ate the weeds growing there. They didn't step into the paddies to nibble on the succulent looking rice, which must have tempted them. The ponderous dark water buffaloes stepped carefully in the rice paddies, only in the rows between the rice crops. They all seemed to feel the sacred importance of those crops, which kept everyone alive.

The expanse of the greater temple ruins spread out for what seemed three city blocks square. It was all scattered black lava stones, delineating forgotten foundations.

Still, there were two fierce temple guardian figures standing twenty feet high. They must have been as old as many of the temple guardians I'd seen in China, and they had the same frightening aspect. Their ugly faces glared, their Indonesian style swords were ready for action. These figures stood guard over the expanse of ruins as stony reminders of times long past. It seemed ironic to me that the guardians lasted so much longer than the temples they guarded.

I had for a short moment, a flash of another temple complex in Mexico, where I'd wandered alone seven years before and seen similar guardians. They too were watching over ruins. I wondered if perhaps I was guarding old memories of my own, no longer useful, but with the same rigid intensity, or perhaps I would not keep meeting these same symbolic statues.

Ruins remind me of old, no longer useful thoughts. They remain hanging on by a thread of existence till taken up again in some new time, resurrected and given new importance. Our thoughts, too, sink into invisible ruin in the recesses of our memory until some flash or insight rediscovers them. Then we call them back into our active lives, giving them new value. Maybe that's what I was doing symbolically in these travels: resurrecting memories of my ancient self. The guardians of my mind were still standing watch over the ruins of forgotten memories I must have been afraid to reconstruct.

The regular rains in late afternoon sent ducks and farmers scurrying for shelter, and me back toward the bus and "home" to my hotel.

Chapter 8 - Chinese Carnival

I had arrived in Indonesia just in time for the celebration of Mohammed's birthday on the 8th of January. They celebrate for a full week. Every hotel was crowded. Students from Jogjakarta University were everywhere, and it was obviously the season for Indonesian tourists.

The Sultan's Palace was down at the end of the main street, within easy walking distance. On the grounds nearby was a great Oriental Carnival in full swing, as a part of the festivities.

The following morning, I walked the half mile to the crowded outer grounds of the Sultan's Palace. Salesmen under bamboo pavilions, juice stands and souvenir booths presented the usual gauntlet of competition for my money. I was overwhelmed by the noise and crazy carnival atmosphere, and almost turned to run away, when I heard sounds of the gamelan players.

I plowed my way through crowded aisles between banana and refreshment stands, and discovered an inner courtyard where eleven men were seated in a raised pavilion with sets of spherical gongs arched in a horseshoe curve around each player. They beat the gongs like a xylophone with padded mallets in complicated rhythms, totally beyond my grasping.

Slowly, one player after another would strike a note. After a pause while the ringing faded, another player would reply. At first the interplay was deliberate, and each tone was or seemed isolated from the next. But the ringing picked up speed that increased in intricacy and tempo to a wild crescendo, then broke into a sudden silence. Next the deliberate slow single gongs would begin again. It was as if the silences between sounds were as important as the compelling ringing, singing of those brassy resonances.

The crowd listening was huge. All stood respectfully as the players continued. Each time after a build-up and silence, the crowd dispersed and new people clustered round.

There was a set of stairs leading to the raised platform, and people had "parked" their small children there. One little girl, serious and serene, sat without restless motion quietly watching the crowd, listening and peaceful, for the 45 minutes that I stood there. She couldn't have been more than 3 years old.

I was enchanted, listening to the sounds that seemed as complicated in their relationships as the old change ringing of British church bells. Were they of the same tradition some place back in lost time? The same "quiet mind" of zazen slipped over me as I listened. They somehow lifted me to a different state, a dream-like objectivity where the crowd and I became one listening ear together and the sounds vibrated through us all as if we too were the gongs.

I pulled myself away to give room for other listeners and wandered in a detached peace through the chaos of people. I was almost ready to turn back when I saw a young boy, perhaps 10 years old, dancing with a horse's head mask over his head and shoulders. There was a sort of a drama being performed in a large circle enclosed by people. It seemed to be about the catching and taming of a wild horse, danced with enormous strength, grace and intensity by this young boy. He then performed a fire-eating act where he thrust great sticks swabbed with oil into his mouth, exhaled fire and "swallowed" other flaming tips. All this he did with the calm assurance of a long time performer, and gripped the audience of nearly a hundred with the skill of an adult professional that many an actor in the U.S. would have found difficult to duplicate.

I'd had enough of the crowds. Back at the hotel, the proprietor told me the gamelan players were a very disciplined group of men. Their performance was a religious act, and before playing, they would fast for at least a day, sometimes for three, to be pure enough to play. He also told me the gamelan players accompanied the dances and the puppet plays.

I'd wanted for years to see the Indonesian Shadow puppets. I learned I could watch a rehearsal in an afternoon performance.

With the help of some young boys on the street, I located the rather obscure theatre where performances occurred every afternoon. The room was nearly empty. There were more people in the gamelan orchestra than in the audience, and the entire puppet production was performed by one man.

A large ten foot square screen divided the room. Chairs were placed on both sides, inviting visitors to shift sides. Both sides intrigued me as I switched from "front" to "back", watching the effects. The puppet master operating the gilded puppets and the gamelan players were on the back side, providing a colorful and action-packed reality. In the front, only the simple silhouettes moved like dark blurry ghosts across the white screen.

The gamelan ringing had the same effect on me as before. I floated into a very detached mood where I watched and listened from a place slightly outside myself.

The puppet master is said to go into a trance state where he becomes the gods and forces that he acts out. He sat before a large screen with at least 75 different flat puppets lined out on either side of him, some of them three feet tall, ornately painted and supported on a spine or thin stick he used to hold them up.

The unreality of the shadow side, I'm sure, carried the religious significance more fully. I alternated my seat, first from back to front, since the stage was set up just for that, and since there were only seven of us in the audience. I sat looking at the shadows, listening to the rhythms of Indonesian phrases intoning in staccato rushes with descending tones. Because I couldn't understand the meaning, I recognized the familiar speech patterns and even voice resonance.

In Eiheiji Betsuin, the monastery in Japan, the Roshi or Zen Master had read us daily a lecture story, or "Tessho" in the Japanese language. They were old traditional "Koans", or stories passed down for centuries, and I felt as he read them that he was using a delivery pattern which must have been just as traditional.

Now, here in Indonesia, in a puppet performance in a totally different language, the same cadences, same voice tone, same rise and fall of voice, short rapid gushes of words, made up the presentation. This puppet master could have been reading to me an Indonesian "Tessho"! Again that weird haunting awareness of similarities of religious practices and customs, this time in sound, rushed through me.

That evening, I wanted to see the famous Indonesian dancers. It was raining, and I found a rickshaw driver among the many sinewy, bony, weary-looking rickshaw drivers that lined the streets with their oversized tricycles near the hotels, competing with each other to drive me. I'd discovered early on that if you don't bargain, they feel a sort of disappointment and contempt for someone who doesn't know the value of money. I felt a bit uncomfortable, as I had talked my driver down to about fifty cents.

We set out. I had no idea it was well across town. A drenching cold rain was falling. I was under a plastic hood, but he was out in the torrents, getting splashed by the passing cars. His sinewy old muscles glistened in the street lights as he peddled the slow rickshaw through bumpy puddles of water, over uneven street stones, down long back streets. When we arrived, I tipped him enough to equal the price he'd asked in the first place. This pleased him no end, but left me fully appreciative of the great effort he'd expended to get me there and how little he received in pay for that effort!

Again the sound of the gamelan chimed through me as the same players I'd seen at the puppet play performed for these dancers. They wore their uniform, a green turban-like hat along with their western style batik shirts. The dancers brought to life all the carvings of dancers on temple walls at Prambanan. All my later wanderings through temples were enriched by the recognition of their stylized motions, the ornate head gear repeated by these fresh skilled dancers acting the Ramayana dance which must have been passed down for centuries. Their disciplined motions, curled fingers, swaying bodies took me through all the adventures of the Monkey King, Krishna, and his consort. I was watching all the still figures frozen in carved stone at Prambanan come to warm, breathing, graceful life.

Chapter 9 - Borobodur

I was still staying in the Rama Hotel, with a vague feeling there was some special reason why I had come to Jogjakarta, when the proprietor recommended that I go see Borobodur, a Buddhist temple built in the eleventh century [Editor's note: actually, in the 9th] that has been recently reclaimed from jungle growth and moisture damage and is being rebuilt. Though I had not heard of it, except to see a few mysterious pictures of the great dome, I had come to Indonesia on the insistence of my travel agent, who said it was one of the most important Buddhist places in Asia. But I had forgotten the name. It was now two months since I had set out so hastily. I knew I'd come to Indonesia to see something more than the puppets and was hoping I would be reminded of that purpose before I had to leave.

So, full of gratitude to the proprietor, I set out the following morning at 6:30 to take the early local buses for the hour and a half ride to Borobudur. I had to stand for 45 minutes on the first bus crowded with farmers and working people. Then I changed to a less crowded bus farther out in the country. All the farmers, mothers with children, women and market baskets patiently jostled and balanced as the bus stopped at village after village.

As we hobbled along, a big tour bus with large glass windows and upholstered seats swept by us with many comfortable Indonesian tourists inside. Since I was going to a temple, I felt better somehow to be coming as an ordinary person with no special comfort arranged for me. I found myself thinking that farmers, tourists, pilgrims, and business people travel the same roads daily, but there seem unimaginable worlds between them.

The bus dropped me off in the middle of a marketplace. It seems that places attracting pilgrims soon draw tourists and the commercial atmosphere that follows in their wake. At almost every temple site I'd visited so far, in China, and Eiheiji in Japan, there were sometimes whole streets leading to the temple, crowded with people making money on souvenirs, food, antiques. Perhaps pilgrims are tempted to acquire some physical reminder or evidence of being in a special place. Then, inevitably, tourists also come to these spots because everyone "should see" them and pile up post cards, ash trays and snacks, as part of the experience.

Maybe I was just seeing the magnification of that souvenir buying mania to which I, too, had succumbed in China. Our group had gone to a beautiful temple where Dogen, a Zen patriarch, had experienced profound understanding some eight hundred years ago. The old resident monks there had been compelled by the Communists to make chopsticks for their living and had given each of us a box. They were also selling mementos at a small store but I had been wandering around the temple grounds and when it was time to go, the tour guide said there was no time for me to buy anything.

I had wanted to bring something back for all my friends at home who didn't have the chance to come. I became curiously agitated because I wanted so much to share this experience. I was totally focused on the chopsticks when the whole meaning and energy of that place was already with me! Such misplaced attention! I was brought back to proper perspective when a very compassionate companion on the tour saw my concern and generously gave me his box to share with my friends.

Anyway, now I had to walk for three blocks through an array of canopied stands selling drinks, bananas, postcards, statues, miniature Borobudurs. I didn't feel like buying anything. Prices even for a banana were prohibitive, so I ended up going on an empty stomach to see this fantastic temple. It was a better state for a pilgrim than I had intended. Maybe accident was teaching me what my own inclinations would have omitted.

Borobudur is a very old Buddhist temple (1000 A.D.), built in a Moslem, and at an earlier period, Hindu, land. Through the years it has been cared for, neglected, rebuilt, and treasured again. When I first climbed up the hill, it was hidden by nearby trees, just as an enormous mountain hides behind nearby hills. I could see little but a high stairway leading upward with ornate, almost Gothic, arches. It was as if I were an ant exploring a giant elephant, the way I began to climb the narrow stairs, discovering that it was made like a gigantic layer cake.

The first layers looked somewhat like the pyramids in Mexico: square with a wide walkway around the outside rim of each successively smaller layer or terrace. Against the inside wall were marvelous carved panels of thousands of scenes. Lovers cavorted, luscious grapes and wines were devoured, money was piled high on tables. All kinds of earthly pleasures were depicted in bas-relief on the ancient limestone, which was in various stages of mossy decay. Sex, food, adventure, power, fame, and wealth: all the realms of earthly desire were artistically presented here.

I didn't notice until later that as I climbed up higher from one terrace to the next, the nature of pleasures carved on the panels became less those of the body, and more those of the mind. I was especially taken by one panel with a full-rigged ship, like those of the early explorers, tossing on realistic seas. Even in the artwork I recognized my love of adventure, my own special form of desire.

By the time I had climbed up over the first four terraces, each about seventy feet high, I began noticing Buddha statues seated peacefully staring outward from the wall which served as a railing. Every one of these serene five-foot-high statues had the straightest backs I had ever seen. Even the head was flat with the back, as if a board had been molded to the back and only recently removed. Since I had made an effort at Eiheiji Betsuin to sit with my back aligned along a guiding stick that a monk had placed against my back, I was fascinated at the incredible straightness.

On the next two square layers more and more of these Buddhas appeared. They flanked the stairs and sat with peaceful faces everywhere. I must have been approaching heavenly realms. Then suddenly at the seventh level, the shape of the layers became circular and the Buddhas sat on a wider walkway. They were encased in in latticed stone bell-shaped stupas through which I could peek to see the serene Buddhas meditating cross legged in private.

Reconstruction was going on, so fences prevented me from walking all the way around each level, as pilgrims usually do. Also, even though it had just opened, people were everywhere along the narrow walkways, running up the stairs on a true vacation outing, taking pictures of each other against the wonderful carvings.

Several Indonesian tourists asked if they could take a picture of themselves with me. So, with a familiar arm around my shoulders, they posed as if I had been their friend for many years. A whole class of 100 high school students from Jakarta came rushing past me up the stairs, crawling like jubilant monkeys on every surface, despite the requests in English and Indonesian not to stand on the stone stupas.

Still the students clambered past. As I stepped out on to the first of the round terraces that began depicting the three heavenly realms, the students were running around as madly as any bunch of speed-crazy teenagers in the United States. I asked one young man who spoke English why they'd come. They had been taking Buddhist Studies in Jakarta, and during winter vacation they were on a field trip here. It was a lark, obviously.

This served as a gift to me because I might have let their monkey-like pace overwhelm me. I could have agreed to have them take their pictures with me and be done with it. But the power of the place was getting to me. I asked them if they'd lost the quality that Westerners are trying to develop now of the Oriental intuitive way of sensing the feeling of a place. They seemed more bent on acquiring all the attitudes of Westerners. All had jeans and T-shirts, many with meaningless English words stamped on them. Some were sporting radios and cameras. They seemed a typically Westernized Coca-Cola drinking bunch of kids.

Yet somehow they would be missing what they came to see. One boy was rather startled when I asked him if he could feel the place. There were seven students with me as I gazed around that lower tier. Thirty-two Buddas sat in their stone latticed stupas on this level, with straight backs and peaceful faces. Each sat within a "bell". They looked to me like gigantic bells—with Buddhas as the clappers. I asked if they could hear that powerful silence ring across the jungles below us. Puzzled, they paused to listen and fell into a quiet so we might all feel the ancient silence. What a wonderful moment—a group of young Indonesians aspiring to all the progress of the Western world suddenly recognizing an inner quality they'd almost blocked out—reminded of it by a gray-haired Western woman seeking to develop that very quality which was innately theirs, the true Asian spirit they might be trying to deny.

The students drifted off and I walked to the top level, which I had to myself for a while. I was right next to the great round solid dome that tops the stupa. It too was shaped like a giant bell. I sat without thoughts for a while, just content to be there, grateful that the cacophonous band of youths had helped ring those bells of silence so meaningfully for me.

When I finally climbed down all nine terraces to the main entrance again, someone told me there were two other lesser temples that were a part of this complex. I decided to walk the six kilometers between them.

After walking along a wide leaf-spattered path which wasn't used much, I came to a small empty temple. Inside the empty interior, incense was burning and flower petals lay on the spot where probably a Buddha once stood. On the outside wall were carved figures like the Greek "harpies", half bird with human heads, that I'd also seen carved on the Hindu temple, Prambanan. What did Greek mythology and the Buddhist-Hindu traditions have in common, that these symbols should appear in such different quarters of the world?

A longer walk brought me to Mendut, a tiny temple twelve or fifteen feet square, with a steeply pointed pyramidal roof, seemingly a hundred feet high. Three stone figures sat not cross legged but on chairs, which was the first time I had seen this representation. In the center was a Buddha with his hands forming the mudra of teaching, which was so beautifully carved it caught my heart. The carving was so delicate that it depicted the gauze folds of the robe with the same skill that the Egyptians used. The two figures on each side were equally splendid pieces of sculpture.

I felt a strong impulse to make an offering to these . Nearby there was a fruit stand where some warm-hearted women sold juice while they painted umbrellas. When I pantomimed that I wanted some incense, one woman went off while I pantomimed a conversation with the umbrella painters. She came back in a while with three long fragrant sticks of incense she had already lighted for me.

By the time I walked back to the temple, an English family had stopped to look in. When they came out, I went into the dark quiet room with my eyes still blinded by the bright sun outside. I offered the incense before these beautiful peaceful figures. I think I was acknowledging the long line of teachings that helped carry a quiet mind state to this present time, paying tribute to that compassion and inner calm that helps all conflict subside into nothing, all fears and desires appear as merely illusory and thus fade away.

I sat down on a ledge to the side, feeling the beautiful peace. I thought I was alone. Then out of the shadows, on the other side of the door, a boy about ten years old stood up. He'd been watching me. Obviously he'd also been struck by the power of those three beautiful peaceful giant figures before us. I shared with him that these seemed to me as beautiful as anything I'd seen in China. I felt that we were looking at a very great work of art arising out of the best qualities and dreams of men.

As we sat there, I asked if he or his family belonged to a church. It appeared they had no formal religion, but I could feel he shared my deep respect for the seeking self in all of us, no matter what form that reaching takes. We both sat there for a while listening to those silent teaching Buddhas, experiencing a strong closeness to each other.

Then we went out to join his family, who were waiting on the steps outside.

I may never again in my lifetime see that beautiful set of Buddhas or that young boy, but I treasure the moment we shared in that quiet temple. I was thankful that I was alone to take this time with someone I didn't know. If I'd been with a friend, I'd probably have been so busy talking I might have missed this.

I later learned that pilgrims long ago would visit Mendut first, then, under a long covered passageway, they would walk to the second temple with the "Harpies". Then, being purified, they would at last go to Borobudur. I had walked in the reverse direction, but felt uplifted anyway.

In Mexico there are straight lines from one temple complex to another across large valleys. Long ago, people walked in processions between them. I hadn't seen such a steep roof on a temple since I'd been in Uxmal in Mexico. Was I blending memories?

Chapter 10 - Facing Fear

After Borobudur where to go? The crowds of Jogjakarta still celebrating Mohammed's birthday felt too chaotic. My proprietor had told me of a beach where the Muslims go to have retreats and meditate, so I decided to go there for a few days of quiet.

There are jeeps that go to some places only as soon as you get enough passengers crowded in. After taking a bus to a street corner where these jeeps congregated, I sat for perhaps 20 minutes waiting for others who wanted to go in the same direction.

By this time I was used to people crowding around wanting to practice English, so I didn't think much of it when two young men climbed in the jeep and started talking with me. They were also going to Perangtritis. One was a student, wearing glasses, very scholarly looking, who spoke English extremely well. The other was a swarthy mesomorph, with muscles he was obviously proud of glistening under his dark skin. They offered to help me find a place to stay at the beach, but I thanked them, and said that I could manage by myself.

We bumped along a country road to a river where we got out. There were women carrying hundred-pound loads of rice in cloths, the corners of which were tied together in a knot. They slung these over their shoulders and nonchalantly waited for the "ferry". A large bamboo canoe-type boat was being poled across by two men, one at each end, with people crowding the center — all with baskets full of coconuts, taro root, and bananas for marketing in Jogjakarta.

I was surprised when the two "companions" with whom I'd been talking wanted me to pay their fare across. I explained that I had no desire for guides and if they thought they were guides, the best thing they could do was go back. No, they insisted, they were going on their own. So we crossed in the boat with the farmers who had been waiting on our bank of the river, with their enormous rice bags. Water came through the slats at our feet, but the boat floated and no one seemed concerned.

The proprietor had told me how to go when I got across, so I intended to walk the five kilometers to the beach village. My two "companions" wanted me to hire a carriage waiting there. I proposed they take that method, I had plenty of time. It was here that the student told me he had been intending to go to Borobudur when he saw me. I clearly told him I'd not invited him along, that I wanted no companions and that if either of them had become because of me, they had best turn back, because I had no need of them.

The student said he just wanted to visit the beach for an hour or two. The one who reminded me of Bacchus, with his slightly dissipated plump figure, said he'd come for the mushrooms. He offered to share some with me and show me a cave on the cliffs. I chose to ignore them as I walked along the road lined with coconut palms. "Bacchus" was full of exuberance and show-off. He tried to climb the coconut palms and steal a coconut, but thank goodness the trunks were all carefully wrapped with prickly bamboo branches and thistles to discourage such efforts.

It was noon. Every tuft of shade from the spindly palms was like an island of cool. As I walked, flanked by my unwanted "guides", I kept slowing down to lose them, then speeding up, ignoring the bravado and lackadaisical mischief of the bearded Bacchus as best I could. I couldn't shake them. When we finally got to the tiny village of perhaps ten bamboo huts by the beach, I discovered that despite my protestations, the two expected me to buy them lunch. When I made it clear that I wanted to be alone, and had no idea of buying anything for them, the student wandered off. The Bacchus sulked and told me he had no money. I found myself clearly telling him that it was his problem as to how to return. He finally wandered off in search of his mushrooms.

I'd had an idea of finding a thatched grass hut by the beach, but the heat baked the inside of the open bamboo restaurant. I ate, wondering if I'd been a bit stupid to turn down the offers of my companions. Then a fine looking young man sitting nearby asked if I would have the time to read English into his tape recorder. I liked his looks, said I'd come to write and meditate, but that I could find an hour or two in the next few days to help him.

He said he knew where I could stay when I told him I wanted something away from the village. We stopped first at his "room", a windowless cement cell which he said most of the rooms for rent resembled. He picked up his book and walked with me along the narrow paths framing the rice paddies to an outlying "resort" hotel where at least one room had windows. The rest had only a row of screened holes three inches in diameter near the ceiling. The room he showed me had windows on three sides. One looked towards the sea across dunes, the others overlooked rice paddies stretching to lava cliffs beyond.

Mahmud, my English "student" as he kept calling himself, left me to settle in, promising to leave me to my meditation and writing till one o'clock each day.

At dinner time, I sauntered back along the raised gravel path past some Brahma bull calves tethered under a bamboo shelter, past rice paddies full of ducks, and banana trees flapping in the evening air.

I had a dinner of rice and meat sauce—mostly rice—and watched the hungry dogs, at least thirty as far as I could count, foraging for an uneaten banana in the heap of coconut husks and garbage tossed out by all the concession huts into the common "street" that opened to the sea. Goats and chickens scattered when the dogs came. One poor dog, obviously the runt, pushed in his hunger too far, and a whole pack of dogs chased him howling into the village houses behind the open restaurants. It looked as if there were more dogs than people in this outpost.

I watched the waves on the expanse of beach, then turned back towards my little hotel. On the way I met two young women with whom I had a pantomime conversation. We were giggling at our efforts to talk when the "Bacchus" of the morning came staggering along. He was obviously following me. Thank heavens I'd stopped to talk, or I'd not have known it. He came up foggy eyed, I presume from mushrooms, obviously sure he was God's gift to women. Luckily the women were there to disapprove of his leering manner. Again I told him I wasn't interested in him and suggested that he go find someone else. He insisted on trying to get close to me as I clearly showed I didn't want any "loving". One of the women said something to him in Indonesian and he resentfully turned and left.

As he went away, I had a leap of unreasonable fear. What if he went to one of the magicians I'd heard were thick around this place? He was angry enough. I thanked my new friends and hurried back to my empty hotel. There must have been five other units, but it was deserted. There was no one around who might help me if he returned.

As it got dark and my nervousness increased, the "manager", a boy who appeared to be about sixteen, appeared with two tiny oil lamps. He couldn't speak English well enough for me to tell him my fears. He only indicated to me that when I went out I must shut my windows or the farmers would come in. He snatched the sweater off the chair to illustrate his meaning. I pointed to the jail-like, half-inch wooden bars across the windows, but he simply made a sawing motion with his hand. This didn't make me feel all too secure.

By this time my heart was beating and I felt sweaty, though I tried to tell myself all my fears were silly. At least I could take precautions. I locked my door and carefully closed the windows overlooking the sea. It was still light enough to see out across the rice paddies and I would be able to hear someone approach if they had to wade through the water.

I forced myself to read Thomas Merton's "Asian Journal" and pretended at least to be calm. Then as it got dark, I looked up to see a tiny green light dart across the window outside. My heart leaped. What if it were some magician peering in? All the stories of the Rama Hotel proprietor, and those of his son, about black magic came thundering into my thoughts. Stories of projecting astral bodies and transforming into animal disguises were all I could think of. Raw fear gripped me. Not all the reason I could muster would disperse it.

I told myself that if it were a firefly, though I'd never seen a green firefly here before, there would be loads of them flickering over the rice paddies. I got the nerve to look out into the dark. There was nothing. Not even the little green light. I began closing the big rickety shutters to the windows, locking the little flimsy hooks into place and feeling they were no protection at all. Just as I got the last shutter almost closed, the light came darting into the room. Strangely, I shut the shutter anyway.

I was shut in with the little green light. Pure panic had me at this point. The two tiny oil lamps gave out such weak light. I tried to turn one up and it went out.

Summoning up all my reason, I decided to go on reading though my pulse was beating so hard the words on the page danced. Nothing else was going on, just my own fear. All I could do was watch it. I felt this was an opportunity to face my fear. Was I afraid of evil? All my experiences had brought me into contact with the loving kindness of Buddha, St. Francis, the kindness of people all over Japan and the Philippines, even in Indonesia. It was a chance to experience faith and confidence in all the teachings of Buddha, Jesus, St. Francis, to have calm within myself, fear no evil, and trust in the power of compassion.

I kept trying to figure out why I had drawn this Bacchus into my experience. What was I putting out? Did I really want his amorous attentions? I felt sure I didn't, and that perhaps just my being a single woman traveling alone had raised his hopes beyond bounds, despite my repeated objections. I tried to meditate, but my mind was whirling. I could only pray that this young man find some satisfaction elsewhere and forget his frustration.

I collected around me all the protection objects given me. I had a tiny Buddha given me by my teacher, a big St. Francis cross given me by Sister Fe, a small one by Sister Carmen. I propped up the book of Thomas Merton's "Asian Journal" open to a picture of himself and the Dalai Lama. But it fell down. The cover of the book had a picture of the beautiful peaceful reclining Buddha he'd seen in Sri Lanka. I set that up. Then I sat calmly for about an hour and blew out the only light.

Just at that moment, the green light settled on the narrow ledge in front of me, next to the lamp. In the dark I saw the glow of the light. I was much calmer. I gently picked up the firefly and put it out, even if it were some spirit. I knew I was putting out my fear with concern for a poor trapped firefly. Crazy the nature of fear and what makes it subside. I think I passed another test that night.

Chapter 11 - Perangtritis

The rest of the time spent at the beach was calm and delightful. I sat each morning till dawn. Just as it got light, I could hear the sounds of the farmers wading in the paddies at 5:30 each morning. I was trying to catch up with writing my diary, but I spent much time gazing at the farmers as they worked.

One man spent two days in his bare feet stepping on the dry stubble left from the last rice harvest. He pressed each patch down into the muddy water to disintegrate and provide fertilizer for the next crop. The sound of the steady slurp of his feet as they rose from the mud, the squash as he shoved down another clump, was the only sound besides the crashing waves in the distance.

I watched a young boy of fourteen or so, perhaps the farmer's son, ride on a long pole dragged across the slippery mud by two white patient gentle cows. He talked kindly to them and they turned back at each row's end without apparent guidance. Back and forth they went monotonously, slowly, till interrupted by a drenching rainstorm. Both the farmer, who had been sitting on the narrow ridged edge of the paddy, and his son, retreated to a thatched shelter which was three paddies away, leaving the two placid cows standing where they stopped, while torrents of rain poured down their white flanks, leaving them a soggy gray.

There seemed to be no hurry to this rhythm. Sometimes the farmer would stand or squat on the edge of the paddy, staring off into space for long periods. They worked smoothly, unhurriedly, touching the earth without apparent effort. They hoed precisely, forming the walls between paddies using a bamboo pole for a straight edge. The women planted their rice lined up in straight rows with the bamboo pole as a gauge. Women in lines, each with a clump of rice sprouts in one hand, bent their backs in unison and shoved the plants beneath the water into the mud. They moved in rows, backing up together as each row was planted, not straightening up for hours. Even in the gentle rain they continued. Only in the downpours did they seek shelter.

I read a quote in Thomas Merton's book: *"Whoever hath lived in accordance with the law of discipline in gentleness and purity will, having transcended deaths and births, put an end to his sorrow."* ....From a Tibetan script.

Could it be that all these farmers and their gentle cows have already attained that state?

Each afternoon Mahmud, who told me he was on the Political Science faculty at Jogjakarta University in the Political Science department, came to have me read English aloud from his book into his tape recorder. He had a book of lectures given by Sidney Hook in 1976. It had the English translation on one page and the Indonesian version on the facing page. He had obviously read and reread the English side, by the look of the underlined pages in different colored inks. He wanted to learn an American accent, not an English or Australian one, and was delighted he had found me.

An odd experience occurred as I read the cadences of Sidney Hook on Existentialism, Ethics, and Marxism. I had always steered clear of these subjects in school, feeling incapable of understanding them. Now with only the necessity of pronouncing the words correctly, I began to absorb the meaning sideways as I read aloud.

There is a professional cadence and language structure to the speech of academicians born in the early 1900's which Sidney Hook's vocabulary and expression reflected. As I read aloud these familiar phrases, I could hear my father, a Professor of History at Ohio State University and Columbia, echoing in my intonation. It was like hearing a lecture by my father coming from my own mouth.

I knew my father was an acquaintance of Sidney Hook. Whether they were friends or not I didn't remember. Yet here in Indonesia, clear across the world and twenty years after my father's death, came thoughts, words, and phrases I'd been too afraid to examine for fear of my own ignorance, in my father's expressions and idioms, laced with the same ironic humor. From that distance both in time and space, I was able to grasp the meaning and to enjoy the interplay of ideas I'd shrunk from so long. So, from an effort to help Mahmud with his English came a gift to me, perhaps from my deceased father who, I had an uncanny sensation, might be somehow looking on with his amused objectivity!

There was a reference to Zen meditation in one of Hook's articles, and Mahmud was very interested in zazen. So after a bit of instruction, Mahmud and I sat zazen in that tiny room together with only the sound of the waves crashing outside.

Mahmud kept calling me "teacher" and kept trying to pay for my room while I kept insisting he was teaching me! I was so very much impressed by his curious mind and eager discipline that wanted to tackle such complicated ideas in a foreign tongue, when my lazy brain had not been willing to grapple with the subjects in my own language! Mahmud seemed to me to represent the intelligent, diligent, ambitious spirit of the students of Indonesia, eager to absorb all the best the West has to offer, willing to undergo the effort and struggle to attain it.

So many young American students, already surfeited with opportunities for learning, are too lazy to apply themselves to such subjects as these Indonesians devoured. Sometimes, I feel that they will soon outstrip the undisciplined and lazy minds of our own country, and we'll be the ones to look to them for example. What a funny world it is!

From my diary, Jan. 7, 1982, 6:30 a.m.

I'm sitting high on a volcanic cliff overlooking a beach that stretches to the right as far as I can see, with the rolling waves crashing line after line, roaring in their own destruction. As I sit, listening, I become aware of a high pitched sound, almost like crickets above the lower cadence of the waves. I realize it's the bursting of the myriad tiny bubbles of foam left on shore to pop as each wave recedes. What a fantastic din they all make together. Each infinitesimal bubble inaudible against the gigantic low pitched roar, but together they fill the air with their bursting!

I gaze out contented, sorry others can't see this, but knowing somehow we're each doing something for everyone else . Right now, I'm sitting watching waves for everyone. The farmer who comes splashing through the rice paddies outside my window at the end of my zazen at 5:30 this morning is planting rice for me, bending his back all day in ankle deep water for everyone! Mike, my son, is mountain climbing for everyone, my weird Bacchus is stealing coconuts and eating mushrooms for everyone! The big bumble bee hastily gathering honey from the blooming touch-me-nots before the rain comes is doing it for everyone. How close to everyone I feel today!

There's a storm coming and I must go down. Rain will drench this book and me for everyone!

Among the interesting people I met at Perangtritis beach was a young British helicopter pilot who was teaching Indonesians how to fly. He told me there was a full scale war going on right off the coast of Java, where Indonesians were fighting to take over a small island. Hospitals were full of casualties brought in daily. This young man told me that he had been afraid he was getting too old (he's in his thirties) to travel freely round the world. Seeing me in my fifties gave him encouragement that there was always time to do it!

I also met a very blond young English woman, a teacher, who had started traveling two years before, and was still on her journey. She was, at the moment, with a beautiful dark young man from Borneo. This was frowned on by the Indonesians, and she felt relieved to talk with a person who felt no judgment. They seemed very happy and affectionate, were both benefitting from the other's culture and viewpoints.

He had been sharing his practice of "yoga walking" with her. He walked with his mind fully attending to his muscles, the feel of the sand, the motion of his body. This sounded very much like "mindfulness" as practiced by Theravadan meditators in Thailand, Korea, and Burma. He had shaved his head several times in sympathy with Buddhist monks.

As we watched the sunset on the beach together, he recalled memories of his early childhood on Borneo. He used to go on fishing trips with his father and brother in a little canoe. He remembered the feeling before Westerners had come into his life. He seemed to like both past and present. He looked to me very Mayan in his features, and when I commented, his girlfriend burst out with the same feeling. "If I didn't know where I was, if you forget geography, I'd think I was in the middle of Peru somewhere."

I had already begun to notice that no matter which country I was in, there were people with the features of almost every other country in the world. I wonder more and more at the apparent unity of the world despite our feelings of difference.

Peaceful days of sitting, climbing the cliffs, watching the farmers plant a whole group of rice paddies, watching children play. I watched two young girls who obviously had been given responsibility for their baby brother while their mother cooked. They laid him down on the sand, arranged his clothes as if he were a big doll, laughing and teasing with him. One sister, about eight years old, lifted him up and carried him on her hip as casually and expertly as any adult. He lay or rode contentedly, enjoying their affection and attention like a live plump doll. Loving and relaxed attention, such natural occupations. Who needs a doll when responsibility for a live child brings out kindliness and caretaking?

Do we, in our cement and steel houses, feeling so remote from those days, farm our small plots to recapture some of that spacegazing ease of the rice farmers? Do we, when we fish by a silent stream or play with dolls, exercise a vestigial muscle in us that still echoes those days of peaceful Eden?

On the last day of my peaceful visit to this meditative place, I walked two and a half miles along the endless beach and back, with the clear early morning light shining on the glistening sand as the waves receded. There's a period just before the wave turns when a soft mist of drops forms over the curve like a halo or a frosty breath before destruction. Even the waves reflect the state of our lives.

It was Mohammed's birthday. My beach was crowding up with visitors, and I felt it was time to be moving on. Full of quiet peace, I left my retreat. After we'd crossed the river in the canoe, I rode in a jeep all the way into Jogjakarta with a miserable dog crouched in a burlap bag. Its white tipped tail stuck out from a hole in the bag. The poor dog howled and yelped continually as the indifferent farmer — guardian of the bag, stared at the scenery.

I suddenly realized why there was such a large number of dogs. They were to be the tasty dishes to celebrate this special occasion!

The white tipped tail reminded me of my own rather pampered dog, Bub. How differently cultures view animals. All the dogs on the beach seemed to recognize Westerners and flock around for affection and play. The Indonesians treated them the way we treat pigs and chickens. While Indonesians associated equally with dogs, pigs, and chickens, till time for slaughter, we pen up pigs and chickens, creating a distance from our prospective dinner. Odd, that I should catch a wakening glimpse of our own way of life in such a startling way!

Chapter 12 - The Dieng Plateau

Back in Jogjakarta, the Rama Hotel was packed full with celebrating vacationers. The proprietors let me use their son's room since I had become a friend of the family, having met all but one of the nine children.

His very tiny room was on the first floor. It could have been the room of any 19-year-old college student. Books—many in English—posters of skydivers, motorcycles, horses, an enormous TV and stereo system that took up almost all the room except for a single bed above a storage unit of drawers. The room belonged to the son who was causing the proprietor so much concern. His modern inclinations seemed directed toward wiping out the deeper values of Moslem tradition.

I had washed my clothes in the cold water by the enormous well in the inner courtyard, and while they were drying on the line on the roof, again I talked with the family.

The wife was Hindu, born in India, obviously very happily married to her gentle, wise Muslim husband. They had raised the whole family while living in the hotel. All the children were educated, and each had been encouraged to carry on his own religious practice. The oldest daughter had learned Moslem Yoga from her father and practiced daily, besides studying to become a teacher. She had traveled to many places in Java and showed me her pictures. She loved the Dieng Plateau, way up in a mountainous region of central Java. The pictures of the rising sun were beautiful. She also assured me it was cooler at the higher altitude. I decided to go there, and as soon as my clothes were dry, I started off for the "bus station", leaving most of the contents of my pack with my friends.

Bus stations are rather disheveled affairs in Asia. I remembered the Greyhound bus station in San Francisco which, in 1979, was a tawdry thing for the U.S., with shabby walls and tired equipment, but it was thirty years ahead of the bus system in Asia. All the buses seemed on their last wheels, chipping paint, dented dull luster metal bodies. The overall impression I had was epitomized by one old wall plastered with posters peeling and mutilated by passing vandals.

Indonesian buses are made for smaller, less well fed bodies. Where a seat in U.S. would accommodate two people, three could sit easily on an Indonesian bus, and when the bus got crowded, a fourth could perch on the end with feet in the aisles.

I took the bus to Wonosobo, flanked by two other passengers. By the window sat a disgruntled New Zealander who'd been working in Melbourne in a factory making plastic bags. He'd suddenly quit his job to go traveling. I sat with my cloth purse resting on my lap, my camping pack at my feet, and the sandwich bag with my money buckled around my waist, pulled over on the side next to the New Zealander, thank goodness. We talked animatedly, and I was only aware of the person on my left when he got out and another passenger sat down beside me.

Two hours later, when we arrived at the end of the line, I got up to leave the bus, and things began tumbling out of my purse. It was then that I realized that the person next to me had cut a clean slit through four layers of quilted cloth just the size for a hand to feel around. Nothing was missing. Such discrimination! I had most of my money, traveler's checks, air ticket, along with my passport, all in my waist belt under my blouse. The potential thief wanted none of my less interesting possessions, address book, sandwiches, pens and the usual traveler paraphernalia. I was puzzled that though my bag was wrinkled, and folded in my lap, the cut was straight and clean, as if it had been held straight. Could this have been one of the black magic artists my hotel friend had warned me about?

Thankful I'd lost nothing, I got out to look for the bus going up the mountain the rest of the way. One of the Indonesians standing at the platform, obviously waiting for a bus, told me that there were no buses going to the Dieng Plateau; I must hire a bemo or jeep. The proprietor had told me there were indeed buses, so I stubbornly kept asking where the bus stop was. There was a bus, but it was obvious that the native people here felt differently about tourists and didn't welcome them here. I learned why soon enough.

There was a large parking lot full of bemos nearby, and I was crowded by bemo drivers trying to bargain with me for a chartered ride.

By this time a group of five Western travelers had gathered. We were all going to the same place. I tried to go by myself, as I was still hoping to travel more with Indonesians. I found a bemo with three Indonesians already seated, waiting to fill its capacity. I got inside. The Bemo driver came over and spoke to two passengers in their own language. They politely got out of the jeep. When I looked concerned, the Indonesians merely smiled and said everything was all right. By that time I was crowded in way at the back, and it would have taken unseating all the rest to get out. He drove off and left the two Indonesians standing, waiting for another jeep. I'm sorry I didn't get out, but at least I objected to the driver, who had spoken very good English before, but now professed not to understand me. I felt it was terrible that he'd ousted those people in order to accommodate us. It was obvious he did it to make more money.

The ugly head of greed, that had been showing an eye here and a tooth there, now rose fully before me. Most of the transportation people in Indonesia seemed subject to this temptation, which I admit must have been enormous.

Apparently Australians, who are the closest geographically, come in droves to Indonesia for vacations. They have a fairly high standard of living. Seeing the discrepancy in life styles, they tend to be generous, almost always chartering jeeps instead of riding buses, and not participating fully in the bargaining that is culturally a part of every transaction.

This "easy money" has two results. One effect is that most Indonesians dealing frequently with tourists, such as the handicraft salesmen and transportation people, develop a contempt for Westerners who "don't know the value of money". They enjoy the bargaining transaction, which provides a way of relating to people they would not ordinarily meet, a way of appreciating each other's sense of humor, endurance, interplay, as well as their patience and control. It is a way of respectful transaction. All of that is cut out by agreement on the first price asked. Even if it is exorbitant, the seller is disappointed if denied the enjoyment of a human relationship in the bargaining.

The other effect is to develop an appetite for money for its own sake. Since it is so easy to get from the Australians, some jeep drivers lose all sense of discrimination and demand high prices from everyone. If refused, they turn away in contempt and leave you stranded. This I experienced to extreme in Bali.

We rode up the winding way past terraced hillsides where potatoes and cabbages speckled rich dark earth with different shades of green.

Farmers, wearing the pointed coolie hat and carrying two baskets on a pole supported across one shoulder, were cutting the weeds and grasses along the road to take to their goats. It seemed a neat way to take care of the road and feed the local livestock at no cost for road maintenance. How much healthier than our way of spraying vast areas with poisons to kill unwanted weeds.

Despite my wish to travel separately, I found that all of us had indeed become a group by the time we arrived in the mist at the top of the mountains. There was a "Hotel" near where the bus stopped, and since we were all looking for a reasonable place stay, we decided to share the few rooms there were.

Three young Germans, a Dutch girl, the New Zealander and I, filled all the rooms in the empty hotel. It was rather an enlarged house. The living room had been converted into a rather stark dining room with picnic tables and benches in it. The rooms were, as usual, small quarters with only a two-foot space between bunk beds, a chair and small table. The proprietor issued a padlock for our rickety door.

The tiny hotel was perched on one lip of the gigantic caldera of an ancient volcano, with a great expanse of valley stretching out before us. In the middle were the ruins of a great Hindu temple complex, built in the 11th century. Nearly all of it crumbled to the ground in indistinguishable ruins because of the innumerable earthquakes. Still, several small buildings stood black against the green fields. We set out to explore these.

Tiny chapels faced what was once a street. Each building was empty, yet each had evidence of flowers and incense being offered regularly by respectful famers. It looked as though the farmers were continuing the recognition made centuries ago of the special nature of this spot. They seemed to serve as lay custodians in the absence of temple priests, carrying on, in abbreviated form, rituals from another era.

Then we walked further on up to an opening in the obviously still active crater. Fumes of sulphur wafted out to us long before we got to the spongy gray lifeless soil that usually surrounds hot springs. Here was a fifteen foot wide pot, boiling with such fury that great blobs of sulphur and steaming water shot six feet up in a thick fountain full of gurgling, coughing, hissing clamor. We stood in awe at the edge of this erupting boil, aware that the illusion of the solidity of the earth we walk on is only by permission of the inner core, which hides politely in its caverns beneath the seemingly secure crust we call solid rock.

It began to rain. None of us wore rain gear, so we splashed soggily back to the hotel where some of us changed clothes. There was no fire, no hot water for a shower. Thank heavens our proprietor had a few extra blankets. We shivered in the blankets as we drank tea in the dining room, and watched the proprietor's wife chew betel nut. In the streets of Jogjakarta, I'd seen the old women selling oranges, seated in squatting positions with the whole betel nut, about the size of a walnut, in their mouths while little rivulets of red juice ran down the corners of to their chins. Here there was a more sophisticated ritual of chewing the fruit.

The proprietor's wife had a little bottle of white paste. She spread a little of this, like butter, on a leaf using a stick. Then she cut some of the dry betel, wrapped it all up with a bit of a twig inside and, grinning, chewed till the juice had her teeth and lips all red. Christian and Caroline tried it, but I guess my sense of adventure met its limit here. They said the effect was to make their gums and jaws feel numb.

The next day we all took the 12-mile hike out into the terraced fields to visit more of the sulphur springs that reportedly heated whole lakes to tepid temperature even though the air was cold. The air was a refreshing cold for me, since I'd been literally sweating in the Philippines, and suffered from the heat everywhere at sea level in Java, which is just below the Equator. Here in the high mountainous area, the rain and cool air felt like a brisk September, though it was actually January. We were again caught in the torrents of one of the seasonal rain storms. We sought shelter with some farmers under an open thatched roof like the one the farmers used in Perangtritis.

One farmer could speak a little English and, to pass the time, tried on my Japanese jacket and posed proudly for a photograph. He said he wanted my jacket. This was the first time someone asked me for the clothes off my back, though it happened daily in Bali. I was still full of the respect for the spirit of St. Francis who repeatedly took off his own robe and gave it to beggars. I watched as I prudently held on to my own. I had no followers with me to go about obtaining a new jacket. So in a way I failed that test of my belief that "when there is a need, it will be answered". I chose to keep myself equipped even if simply. I had at least loaned my sweater to the shivering Caroline, the Dutch girl who had left the hubbub of Jakarta spontaneously for a weekend in the mountains without any extra clothes.

To pass the time, I began to read the palms of my companions. Then the farmer who had tried on my jacket, reached for my hand. With great seriousness, and with the help of his friend's translation, he pretended to read my hand. Pointing to my hand, he said: "You should go back to your own country and get a job, and not wander uselessly around the world like this." He clowned in the air like a fortune teller while his companions laughed. I got his point. He reflected the view many villagers must have, who see strange foreigners who spend weeks and months in seeming idle wandering with no sign of having to make a living. What could I say to him? I only grinned recognition.

The rain kept pouring in sheets of silver, dropping in great muddy pools around the edges of the dry shelter. It looked like an all day rain. We finally decided to continue our walk in the wet. We were soaked through when we came to a small village where we could warm ourselves in a tea house. Two women ushered us into their kitchen where a charcoal fire burned on the floor, heating the room as well as the water for the tea. Both women wore beautiful long batik skirts and very fine silk blouses. What a contrast between the grimy smoke smeared walls and floor and the beautiful dresses they wore without aprons. I noticed they squatted to do the cooking, not needing chairs.

After warming ourselves with tea and some delicious cinnamon crackers, our group waited in the sheets of rain till a driver stopped, laughed at us, and offered to give us a ride in the back of his pick up truck under a huge tarp. Gratefully, we all crawled under. We could feel the cold wind, though at least we were dry. I could look out through a small hole in the tarp to the road where, despite the downpour, the workers were trudging along the endless hills carrying their loads of cut grass or vegetables on poles. They were thinly dressed and barefoot, drenching wet, and I knew how cold they must feel. No one stopped to pick them up. How was I so lucky not to be walking under their burdens?

Again, we shivered in the cold "dining" room, drinking hot tea and eating puffed rice biscuits, and talking of volcanoes. Christian had been at Mt. Saint Helen's four days before it erupted. We seemed to be the only tourists sitting there on the steaming caldera. We couldn't help wondering what had brought us all together here.

All of us on budgets watched our New Zealand associate devouring the expensive rice cakes and nut brittle conveniently placed in jars in the middle of the table. The others of us ate sparingly, counting our own expenditures. It was interesting to watch when we all settled accounts how he'd "forgotten" to count his. He had been eating blindly, reaching for what was in front of him till it was gone, with no thought of sharing or for assuming responsibility for his amount.

There have been times when I've caught myself in this greedy pattern of eating. Thank goodness I was more awake at this point, but I got a picture of it in full color none the less. What a difference between the attitudes of travelers on this earth! There are those who are aware of others and assume their own responsibilities, and there are those who are completely oblivious of their surroundings no matter where they are: two different mental states wandering around the world.

Before dawn on our last day, I got up to walk to what was reported to be a spectacular overlook for viewing the sunrise. I walked for nearly five miles, greeting the surprised villagers as I passed, to discover a mist so thick there could be no "sunrise". As I turned to go back, a young man wearing a hard hat picked me up and offered me a welcome ride back. He was a geologist, a graduate of Jogjakarta University, working in the area developing geothermal energy.

On the way back, he stopped to drop something off at his "plant".

We drove off on a side road, and suddenly we were in the midst of cranes, trucks, metal storage tanks as big as those in U.S. refineries. It was a blast of big industry hidden away just miles from the easily visible rural rice paddies and vegetable terraces. I had just come over the hill fresh from a village of grass and bamboo huts where water buffaloes grazed on the weeds and women were carrying their wash out to dry.

As we rode back, I talked with this curious, intelligent young man. I got a glimpse of Indonesia's future, where human effort towards our "progress" in industry will cause a great change. Will they, too, have to experience all the accompanying ills resulting from material gain which we have pursued so single mindedly ourselves, or have we learned anything from our mistakes along the way that can be passed on for others' benefit?

Our whole group went back to Jogja together. There we separated with mutual affection gained on the trip. I was glad for a short interlude of companionship.

Before I left Jogja, since I was already feeling ready to move on to Bali, I took one last bus ride out into the country. Then I walked between the rice paddies, watching boys herding ducks, and farmers shoveling new low walls from the crumbling edges of their plots. They piled up the soft mud in precise lines, smoothing the edges with the shovel till they were as straight as the bamboo pole they used as a guide. Some men and women were barefoot, standing in the mud while planting small shoots of new rice. They waved to me as I walked by, smiling at my coolie hat, and gave me the thumbs up gesture of approval. I was tempted to offer to help them. But to my regret, I passed on by.

On the bus ride back, I saw a whole series of shops displaying grave stones. It seemed to be the main business of the area. Maybe these stone cutters were the descendants of the artists who cut the stones for Borobudur and Prambanan. Once these people were great artists carving the exquisite bas reliefs of Ramayana stories and Buddha. Now they carve the symbols of leaves or flowers on tombstones in the same black lava and marble rock that built those great monuments.

I had one flicker of recognition that I, myself, was the descendant of well known people, yet I dabble in smaller activities than either of my parents. Just another sign of the breathing out and breathing in of the world.

One more night in Jogjakarta. I was going to miss the sounds that had become so familiar while I sat in meditation.

Insert from my diary: Sitting sounds in Jogjakarta

4:00 a.m. - Time for Moslem prayers. Voices calling out from loudspeakers, first from far away across town; wails, like wolf calls in the dark. Then more and more minarets take up the cry, and the sound becomes louder and chaotic as the chorus of cries mingle and float in variegated call to prayer.

Then silence.

Next, the steady scrape, scrape, scrape of someone sweeping the street. The stiff spines, taken from coconut leaves, tied together, scratch with a bristling, persistent rhythm. Sweep, sweep, pause, brush into dustpan, sweep, sweep, sweep again.

Then a child's voice singing a sing-song tune like a verse accompanying a bouncing ball or rhythmic clapping.

Traffic sounds in the streets begin. Buses roar, bemos honk. There are sounds of sticks struck together, gongs gonging, high pitched bells ringing, announcing that different street vendors have come, wheeling their carts full of cooked breakfast buns or juice.

Later sounds as I go out: "Hey, mommie, where are you going?" from the rickshaw drivers. Hooves pound and wheels splash suddenly into pothole puddles on the rough gouged street.

"What's your name? Where do you come from?" from all sides from anyone trying to practice English. Little children call "Hello- Salamat Bagi" (good morning) in sing song voices making fun of foreign accents.

"For you, very cheap! 3,000 Rupees" from vendors along the way (Not cheap at all). Then the high wet sound of pouring rain splashing on shiny streets, slapping against ponchos and metal buses, dripping from eaves in high pitched continuous sighs.

I said goodbye to the proprietor of the Rama Hotel and his fine family. I felt privileged to grasp the feeling of a sincere Moslem way: a generous, compassionate and gentle way devoted to meditation and self development of one's kinder instincts and self control of one's hurtful tendencies. It's no different from the deeper reaches of any religion into the hearts of its followers.

Chapter 13 - Bali, and Money

While flying to Bali, I wondered again at the odd fluke that had me rerouted to a place I had intended to avoid, and ever since I'd started traveling I'd heard from many people that Kata Beach was to be avoided. I had already given Sister Fe the money I had allotted for a stay in Bali. In spite of my intent to bypass it, the airlines had rerouted me there anyway. So what was going to happen? This open curiosity was really a bit exciting.

As I got off the plane I asked one of the airline stewardesses if she knew Dini, my friend from Jakarta. She beamed in delight and said, "You must be Ellen!" She wanted me to come to her hotel to visit, but I suspected it was too expensive for my budget. I suggested that I find a place in Kuta and meet her for dinner, not dreaming of how far away her hotel actually was.

So I got on a jeep that dropped me and several other travelers off on the main street in Kuta. I found myself in a dismal lane bounded by stores selling tape recordings of American rock music, stores selling clothes, paintings, wood carvings, bathing suits, a veritable barrage of chaos that tourism seems to draw together. I walked, pack on my back, through this noisy confusion in a sort of shocked daze.

It was still three in the afternoon so I had some time to catch on to the way of the world here, but before I even got to a tea shop, a quiet voice from among the sales ladies along the row asked: "Are you looking for a room?" I answered, "Yes, but not in all this noise. I want a quiet place." "This is a quiet place," she answered. "It's a bit away from here. Would you like to see it?" There was no choice but to look. She had to find her brother, who had a motorcycle, so I waited patiently for an hour, fascinated at my trust that this would work out.

Her brother arrived. I climbed on the back of the motorcycle, and we splashed along streets with great potholes full of the recent rains. Then we drove off the main street through a coconut palm grove to a small cluster of cement units. Florida motel style, I call it. Here, among one of five units, was a clean room, with a western toilet, a big delight I must say. It cost less money than my room in Jogjakarta. What a gift!

There were only six rooms in my lodging unit, constructed in a row, motel style, surrounding an inner court where a pavilion under a bamboo roof provided a "temple" for the Hindu family that owned and ran the place. As I woke early out of habit, I heard the delighted cries of the proprietor's one year old baby as she toddled along the walk. Her mother was following her with a wash basin, splashing water over her slippery soaped up body when she could catch up with her.

Our set of rooms was less than five minutes' walk from the beach, buffered from the crowds and denser housing by a quiet coconut grove. Beyond the grove, the road was already the gateway to the swift paced world of tourist infested Kuta.

My memory of Bali is inseparable from the memory of the hassles with transportation people. Here the opportunity to gain money from tourists presents the greatest temptation. Bali was an exaggerated example of what the beguilement of "riches" could do to enhance the personal characteristics that usually accompany greed. Most of the Balinese people seemed generally a gentle, kind, patient, and thoughtful people. But the people involved in transportation that presented themselves to me on every corner seemed a different breed.

There are no public buses in Kuta, only bemos that everyone uses: the shopkeepers, the farmers, the working people. These for the Balinese are fairly cheap, 200 rupees to get to Denpasar, about thirty miles away.

The first time I stood on a street corner to catch a bemo (a big passenger jeep), a young American woman who ran a dress shop in Kuta was there with me. She knew the local fee for transportation and was refusing to pay a higher one. For two hours she'd stood on the corner as taxi drivers called out to her in derisive tones, "2,000 rupees" almost like children teasing. These bemo drivers passed us without picking up anyone—even the farmers waiting with us, which must have endeared us to them. If a driver stopped, it was to demand 500 rupees of her as others got on. I would have expected her to be somewhat exasperated after such a long hassle, but she was determined not to pay more than the listed fare, and finally a bemo picked us up for the 200 rupee rate.

She told me that you can get on a bemo, and if you know the rate, can pay it at the end of the trip as all the natives did. If they stated the rate for you before you got on, you had to pay that amount.

Drivers didn't look at my pack and clothes. They only reacted to the Western face and hiked up the fee almost automatically. Since I had already given Sister Fe, in the Philippines, the money I'd allotted for a month's stay in Bali, I was living on a tight budget, figuring maybe I could spend just a week here. If I had spent what the bemo drivers so frequently demanded, I'd have lasted maybe one day.

The proprietor of my lodgings had already briefed me as to what I should expect as "reasonable" fares for each section of the trips I wanted to take. I decided I would try to hold to what seemed a fair price. What amazed me was the enormous mark-up the bemo drivers were demanding. When I refused, they would drive off with contemptuous, "Oh, you have money!" I watched as they callously demanded 100% mark-ups of Western travelers. They showed such contempt and seemed to enjoy such a sense of power as they drove off, leaving helpless tourists to stand and wait for yet another bemo.

If I'd been willing to spend the money, I easily could have chartered a bemo to any place in Bali, as many tourists did. Others split the fee, and therefore felt they were spending less. But on one ride that I shared, a group of four people had agreed with the driver to pay 10,000 rupees for what my proprietor had said ought to be only 800 rupees, and I had estimated a mark-up of perhaps 1,000! One bemo driver on the main corner, who continually demanded high fares from me, tried to persuade the other bemo drivers not to pick me up as they slowed down. He became angry when I would not accept his price. Odd, that he was the one in a fury. I found myself patiently waiting for a better arrangement—which usually presented itself in a half hour.

As I write this I'm aware that I'm reflecting the focus forced on me during my stay in Bali—MONEY! But I also learned a very good lesson—how to be patient, firm and good natured in the presence of demanding contemptuous people. I had time, and was watching myself deal with a potentially frustrating situation in a pretty calm manner. I felt these bemo drivers were the best teachers I had on the whole trip. I felt myself becoming strong. I don't think there was any more powerful learning than this patience, holding to what I believed was fair, in the presence of emotional pressure and what could have been the urgency of "time".

I also experienced the feeling that so many minority people in the United States must have when the reaction to race blinds any perception of the "individual" in any situation. I was always surprised that most of the bemo drivers treated all Western faces alike. There was no discrimination between those who were more expensively dressed, obviously in the habit of overlooking the cost of things, and the shabby jean-wearing traveler who counted every penny. Their thinking seemed to be that all Westerners have money, or they wouldn't be in Bali, which was true in some sense.

I watched prejudiced behavior become exaggerated when concern for money was uppermost. As I watched the innately generous Balinese people step into the world of progress and finance, I caught a glimpse into the origins of the sense of separation between people in the U.S. Greed for money and power seems to blind perceptions. People who choose to extract money from others often pull away from them, lump them together, and treat them all the same, no matter what the individual circumstances may require. This seems to be almost a corollary of our economic system when applied without some ethical philosophy, given the temptations to our human spirit.

I had learned, through conversations with many young people in coffee shops and on bemos, that the well meaning Australians vacationing in Bali are contributing to the change. They make very good money. Australians generally come to Indonesia for a three week period. They spend lavishly, feeling, perhaps, that they can share some of their money with the poorer population. The result of this generous spending has not been to raise the living standard of the poor. It seems to develop a new class of people: those dealing with tourists, who then become a rich class. The tour guides and those working in hotels have carefully learned the manners and customs expected by tourists. They may feel a bit of contempt for the helplessness of the general tourist and his lack of a sense of the value of money, but they have learned how to glean their share through polite behavior. My proprietor at the Rama Hotel had told me of a popular saying: "Beware of an Indonesian Smile".

The bemo drivers, a step or two down from the hotel people, feel no need of masking their contempt for the individual traveler because their greed has become insatiable, and it can only be mollified by money.

Chapter 14 - Kuta Beach

Note from my diary, January 17, 1982 - Kuta Beach at 5:00 a.m.

I walk through the rustling palm grove, leaves lashing in a high wind. It feels like a storm coming. The sea is just over the rise, but its roar is blurred and distant. I splash through the edge of a rice paddy beside a cluster of bamboo houses. Then the sea. There are lights still on along the shore to the left. The sky is still dark, softened by the coming dawn. Low rolling breakers crash in an edge of white. This time the tide is coming in. Yesterday, the sun glistened on the shiny sand where coral and broken shells were discarded by the receding tide. The sea is green with a misty grey transparency as the waves curl before crashing.

Many Balinese joggers spread out along the shore, gracefully striding along the line above the white froth, dark skins silhouetted against the beige sand.

One young man with a temple sash tied round his waist wades into the water and washes his legs. Is it an early morning purification?

I sit along the high tide line. Coconut leaves, seaweed, plastic shoes, and suntan bottles mingle in a tangled frame along a sea-swept beach. There are fifteen dogs now clustering around me, companionably rolling over each other, chasing along the expanse of quiet sand. They keep me company, as did the dogs who walked with me at home in California.

I gaze at the rising waves rolling, pouring over themselves in the same way that I gazed at the waves of fog pouring over Black Mountain in California. Am I so far away? So hard to write about what's happened and past. So hard to write about what is. First I stopped taking pictures because I had to pull myself away from the happening. Now to write, I must take my eyes away from the succession of waves moving towards me, never reaching me— always appearing to move forward, but like Alice, staying always

*where they are. Maybe that's me too—only seeming to move on.
Something is changing, but I stay the same.*

*I'm joined by a crusty woman who each morning has offered me
a "smoke" which I regularly refuse. Today she will not move on.
Squatting down beside me, she says: "No smoke, no good". Her
eyes are lovely, she has cheeks like Katherine Hepburn. She says she
wants white skin; wants my shirt. "Indonesian shirt no good."*

*She wants a tourist boyfriend. "They all kiss. Good food, a place to
sleep", then when they leave her at the airport, she cries—"many
tears", they offer plenty money, give address, very nice". Indonesian
men all kiss, kiss, kiss, I ask for money, they say, "Later, Later". Then
get ready to go. NO money. No address. Not so good."*

*She rocks back and forth beside me. I'm reminded of Patricia, a
friend at home. How close I feel to her. I walk back along the shore,
sun already getting hot at 7:30.*

*I meet an older Indonesian tourist, expensive camera round his
neck, from Los Angeles. He's come back "home" for the first time in
fifty years. His home is gone, a big building is there. He's had a big
shock, it's all changed so. And people here talk of the change in the
past two years! He used to live in Magalan near Borobudur. That's
changed too. He's going home to Los Angeles.*

*I mention I'm going to Thailand: "I've been there, too, as a prisoner
of war of the Japanese." We talk of war. I mention Hiroshima.
He was there when the bomb dropped —"Near. I survived. My
associates didn't." To survive seems all.*

*I remember Caroline whom I met on the Dieng Plateau, whose
mother grew up in Jogjakarta. She told me she had visited the place
where her grandfather had sat in a school courtyard, a prisoner,
awaiting death by firing squad. Memories sweep like shadows even
across the beaches of Bali. Was it our greed for power and money
that prompted international invasions of even peaceful Bali? Did
it spark the seed of greed lying dormant under a simpler lifestyle
where temptation is not so great? The tourists come and the
Balinese change to be more like us!*

Until about 7:00 a.m., Kuta Beach was quiet the way I saw it. After that more and more tourists started arriving and I always left. I never saw the beach in "full swing", so for me, it was the beautiful beach it was when it attracted all the tourists in the first place. But from conversations I had learned the beach was "ruined". It was transformed into a crowded Western pleasure center with crowds and radios blasting. This seems to happen wherever rich Western tourists come. They bring their lifestyle with them, and as soon as the place becomes "spoiled", they move on to the next discovery, leaving the wreckage to be enjoyed by flocks of tourists who've heard of the reputation and come in crowds to see what's left of a beautiful foreign land. So the "nicer" town was Sonal, on a beach further away from Kuta. Kuta now collects the dregs.

How lucky I was to find my quiet lodging with the kind, intelligent Hindu family. They could have succumbed to the desire for more money, but preferred to pick their customers and ask for just what they needed to live comfortably, and keep the quiet, devout atmosphere of their own lifestyle.

Chapter 15 - Bali Temples

The proprietor of my "palm grove motel", a gentle, helpful young man, told me about several nearby points of interest. I liked his inner courtyard temple. He told me every family in Bali owning land had its own temple. Besides these, there were many big public temples within close range. I decided to visit these, since so many of the other tourist attractions were expensive.

He told me about Uluwatu, a temple on a tiny peninsula that I could reach fairly easily. After the usual delay trying to get a reasonable bemo ride to Denpasar, I got to the city in the very early morning. I was let off at the beginning of town. The bemos I needed were located at the far end of the town. Drivers of rickshaws called out to me, but I chose to walk. I had promised myself not to spend money on transportation when I could walk. The tourist map I had of Denpasar was drawn out of proportion, probably for the benefit of taxi drivers. What appeared on the map to be a distance of a half mile was actually only two blocks long, so I had much less to walk than I had estimated.

The walk provided benefits! As I went slowly along the streets, I peered over old five-foot-high brick walls into large, private yards where temples stretched their tiers of thatched pagoda-like roofs up as high as fifty feet. There was a stone temple structure on nearly every block, some enclosed by brick walls with open gates.

I wandered through an open gate into a neglected, weedy yard where a red brick tower rose, with big round Dutch china plates decorating its square façade like giant gemstones. There were gargoyle guardians at the corners looking somewhat fiercer than the already fierce temple guardians of China and Japan. The winged eagle "Garuda" god, that reminded me of the Mexican eagles in Aztec temples, was represented here too.

Weeds, ferns, and moss were growing out of every crevice,

but I discovered some incense, newly lighted, burning on a little shelf or offering place. By the look of the unkempt lot I had judged the temple a deserted remnant from times past, but just as in Borobudur and temples in the Dieng Plateau, people were still offering incense here, though they seemed to feel no need to keep the courtyard neat. Was this a shadow or projection of my own way? I had to look hard at this. I sometimes pay attention to what I think is important, neglecting the surface things which to others are so obvious but which escape my mind's eye.

As I walked further, I passed a whole procession of women and men carrying offerings in baskets balanced gracefully on their heads. They were making their daily rounds to give offerings at various temples. My landlord had explained that they always wore red, yellow or gold when going to a temple. The women wore long gold embroidered red skirts, the men wore only the familiar temple sash around their waists over their everyday clothes.

Everywhere I walked there were people, most often women, gathered at street corners and in front of shops, weaving little square baskets from flat bamboo strips, and arranging beautiful flowers and rice cakes in them as daily offerings. I felt I was observing the origins of religious patterns that I observed in Japanese temples. I had first seen this practice at the home and temple of Kobun's brother in Japan, where his wife had offered rice at the altar and to the ancestors each morning while we were chanting the morning service. Ever since, I have felt that to be a wonderful way to begin a day.

I found the marketplace and after some search, located a driver who would go at least as far as the last town on the island. The temple, it seemed, was situated on a small outer island attached by a causeway. He said I'd have to negotiate on my own from there. Suddenly he asked me to wait and disappeared in the crowds.

Since I didn't have any idea how long he would be gone, I didn't wander far into the wonderful chaos of early morning commerce. Several streets had been blocked off to traffic. People, baskets of vegetables and fruits, and bags of rice were crammed into every space available in a general friendly hubbub of exchange.

After 45 minutes, the driver returned with a high stack of little square baskets piled one on another, each full of rice and flowers. He explained that the route was not heavily traveled by people who wanted to visit the temple. Mostly surfers chartered bemos to go there. Since I had wanted to visit the temple, he had taken advantage to make his own offerings to the spirits of the temples we passed on the way.

As we sped along the country road, I was surprised when he just tossed a basket out of the window. It landed on the street and skidded, leaving flowers and rice scattered for the next passing car to run over. We had just passed a temple on the side of the road. Each time we passed a temple (and there were nine) he dumped another basket casually out the window.

I asked him if this was customary. "It doesn't matter where or how the offering lands, it's the spirit of the offering", he explained. As we rode, I noted remnants of other offerings scattered like garbage along the road. The once green bamboo baskets were brown and dry, flowers crushed by cars.

He dropped me off at a rural marketplace under large canvas canopies. Stalls with bushel baskets of bulk dry fish, fruit, rice, baked sweets, and ready-made offerings filled the air with a fragrance of dry fish and honeysuckle. I decided to go with the spirit of things and bought an offering. It cost about a dollar and was all full of pink and white blossoms, but no rice. Then came the problem of getting a bemo to take me out to the tip of the next island. Not so easy. My proprietor had told me that 500 rupees would be plenty, but everyone wanted 2,000 rupees. I guess it was the usual fare for the Australians with surfboards and lots of money who wanted to get to the waves, but I felt that this visit was more a continuation of the pilgrimage I had started in China, and I didn't feel the need to spend lavishly. So I decided to walk. I set out along the road determined to walk the 15 kilometers if I had to. It felt good to walk in the countryside, past farmers, bamboo houses, cows, and many great banyan trees.

All over Indonesia, but mostly in Bali, there are giant trees the size of the biggest redwoods. They seem to have been preserved, as building and farming wiped out nearly all trees. The feeling of reverence they inspire is reflected in the tiny offering shelves erected on the enormous tree trunks. Frequently a stepping stone path leads up to them. Always there are fresh offerings, usually burning incense.

I walked up to many of these old guardians. Their branches sent down aerial roots that in time had become thick tree trunks themselves, until the original trunk and all the new "saplings" melted into one mass. Standing close to these trunks, I felt like merging into the tree myself, to experience the quiet peace of these old souls.

I've always loved trees and have helped many children in California to develop a love of trees. It felt as if what we had to teach consciously was an accepted part of life here in Bali. The spirit of affection and respect for the plant world has taken on a visible form for all the adults to practice in their daily offerings to the spirit inside the tree.

I felt a "bleed-through" from my experiences in Japan. I remembered the way the Japanese felt about trees. In Tokyo, many tree trunks had fiber wrappings around them for protection from changeable temperatures during the winter. Parks had old trees with thick rope belts around the trunks, hung with bells and tassels to denote honor given to their ancient spirits. Here on this island in Indonesia, I could see where that spirit originated, which persists through all the modernization and cultural refinement. The Japanese people are spiritually not that far distant from the Island peoples. They express deep caring for growing things in their more restrained way. The meticulously manicured gardens show the same reverence for the plant world.

After I had been walking for nearly an hour, a young man rode up on a motorcycle. He offered to take me the whole way to the temple and back to Kuta for 2,000 rupees, so I accepted with relief. Besides, I wanted a ride on a motorcycle. We went through several small villages. Young girls in uniform were walking to school, books under their arms. They all seemed to know him and stared at me with surprise. Farmers carrying baskets of taro roots walked along the road, but otherwise the road was deserted.

As we rose up a hill, I could see the ocean, and greater expanses of unpeopled terrain. I was lucky I'd not had to walk the whole distance. When we finally got near the temple, he told me he couldn't ride the motorcycle any further, so he dropped me off at a tourist refreshment stall under a canopy, saying he'd pick me up in several hours. I was already thirsty, but all there was to drink was the horrible orange pop, Coke, and beer, at exorbitant prices that must have been easily affordable by the Australian surfers who frequented the place. I decided to wait till I was really thirsty.

I walked along a trail to the spot where an old stone gate opened to a long set of steep steps leading to an inner court. I felt the same feeling I had had years before while climbing up the steps to a sanctuary at Chichen Itza in Mexico. I felt as if I was rising out of my own past into a higher level of awareness.

A wizened gardener met me at the top, as if he'd been waiting for me. He put down his sickle when I said I'd come to make an offering and to meditate here. He pointed to the little offering basket which I'd clutched tightly during the whole walk and motorcycle ride, and asked "Did you pay for this?" Of course I had. He was disappointed, but indicated it would be all right to offer it to the god at the entrance.

In all the temple complexes I'd visited all over the world, the most reverent spot is the last you come to, so I realized sheepishly that a purchased offering was not good enough for the god inside the temple.

He stuck a flower behind my right ear and showed me how to bow low with palms together, touching my thumbs first to my third eye, then throat and heart. I left my offering before a statue of a stony figure carved in the ornate style which seemed reminiscent of the Mayan art of Mexico.

Bowing before these "gods" seemed natural, almost as if some part of me had long since done this. It was a gesture of observance to the spirit in us all that helps us aspire to the best that we can achieve, the most compassionate part of ourselves. I bowed, too, in the spirit of a pilgrim offering respect to religions derived from a common source — respect, gratitude, and wonder.

We progressed through a grassy yard to the final court. Here I found the now familiar pagoda with intricate wood carvings around four sides. The front had a set of closed doors (behind which, presumably, the god sat). A series of thatched roofs rose in tiers twenty feet high in a courtyard paved with coral blocks. I remembered again the church in Zambales in the Philippines. It was also made of blocks cut from a coral reef. A short wall enclosed the promontory. I could look straight down at the blue surging sea seventy-five feet below.

The gardener, who assumed the role of teacher, picked a flower, showed me how to hold it between the tips of my fingers, palms together, and touch again my forehead, throat, and heart. So it was not my ornate basket that I offered here, just one simple blossom, and I felt better!

The gardener left. I sat down on the hard coral floor and settled into zazen. The waves crashed incessantly against the cliff, the shadows of the sun moved slowly past me till I was sitting in bright, hot sun, and I felt it time to move on.

Some Indonesian tourists came as I was leaving, and asked if they could take a picture of me with them. They didn't ask my name, just collected a picture of a grey-haired woman from the U.S. I wonder what they told their friends! Back at the concession stand, the motorcyclist was waiting as he had promised. I was very thirsty, but still 300 rupees was too much, so I decided I could wait longer.

This time my motorcyclist drove me by smooth roads all the way to Kuta, no hassling with bemo drivers in Denpasar. Nor did I have to pass those giant posters, 200 feet long and 15 feet wide, displaying the sexy, violent story of some movie in living color so much bigger than life that the nightmare of some screaming, bleeding woman or some angry face of a man behind a gun lingered in my mind, as it did the last time I was there.

No wonder most tourists succumb and pay the higher prices for transportation. It was really difficult to persist in looking for reasonably priced transportation. I realize if I'd been a native trying to travel this way, I'd have had no trouble. My Caucasian face was now a trigger for the higher prices. I may have been traveling too late. In earlier years, single travelers moved with ease without having to charter rides. Still, by not opting to use the customary transportation for tourists, I had my own adventures.

Chapter 16 - "The Monkey Temple"

By a complicated use of four bemos, I went to visit the "Monkey Temple", where, after passing the usual gallery of vendors selling T-shirts, painted velvet rugs, pop, etc., I saw hundreds of green monkeys sitting in the trees next to the clearing with little old pink faces staring wisely at the tourists and preening themselves in groups.

Here, as I walked through the entrance, a big crafty monkey swooped down and snatched the hat off my head so suddenly, I didn't have time to reach for it. He ran up to the top of a tree and grinned at me. Three women from the concession stand threw bananas at him which he caught and consumed, but he still kept the hat. Then they threw rocks at him till he dropped it. At that point they demanded 500 rupees. Maybe here the monkeys work in league with the concessionaires!

The temple is situated in a beautiful forest whispering with rustling leaves. The trees are as tall as one hundred and fifty feet, with beautiful undergrowth full of the "Chinese Evergreens" I knew as a child. Here they flourished in large, tall, dark green clumps against the brown color of dry fallen leaves.

So many times plants have recalled memories of earlier times in my life. The enormous elephant-eared taro, growing all over Southeast Asia, reminded me of a time when I was six years old. My father had brought me a mysterious taro bulb, which we planted and watched with fascination while this unknown plant developed giant three-foot leaves. Plants touch moments of the past in surprising sparks, unexpected and, like ghosts, a bit haunting. Nowhere in the world are you far from home, and everywhere the past seeps into the present till all sense of time and place collapses.

Strange nut-like seeds were falling from the trees, and the monkeys seemed to enjoy eating them. I collected a handful to offer at the main temple.

The usual ancient "father-time" type man came out of the shadows with a rake in hand to "show" me the temple and collect my "contribution". There seemed to be no evidence that this ancient soul did any maintenance, though. Moss, leaves and grasses grew all over the aging blocks of the temple. The giant winged Eagle, the Garuda, that guarded the entryway was encrusted with barnacle-like lichens, but still was an awesome sight, standing higher than my head as I passed around him into the temple. I had the recognition that some part of my own mind, all crusty with forgotten memories, stood here.

The sinewy old man with a turban on his head gave me an approving "thumbs up" gesture when he saw my temple scarf tied around my waist. The scarf, as indispensible as a hat in a Catholic church, is a sign of devout respect for the temple visited.

Monkeys sat on ledges everywhere, preening themselves. They were a whole congregation of little beings to attend this temple, which must have drawn many worshippers in the past. Rather than studying the carvings hidden in the mossy stones, I just stood in the open court feeling the nature of the spot. I'd seen so many moss encrusted temples full of silence. Was this symbolic of the silence within me, so neglected by myself that only my monkey mind can delve into it?

Other people began to arrive, and after feeding the monkeys the nuts I'd gathered, I was ready to leave.

I had a hard time locating a bemo that went in the direction I wanted to go. By a wonderful accident, the "wrong" bemo deposited me at the "Mengui" temple, the largest one I'd seen so far. It covered about three city blocks in a plan similar to temple plans in Mexico. Innumerable lesser gods in small pagoda houses flanked the main walk to the innermost house of the most important deity. I felt that on a smaller scale, with the scenery changed somewhat, I could have been walking along the road between the temples of the Sun and Moon at Teotihuacan in Mexico.

At first I was alone. As I sat wondering in the silence, a woman with two young men, who were apparently her sons, came in. We began talking, and she offered to take me to Tanah Lot, the temple on the sea that I'd been interested in but had given up trying to reach because only tour buses and chartered bemos went there. She had hired the taxi for 15,000 rupees for the three of them. I accepted the offer. We drove through the countryside past large fields of just harvested rice where farmers were piling the stalks up and burning them. The hazy smoke lent a dreamlike quality to the landscape as they prepared the ashes to fertilize the next crop.

The taxi drove up to a restaurant with a fake plastic thatched roof made especially for tourists with glass windows and tables neatly covered with starched cloths. I had no choice but to eat with my hosts, ordering the cheapest thing on the menu, which was more expensive than my night's lodging. We spent an interminable time waiting to be served and eating, even though the conversation was delightful. I felt a bit helpless in that we were trapped by the taxi driver who had chosen to bring us here. I had no idea how far away Tanah Lot was. Then when we had finished, we drove one little block to the site of the temple! Had I known it was so close, I'd have opted to walk on and spend my time at the temple instead of frittering it away in eating, especially in a fake atmosphere. This seems to be the fate of many tourists who surrender to the guides and transportation people.

Gigantic waves were smashing in splendid force against a black lava pinnacle by the shore. Rising from the top were the small tiers of the temple's thatched pagodas. It was late afternoon and many people had gathered to see the sun set. The tide was too high to cross the distance from the shore to this black island, and the white spray of those magnificent waves shattered all over it. I stood and looked with awe at the choice of such a location for a temple, feeling the power of the place. I had no film, and watched the white force of the waves against the black, still lava, happily free of the need to capture the scene with a camera.

I had expected we were going to watch the sunset. The sky was already melting into a peach hue, but no, the group I was with had to leave. They were scheduled to see a fire dance. I debated about remaining, but knew there was no other transportation back. I knew I'd be a prime victim of marked up prices. I promised myself I'd come back alone and spend as much time as I wanted. We'd had perhaps a little less than an hour here.

We drove through the hazy rice-ash air caught by the late afternoon sun, watching rice paddies turn golden as the farmers left their fires to smolder in the dark.

It was night, and again I had no sense of where I was going. Pretty soon we entered an area with crowds of camera-laden people, gathering for the dance. Chairs were set up in an open courtyard before a real temple gate. The seats were all full except for two empty ones in the second row, so the mother and I edged our way to our orchestra seats as if they'd been waiting for us!

All the temples I'd wandered through in Denpasar came alive that night. The "gate" was a fine backdrop for dancers. There were entrances in the center and on the sides from which costumed dancers could emerge suddenly and dance down the steps to the open space in front.

No lights. Only a fire glowed in the center of the courtyard, and many dark shadows slipped into a semi-circle around it. A throbbing drum beat like a thumping heart, and the mystic clang of the gamelan churned up sounds from the gathered group. About 25 men swaying sidewards, hissing, uttering percussive "ugha! ugha! ugha! click! click! click!" sounds melted with a sighing, groaning unison into a terrible dragon in the dark. How necessary the temple guardians, the Garuda; the lions seemed to guard against the power of such imaginary beings! It called up the terror and awe that must have ruled this land for centuries.

Two young girls about ten years old danced in perfect synchronization with eyes closed, in a trance that seemed to give them all the grace and precision of dancers who had spent lifetimes disciplining their bodies. They moved to the music with a grace that enraptured the whole audience.

Then a man, his sinewy dark body wrapped only in a white loin cloth, stepped, kicked, stamped, and danced unhurt on fiery coals that scattered and sent the crowds on the edge shrieking back as some were burned by a truly hot fire. The drum compelled all into mental participation with the dancers.

I had at last seen a Bali dance! Then we piled into the convenient taxi, no sign of any other available transportation, and rode back to Kuta. I saw the hotel where my friends stayed. It had a lobby, sheltered garden, big driveway for the tour buses to pick up and deliver clients to their doors. But content, I set off for my simple room with the necessities of life; a place to wash, a place to sleep, and a place to store my pack.

Chapter 17 - Tanah Lot Adventure

The proprietor had told me of a small temple on the beach two kilometers from our palm grove, and after sitting at 4:00 a.m., I set out, barefoot, in the dawn, along the silent beach. Waves crashed ferociously on my left. A cool sweet wind was blowing.

From my diary.

The wide expanse of sand stretched endlessly, with so many places to stop. Little openings in the underbrush led to sacred trees with paths up to giant trunks where traces of past offerings, bamboo boxes turned brown, woven birds and cloths of woven bamboo droop by the many remnants of burned incense.

I feel the urge to bow to these ancient giants, whose roots start from the branches and in time merge with the trunks in one huge mass of sinew. I feel as if I am walking inside the sinews of my own arm!

There are fresh-water rivers where prickly green thistle growth comes close to the ocean shore. Then enormous grandiose hotels with ostentatious bamboo pavilions. At one, a waiter is busy setting tables covered with white cloths on a grassy patio with gardens leading to the sea. I ask if they serve breakfast. "Not today, we have a big buffet this morning."

So I go on, still thirsty, till I finally come to the river. There is a bamboo bridge and a red brick temple gate rising beyond a wall, just up the rise, as my proprietor had described it to me.

An old codger comes up to me with open hand for "donation". He shows the way Balinese gassho for 300 rupees, but he wants to show me an inner temple for 500 rupees. I decide I've seen enough of the open temple. He offers to give me a massage, which I turn down, but he insists on pressing my elbows. When he playfully squeezes my breast, I call it quits and wander to a single small refreshment bar nearby. It's open, and the gusting wind keeps blowing over a bamboo barrier which the vendors keep erecting with no firm support and which immediately blows down again. No one talks English. We smile. They overcharge for a drink.

Then I sit zazen alone under a great banyan tree, with the sounds of a water buffalo crunching grass on the other side of the wall. I decide Tanah Lot is not so far, only 13 kilometers to go, and the waves are magnificent.

So I go on, barefoot, waves lashing at the shore, a hot sun making it impossible to step on dry sand. The high wind keeps me cool, but it blows sand in my face. I have to hold my Indonesian farmer's hat on my head. The sun is too hot not to wear it, and the strap has been broken since the monkey ripped it off my head at the monkey temple.

I push on, wondering why I should do this crazy thing, but going on. I pass countless little square plots of temples, sometimes no bigger than 15 by 15 feet, enclosed by old stone walls. There is the thatched pagoda with carved wooden doors closed to shelter the deity. Sometimes I run across the hot sand and green prickles to the quiet courtyards, to gassho before the gargoyles and race back to the tide-swept, cool, firm sand, which I can walk on.

I pass a set of 70 or more brightly painted fishing boats sheltered under thatches. I can picture people racing with them into the waves, launching these sleek hulls for fishing trips.

I sit and watch the great green waves rise and crash, letting time pass in a deep stillness. Then I move on.

Three men are standing by a temple off in the underbrush to the right. I wave and ask permission to look at the temple. They invite me over. I run over the blazing sand across the dry area to the grass.

Two men wear turbans and all wear yellow sarongs. The third wears a sarong of batik and a western style shirt. They seem glad to see me.

I walk around examining the guardians and stone carvings. Ancient mossy turtles catch my eye.

The young man in Western clothes says they're going to have a purification ceremony since he has been sick. Would I please join them? We sit before the hut which is the main altar, three of us, one on each side of me. The third man stands in the doorway of the pagoda on the steps. He offers incense, prays, chants, pours water, and scatters flowers. Then he takes baskets of flowers, blesses them, and brings them down to us.

Incense burns, and the young man holds out his hands. The old priest pours water three times into his open palms. He sips it three times, then washes his hair and face. With a flower blossom, the priest dips into the water and touches the crown of his own head, then the crown of the youth, and splashes water on us all.

I think of priests splashing holy water and burning incense in Catholic churches and in the Buddhist temples in China. Are any of us so different? Somehow it unifies me with all the ritual of the world, and I feel as if some passage has been celebrated here on the beach. It feels much like a dream.

Then the priest comes to me. I sip the water three times, wash my hair and face three times, and they motion it is finished. Time for me to go. Is this some chance happening or have I just been purified? It feels right to go with this spirit to Tanah Lot.

I pass a dune covered with bristly frond-like growth, and a strange wailing sound stretches out to me. It rises, falls, pauses, and sings out a long low call against the strong wind. I come closer, curious as to what it is. There on the top of the rise are bamboo pipes, hollow, standing vertical like some aboriginal organ in the wild, the wind blowing the melody to a silent deserted universe with only me to hear it . It feels again like a dream.

The day is wearing on. It's odd I feel no worry about what I will do when night comes. I reach a place where some ancient lava flowed in a wide black band out to the shore. Here on the wave-worn surface are vestiges of foundations of what must have been an old temple carved in the flat black rock and long since worn away by the raging waves. There are still offerings being made to these temples that used to be. All kinds of green bamboo boxes float in the tidal pools, and fresh flower petals dot the dark rock. Such a reminder that what we see isn't all there is. Someone seems to be paying tribute to another dimension.

I'm beginning to be tired, and ahead I see a river too wide and too deep for me to wade across. There is a tiny bamboo shelter just big enough to crawl into to hide from the heat of the sun. Just as I get my weary bones settled, a man comes along. It's his shelter, so I move on like some weary vagrant, no place to rest.

I can't cross the river, though I must be very close to Tanah Lot. It is so deep I would have to swim, and I don't want to wet my camera. I've no choice but to cut up to the right into that wide expanse of fertile green rice paddies with narrow raised walkways between them stretching in maze-like zigzags. No direct way to go.

I find a wider roadway that passes little shrines where farmers have left their offerings to the spirits of the paddies. One young girl comes out to leave a flower at a shrine, points the way to a village, I think. She speaks no English.

At first the dirt road is soft dusty clay which feels like velvet to feet rasped with walking on the wet sand. Then the villagers must have begun to pave it. Sharp, jagged stones stick their points up like spiked cobblestones, waiting for sand to be sifted round them. These stones slow me to a meticulous picking for some flat unjagged place where I can put my tender toes or make quick agonized leaps past points unavoidable to some more gentle surface. I've no alternative, for the road is edged by planted rice paddies full of water.

This weary gray-haired Caucasian staggering through their rice paddies arouses curious expressions from the first villagers I meet. But no one speaks English. They watch me trudge along.

At one village there are benches at a juice stand under thatched canopy where I wearily ask for a drink. There is only Coca Cola, though the sweet sticky taste hardly quenches my thirst. The water is not boiled.

Droves of children come out of nowhere to stare at me, giggling and hiding shyly when I smile at them A young man who works in Kuta and talks English comes up. He says I'm so far off the beaten track few Westerners come here. I'm sure not many, at least. Mothers with small babies appear and hold them up to look at this strange person.

I was still hoping to reach the main road by dark, so, thanking everyone, I moved on. I was painfully picking my way between the rocks, balancing on the narrow ridge on the side of a road like walking on a two-by-four, when children appeared to watch me. One small boy, maybe six or so, laughed, and stepping gingerly on imaginary hot coals, began to sing a taunting song. They were all laughing then.

I was so tired and my feet hurt so, I could have sat down and cried. I could have gotten angry at my tormentors, but I just grinned helplessly at them and continued on my way with the boy gingerly mimicking behind me.

At the next village, about a football field's length farther, a man stood in the middle of the road holding out a pair of plastic thong zoris that everyone without much money wears! It seemed as if it were a reward for my assuming the right attitude. There could not have been a more welcome sight. I had to control the tendency to cry in relief!

Here in a little store under a canopy like the other stores I had passed along the way, shoes lined one side and the familiar gallon glass jars full of biscuits, candy, dried shrimp and cakes, as well as the Coke and 7-up bottles, filled the wooden shelves at the back. This was all they sold.

I sat down, grateful for a rest. Crowds of children and young adults came out of nowhere. A young man who works in Kuta translated for me. He invited me to his family home to spend the night, since the sun was already setting.

With great relief I accepted. I felt so thankful for whatever "magic" was still giving me a close view of how people lived.

I walked back with him, in my newly acquired shoes, along the road to a house on the edge of the village right next to the rice paddies. We went through a gate of cement in a five-foot cement wall. Inside was a nice courtyard. Small open sheltered rooms comprised a kitchen on one side and a family gathering place, a "living room" a the end of a neat cement walk. There were flat wooden benches built against the wall, which I discovered were the beds for the children.

We sat around a table under a Coleman lantern and talked together. The young man was the only one who could talk English, but I learned his sister and aunt had high places in the leadership of the village. They were working on developing their house as a demonstration house with government funds. All of the sanitary system, the well, the open ditches for waste water, I saw, were new.

Tomorrow they were expecting an inspection by government officials. They invited me to come. Most of the village people still lived in clay houses, but cement ones were being built in every village. The waste water still drained out to the rice paddies.

The grandmother, father, sisters, and brothers soon joined the 35 children to stare at me, and smiled as they offered me tea. I ate my first meal of the day - a rice dish with green vegetables cut up in a spicy sauce.

Finally, they showed me to a room, a cement room with tiny portholes at the top of one wall, a table, a platform with a grass mat which was the bed, and one chair. This, the young man said, was his room. He would sleep outside with the children. Despite my protests, he insisted I sleep there.

I found the bathroom across the court, a cement room much

like rooms near swimming pools here in the U.S. There was a tiny stall with a very clean Asian toilet, the tiny hole and the two uplifted foot platforms, with just enough room to squat without bumping the sides. There was a square cement "box" holding water, and the usual plastic dipper. Off from this there was a bathing room, with a larger square tank nearly four feet high full of water. There was a hook to hang clothes on. The water drained into a two-inch wide channel out to the rice paddies on the other side of the wall.

I was so tired. Even though the grass mat seemed hard, I slept like a rock till five. Then the sounds of the children giggling and sweeping came to me. No one else seemed up, only the children, three of them, doing their morning sweeping in the courtyard.

The inner courtyard was surrounded with all kinds of plants, banana and papaya trees.

The women were up later cooking in their outdoor kitchen under a bamboo thatch. Smiling, they handed me a metal dish of rice with chopped chardlike greens again, and tea.

Everyone ate with their hands, and though they handed me a spoon, I ate as Dini had taught me, shoving the rice into my mouth with my thumb. I was a bit awkward, but they were pleased to see me try to eat their way.

I then helped the young men sweep the family temple before going to the "mother temple". Their shrine had to be swept of the offerings of yesterday, along with candy wrappers and plastic toys from a day's use by children playing there.

Before I could sweep the big village temple where all the big ceremonies were held, I had to undergo another purification. My friends offered water three times, which I used to wash head and face, then sip three times. Then they threw flower petals over my head. Later, as I saw villagers walking in Denpasar, I recognized the same flower petals clinging to hair and shoulders of nearly everyone I passed. This is a common daily ritual with everyone.

The temple was made of ceramic tile, and glazed gargoyles of bright red, greens and blues made ugly faces at me as I swept the corners. At least my temple world was no longer symbolized by decaying moss!

The young men were going to play the gamelan later. They proudly showed me their small village sets on a smaller scale than the ones I had seen in Jogja.

Then we walked to the big gathering in the next village. Villages clustered along what would be the distance of every twelve city blocks, and today the whole way was decorated with bamboo staffs stuck upright in the ground with intricate bamboo loops like fake flowers topping them. [N.B. -These are penjors, erected 2 days before the major celebration - Galungan days].

Many village people walked with us. They already knew about me. They were dressed in beautiful gold embroidered clothes. All had their bright temple sashes tied on around the waist. They emerged, along with sway-backed pigs, from houses on side streets to walk along the dust and mud road, which was paved at this point, that is, the stones were buried in mud.

It amazed me how clean and neat they looked, coming out of the dirt houses with dirt floors. I saw later that they all pre-ferred to squat rather than to sit on the dirt. They gathered under canopies on wood platforms along with others who were already seated on the edge or squatting.

When we arrived in the next village, the dancing was already over, but there were speeches. Most of them were delivered by the village women. My friends were talking with others while the speeches droned on in Indonesian. I had no idea what they were saying.

The whole procession moved back to the village I'd slept in. The officials, dressed in ornate embroidered skirts and blouses, rode in big army trucks. Then there was an hour of gamelan play-ing. My friends played very well according to my unpracticed ear.

I began to see that this ceremony would last all day and that

I would never make it to Tana Lot, so I bade goodbye with many thanks to the family and walked on along the decorated road. At a crossroad sometime later, a bemo stopped for me and took me to a second road to change into yet another jeep. The fares were the usual Balinese fare, thank heavens.

Tanah Lot was no exception. The postcard vendors, the drinking stands, and souvenir shops lined the approach. Since I had to walk, I was followed by 10 or so children of ages eight to twelve all pitifully begging me to buy postcards or demanding forcefully that I do so. They all giggled happily when they didn't know I was watching them.

Finally, I reached the shore again and there was Tanah Lot, the temple on the lava island with the waves crashing less ferociously than the last time but still as beautifully. It was low tide. There was still just time to wade out through knee deep water with a strong current that could have swept me into the water. I bypassed the chance to see some "snakes in a cave" offered by some turbaned types dressed like priests.

With the guidance of a man who knew the shallow spots, I safely reached the island offshore.

On the trail up the steep hill were some more men in turbans collecting "donations". At the top, there was a temple deity behind the carved wood doors in the usual pagoda-shaped tower. I started to bow my respects to the sensed holiness of the place.

While I was in mid-bow, an Indonesian tourist came up to me and asked, "Where are you from?" The shock that he couldn't wait till I was finished startled me. The full impact of the Indonesians' view towards foreigners struck me. We are such an opportunity to practice English that the Indonesians don't stop to see who they approach. They just rush up in an aggressive way and ask the staple question, almost a formula, "Where are you from?" I wasn't even sure if he even wanted an answer or if he just wanted to show he knew English. Somehow I blurted that I'd just walked from Kuta to see this temple and wanted to catch a glimpse of it in peace, and that perhaps he too might take time to notice the nature of the place. He looked so surprised! The more wealthy Indonesians seem to tour their country, visit shrines, but the feeling is more that of a sightseer. Could they have learned that spirit from the foreign tourists?

Later we talked. He was a businessman from Jakarta on vacation. He came to see the temple because "everybody does". It's a nice spot.

He hadn't even stopped to think what it was, despite the temple "priests" with their little baskets for "donations". Strange feeling.

Even so, the wind carrying spray of the roaring waves, the blue sky and black rock, the little enigmatic figures on the pagodas brought me back to the recognition of the special nature of the place that caused the temple to be built. I could feel that awe for the unpredictable fury or placidity of the sea goddess who rendered all islanders her subjects, helpless in the face of her caprices. That stronghold of black lava, defying the everlasting attack of the waves, somehow held promise for stability. In our modern houses we feel protected from the wildness of weather. How easily and quickly we forget the forces of nature that must have dominated this little island.

The tourist wants a photo of me at Tanah Lot and gets a priest to take the picture with his arm around my shoulder. The tide is coming in fast. It's time to wade back or I'll be stranded for 12 hours till the next low tide.

I wade back, or rather stagger back through the knee deep water lapping at my rolled up pant legs, and get to shore just in time before a great wash of water floods the little causeway.

I have no film. It seems to be my fate, that at the most impressively beautiful places I have no film or the camera breaks. I must record in my memory the white power of the frothing waves. I sit on another grass covered promontory overlooking the temple, watching the huge waves coil and spill over, rise, smash, and meet each other, falling back. The white mist in the air and the green water breathe for the sea goddess. I can fully see her thirstily lick-ing her chops at the prospect of devouring the black lava rock!

Then past all the concessions, including coconut hulls gaily carved into monkeys with enormous eyes, past the triumphant bemo drivers, who refuse to drive me back to Kuta for less than 4,000 rupees, I walk with optimism. I find a group of American tourists going back to Kuta who will allow me to make a 1,000 rupee contribution towards their own charter. I go home to my peaceful palm grove and Hindu family.

I'm tired of dealing with the hassles of Bali, and I've spent what money I could afford. It's time to move on.

Chapter 18 - Medan

Transportation struggles again. From Denpasar I land in the International airport in Jakarta. I can't just change planes, the domestic terminal is clear across town. Many taxis offer rides, but I insist on walking about a quarter of a mile to a bus station, where luckily someone helps me find the right bus. I have no idea how far it is to the other airport. The Garuda ticket agent has told me that the last plane leaves for Medan at 4:30 pm. It's 2:00 pm, but I guess I have plenty of time. The bus stops at every block and people pile in and pour out interminably. For two hours I ride, trying not to return to the agitated mind that comes with schedules. We arrive at the airport at 4:15, and I hastily rush to the counter hoping I do not have to spend the night here.

The ticket agent smiles and tells me there's another plane in an hour. Why didn't they tell me about it in the other airport? Glad I didn't take a taxi as an emergency tactic, I sit in the plastic upholstered chairs and wait. I talk with an American, a retired executive, who came to teach Indonesian executives. He's amazed at how I've been traveling. "You must have a lot of courage and an iron stomach!

Again the contrast greets me—the shoddy, peeling, over-crowded bus, and the serene waiting room in the airport. There's nothing fancy in the cement room, but it's clean. The toilet on the other hand is filthy. There are always Indian women in saris waiting for a "contribution" for giving you a towel; certainly not for washing the toilets. Then another 45 minute leap and I'm in Medan in Sumatra. It's already getting dark. I was hoping that there would be travel information available, but there are only hotel people trying to divert you to their hotel—"Very reasonable", 90,000 rupees.

The taxi drivers all want 10,000 rupees just to take me to a hotel. I go out, pack on back, to the loading platform as hopeful taxi drivers maintain there is no other form of transportation. I say I want a cheaper hotel, and someone sneers, "Oh yes Ramma Hotel. Verry cheap!" I go inside and a long haired attendant shows me a map on the wall and we locate the hotel. It looks as if it's not more than two miles. So I decide to walk. To the surprise of all the greedy taxi drivers, I set out. I walk a half hour along an unlighted road, thinking maybe this time I've been really silly. But I walk on wondering how it's going to turn out. Then, to my surprise, the long haired attendant that had helped me with directions in the airport, rides up on his motorcycle and offers me a ride, which I gratefully accept.

We ride for fifteen minutes. I realize what a long walk I would have had. Then we drive up to a dingy alley, and he drops me off at the entrance. I see he stays waiting to see what happens. I think he's curious what I will do. The waiting room lobby smells of marijuana, and I wonder myself. As I walk to the desk, I pass a nice Swiss couple, a pretty blond girl, waiting to be shown their room. I decide if they can hack it, so can I.

The room is cheap, 500 rubles. It's a dormitory, smaller than the youth hostel room in Manila. There's room for only two bunk beds and a fifth bed along a wall. There's an aisle three feet wide between the beds.

The Swiss couple and a Japanese man are already settling in. So it's co-ed. Oh well, I figure I'll get along OK.

Thank heavens I get a lesson from the Swiss girl in how to change clothes gracefully on such occasions. She puts her head through a tent-like mumu and calmly changes quickly underneath. I wrap my long skirt around my neck and do likewise.

They go out to eat. I've eaten on the plane, and use the extra snack peanuts as my meal.

The Japanese boy is a drop-out from college in Tokyo. He's been traveling for two years with no inclination to go to "work".

I go to sleep with my ticket, money and passport tightly tied to my waist though it's incredibly hot and stuffy in the room.

In the morning I wake at five o'clock again (I can't seem to help it any more) to discover another young man in the fifth bed. Since everyone is asleep, I go out to a seat in the "hallway" to write in my diary.

This is a Muslim hotel, with the usual Asian toilets; no shower, only a dipper in a room with a deep four foot square cement box-shaped tank full of cold water and a drain to catch the water you pour over yourself.

The whole building is cement, drab gray with grimy finger prints. There's an open courtyard similar to the layout of the Rama Hotel in Jogjakarta, with rooms along the sides. The rain pours into the central opening, but the covered walkways just outside the rooms prevent the rain from blowing into the rooms. There is a stairway leading to the roof with no view - only cement sides of other buildings. People's clothes stretch out on the lines.

As I sit and write, people emerge from other rooms, probably not dormitories. Indonesian businessmen groomed and clean, in Western suits, emerge from the scantily equipped "showers". Their plump wives are beautifully dressed. They don't seem to notice the drab surroundings.

When I was in China, I noticed the similar pattern. People were always well dressed and clean, but content to live in extremely sleazy housing. It seems they are satisfied, that they don't expect much of their surroundings. This kind of traveling could be very hard on some people in the U.S. used to shiny interiors. I'm glad I can just sit and watch.

I walk around my section of Medan, an apparently depressing, dirty, drab, cluttered town. Trash is everywhere. Most of the sidewalks seem to have undergone great earthquakes. The huge cement slabs are crumbling and tipped at odd angles with dirt gaps between, sometimes as big as six feet. They are treacherously muddy in the rain.

On the main street, all the stalls have greasy finger-printed doors. Grime is everywhere. I walk five blocks past dingy coffee shops where people in business suits chat around tables placed on linoleum floors that haven't been mopped in weeks. Is this a hangover from the bamboo psychology, where typhoons crash down old buildings and new ones replace them? Cement doesn't blow down, but still people don't notice the dirt.

I walk down an alley where poor people cluster, getting up from their beds outside in front of the shops where they work. There are "shops" every 20 feet, repair shops, with corrugated metal walls. Children, half clothed, run among the free wandering chickens. The street is unpaved dirt.

A woman with one eye cloudy, her face a mass of wrinkles, is obviously the matriarch of a whole cluster of young mothers with children at their skirts. Are they her daughters or just whores? Through the confusion of racing children, she says, "Good afternoon" and extends her hand firmly demanding money. I don't know why, but I gave her 1,000 rupees, indicating it is for them all, and that I trust she'll manage it well. Strange how I sleep in such crazy places and then give away twice the price for a bed! Perhaps it's the sleeping in such places that makes me aware of how people have to live, and provides the money to give away.

Everyone is always busy sweeping. Maybe they just shove the dirt around to redistribute it. I have that dreamlike feeling again, that somehow this is the clutter in my own mind that I never seem to be able to clean away, only shove aside to a less noticeable place.

People here don't seem too friendly towards travelers or want to help. A man tells me that the bus to Lake Toba is two kilometers along the road. Something occurs to me to ask someone else after I've lugged my pack for a block further. I discover that the local bus goes right along the road I walk. My pack seems to get heavier when I walk city streets, so I'm grateful. Finally, I find the bus, crammed with farmers and rice bags, chickens, and hoes. Perhaps the earlier instructions given me were to a station for tour buses.

We have a bumpy six hour drive, the bus driver believing, I'm sure, that gravity doesn't exist, that all obstacles we meet will dissolve before we get to them, and that steep curvy mountain roads are no different than flat plains; no need to slow down. We pass many villages with shabby shacks much like Appalachian shacks I remember from forty years ago.

I have my first view of rubber plantations where rows of tall thin trees each have white chevron grooves in the trunks, with a little cup hanging below the V to catch the white rubber sap. Groves and groves of mango trees sweep by. I marvel at what I thought were pineapple plantations. I learned later those trees produced oil for margarine.

Chapter 19 - Lake Toba in Sumatra

From my diary:

The bus lets me off in the center of town near Lake Toba. Everyone offers to arrange "a nice hotel" for me and a trip to the Island next day. For some reason I refuse. I walk one more kilometer down to the edge of the lake where the fishing boats are moored to transport people to Samosir Island. I'm too late for the ferry boat, but one young man says he'll take me to his own village when he goes back in the evening. He knows a place where I can stay, not at a hotel.

I'm left with two hours to pass, so I go to one of the local "restaurants" by the lake; it looks like a beer hall. It faces out onto a large open paved parking lot that would easily compare with any shopping center parking lot in the United States. It seems unnecessarily big for the number of motor vehicles I've seen so far.

A woman who owns the restaurant cooks me a meal in her wok over charcoal: fresh vegetables over rice. Her daughter, carrying an eighteen month old baby, sits near me. The child climbs up on the table and we talk, in broken English, of children. The grandmother, who is smoking, takes the cigarette from her mouth and holds it for the baby to take a puff, as if she's been smoking all her life!

Just outside, there is a young girl, maybe eight years old, singeing a chicken by holding it in her bare hands close to the flame of a primitive gas burner on the floor.

Some young men are singing to the accompaniment of a guitar. It sounds like South American or Mexican music. I enjoy their sheer pleasure in the rhythms as they drink beer and joke together. I wonder where they heard these melodies, but they insist they are playing Batak music, native to the people on the island.

As I sit there, I have a vague feeling that someone has pushed an enormous finger through the earth, and that sitting at this table are a few young men from South America who've just poked up on this side of the earth. They tell me that many travelers are struck by the similarity of their music to that of South America, but none of them has heard anything but the music of this island.

Finally we cross to the island in a small motor-driven gondola. The sun is setting and the sky glows red behind the steep cliffs of the central mountain range, reflecting on the smooth swirls of water.

We arrive at a tiny dock, and my guide leads me for a few minutes, in the dark, to a barn-like "house" where a couple in their eighties keep three rooms for guests. Electricity shuts off from the central station at 11:00 pm, so I'm given an oil lamp. The proprietor, a frail man, indicates I must close the windows which look out over the lake. There is no space for air to come in.

I don't feel like sleeping now, and another group of young men is gathered around the small table in the open hallway, singing delightfully joyous Batak songs. They are obviously enjoying themselves, practicing new arrangements, singing freely with much laughter. So my first night in Lake Toba goes quickly.

In the morning, after I've sat zazen for my usual time, I hear women's voices outside in the early dawn. They are doing their laundry.

They have enormous baskets of clothes which they leave on shore, wading out to the rocks off shore, to wet, soap, and knead the clothes on a flat rock. I go out and watch till they are finished, then wash my own with a bar of Fels Naphtha soap I have left from the Philippines. Then I wade out to deeper water as they did, to rinse them. They are surprised the cold water doesn't bother me. None of them talk very much English, but we're comfortable together.

They bathe here too. I've my six-foot length of batik cloth I bought in Jogjakarta. I've been using it as a sheet. It's a skirt for men, but it makes an excellent sarong and bathing suit. We laugh together and watch the sun rise across the lake.

It's market day, and the proprietor and his wife ask if I'd like to go back across the lake to the village. We pile into a crowded boat, large enough to hold about fifty people. I squeeze in with baskets of yams, rice, carved wooden guitars, beans, and lithe women, sinewy men, all dressed in their best clothes. There are many old women grinning contentedly at me while chewing betel, the red juice sliding down the corners of their mouths.

One old woman has a whole kit for betel chewing, the tiny jar with a white salve, a box of leaves and twigs, and a mortar where she pulverizes the hard nut into the pasty white salve. She spreads it on the leaf, adds a twig, and rolls it up and stuffs it into her mouth, chewing like a serene cow as we sway in the rocking boat.

We finally arrive at the pier from which I left the day before. I find myself climbing up the steel ladders to join the masses in the market. The whole vacant "parking lot" I'd seen the day before is alive with makeshift portable canopies of bamboo and burlap. Farm women have spread square burlap cloths in neat long rows, leaving tiny aisles of about two feet so shoppers can walk between the rows. On these cloths they've arranged incredible varieties of abundant fruits: apples, bananas, and oranges, lichi nuts, and fish: tiny minnows curled and dried, shrimps, larger fresh fish. There's a whole area under makeshift canopies with butchered pink pork meat, red goat legs, ribs, and hearts, waiting for people to buy them and have them wrapped in newspaper packages ready to plump them in the market baskets on everyone's habitually crooked arm.

Snack food is everywhere. Cold rice mixed in a yellow curry sauce, or hot with chili peppers, is stuffed into pita bread pockets. Sweet cakes stacked up in pyramids are tossed into envelopes made of used typing paper.

Children of all ages work along with their parents packing goods. One young boy hands down enormous stalks of bananas to his father from the top of a truck parked at the edge of this milling confusion.

I wander along, not buying anything, just taking in the color, the gaiety of the market people, the poise of the children full of *responsibility.*

There are separate sections for hardware, yard goods, clothes and books. Children must buy their own paper bound school books. Many children can't afford to go to school because they can't afford the uniform and school books.

The grandson of Mr. and Mrs. Sidebatur, my proprietors, wants books for school. His sister, a sweet eight-year-old who can't talk English, must need them too, but he doesn't mention her. I go with him to a shop where paper books, stapled together, are stacked in piles. He points out the books, and I buy them. They're terribly drab looking texts using bland linear illustrations that would easily squelch my own curiosity for learning.

The grandson says he's taking time off from school for market day. It seems most of the village children are occupied, and are necessary to help their parents on this busy day.

All day there is a running humorous commentary going on over a loudspeaker, which raises the din to the level of shouting. Everyone seems to enjoy the noise, and periodically group laughter bursts out over the clutter and chaos.

Somehow, with all the things to purchase, I buy nothing except a pineapple, some fish, and small pieces of pork to add to the community table at my establishment. As I'm the only guest, there are not many to feed.

Then wearily, everyone packs up what's left of their produce, and as we leave at 4:00 pm the open square is already returning to its original drab condition. Carts pulled by water buffaloes, old rickety trucks, and many pedestrians with wares in baskets fan out through the streets. Quiet returns.

We go back across the water in the wonderful market ferry boat.

This time the large bags of rice have turned into small packages of needed supplies. They're more awkward to step over, but miraculously we all cram in together.

Next day I decide to go somewhere quiet. Even here are many people trying to practice English who stop you, come visit the guest house, follow you insisting that you talk with them.

I refuse several offers to guide me to the mountaintop because they ask extravagant prices. When I turn them down, I realize I've earned a bit of respect. I don't carry my camera in sight here. Everyone is so poor they would have to work half a year to buy a watch. The young men practicing English are hoping to get jobs in Tuk Tuk, the next village, where they can earn lots of money at tourist hotels. I can see the nature of this peaceful island will soon disappear as the tourist trade takes over.

I walk up into the rolling hills. Along the road a herd of water buffaloes comes trotting along, shepherded by boys. They have enormous horns, but very gentle looking eyes. They pass me as a group of boys comes around the bend. A woman with them hands me her stick, warning me that they are apt to charge. I feel a bit silly with the stick, but accept it.

As I rise higher, the dry cracking earth, which was plowed when it was moist, is now a mass of huge, brick hard clods of black dirt waiting to be softened by the rain already delayed too long for this season's rice crop to be planted. I pass some rice farmers, a whole family, methodically chipping at the hard clay with hoes. They will carry their water from below, bucket by bucket, because they must grow their rice in order to eat. We talk in interrupted English. They offer me some tea. I'd forgotten to bring any water, and gratefully sip a tiny sip, realizing that this is their water for the day. As I leave, I leave a contribution for the tea, thanking them for their hospitality. They are delighted.

I climb on up further on the hill and come to a church. Inside of Muslim Indonesia, on an island in Sumatra, where they sing South American sounding songs, the natives are Christian. The houses in the village nearby have steep roofs, sway backed with bull's horns reminiscent of Vikings' homes. Nowhere else do they live in homes like this.

As I pass, I wave at children playing among the free wandering pigs and chickens in a school yard nearby. I've been listening to their voices chanting their lessons in unison as I've been climbing.

I find what I think is the trail to the top of the hill that Mr. Sedebatur described. It rises into thick jungle, getting narrower and narrower. I come to a great pineapple tree which has a large clearing around it, and realize that the trail led to this and was used only at harvest time. It's not the right trail, but I'm used to following animal trails, and see the rudiments of a trail that leads further.

By now I catch glimpses of the valley below, to the blue water of the lake, and the small Batak village of swaybacked houses. But the jungle growth gets thicker, and I'm hot and sticky. I wonder if I shouldn't turn back. I find a huge pile of brush blocking the trail. On the other side, it's clear, so I try to bypass it. In swinging out around a tree trunk my foot slips and I slide ten feet down a steep drop-off. I'm stuck on a small ledge on the side of a cliff which feels like hundreds of feet above a larger level shelf, and the soil is soft, crumbly, and dry like powder. It slips each time I try to climb back. I'm really in a pickle.

There's no way anyone can hear me, and I'm still a bit ashamed about following an unknown trail so far into the wilds. I've got enormous blisters on my feet, and I'm getting to feel a bit desperate.

Then I see that a great number of the plants clinging to the loose soil are my old friends the Bracken ferns. I have loved them in Yosemite, where they sometimes grow to shoulder height, and in the hills where their fiddle heads have been a source of wonder each spring as they uncurl.

If ever there is a time to speak to the plants, this is it. I humbly ask their help, praying they will cling to the loose soil while I try to pull myself up. They are loosely set in the crumbly earth, and perhaps I might have pulled them out in some other circumstance, but thanks be to all the beings of the plant world, they hang on, and with enormous struggle and much faith, I drag myself up to the rough path again. My heart is full of gratitude and a sense of kinship.

*For years I wandered daily in the hills of California, feeling like
a brother to the ferns, grasses, trees and shrubs. I knew each
and loved them. But here, in Sumatra, in this wild space, the
plants are all foreign to me. The prickly palm-like fronds, an alien
undergrowth, fascinated me and had drawn me this far into the
impenetrable tangle of jungle. But the familiar Bracken fern has
appeared in my moment of need and aided me in a foreign land. I
am swelling with the oneness of the earth.*

Sheepishly, with hair tangled, hips bruised, and dust bespeck-
led, I returned along that precarious trail, grateful that I was not
destined to become a skeleton in that unfamiliar terrain.

As I cross the yards of the Batak village, trying not to get in
the way of the swaybacked pigs, someone calls to me in English.
She is the school teacher who had seen me walking up the hill
earlier. She invites me into her home. Batak houses have ladders
leading to a second story which is the living space. She shows me
the one large room warmed by a charcoal stove. Great beams of
wood hold up the roof. Incongruously, the living room has two
overstuffed chairs, a coffee table and a sofa. How did they ever
get them up the ladder?

My hostess, though obviously more well-to-do than her neighbors, was worried because she didn't have the income to take care
of their coming baby. Her husband, she said, walked all the way
to the school two villages beyond Tuk Tuk (about six miles) to do
janitorial work in the school. He was an excellent wood carver.
She showed me a cane he'd carved with complicated designs,
but he made most of his money at the school. As we talked, he
came home, mentioning the bus was late. They offered me dinner, continually talking about how poor they were. I began to feel
the effect travelers have, even in this outpost. People didn't feel
uncomfortable about asking openly for money from foreigners.

Here again was the specter with which I've not fully dealt. Of
course, I had more money than any of the people here, and obviously I was aware that their standard of living was much less than

nearly everyone in the U.S., but how could I help to change that inequality?

This family could talk English, had better jobs than most, could beg for help more effectively. I could see that any direct help I would or could give would not go to the rest of the people less well off. I also saw that any money given would only lead to more begging. I had met children on the road as I walked who said without looking at me, only at my pack — "Hello, bonbon?" "Hello, pen?" "Hello, pesa?" They reached hands out begging openly, though they were nicely dressed and carried school books. I realized they had more money than those children who couldn't afford to attend school.

By open begging, the whole community on the island had begun to acquire an improved way of life. Somehow, there must be some other better method of redistributing money and things.

The greeting of "Hello, bonbon", was not a greeting to me. I was only a possibility for some money. These children usually looked surprised and pleased when I held out my hand and said, "Hello, friendship?", asked their names and talked with them. The contact would have been empty if I had handed them money, though they expected this shallow interaction when they saw me. Is this what we're accomplishing all over the world by our financial assistance?

Anyway, I took the address of the school, hoping to establish a friendly relationship between the children of our two countries where help might come in some meaningful way.

It was late already and I was exhausted from my wild climb. I still had a long way to go, and it was getting dark. So I dragged my blistered feet on down to the valley floor and gratefully entered my cubicle with the closed shutters. I had had a fine adventure in the wildest terrain I've ever seen.

In the evening, I chose to write in my diary, catching up on events in Bali while the two grandparents and their grandchildren went to the next village to watch television. Mr. Sidebatur asked if I felt safe, told me to keep everything locked, and went away.

I wrote with the window open, looking out at the lake in the darkness, the oil lamp giving plenty of light. Then I was interrupted by "Flower", one of the young men who had played songs on the first night I was there. He'd come to "practice his English" and in his words, "Make you a little happy, make your life longer". It became clear he was making an offer to make love. As he was climbing in the window, I asked him to leave, finally closing the windows with a firm message that I was not interested. I wondered if that was the reason the whole family had left for the TV, that perhaps they thought I'd appreciate such an opportunity.

After Flower had gone, I walked along the lake shore a bit under the brilliant stars. They were so beautiful, I decided to sleep outside. I got my sleeping bag, and had lain staring at the clear stars for perhaps two hours when Mr. Sidebatur came and said, "Sleep here, no good! Mosquitoes!" I said I'd found it wonderful to be under the stars. He again insisted, "Sleep here, no good. Mosquitoes!" There were no mosquitoes, but since he was not happy with my sleeping out, I finally went back in to my tiny cell where with the windows closed, there was no light at all. Was it the fear of evil spirits which prompted such precautions?

Chapter 20 - Tuk Tuk

I walked in the other direction to Tuk Tuk the next day, following an inland trail. On my left I could look up to the high escarpment rising hundreds of feet above the open valley. I could imagine the deep grooves in the rock raging with waterfalls, which must have been a magnificent sight in the rainy season. Young girls were tending water buffaloes grazing in the flat crusty dry rice paddies stretching out on my right. I had told the teacher in the Batak village that I had worked with children in an elementary school in California, and everywhere people would stop to ask, "Are you the teacher?" This area was almost ten miles away from where I had been the day before, but news had obviously traveled fast.

I was going rather slowly because of my blisters, and a whole family walked past me. First came a young girl about eight years old carrying a baby on her hip. Stumbling close behind was a younger brother, perhaps four. Then came the parents. The mother, quite pregnant, was carrying a huge bag of rice on her head using a square ceramic "plate" on which the bag rested. The husband carried nothing at all. We greeted each other, and I watched them go down the hill far faster than I could. At one point, the man stopped and reached for the bag of rice. I thought with relief that he was going to take his turn carrying it, but I saw he only helped readjust the weight of the bag so it could be more balanced on his wife's head. Music was not the only thing held in common with South America. But then it seems women are considered beasts of burden in many places on this earth.

Along the way was one of the most fascinating of the ancient banyan trees I'd seen. Circling the nearly twelve foot trunk and out about ten feet were a series of lesser "trees" propping up the horizontal branches of the original tree. Each subsidiary trunk was really a tap root, sent down who knows how long before, now grown to a foot or more in diameter. Like palatial pillars, they circled the inner tree, creating a natural temple. There was a spot inside these pillars where the great convoluted roots stretched like great fingers clutching the earth. Here incense and offerings rested.

Again I had the feeling of exploring the tendons of my own limbs, as if I were some tiny corpuscle. The sense of serenity inside this enclosure was as deep as any temple made by men. I stood there, not knowing which was up or down. The trunks pierced the soil and could have been holding up the earth from the arms of some great hand like that of Atlas.

As I sat spinning in my own mental state, an old man approached me. The temple codger again. He spoke no English, but pointed to the offering spot. Then, as I had no incense or flowers, to my purse.

I grinned at him, took out a rupee and placed it among the ashes, gasshoing my thanks. He reached down in one great swoop and scooped up the rupee and our eyes met in one amused twinkle. This tree must also be revered for its provision of income for the impoverished people here.

When I got back to my little windowless home, I noticed that only two of the three dogs who lived there greeted me. They were Batak dogs, a buff colored terrier that I've never seen anywhere, full of affection and loyalty. They had guarded the entrances and were lovingly treated by my old proprietor and "Mama", his wife. When I asked about the third, there was no answer. I wondered if he had met the fate of dogs in Bali.

I've been told they taste very good, but my appetite diminished. Here, the pigs and chickens too are treated as friends, free to wander, forage and be free, till the need for meat brings about their demise.

I thought about my own distinctions, that pigs, cows and chickens were OK to eat, but not dogs! Why not, if I was going to eat a being? It seemed to me a more respectful way. These meat-eaters honor the being till time to eat it, no matter what it was. Certainly the understanding of vegetarian practice became clearer to me than it ever had before. I felt a sense of shame at how I made my own distinctions in order to permit myself to eat pigs and chickens without conscience!

I stayed at Lake Toba four days, washing at dawn in the lake with the women, walking along the trails into the hills, resting from the hassles of Bali. Then I knew it was time to move on. I found a young man who would take me over to the mainland for a reasonable price. But as we pushed off from shore, he called out to me, "4,000 rupees!"

Oh, no!, I gasped and moved in one quick motion to the side of the boat. I almost jumped into the quickly deepening water, pack and all, when he just as quickly said, "Oh, OK, 400 rupees". It was as if I'd passed the last test with these hard-working people. I realized they'd accepted me as a friend when I was greeted all over the island with recognition and questions, "Are you the teacher?" They knew I had not chosen to stay in the imitation Batak houses created for tourists at Tuk Tuk, that I was content with simply walking through villages, but did I really know the value of a rupee? They had a real contempt for the tourists who accepted exorbitant prices for tours around the island and paid for high priced meals. Yet, they readily took their money. With this last act, the young man and I became very close in some inexplicable way.

He waited with me at the station till my bus arrived, two hours later, telling me of the family clans on the island, where very strict rules existed. He had met a young woman from the other end of the island to whom he was greatly attracted, but when he heard her name, which indicated she was from his family clan, he knew that was it—he could not marry her, no sense in getting attached.

The bus raced back over the terrifyingly winding road. I'd been delighted that there was a seat at the front so I could look through the large windshield. I must admit that the image of myself flying through that membrane of glass occurred to me several times as we speeded around curves where centrifugal force and the laws of nature should have propelled us over the cliff, hurtling us into a steep canyon. But the confidence of the driver, and I'm sure the prayers of the passengers, seemed to hold us on the road.

Bus ride back from Lake Toba to Medan, Jan. 27, 1982

Broken plastic seats, the stuffing oozing out of the flaps. I sit in front, feet propped up to prevent me from flying out the windshield as we whiz around curves.

I feel the yawning mouths of canyons full of jungle trees like teeth ready to devour us in the dark if we should pitch of the road. Then we're on level ground again and the enormous orange rising sun shows for an instant with grey cloudy streaks across it. Then it is lost behind Batak wood frame shacks with corrugated metal roofs. The wood is the same color as the muddy buffaloes and pigs.

At 7:00 am, children are already bound for school, some wearing white uniforms, some dark brown pants and skirts with pumpkin shirts. We sweep past groves of planted trees, dense forests, Bracken fern, green underbrush with tall step ladder trunks, where wide leaves have been sliced off, year after year. Some are curved with the weight of the frondy tops blowing in the wind. We ride through market towns where women haul heavy baskets on their heads. One short old woman drags five bamboo baskets as large as she is across the street. No one helps her.

Two children strain to pull a big two wheeled cart full of bags of rice, no sign of adult help. A woman seated on the ground by a pineapple stand eats rice from a banana leaf "plate". Children stand wrapped like cocoons in plaid, tube-shaped blankets in the morning cold. Pigs root in gardens and bushes along the road. One great sway-backed, prickle-backed, pregnant sow, stomach dragging on the ground, stops to look at us as we rattle past.

More children, some carrying coconut spine brooms. Motor cycles, bemos, honking horns.

We arrived in time for me to take an evening flight out of Medan. I was spared another night in the "verrerry cheeeep" hotel.

Chapter 21 - Penang

I arrived in the Penang airport. It was late afternoon, and again airport efficiency greeted me. Everyone was glad to help me find a costly hotel, but no one knew of more modest housing. An agent directed me to a bus stop a half mile away where, after walking, I waited for a bus for an hour. Then it took me another hour to get to the center of town on a crowded bus full of people in business suits and western clothes, commuting homeward after a day's work, probably in the computer companies and other western establishments we passed on the main road.

When I got off, I discovered Penang was in the middle of Chinese New Year celebration, and all the hotels were either full or the price had been doubled.

I was always astonished by my stubborn insistence on reasonable prices in unreasonable circumstances. I'd been up since 5:30 am, had ridden the bumpy bus for eight hours, taken the hour flight, walked with my pack for half an hour, then stood on the one hour bus ride into town. I was tired. Still when the clerk at a hotel a rickshaw driver had promised me would be cheap, asked for twice the quoted price, I refused to pay even though I could have, at the expense of a shorter stay.

I walked in a tired daze down the brightly lighted streets that looked like Chinatown in San Francisco. Festive decorations of bright lanterns and colored paper cheered the crowds milling in the streets. All signs were in Chinese, so I couldn't identify a hotel if it had been right in front of me.

I realized I was going to have to ask someone, and out of the sea of faces, picked a friendly female face. Like some wonderful miracle, she spoke English. She was visiting her brother for Chinese New Year. She stepped inside a shop to ask him for information and came out with an address. She and her sister insisted on driving me in their car, the first car I'd ridden in in months. I gratefully accepted and rode in style to a section of town much further away, not knowing where I was at all.

We stopped. She spoke to the hotel proprietor in Chinese, and an acceptable fee was arranged. She and her sister, who were both teachers in elementary schools in other parts of Malaysia, were like angels out of nowhere. We laughed at my good fortune and they returned to their brother's house.

I went to my room, equipped with a sink, a fan, and a hard bed. The walls were the usual dingy gray fiberboard partitions with paint dirty from years of non-washing. I had by now become accustomed to the usual condition of cheap Chinese hotels.

I slept like a rock. I was aware that celebrants of Chinese New Year were drinking, playing a game of Mah Jong, and talking in loud voices just outside the door, but nothing could disturb the sleep of a weary traveler luxuriating in the comfort of a shelter and a bed. How marvelous are the simplest things we take for granted—shelter and a place to sleep. How wonderful that in a foreign land there are generous, helpful people to guide a weary traveler. The experience of that awareness colors all other impressions of Penang.

The following day I did the "tourist" things, but by bus, so it took four times as long because of the local stops at each street. I had no real energy or desire to experience Chinese New Year celebrations, and the crowds of people only propelled me into a dreamlike state where I stood aside and watched. I wandered along the sea coast, took a tram ride to the top of the mountain to watch the sun set and to gaze out over the town below as the lights came on, and I visited the third largest reclining Buddha in Asia.

I wandered into the grounds of the temple where the reclining Buddha was. With a strange detachment, I watched the picture-taking tourists (mostly Chinese) crowding around. They lined their children and relatives up against the giant green dragons guarding the entrance, and took photos of the grinning family. How similar are groups of people no matter from what nationality.

Tourists everywhere act the same way. There is a common bond between them.

Inside the temple was the giant Buddha, stretched out 105 feet long, like an enormous plaster doll. His feet were ten feet long, his head had the vacant stare of plastic dolls. People were offering incense before it and prostrating in devotion, so I respectfully wandered around to the back to examine a row of other "plastic" standing Buddhas placed around the outside wall. In front of each was a collection box with a plaque that stated in English, "If you pray to this Buddha, you will have wealth", the next, "If you pray to this Buddha, you will have fame". On each was the attainment of something: success, health, good fortune — all the things Buddha taught not to seek after or get attached to! I wonder if ever that giant reclining Buddha tosses in his doll-like sleep!

Set around the raised platform supporting the big Buddha, I noticed some beautifully carved, dark wood panels telling the story of Buddha's life. There was one magnificent panel depicting Buddha after his time of ascetic practice. His body was reduced to a skeleton. I gazed at this for a very long time, oblivious of the crowds. The artwork was excellent, but it seemed to convey much more than a picture. It was Buddha himself, waiting for understanding. It was, for me, a very compelling experience. I had seen pictures of Nazi concentration camp inmates whose hollow eyes, sunken cheeks, protruding ribs, and large knees impressed me deeply with their suffering. Here was someone who took this on by choice to deepen his understanding.

Buddha taught that all suffering is due to desire and greed, for food, wealth, fame, success, power. Certainly it must have been the pursuit of these desires that brought about much of the suffering in World War II. Now, in Asia, the followers of Buddha pray for attainment of just these things. Funny how we twist teachings to suit our own desires. That meditating skeleton spoke to me across all the centuries that the understanding he had reached has validity. His enlightened transcendence of all the mind traps of this world could help us all.

Odd, now I look back, how in that hall of the plastic Buddhas, where the daily devotion had drifted so far from the teachings of Buddha, that such a profound experience of the practice of the real Buddha should come to me. Always that panel will stay in my mind.

The rest of Penang somehow didn't capture my imagination or interest. I was glad to move on after two days.

I remember one odd experience. As I was walking around the city blocks, I passed a beggar half squatting, leaning against the wall next to the sidewalk. I had to repress my spontaneous "what are you doing here?", since he looked exactly the way Trout, a friend of mine, usually looked after a long day's hike in his ragged shorts. He was grinning at me out of his dark face. The same curly hair, features, expression — an exact twin of Trout, begging in the streets of Penang! It always amazed me how my long distance friends kept popping up into my awareness in such a vivid way!

I was up next day at 3:30 a.m., riding in a rickshaw to the ferry through the drab wet streets. The ferry ride with commuter people, lights shining on smooth ripples, dark tankers and freighters against a dark sky, painted my memory.

Impression.

By the shore in Penang. School children, Hindu (?) in neat uniforms walking along towards home. An old man, perhaps in his seventies, carries six school packs and trudges along between groups of children. Six children follow him, carrying no bags! They begin early here to learn superiority and escape from menial tasks!

Chapter 22 - Cameron Highlands

I head for the highlands to cool off a bit, and let the jangle of Penang drop off. More bus changes, rides along roads banked by palm trees and banana plants, wood frame houses on stilts, the inevitable free-wandering pigs and chickens.

On the rickety bus that climbs the steep winding hills to the Cameron Highlands, past canyons where wild banana trees shake in the wind, I talk to a young Hindu farmer. He tells me his grandfather came to the highlands to supervise the tea plantations and brought many Hindu experts in tea processing with him. Now the population of Malaysia is one third Hindu. one third Chinese, and one third Muslim natives.

When our bus breaks down and we stand along the road waiting for another bus or some assistance, he sees Chinese families whom he had helped before pass us by. They seem not to notice him. He speaks of the prejudice. The Chinese, who are "inferior" to the Malaysians, look down on Hindus with contempt.

This young Hindu finds himself in conflict with his own customs as well. His brother is very wealthy and recently got married. My Hindu friend and his family had gone to the wedding and were just now returning. It is the custom for the guests to buy new dress clothes for the wedding couple, and for the couple to supply each guest with similar new clothes. He had suggested that they dispense with that custom, since many of the family members could ill afford the purchase of clothes they could not wear on ordinary occasions. His family had been shocked, and he was nearly disowned. He reminded me of the young man in Bali who'd gone into debt for five to ten years because of his wedding reception.

Finally a truck came by and offered to take us to the next town, where I would have to change buses for the final ride to the top of the mountain. I'm glad I didn't succumb to the temptation to try to hike. My pack was feeling heavy with unnecessary burdens as I had carried three thick books, hiking boots for trekking in Nepal, plus a sleeping bag that I had not used in all the sweltering places I'd visited so far. It was the end of January, and in the Highlands it was just comfortably cool.

The hotels the Hindu friend had recommended had been "full", though I realized they were for native people and the proprietors were suspicious of tourists. I found a hotel "by chance" when a traveler I met in a small café told me where she was staying.

Tourists come in droves to this area, staying at incredibly pretentious hotels, costing one hundred dollars a night, which were located in a cluster around a beautiful golf course, further along the road. Being self-contained, they rarely entered the tiny villages. I had to walk for half an hour uphill to the hotel where I stayed. It was a dilapidated former summer home now rented to students and other single travelers like myself.

Many Western students were staying there. It was already full, but the Hindu proprietor said I could sleep outside for two dollars and that there would be a room the next day. I was delighted. At last I had a place where I could sleep under the stars in the clear air, which made up for my frustration at Lake Toba.

I hoped this interim was a time to replenish myself from the dull erosion of Penang's crowded grubby streets. There were "jungle" walks nearby and I sauntered through very civilized trails overhung with enormous split leaf philodendrons and other tropical foliage, which was made up of our familiar house plants but growing wild and to gigantic proportions. My favorite time was spent sitting by beautiful streams and drinking in the stillness.

Excerpt from my diary, Feb. 2, 1982

What do I do when I look at a stream? watch the foam. White bubbles catch along the side of a rocky shore, race with the flowing stream. Some tarry in an eddy, circling, then run on to join the rest, swishing, giggling—gone.

Then, for long periods I watch the white torrent splashing indistinguishably. White pulp of water glows white in late afternoon long after the sun stops catching it. Forever curling, bubbling, spurting on, on, on. I watch hypnotized by its changing changelessness.

Then my eye slides to the places where the water slips clearly over the chiseled polished rock, cleanly. No sound. No torrent, like glass, glazing the surface. It pours immovably on till it breaks into the stream once more and becomes noise and rush.

I watch the various mini-falls where water leaps over a smooth surface like curled tusks, downward in a shiny curve of streams, air bubbling beneath the crystal surface.

I stare at the rocks. Some moss covered, some dark with stains of water, some smooth like velvet or agate, some still jagged and opposing the onrushing stream which crashes, laughs and moves on, unbothered by the obstacle, taking with it at each moment infinitesimal minerals, wearing away with the gentlest persistence and patience. I watch the rugged stubbornness of Time—holding firm against the cutting chortle of the water.

Then I watch nothing—just sit like some dumb leaf listening to the cacophony of sounds, the high song, the low roar, the endlessness of passing that sounds like the wind in the trees, or rain, or roaring engines.

Then sounds fade, light fades, and I awake aware that Time has passed and I've been doing nothing!

Time to move on myself, still with the singing water in my heart.

Five months, I've traveled so far. It's time to allow a healing moment in nature. I wander through the small villages, sit in tea shops where occasionally army personnel casually wander in, plunk down great machine guns on the table as if it were a pack, eat, laugh and leave. Here in the midst of the sweetest serenity are reminders of the military mind.

I join the students in their evening meals. We contribute a fish or potato, and we all take turns cooking for everyone. I meet a Turk who reminds me of a friend, a young German interested in meditation, a group of Swiss girls traveling together. One says of me, "My mother would NEVER travel the way you do." She's astonished at my pleasure in this type of simple travel.

I'm taking leave, and I tell them that my next destination is Thailand, where I was hoping I could meditate in a temple, but still, I have no idea where. The young German gives me an address of a monastery that a Tibetan teacher had given him. He has no idea where it is, since he didn't go there. He has already been to Thailand and leaves me his map printed in English.

This is my last night in Malaysia. Funny he should supply me with the next place to aim for—just as I need it!

Chapter 23 - Thailand

People crowd on the train. There are no reservations where I sit. Still I find a seat by the window. While I'm standing stuffing my pack in the storage rack, someone sits in my seat. I laugh, and two women already buried in boxes of cookies and bread make room for me. I hold four cracker boxes, my feet rest under four more. Everyone seems to be a small merchant carrying wares from Malaysia to Thailand.

At the border, we pour out for passport checking. Barbed wire, soldiers holding machine guns watch us as we stand in line. It takes two hours. There are random checks of packs and bags. Few have suitcases. Everything is packed in cardboard boxes held together by strings which must be unknotted and retied. There is a foreign exchange window behind iron bars. There's more waiting till we get through this second line.

This time two middle aged men, one an Arab, one from Bangladesh, sit opposite me. I'm still buried in cracker boxes. The Arab spent several weeks in a Thai detention camp because his visa had lapsed. There seems to be a strong drug traffic. Before we start, soldiers board the train, randomly pointing to packages which must be opened and examined. Everyone accepts this calmly as a customary thing. The machine guns still give me the creeps. There is one more hour delay for this inspection.

At the next stop across the borders, windows are flung open and wares are passed and tossed to people waiting alongside the train.

The woman who owns the crackers reminds me of Merlina Mercouri in "Never on Sunday". She has a hearty manner, beautiful, with her bare shoulders peeking through rips in her ragged dress. She talks in animated joyful tones to all the men and many of the women around her. She's full of the vitality of life. She tosses her cracker boxes out the window, fondly embraces everyone in reach, and leaves with the rest of the vendors. We're in Hadjai, and I get off.

Everywhere people approach with barbecued chicken, fruit, and grubby cups of tea. The train station is chaos. Thai monks are everywhere; saffron robes and bare right shoulders. Vendors selling umbrellas pack the sidewalks. No one seems to have heard of the monastery, Watt Thom Sua, or Krabbi. It must be my pronunciation. This is not a tourist spot. I'm the only Caucasian, and there are no provisions for travel information in English.

I go into a restaurant and order a cup of tea and study the map which was given to me by the student traveler in Malaysia. Luckily the place names are in English. Finally I locate Krabbi. It's a long way from Hadjai. I see that no trains go there. I must take a bus. My first inclination is to spend the night, but the hotels which seem as if they would be inexpensive demand twenty dollars a night.

I lug my pack several blocks to the bus stop to wait. Here I'm beset by women and men offering to take me to Krabbi—"You charter, no take bus!" I say I want the bus, which fortunately drives up. I has an English subtitle next to the Thai caption stating "Krabbi". I'm halfway in the bus when someone grabs me off balance and drags me off, stating in commanding tones, "You charter". Again I refuse, and wait for another bus.

Many local buses come by, all with the enigmatic Thai writing which no one will decipher for me. Someone tells me there are no more buses to Krabbi today.

Finally, acknowledging my predicament, I sit down on the sidewalk. The tendency to cry is welling up. I'm tired, don't know where Krabbi is, don't know if there's a monastery there for real, don't know if they'll take me in. Am I totally off kilter? Should I go back to the train station and continue on to Bangkok and forget the whole adventure? What next?

Quietly, I feel a touch on my dejected shoulder. I turn to see a kind woman who's been selling oranges close by and who watched the whole episode. She points to a bus coming up to the sidewalk. I thank her with a gassho and run, grab a firm hold on the entrance pole which withstands the aggressive would-be-tourist-agent's effort to pull me off. He repeats, "This bus doesn't go to Krabbi. You must charter." He shouts that the bus goes to Petaluma, that I'll get there at 11:00 pm. But I settle in next to a man carrying a disconcerted rooster that crows confusedly every time the light changes as the bus turns into or away from the sun.

No one speaks English, but I gather that I must change buses in Petaluma, and go to Thrang, I see these listed on my map. They're in the direction of Krabbi, so I rest and watch the country-side, amazed at my own stubborn determination in the midst of such obstacles.

At Petaluma, the same scene occurs. A sturdy woman in a uniform commands, "You take taxi. I take you to Thrang!" She seems as powerful as a woman jailer, but I thank her kindly. A bus drives up, showing the word "Thrang" in English on the front! I gratefully board and ride on.

Then Thrang: a veritable metropolis with skyscraper buildings of four or five stories. Shops with plate glass windows look out on a street that even has a curb. It's 4:30 pm. Krabbi is still two hundred kilometers further. I have a strong inclination to seek out a comfortable hotel and try again the next day. Then a bus stops in the middle of the street. The driver leans out and calls, "Krabbi?" It's the bus I was dragged off in Hadjai. Two men jump out, one takes my pack, one helps me up the steps. They're glad to see me and, I think, surprised I've stuck it out. They seem to pay me kind respect. Again I feel the camaraderie with foreigners who take the common path, not yielding to the expensive comfortable way. Is this something that occurs just for me, in a sort of reinforcement of my beliefs? All I know is I feel close to these strong men who jumped out to help me. It wasn't even a bus stop!

We drive through desolate flatlands of grass and small shrubs. There are very little signs of habitation. I wonder where I'm going. It looks like a tiny crossroads. There's a "hotel" they point out to me.

I walk over to the desk which is open to the street under a thatched overhang. They want 70 Bhat. Actually, this is reasonable, about seven dollars, but I've just come from Malaysia where the exchange rate is very different. I miscalculate the price, which seems exorbitant to my weary mind. I turn away, for the first time wondering if I will have to camp out in my sleeping bag, and if so, where?

I cross the street to where three restaurants are open in the night air. For some reason I pick one, go in and sit down, and order tea. This is the second time I meet the overwhelmingly sweet tea common to Thailand. They fill the cup one third full of sweetened condensed milk and pour in tea to the top. It's sticky sweet, and when you're overcome with thirst, it's no quencher.

I show the waitress, a young Chinese girl, the address of Watt Thom Sua. She puzzles over it, takes it to some men at another table who puzzle over it. English writing must seem as exotic to them as the Thai script does to me. They couldn't read it. Again I pronounce as best I can, "Watt Tom Su". "Watt Tom Su", "Watt Tom Su", they repeat in a vague way. Then one lights up. "Oh, Watt Thom Sooa!", and they burst into gales of laughter.

No further interaction. They resume their eating. There is no help offered. I continue to drink my sticky tea, maintaining my "What's next?" attitude, more out of tired baffled vacuousness than out of any concerted effort.

Then from across the room comes a voice in English asking: "What do you want to do at Watt Thom Sua?"

"To meditate", I answer, expecting another peal of laughter. As it turns out, this handsome young man in his thirties invites me to join him at his table. I come over as he orders food, and we begin to talk. He is well read in Michener, Tolstoy, Robert Frost, and other Western authors translated into Thai. He is curious about my meditation practice, has read about Zen meditation, but has never tried it.

After listening for awhile to my experiences of sitting in Japan, the travels in Indonesia and the Philippines, he says: "I'll take you to Watt Thom Sua. I figured when I saw you that either you had problems or you were a very courageous woman. I've decided you're a very courageous woman."

First I eat the food he offers, which I had thought he had ordered for himself, but which he insists on giving me. Then we go out into the dark, get in his jeep, and start down the desolate highway. We drive for many minutes, then turn off on a dirt road. I realize now that I am totally at his disposal. I remember all the warnings in guide books not to trust handsome young men. Actually I have a good feeling about him, but the thought of my rather vulnerable state still flicks through my mind.

Just about that time, we drive in the dark up to the front of a temple which is an open cave. Loud speakers shout chants into the still air, and I can see with the help of electric lights lines of nuns in white and monks in orange robes seated before an altar, chanting.

A young monk comes out to greet us. Thank heavens for my new acquaintance, who translates for me. The monk asks "How did you hear about us?" I tell him about the young traveler in Malaysia, and that I want to meditate. "For how long?"

Actually I had thought about only sitting the one week of our regular February sesshin, but when I see the cave, I ask for three or four weeks. I tell him I am accustomed to sitting the period commemorating Buddha's death, that I had been practicing Zen meditation. He thanks David, my translator, who disappears, and he leads me up the stairs into the most fantastic cave temple I could have imagined.

On one end, near the stairs, at the entrance, is a small altar with a life-sized, seated statue of the abbot of the monastery, covered with flakes of gold. My focus sweeps past the seated monks and nuns to the greater altar, and to a stark pink five-foot head of Buddha. In the confusion of being newly arrived, I instantaneously am aware of ornate statues, candles, a great throne from which the abbot speaks.

I prostrate three times before the teacher's statue, as is the custom when entering a monastery. I'm thankful for learning the proper temple etiquette in Japan, when I stayed at Kobun's brother's temple for several days.

I sit apart from all the white robed nuns till the evening services are finished. Then the young monk in charge guides me to a wood cabin along an unpaved street of houses where the nuns live. I'm given a room to myself on the second floor, furnished with two grass mats, a tea pot, cup, and pillow. "This is your room, you can practice here." With that he leaves me, and I pile one grass mat on the other to make a slightly thicker mattress, and marveling at the amazing circumstances that led me here, fall into a deep sleep.

At 4:00 a.m., loudspeakers again! A male voice, speaking Thai, penetrates the darkness. I get up, locate the bathrooms by following the old nuns among whom I live. They're cement rooms equipped with the square tank and dipper for "flushing" the Asian style toilet.

I watch a young novice, who sleeps in the room next to mine, fill her cup with water from an enormous ceramic cistern which is full of rain water from the roof. I brush my teeth in similar manner, leaning over an open gutter beside the house. Then under the stars, I follow the nuns gathering from other directions and we walk down the road back to the cave temple.

Electric lights brighten the lumpy overhanging ceiling from which thick, three foot long stalactites hang. The floor is leveled by a wood platform covered with linoleum reminiscent of old kitchens in the U.S.

There is a raised platform about one and a half feet above this floor for the monks. They assemble, spread out a sitting mat and settling down on their knees, sit on their heels — which they do for the entire hour and a half of morning chants and meditation!

Fifty monks and ninety nuns gather while the recorded voice

of the abbot drones on over the loudspeaker. At the proper time, the recording is cut off, and there is profound silence. The abbot is temporarily away in Hadjai, the assistant tells me, but they listen to his recorded lectures in his absence.

Then we chant. A musical resonance of male and female voices echoes under the enormous overhang and bounds into the dark. I have been used to monotone chants of the Japanese monasteries, and the repetitious rhythms of the "Hail, Mary's" of the Philippine nuns. I'm surprised to hear the rise and fall of Thai tones, which give the quality of song to those early morning chants. Microphones have been placed in front of a nun and a monk who lead the chanting together, and reinforce the sound.

As we started to the temple, someone handed me a thin cotton cloth "rug" on which I am to sit. I wriggle uncomfortably as my unaccustomed ankles became numb. My knees, unused to sitting flat without a cushion, roar their protest. Still, I had the impulse to sit "sesshin". I knew that my friends and fellow practitioners of zazen would soon begin the week long sitting at home in California, and it feels right to begin this practice now in Thailand.

After the chanting, voices fell silent. In that great cave, everyone meditates. There is an odd "coo, coo" sound that occasionally cuts the quiet from nowhere in particular, and I only later learn it is the cry of the iguana who lives in the crevices of the overhanging rock. There is a power that impels stillness when you stand or sit in a cave. I agree with hermits who seek caves for meditation in every age and across all religious practices.

I marvel at the good fortune that guided me to such a wonderful place!

Just as the stillness closes out the chill I feel in the morning air, nuns and monks began to stir, rise, and file out into the dawn. There is little talk, and many of the young nuns pass by me and smile in friendly greeting. Here, the gassho, hands pressed together while we bow to each other, is such a comfortable practice. I feel I've been bowing that way all my life.

I go back up to my room, and continue sitting since I don't know what else to do, and no one talks English. This time I fold my soft sweater under my ankles against the floor, for the comfort of a padded mat while I sit. I use the pillow to sit on and sink into quiet.

Later, when I go downstairs, headed for the bathroom, I find five old nuns with wrinkled faces who live in the rooms below me. They're seated on grass mats laid out on the cement outside, eating together. They motion for me to join them. They have rice and cooked ferns in a sauce. They insist on piling rice high on the metal plate they give me.

I squat on the grass mat and eat with my hands under their approving chuckles.

A young nun finds me and tells me in broken English that I should come to the temple at 8:30 when they all go for food. I sit upstairs till again the loud speaker, apparently playing another lecture, appears to announce the time for everyone to go to the temple to receive offerings of food brought by the townspeople.

The nuns have prepared fruit and rice to take to the temple, and a lithe tall nun, perhaps in her fifties, motions for me to carry the offering.

We go together, prostrate before a group of monks, and place our offering on a cloth that one monk spreads out on the floor. They go to great lengths not to receive anything directly from a woman's hands. We prostrate again, and find our seats.

I spread my square cloth kneeling mat way to the side where I look directly at the statue of the teacher. There is much bustle as the monks assemble in two long lines facing each other, sit down and casually begin to read the morning paper or chat with one another. Their enormous buddha bowls sit in front of them, ready to receive the packages of food tossed into them by attending monks. The food is wrapped in plastic bags which kindly separates sauces, fruits, rice, and things wrapped in intricate bamboo leaf packages or rolled in banana leaves. There is a period of chanting: the meal chant, I recognize, similar to the chant we do during our weeklong sittings. Then the monks begin eating. After they have started eating, the nuns, who have been sitting waiting, are served.

They have stacked enamel dishes called pintos, which contain separate foods. Large hunks of food like watermelon or pineapple are on top. This is their food for the whole day, which they will eat before noon because they have taken a vow not to eat after 12:00 p.m. Someone brings me a stack of dishes full of food firmly held firmly together in a neat cylinder by a small handle that I can carry out of the temple without worrying about spilling anything. Then, carrying our stacked enamel dishes, we file out to begin the day.

Chapter 24 - Islands in Thailand

The next morning, I said a temporary goodbye to the nuns, making sure they knew I would be back. David arrived in a jeep full of charming Thai women high school teachers. We set off in the morning mist, picking up twenty teachers who lived in the area. A drive along barrens to the coast gave a slight hint of what waited for us. Occasional single limestone mounts rose up from the flat plain like strange vertical loaves of bread covered with hanging vines and trees. They made a startling effect poking their rock noses up through the flat earth.

There were many dark gray water buffaloes grazing on weeds by the side of the road, serving as the usual road maintenance gang that I had seen in nearly all the Asian countries I'd visited. Other buffaloes had been wallowing and were caked with a stiff cracked layer of mud.

As we drove over a rise the open sea and sky, blue on blue, hung before us. Stretching out across the expanse of water, like the waving spine of an ancient sea monster, blue mountains jutted up in a line, each steep and grizzly with the green verdure. The sea was as still as a lake.

We watched from the shore while fishermen unloaded a great heap of shrimps from the hull of a small fishing boat, packing them in barrels. Others were crushing great blocks of ice in a simple hand crusher to preserve the fish during the trip back to Bangkok. Then we were invited to board this same boat. The aroma of shrimp pervades my memories of this idyllic trip.

As in some unbelievable dream, we glided across the swells of water towards the line of islands. They rose so steeply from the water that the sides were like upright walls with no inclining shore. Even the trees were clutching desperately to the rock, straining against gravity in their effort to keep upright. The memory of the musical chanting of the nuns rang in my ears as the wind brushed past, smooth and sweet.

Once, in California, I'd sat on a mountain ridge overlooking the sea while fog filled the valleys, leaving only the peaks of the mountains standing like isolated islands. Now, as the sea washed the feet of these rocky cliffs, I could have been back there, and I had a misty "nowhere" feeling.

We glided to the shore of the only horizontal island in sight. The others were limestone, gray and jagged with erosion like living Chinese brush paintings. This island was black lava rock like some sleeping monster in the midst of standing giants. Some people were already in swimming as we glided up. We jumped out of the boat into the water. I got into my "sarong", the piece of batik I used for my sheet, and went in swimming.

I wondered what it would feel like after two days of meditating to be with such a large group of people. Few of them spoke English, and David was engaged in charming two pretty teachers, so I had time to myself.

There were several snorkels, and after much giggling about the feel of the rubbery mouthpiece fitting around my gums, I slid into the silence of underwater with that raspy, exaggerated, rhythmic breathing which was my own. I floated over dark crevices and rocks where strange wormlike, many-legged beings darted for cover, where striped and spotted fish swam curiously up to my nose and stared at me. I was doing what I had always wanted to do after seeing wonders of coral reefs in movies. I would never have gone to the expense of a tour that included this, but here it was, flooding me with secret splendor. There was much debris, brown "dust"-like silt that rose as the "millipedes" flipped around the ledges. I could see what Cousteau meant when he said the sea is dying. There were barnacles and other coral-like things that had been clogged with the brown silt. There were fewer fish than in the movies. It was sad but still the most wonderful experience to slide silently past forms that took shape in the watery distance and took on detail only when I glided past.

I felt as if I was doing some other form of zazen where I could watch my bubbly breath while visions rose and disappeared in my awareness. I could have continued forever, but others needed turns using the snorkel, and I was in danger of burning my back. So I stood up and climbed out like some upright amphibian, dripping in my wet sarong, to join a picnic feast.

A six year old boy was piercing fish onto a stick to roast over a fire with all the coordination and confidence of any adult. I wondered if any six-year-old in our culture could have handled that task so capably. Sometimes it seems as if we educate out all the natural coordination of our children.

When everyone began to take naps, I set off to explore the island shoreline. I experienced the strong disorientation of space and time again as I walked along the black lava shelves that jutted like tongues into the sea. There is an island I love in Bar Harbor off the coast of Maine, where black lava just like this made cliffs for the white surf to crash on, where barnacles and limpets cling to the tidal layer of smooth stone and clams dig deep into the sand. I felt gifted to stay on that island, feeling there could be no place on earth as beautiful. Now here was a replica, but more like a vision of what Bar Harbor had looked like eons before the glacier polished it smooth.

There were great "plates" of an iron-tinted coating on the gray and black rock, like some crusty scales on an antediluvian monster. The whole island felt ancient. As I climbed among the jagged rocks and walked on sand, I traced great tracks of webbed feet with dragging tail marks of what I learned later was a six foot long iguana that had crawled out of the jungle in the center of the island. The limestone rocks were embedded with oysters; strange roots stuck up from salt ponds like five inch high stalactites. Palms and fronds of all sorts leaned over the beach. Dense forest came right up to the sand.

In the beginning of my journey, I had spent one day in Kweilin, China, where limestone mountains pierced the flat plain like this, and wished I could spend a lifetime there. Two places on earth with the same magic vertical mountains piercing earth and water.

Were all the fantasies of my favorite spots on earth merging into one?

I met two teachers who were walking in the opposite direction, and we three stopped to dig for tiny one inch clams in the sand.

Then it came time to leave. David caught up with us, and we walked back to the boat, he quoting Saint-Exupery, Richard Bach and Michener.

From my diary:

We load our gear into the small boat, and push off as the sun is setting on our left. The white moon, one day short of full, rises on our right above the island, as we glide away.

Soft clouds turn from white to gray to pink, unaware of their own splendor. Golden stepping stones dance towards the setting sun on the smooth rising swells of darkening water. We slide with the putting of the motor through this great unpeopled expanse, past dark islands up to the island of the "grandmother".

In the dark, we glide up to a long dock where a two-masted galleon is moored, like some ghost out of the 17th century. As we glide past its great hull, rough with flaking paint, a dog barks from the cabin, perhaps to call us back to reality. I had been expecting a whole troop of pirates to pour out of the shadows and dispatch us all.

We each claimed our packs and walked up to an enormous three- story Chinese mansion. Would the surprises of this trip never end? In the reception hall, one of the group, a lawyer, greeted his grandmother who stood to welcome us in silence. She had had a stroke and couldn't talk, but watched us with kind and friendly eyes.

We walked through a long wood paneled dining room hung with pictures of the Thai president shaking hands with the grandmother in younger days. The dining room table was twenty feet long, with chandeliers and a white tablecloth. Up the stairs were two floors of rooms now unused, but with rooms for male guests on one floor, female on the other.

The kitchen area was as big as a whole house, with cement floor and drains so that the entire floor could be cleaned with a hose. There was a counter where four or five enormous woks could cook on charcoal fires. Showers and toilet were in one corner. In a bustle, the teachers gathered to begin cooking chicken, shrimp, the clams we had dug on the island, and fish in sauces over large charcoal fires set up outside next to the kitchen. In no time a banquet spread down the twenty foot length of the table, and we began to feast.

We each took a turn riding on a Chinese fishing boat, propelled by oars which crossed so that the right hand operated the left oar, the left pulled the right oar. Time collapsed again for me. Only six months before I had been boating on a pond in Maine under the full moon. Now here I was sliding past a big pirate ship in the silence of another full-moon night in Thailand!

A large man in his fifties, who was introduced to me as the "owner of the hotel" at the crossroads, that I had seen the first night and had thought too expensive. He was an expert at propelling this craft. Through David, he kept sending friendly messages to me, since he couldn't speak English. We felt very comfortable together. Though there was no verbal communication, I enjoyed the group a great deal, and David said I seemed to be at home anywhere, that my friendship was enjoyed by everyone.

When it was time to sleep, I lay on an outside porch, so that I could watch the moon till I fell asleep.

I woke at dawn. As everyone was still asleep, I walked out on the long dock to do my morning zazen. I was aware that a nice young man, a physical education teacher, came to join me. We both sat cross legged and still on the rocking dock in the dawning light. The creaking sounds of the pulling ropes that held the moored ship mingled with the sounds of swirling water as the tide receded. The bubbles of digging clams popped in the mud, and the scuttling of crab feet splashed with infinitesimal unison in the morning air. Little sticky sounds of bird feet slapped across the mud.

When it came time to go, I really hated to leave. It was still early in the morning, and I had hoped we could spend the whole day here. While others gathered their things I wandered through a palm grove where goats were chewing on a mango-like fruit that dropped from the flower of the coconut tree.

Just before I left to go on my trip, I'd lived for a short time in a community where I had charge of some goats, and used to watch them graze. How at home I felt here with the crunching sound of their busy jaws and the flicks of their short tails. I marvel at whatever it is that continues to present me with flashes of other times and places that feel similar to these "foreign" experiences time after time.

I said goodbye to the grandmother, such a beautiful woman. We couldn't talk. I just looked into her clear old eyes and held her hands, feeling a vast warmth flow through me.

From my diary:

I go down to the mud flats to wade through the shallow water to the boat. Last night the boat was even with the level of the dock some twenty feet above us. I'm sad it's all over, savoring the last boat ride through the green water, past the end of grandmother's island, but the surprises are still coming. We drift into a neighboring island where a small bamboo village looks out on the shore. We've come to pick up a passenger.

There is a tall dignified old man standing on shore, and I wave to him a friendly greeting as we wait for the passenger. He waves to me and invites me up on shore. The others grin and encourage me to go.

I gaze at his fine wrinkled wise face and deep good humored eyes as I shake his hands and to his delighted surprise, gassho. Behind him, children are shyly gathering to stare at me, but when I smile and say "hello" they scatter like startled birds.

I sit down on the sand as the chief walks away, leaving me to make their acquaintance alone. I remember my wonderful dog, Bub, who had a beautiful talent for reassuring timid children. She would sit with her back to them, seemingly interested in other things, while they crept shyly up to touch her. When they were fully comfortable, she'd turn slowly towards them.

With grateful thanks for her teachings, I gaze off at some of the bamboo houses while they steal up behind me. Then I turn and smile again. This time they only back up a bit. I pick up a coconut and say my word for it. A woman tells me their name for it. When I repeat it, ineptly, they all giggle and we are friends.

The chief comes up with a huge armload of bananas, and it's time to go.

While we drifted away from the island, I couldn't help marveling at the illusory feeling to this adventure. The chief stood tall on the shore waving at us till we rounded another island, but his wise old deeply wrinkled face and dark eyes burn in my memory even now.

We glided past the close steep walls of islands. The lawyer grandson began to share stories of his early life on the islands. He used to go with that old chief when he was a boy, perhaps fifteen or twenty years ago, climbing up those forbidding vertical cliffs, carrying a machete to cut bamboo growing on the top.

I was still marveling at the wonder of this unasked for adventure, thinking it was nearing its close, when we slid literally into the island we were gliding by. We entered a great opening, and ground into the smooth sand of a beach inside an enormous cave lighted dimly by the reflection of the sun on the water.

David joked that this is the cave for me to do my meditation in. It would have been perfect! Under a ceiling nearly 100 feet above the water, a gigantic white column thirty feet across, with tier on tier of dripping crystals, rose as the "guardian" of this inner temple. The floor sloped steeply up toward the back, where stalactites caught the light of an enormous fifteen foot high pyramid of bat guano. This is an untouched sanctuary with all the vaulted feeling of any cathedral, pulling me deeply into a quiet state where rock and air and I feel all the same.

Time to leave. High tide will cover the entrance completely. When I was young, I read about the Blue Grotto in Naples where only at low tide could you slide inside and watch the phosphorescent water spark as it was splashed. Here, like some composite summation of a thousand day dreams, I left this undiscovered ancient cave feeling I'd seen a secret Blue Grotto.

Still the unbelievable nature of this day continued. Reluctantly we rode over the green glossy swells past the "sea serpent" islands stretching to the misty horizon. Then a dusty ride on the unpaved roads brought us back to the monastery.

Chapter 25 - A Celebration

Back at the monastery, preparations were in progress for the annual celebration of Buddha's birth, death, and enlightenment which takes place in Thailand on the night of the full moon in February. People from the town were gathering along the road where the older nuns lived, bringing large bouquets of flowers. The nuns were seated on the porches of their houses tying many little bouquets including a few flowers, a stick of incense, and a candle in each one.

We sat in the outdoor temple where the monks practiced, with all the monks seated on a wooden platform above the nuns and lay people, who gathered on the bumpy ground around them.

While I was sitting there on the ground, someone placed a small traveling alarm clock on the ground with a note in English by it. It was from an English monk who had been in the hospital with a bout of malaria when I arrived. Jampa had told him about me, and he was offering his clock for me to use.

After the magic adventure on the islands, I had completely forgotten about the watch incident. Now, clocks and watches were tumbling our of everywhere and with them, were opportunities to communicate with everyone. The young monk indicated he would be able to tell me about Vipassana practice at some convenient time, explaining that monks could not speak to women alone; that they must be accompanied by another monk or nun. He also gave me a tiny pendant made of a white composition which held a monk's hair pressed into a mold to form an amulet with a miniature bas relief of Buddha. It was seen as a protection. I'd noticed that nearly everyone in Thailand wore one of these pendants; sometimes as many as five dangled around their necks.

I also felt the reassuring acceptance of the whole community. It was like a welcome home.

The abbot, seated in his chair, gave a talk. Since I couldn't understand the meaning, I fell into listening to his voice and speech patterns. That gentle voice rang out in slow syllables, as if he were giving a gentle caress to each one of the people there. There was a lot of laughter and smiles, and a warm feeling of love spread among everyone there.

After chanting and bows, a growing row of flickering lights appeared as everyone lighted candles and incense from the person next to them. Just as the flickering candlelight increased, the wind blew up, and we had to repeat the process all over again.

As it began to get dark, about two hundred townspeople and their children climbed up the cement staircase, in a long procession with all the nuns, over the lip of the cliff and down into the fantasy jungle valley to join the monks. The whole procession of people, saffron robed monks first, then the white clad nuns, then lay people, began to walk along the narrow path against the cliff that circled that primordial valley.

The great philodendron leaves and undergrowth hung like dark shadows till lighted by the passing candles; the caves looked only like dark recesses in greater darkness.

All was silent as bare feet slapped on the dirt path. There was just the line of bobbing lights ahead turning in a gradual arch. Glowing incense added a tangy aroma to the moist earthy air. Children darted in and out, dropping flakes of still burning incense on the dry leaves along the path. It was amazing to me that, in the gusty wind, nothing caught fire. The older nuns, guided by more sure-footed younger ones, stepped over the great roots extending from the giant tree trunks next to the path. Stones along the uneven path became visible only as we tripped over them. It took nearly an hour to circle the valley.

As we returned to the outdoor temple, people placed the remainders of their burning candles and incense in crevices on small rock altars on the side of the trail. Some of them were still flickering like tiny torches long after the townspeople left to go home at 10:00 p.m.

The celebration continued as monks and nuns chanted, and then sat together in silence. Many nuns were planning to sit up all night. I realized this was an opportunity to sit for twenty-four hours as the abbot suggested, but I was tired from the magic weekend at the islands. Towards 1:45 am, my legs were aching from sitting on slanting ground, and my head drooped and nodded. When a group of nuns got up to leave, I left with them to climb back up over the "pass" and down again to the flat level of the bamboo jungle. I slept deeply till 4:00 am when the morning service call rang out through the air.

Excerpt from Feb. 12 diary

> *Days pass. I go at 4:15 every morning to the great cave after being wakened by the loudspeaker giving an "Amber teacher" talk. I wash in the cement bathroom, splashing water over myself with a dipper. There is a drain hole in the cement floor. The wash water comes from great cisterns, shaped like the hiding places for thieves in the Ali Baba story, that catch the drip water off the roof during monsoon rains. Some water is stored in rusty iron drums. We must be careful since water is getting scarce now.*

> *Then we all walk together under the stars to the big cave temple where we have morning service. The nuns usually arrive at the temple first, since their houses are nearer. They spread their square kneeling mats, and do three prostrations. They sit in two neat lines facing the altar. The monks, who must come all the way from the inner valley, straggle in, casually place their kneeling cloth, adjust it with a toe, kneel, and prostrate three times. They sit in a half circle around the throne where the teacher sits.*

> *We all stay kneeling as the wonderful musical chants rise and fall in a chorus of one hundred and fifty voices. The bats squeak in the crevices at the "noisy" disturbance, and a few unsettled bats rearrange positions in other niches in the convoluted stony ceiling.*

> *The great five-foot high pink Buddha head looks on benignly as do the other life-size statues of the abbot's teachers flanking it. The*

statues are covered with flaking gold leaf squares, the offerings of devout followers.

The abbot speaks when he is in residence. He sits, cross legged, on a high throne, and each time before he speaks, the monks first do three respectful prostrations. After they're finished, the nuns do the same.

After the talk there is a period of silence. Sometimes, he breaks the silence to guide the meditation. Lek tells me later that he gives suggestions to concentrate on your body as a skeleton, or watch the flow of blood in your body.

There is no signal for the end of meditation. One by one, usually the older nuns first, individuals leave, walking out into night, still black at 5:30 am. The moon shines through the clouds. Sometimes, there's a rainbow round it.

In a group we go down a small hill on a newly made path along a new stone wall, which forks out into many directions. Here, white robed nuns fan out to the right toward the bamboo jungle or left along the row of wooden huts. All the monks use the road to get to their practice place in the valley.

Until I discover that this is the time the nuns do chores, I sit zazen upstairs in my room. The talk of the abbot which the loudspeaker plays seems no more distracting than the Spanish songs played on the radios in the neighborhood next to the Zendo in California.

At 6:30, I break my sitting to go down to eat with the older nuns in back of the cabin, where they have a little outside kitchen area with a charcoal stove and a dirt trench for draining water. Ragged woven grass mats, the remnants of larger much used ones, serve as places to sit on the cement. Sometimes they spread a cut up piece of discarded underwear to cover the ground so we can sit. Everything is recycled here till it falls into such small pieces it can't be used.

A beautiful, wrinkled old nun, whom I feel I've known forever, heaps my metal plate with rice, pushes smaller plates with sauces toward me. "Kop koon", she insists, "Eat, eat."

The oldest nun, in her late 80's, bent over double, hobbles out of her door. She squats, takes a handful of rice from the central bowl, scoops it through the sauce, and eats. The nuns hand me a spoon, but I follow their example and eat with my hands too. They all nod approval. We separately rinse our dishes in a pan of cold water, using the ashes from the charcoal stove as cleanser. It works wonderfully!

Then there is free time, to sweep fallen leaves from the open gutters and the road with an efficient broom made of a bunch of rice stalks tied together. As I become more observant, I begin to sweep the leaves off the porch of the old nun who cannot stand upright, and sometimes I have time to do the other nuns' porches on my side of the road.

At 8:00 am, it's time to go again to the temple. A nun shows me a white scarf which she wants me to drape over my right arm, over my left shoulder and across my chest. I show her my temple scarf from Bali. She approves of my using that. The nuns all help me arrange it and pantomime that I should shave my head.

After the meal distribution, I return to my hut in the bamboo jungle. The first four days I went carrying a pillow I wanted to use to sit on. One of the old nuns laughed and shaking her head, "No", gently took it away. I must sit first on the mat as they do, which kills my knees. But I recognize I have chosen to practice with them, so I submit with a grin. As I go down the lane, they all smile and say "Samadhi?" I nod, though it's only a recognition of what I go to do. I don't think I will ever reach Samadhi. I just sit.

The hut, a tiny thatched roof space, looks exactly like the hut Sister Fe offered me to practice in, in the Philippines. Again a strange coincidence, since I wished I could have used it there, but turned it down in favor of my continuing travels. It's surrounded by tall bamboo, shedding leaves that cluster, light brown, on the darker dusty paths.

Sounds while sitting in my bamboo hut.

Swelling breezes tickle the dry crisp leaves outside. I can hear a few fall and scrape along the swept earth till they stop, gently tapping the ground as they fall. The beige sheaths around the green bamboo stalks pop as the circumference stretches. There's a crisp click in the silence The sound of growing.

A bee buzzes by. The swallows nesting under the thatches mumble sweet sounds in the eaves.

Cooking pots clang way off in the distance, and laughter comes from the nuns' huts.

The breezes swell in waves, to a great rustle in the leaves close by, pass through in a whisper that subsides like a breath in the distance.

I can almost hear the clear blue air! I sit deep in my center doing, thinking, nothing. My bones ache, and I get up and walk outside, stepping on the leaves that I heard fall. My thoughts stretch around the earth, like strands to friends everywhere, and a swelling happens in my heart.

Time scrapes by like the leaves. I don't know what I'm doing. I'm just doing it.

Chapter 26 - Life Among the Nuns

Two weeks pass. I continue to walk daily from cabin to temple to my windowless bamboo hut, and sit long spaces of the day.

I wonder if I need a teacher, or if what I'm doing has any sense to it. Each day I've watched an enormous brown spider, his body nearly one and a half inches across, who sits impeccably in the corner to my left. There is no motion. He's aware of me because he shuffles when I come in, but doesn't feel the necessity of moving. So we sit together - companions in this timelessness, letting leaves fall, letting the sun move the shadows, but not moving. I feel that brown spider is my teacher.

I try to conserve water, and only periodically wash my clothes, one set of pants and shirt while I wear the other. The old nuns supervise my scrubbing, amused at my awkward techniques, evidence of long dependence on washing machines! I'm always full of awe that they get their own garments so shiny white when the water they use is so brown from sitting in old oil drums. The water from the great catching jars, five feet high, that sit at the corners of the huts is not much cleaner. Only one time during my month's stay, a big tank truck came and filled the cement cisterns we use for drinking water.

Jampa, the English woman who spent nine years training in Nepal, wears the robes of a Tibetan monk—"not a nun", she insists—returns from her trip, and can at last help me communicate with the nuns, explain practices and be a friend. In late afternoon, after the walking meditation and afternoon sitting are finished, and the lecture by the abbot is over, we talk with the nuns. They are tremendously fond of this clear-eyed woman who lives the equality of men and women not yet openly available to most of the nuns. She tells me that in the whole monastery there are only twelve nuns who have large begging bowls and join the monks in their early morning trips to town for the customary begging practice. The others have the "pintos" or stacking dishes like the one they gave me.

As we sit on the porch of Maechi Im's hut in the shade, we talk and laugh. The women here are much stronger individuals than those who chose a married life of service to a husband. These women are more decisive, more comfortable than their married counterparts.

They ask me if I believe in ghosts. I can only tell of an experience of closeness to my mother-in-law, after her death, with no need to label it as a ghost—or otherwise. They share their own beliefs. Quite a few of them have become nuns in order not to be reborn in the realm of ghosts.

Many people in Thailand experience "Possession", and come to the abbot to chant for them. He exhorts the spirits to leave the person's body. Many have become monks and nuns after such an experience.

The pictures the nuns use to decorated their huts, and to seal the cracks in the bamboo walls from damp winds, are cut from old newspapers, calendars, and magazines. There are "pin-ups" of alluring girls, bare legged, sitting or standing in inviting poses; chaste, but still a surprise to find in the nuns' surroundings. Perhaps it's their attitude that "nothing is profane" which puts a picture of a pin-up girl next to a waterfall, next to an advertisement of a new car - all things not directly experienced in this simple setting, but all OK! not to be excluded.

Among the relationships here, I feel there is a very healthy realism and genuine contentment. These are not people who retreated from the world in one sense, they are full of caring for each other and the townspeople who are always passing through. There is much humor, and their eyes sparkle with enjoyment of life.

Jampa lives in a small cave outside the valley—one of the few besides the great temple cave. She has shared this space with me. We sit together, and I can feel the depth of her practice.

She's interested in the practice of zazen, and I share with her the book by Eido Roshi I've lugged in my pack since Japan. We both have observed the way many of the monks and nuns sit. There seems to be no emphasis on straight backs, though in Japan I learned to hold my back straight.

I always carry with me the image of those straight-backed Buddhas inside the "bells" at Borobadur in Indonesia. I show Jampa the position of zazen, the "empty" sitting posture of the mind, and again we sit in her little cave.

There is an area deep in the back of the cave that I feel is a little creepy. Jampa says that Ajahn Jamnien, the abbot, has sensed a being there.

Chapter 27 - A Climb and a Cobra

From my diary, Feb. 16, 1982

I'm sitting high on the mountain above the monastery, and only Buddha, Heaven, and all ethereal beings know how I got this far!

Yesterday, while I was doing walking meditation, at the end of the fifty foot path I walk, I stopped, looked up at the mountain, and my eye caught the white of a nun's dress high up along the cliff. She seemed to be lost, moving back and forth. After walking period, I pointed out the place to some of the older nuns who sit on their porches. They just laughed as if it were nothing. One pointed to me and pantomimed the walking meditation posture, and pointed to the cliff as if, of course, I could do my walking meditation there.

So I decided to skip the afternoon lecture-sitting and climb. Jampa's cave is just at the beginning of the trail. She told me that it leads to a set of "Buddha's footprints" impressed in the rock on the top. I had been quite curious about these. Teenagers pass on this trail frequently, and picnicking families often climb this and come down as if they had had a nice outing. Cement stairs begin the trail, which I imagined to be like the walking trails in Yosemite—steep, but still foot trails.

I set out, climbing till the steps stopped. The dirt trail became steep. It led to a ladder that leaned on a tree whose branches became part of the way up. I realized it was going to be more difficult than I thought. As I had just negotiated the tree part of the trail, and was again on firm ground, a young nun was coming down the trail towards me. When I indicated I was going up, she pantomimed concern, pointing to the sun that it would be dark soon. Since I had come this far, I just wanted to go a bit further. I wondered whether she was the nun I had seen during my walking meditation who seemed to be lost way up on the cliff.

The trail climbed steeply, leveled off and led to the foot of a fifteen foot rock face with nylon ropes indicating the way was straight up. I stood and studied this obstacle, decided this is where I would have to quit, turned, climbed down the somewhat scarier tree limbs and reached the bottom safely, hot and sweaty!

Jampa was in her cave as I passed, and shared her afternoon Ovaltine with me. She has taken strict vows about foods, and can't eat after 12:00 pm, though she can drink liquids.

She didn't seemed surprised to hear that I'd tried to climb to the top, though she had never done so. We sat together in the evening twilight, and she shared stories of her exploits of the past fourteen years. She'd been to India, wandering like some impoverished monk, to Mother Teresa's place in Calcutta, where she worked for a short time, and Nepal, where she studied under two teachers for nine years. She'd been at this monastery for three years, sitting in the cave, though she felt it was nearing the time she should leave.

Anyway, I decided to try the climb again early this morning. I'd been sitting since the second of February, and needed exercise. So, after I had eaten breakfast of soup and crisp dried fish with the old nuns behind the cabin, I decided to skip my sweeping duties and the time in the temple waiting for the meal offerings, and just began climbing the mountain.

My son, Mike, is a mountain climber, and I had watched some of his mountain climbing techniques. With this dangerous little bit of knowledge, I began.

I was past the cement stairs, and was going up a very steep dirt trail with my eyes on the ground and my hands bracing on roots to keep from slipping, when I heard a sudden "whisssing" sound above me and looked up.

There, not fifteen feet away from me, at the top of this steep section of trail, an enormous cobra had raised himself to three feet in height with his great hood spread out like all the pictures in Rikki Tikki Tavi. In the flash that I glanced at him, I could clearly see the yellow armor plates across his three inch wide trunk, the wide spread hood, the "eye" spots.

Out of me escaped an "Oh my goodness!", and I respectfully turned
to rush back. I got about twenty feet more, but then there was a
steep place I would have to slow down to get over. Knowing that if
he wanted to get me, he'd catch me before this, I turned to watch
him slowly slithering in the opposite direction.

He'd been sitting in the sun when I disturbed him. Obviously he was
used to having the trail to himself at this time of day, since no one
had spoken of him.

I sat marveling at having seen him, wondering whether to go on
or not. I figured I'd wait a half hour. Then, when the squirrels
began racing along, and birds were chirping normally, I decided to
continue—cautiously.

When I got to the rise, I looked over into a steep ravine, and saw him
resting outside of what must have been his hole. I'd doubted my
impression. He couldn't have been as big as he looked—but there
he was for me to gaze at—a full three inch thick body coiled up
below me shining in the sun. No sign of a head, just the long snaky
body which slowly eased over the rock and out of sight into his cave.

I began to realize this climb was like some dream experience, and
that I'd have to use all the inner resources I had. I was surprised
that I was not feeling fear, only alert caution. Perhaps all the hours
of empty sitting had helped me now.

I climbed on till I came to the cliff and stood for awhile puzzling.
I saw a pretty well worn path leading along the cliff to the side,
so I decided to follow that, checking the landmarks of ferns,
bamboo, and mushrooms along the way. This path led to another
impasse—a heap of vertical rocks, but possible to climb over.

I'd been wearing the plastic thong sandals everyone wears, and as I
slanted my toes up, my feet came loose. So I took off my shoes and
proceeded to catch my toes in tiny holes and draw myself barefoot
up over the rocks..

The trail flattened out and then again led to a cliff with fixed ropes. By now, I realized this trip was not going to be easy. But the nuns had climbed it, in skirts, even! As I was studying this thirty foot wall, and praying with all that was in me, the rope began to wiggle, and looking up, I saw an old nun with crusty feet negotiating footholds, slowly edging down by the aid of the rope! She placed both her feet on the ground, smiled encouragement at me, and turned to go on her way down. If she could do it, I reasoned, I can too.

I'd come to realize this climb involved the practice of mindfulness completely, plus the faith in all the strength within. After my encounter with the cobra, it began to feel like a spiritual test. Am I going to pass?

So I went up three more cliffs, all of which looked impossible to scale, all of which had fixed ropes, and all of which I knew the nun I'd met must have conquered. Each time I found myself reaching out with invocations to the rocks and trees, ferns and spirits of the mountain to help me safely up. Each time I pulled up onto a level area, enormous gratitude swelled in me.

Now, I've come to an impasse. There's a narrow log "bridge" over a twenty-five foot chasm. The chasm is not very wide, but only the rope cable at hand level gives balance. I'm not sure I can go further.

I'm feeling maybe I've bitten off more than I can chew—been too foolhardy. I have looked out over the flat plain below, over the steep cliffs that I've got to get down somehow. I wonder at the arrogance that helped me get this far!

I wonder, will mindfulness be enough to get me down? Can I muster enough faith to help me descend safely?

I've already started chanting and am using all the prayer I'm capable of. I think: if I'm a fool, I won't make it down. Maybe that cobra was a reminder of my death.

Thank goodness, I did make it down! After looking over the steep drop-offs I'd come up, I sat down wondering if I'd ever get down. After writing in my diary and thinking it would be my last entry, I could hear the abbot chanting on the loudspeaker perhaps 2,000 feet below me. I didn't think this was the usual time for chanting, and I had a feeling that he sensed my predicament in some way, and was helping me.

I didn't feel so alone, and knowing I'd made it up, I began to edge down the first cliff. I didn't use the fixed ropes much, as they were a bit frayed where they rubbed the rocks, but I hooked my elbow around so I could catch myself on the rope if I slipped.

Cautiously, and very mindfully, I eased my feet into footholds, lowered my hands and fumbled again for foot holds lower down.

Once, I had to circle the outside of a rock. I knew I'd come up another way, but couldn't find it, and eased myself out and around. If I slipped, I'd fall maybe twenty feet. I kept wondering if I'd break a leg. Most of the time, however, I just concentrated on lowering myself step by step, drying my sweaty hands frequently so they wouldn't slip.

I wondered how many 53-year-old women would be foolish enough to try this crazy climb. I thanked my son for the years I'd watched him search for hand and footholds on Yosemite rocks. Slowly, I gained the realization that I had only to try with all my attention and, with care, I could make it. Not one moment could I wander in my awareness. I would have dropped into rocks below or down steep faces. There was no better way to teach me concentration. My life depended on it.

After an hour, the abbot stopped chanting, but I'd made it over the first hurdle of fear, and was only doggedly laboring to get down. I didn't need the chants anymore, though they had been comforting.

When I finished the series of cliffs that made up the steepest part of the climb, I started on what seemed to be the dirt trail through the jungle growth that I'd come up, but I ended at a cliff that looked straight down at the nuns' village. I knew I'd come up another way. The nun I'd seen the first day going back and forth high on the cliff must have been right where I was now. I was getting tired, and the keen state of attention I'd kept up for so long was in a state of decay. I was lost. I looked for another trail but could find none.

I sat down, puzzled. My "what next?" attitude surrounded me. After about an hour of rest, I just got up and without thinking, let my feet guide my way. To my astonishment, I found a trail not far from where I'd gone back and forth only an hour before. I was still dreading having to negotiate the first cliff that had stopped me the day before, but this alternate path mercifully guided me around that rather frightening face. I gratefully sent out thanks to all the rocks, ferns and trees for their help, and to that inner guidance I'd trusted once again.

On the way down the path, I talked and sang in case that old cobra was out sunning still, but I caught no sign of him again.

With incredible relief, gratitude, and weariness, I arrived back on the safe stairs above Jampa's cave, at then in no time at all was back down on the nuns' street.

Even though I was very tired, I immediately went to the cave temple to give the offering of thanks that I had exuded all during the climb.

I found the abbot talking to some townspeople, and Alan, the young English monk, was nearby. I persuaded him to translate for me a thank to the abbot for his chanting. The abbot just looked at me and nodded, but his eyes twinkled with a knowing amusement.

Later, I learned that everyone asked the abbot before they began to climb; then they would find the way. Then they would petition the Devas of the mountain for safe going. At least I'd been duly respectful of the mountain spirits. Perhaps that, too, had helped me.

I was trembling with fatigue, but with a wonderful elation.

In the afternoon the next day, I talked for awhile with Jampa and with the English monk, Alan. He had lived in Thailand since he was seven, had been working with Aid to the Blind in Bangkok, and had decided to become a monk two years before. He was deeply devoted to his teacher, the abbot, and related a bit of the discipline the abbot exacted from himself.

The abbot had spent three years meditating in a graveyard with only enough water to drink — no water to wash with. "Think of the mosquitoes and the flies!" Alan gasped as he spoke. In many parts of Asia, it is a custom not to bury the corpses, but to leave them in a large burying ground to rot or be eaten by vultures.

If this tiny practice of mine had focused my awareness a little, how much more profoundly three years of such hardship must have sharpened and clarified the abbot's mind!

He was now following a vow not to sleep lying down for a year. I had noticed that he nodded occasionally during morning lecture. Alan said no one dared move so as not to wake him up, and that after perhaps three minutes, he would carry on exactly where he had left off.

He walked around the grounds at night checking on who was meditating and who was sleeping. To me, it was amazing that he had so little sleep, because of his great energy and kindness. He always seemed to have patience for everyone, and laughed and worked easily with everyone.

Alan told me that a monk who had climbed the mountain the same day I did, had also gotten lost, and thought he was going to die getting down. However, no one seemed to know about the cobra.

The following day while I was sitting in my bamboo hut, I heard shouting and later learned the cobra had come down among the nuns' houses, probably for water. Everyone chased him away, but they later told me they had not seen him before.

Jampa then told me about two more cobras, even larger than the one I'd seen — five inches in diameter, living next to the stairs we used to enter the temple. No one had seen them, though the abbot, who lived right above them, had a feeling they were there. There was a woman who some time ago had given birth to a perfectly shaped baby four inches long, which died. The corpse was kept in a bottle on the altar. She comes periodically to talk to the child, and the child speaks through her. The abbot had asked her one day to tell him what lived in the hole below his cave house. The woman said she didn't need to ask the child, that she knew two snakes lived down there. Just then two big cobras looked out of the entrance!

Cobras are very frequently depicted in Thai sculpture. There is the story of Buddha while he was sitting, just prior to his Enlightenment. He had vowed to sit and not get up till he was enlightened. A monkey brought him coconuts, an elephant brought him water, and a great King cobra spread his hood above Buddha's head to shelter him from the sun and rain.

The small charm Phra (monk) Alan had given me showed a seven-headed cobra or Naga, forming a diadem above the Buddha figure.

The young assistant to the abbot told me I was very lucky to see a cobra. Strangely, I felt that way.

Chapter 28 - Sitting

The longer I stayed at the monastery, the more at home I felt. Two days after I'd climbed the mountain, Jampa and I were talking in the afternoon. We had been sitting together in her cave. She said she would like to try sitting up all through the night also. So we decided to try together.

In the evening after the abbot had finished his talk, and the meditation period was over, everyone filed out of the temple. But Jampa and I just remained sitting. I managed to sit for a longer period than forty minutes, just getting up to walk when all circulation in my legs had seemed to stop. Then I would walk around the front portion of the cave, slowly, just to stretch my legs. There was a wonderful silence in the cave with the still night air behind us.

Then, after we had already been sitting for quite awhile, the abbot came back with a group of nuns and settled down to talk with them at one end of the cave.

Later he chanted in his musical voice the incredible syllables of the chants. The sound rolled out into the night, rising and falling like the very vibrations of existence, joining all the chants accumulated in my being from Japan, Philippines, Bali, the American Indians. All together, they touched a chord of my being not accustomed to being played. I vibrated in harmony nonetheless, as if a part of me that belonged to primordial time was resonating. Then, though I was still aware of them, the sounds melted into the night along with the bat and iguana cries. The chanting had a wonderful supporting effect on my sitting in the way it had bolstered my confidence in starting down the rock face.

Just sitting, not thinking. Then the chanting ended, the nuns left to sleep, and the abbot walked out to talk to a group of monks. No one seemed to sleep here. It was nearly 2:00 am! We sat in stillness, much deeper because of the resonance of the chanting still ringing in my ears.

I was sitting using the Vipassana mudra, with my right palm resting on my left palm (just the reverse of the Zen practice), and my eyes were closed, though usually during zazen, I keep them partly open.

I was grateful for this when I smelled the cobra. Not till I smelled it this time was I aware of the peculiar odor I'd smelled on the mountain when I startled the cobra there. This time, it seemed very close. I had heard some rather unexplainable thumps earlier, during the silence, and had guessed they came from the back of the cave. I even wondered if they were snakes catching rats. But I just continued to sit quietly, smelling the closeness of the cobra that I had no desire to open my eyes and look at. I was also grateful that I was still enough not to disturb his nightly outing. Funny, I felt no fear, only awareness, and recognition of an odor I'd never forget.

When the odor and sounds subsided, we sat in stillness. I could hear the wind like a breath coming in and going out of the cave.

Then Jampa and I took a half hour break to stretch our legs, drink Ovaltine from her thermos, before we settled down again to sit till the sounds for morning service stirred the whole community at 4:00 am. Another day had started as the nuns began to file in.

The old nuns greeted me with smiles, and after morning service, motioned that I should sweep the temple before the meal chants. Cleaning the temple was a part of the practice I had followed in Japan, so I was pleased to be able to continue to do so here. The temple was enormous, and because of the dry season, dust in thick layers covered everything. There was plenty to sweep. I was full of energy, surprisingly refreshed. I started to clean the area near the statue of the abbot which was on the far right side of the cave.

The "make do" of the altar set up before the abbot's teacher struck me as so reflective of the feeling that nothing is specifically holy, everything is the same — all holy. The offering table, where townspeople and nuns offered incense, was a folding metal TV table, caked with spattered candle wax, since the cave was open to every gust of wind. Burned matches were stacked in heaps along with small used papers left from the gold leaf offerings which devotees rubbed on to the teacher's statue. Apparently the small one inch squares of gold leaf came off a "peal back" sheet of paper like self stick labels.

There was no wastebasket. I set to work with delight at having the privilege of cleaning this area. It was a Herculean task, and I only got a small way before mealtime. I realized again the non-discriminating mind of Asians — nothing is really dirty, no need for our compulsive cleanliness.

One embarrassing note. Before I had begun to tackle the teacher's altar, I vigorously swept the dust off the floor with a broom made of bound rice hulls; full of added energy from the night's sitting, I raised clouds of dust. I finally stopped to do the altar area. When the townspeople came to prepare the food for the morning meal, the dust was still settling.

Later that day the abbot called Jampa and me to the temple. As usual, he was busily engaged in many activities, talking to townspeople and his monks, but he came up to us grinning and holding out necklaces made of colored beads for each of us! He didn't have time to talk, but was obviously pleased with our efforts at sitting. The beads were 7 or 8,000 years old, Jampa told me. They had been collected from old cemetery plots where archaeologists had dumped them from burial urns, where they had lain covered in mud, unrecognizable till washed. I had seen the nuns stringing them, and had no idea one was for me!

The abbot had a custom of wearing bags of these around his waist, letting them accumulate his energy. He also wore many pictures of himself, rings, and charms of Buddha, like the one Phra Alan had given me. When the objects had absorbed some of his vibrations, he gave them freely to everyone. Jampa commented that his teachings were too profound for most of the lay people who came, but these gifts had great significance for them in their lives.

I was very touched and honored by this gesture. I counted the beads, and discovered there were 216 - twice the 108 which is the number of the Buddha prayer beads. Perhaps I needed twice the number!

After the overnight sitting, many of the monks who had not spoken to me before, began to talk to me in fragments of English - always in the presence of others. They were interested in the training that helped me have such a straight back. They wanted to know more about zazen, oryoki practice (the use of meal bowls and service), and our walking meditation.

I explained that actually when I sat with no pillow on the hard ground, and my back slumped, energy seemed to clog up in my back and neck and was very painful, so I had to sit straight. I also mentioned the straight-backed Buddhas in Borabadur, and the experience of the kiosoku (teaching stick) which was pressed up against my head and spine in the Tokyo monastery to help me perceive how to hold a straight back.

There was much interest in zazen among the nuns as well, and they began to ply Jampa with questions about Mahayana practice, and the Tibetan and Japanese interpretation of Buddha's teachings. I felt the enormity of my ignorance. I had practiced the posture Buddha had encouraged in meditation, but I liter-ally knew nothing about Buddha's teachings or the philosophy behind zazen. I couldn't say anything, and was deeply embar-rassed. Thank heavens Jampa could speak to them.

At 5:00 p.m., when the nuns gathered around a banyan tree in a clearing where afternoon meditation took place, the abbot spoke to Jampa and everyone. He said that emptiness of mind could be deceiving, that one could still be deluded. One had to continue to fight delusion.

He said I had reached a quiet place, but that I was still deluded, since I needed his chanting to get me down the mountain.

I knew immediately that he was right. I had felt that his chanting had helped me down the mountain. I had actually realized that this was a delusion when the chanting stopped. By total mindfulness, I had managed the rest of the climb myself. I realized I had much further to go before I gained true understanding.

The whole traveling trip had been, so far, a trip into the nature of my mind, discovering how my attitudes affected what happened to me; how my thoughts seemed to materialize my surroundings. I'd come more and more to realize this as I went along. This was a powerful teaching about my deluded mind, and I was very grateful for it.

I could not answer him about emptiness. I wish I could have done justice to it, but my ignorance was so overwhelming. I could only remember for myself an answer Kobun had given to a young girl who had asked why so many Zen students she'd met were so severe, and apparently stern. He brightened, and said "It's like an unripe persimmon. It's very hard to eat and dries your tongue, till it sits and sits on the branch and becomes ripe and sweet."

I truly felt that some change was happening slowly in me as I sat so much, but I couldn't identify it. I could only continue to sit, ripening myself in the silence of my being. I suspected it would take me a considerable time of ripening for such ignorant fruit, but I continued sitting.

I was experiencing the first encounters with emotional agitation and feeling of inadequacy at my own ignorance on the trip. This is a frequent experience for me, since I often felt stupid in the presence of my father, a university professor. The abbot had truly hit the target. I had to sit with the delusion that I ought to know everything. Then I let it go, just as I let go all the thoughts that came in my mind when I sit zazen, and calmness returned.

The next day, the abbot gave a talk on Vipassana meditation which Jampa, who usually can only grasp part of his talks, could understand completely. But sadly it was lost on me. I began to realize the predicament of being with a really good teacher, but not being able to understand him. However, I had come for a retreat to meditate, and was certainly having the best atmosphere for that that I could hope for.

The second half of the month of February, Phra Alan was in the hospital again with malaria, and I rode into town with the monks who visited families to chant for them. I took food to Phra Alan. In Asian hospitals, it's the responsibility of the family or friends to bring food to the patients. The monks and nuns shared their offerings with patients who had no one to bring them food. The rooms were crowded with people with all kinds of ailments in single cots, dormitory style, next to each other. Many of the weary patients would have perhaps five members of their family sitting and standing around the bed. It didn't look to me like such a restful place for recuperation.

I felt a warm affection for this frail and very compassionate monk who shared many of his teachings with me. He loaned me books on the teachings and life of Buddha. I read about the life of Buddha who, like St. Francis, was also a nobleman. He left home to follow a life of stark simplicity, teaching others of compassion and the cessation of desire, which ends all suffering. Phra Alan also loaned me a book of the chants, and I began to join more easily in the morning service, to the delight of the nuns. The third book was the 300 vows monks in the Hinayana school of Buddhism take when they are ordained. This list is overwhelming in its detail about daily life, yet regularly the monks go to the head temple to remake those vows and confess breaking them in the past.

In the afternoon, I sat sometimes, but I also joined the nuns in digging an enormous reservoir. There were about 55 to 60 nuns able to do this hard labor. They lifted baskets of dirt in a "bucket brigade" fashion out of the deep pit which had been started by a bulldozer. It was cheerful work, and they were all delighted when I joined them. It felt as if I'd worked with these women forever.

I had been at Watt Thom Sua for nearly a month, and I felt the time approaching for me to go. I still had not been able to find the Buddha's footprints at the top of the mountain. Though I'd been stiff from the first climb, I wanted to try again.

Each day was terribly hot after 9:00 am, and I kept postponing the trip. I finally got the courage to ask the abbot if I could try the climb again even if it was almost too hot. He agreed but, he said, I should take a nun or someone with me. This day was even hotter than other days, and none of the nuns could, or wanted to, go. It looked as if I weren't going to be able to do it. This was my last day. Jampa had gone to the seashore for a week, and had let me sleep in her cave while she was gone. I had promised to feed her birds and squirrels.

I was sitting there when three young men paused at the entrance and greeted me. They were going to climb, and I asked if I could go with them. I took a water canteen, three oranges, and we started out.

This time, the confidence of knowledge helped me. When we came to the first cliff that I'd been too afraid to try before, I found I could pull myself up more easily than I expected. Each successive cliff seemed, surprisingly, much less demanding, and we made it to the top before I realized that none of the young men had been up this mountain before.

But we did find the top, where the limestone formation turned into sharp points and I could scarcely walk with my bare feet. One of the young men loaned me his zoris, or I would never have been able to make the last few yards. We discovered the two great elongated "footsteps" indented in the rocks.

There were sticks of incense in front of a small stone altar, ready to be offered. As Lek had told me, I poured water into the indented shapes that did look as if two twenty-four inch feet had pressed into the gray stone. I washed my face with it and offered incense, placing it in a crevice along with other sticks which people had placed there before. There was tremendous gratitude for getting here.

It was a wonderful way to end the month of practice — high on the mountain with a clear view in three directions across a plain to the sea. We retreated down all the difficult climbs I'd struggled with before, with much greater ease. It was actually a joyful descent.

Now I knew it was the time for me to move on. I hated to leave this paradise, but something was completed.

The head nun, Maechi Im, had asked me where I intended to go after my time at the monastery. When I said that I would go to Bangkok and then to Chiang Mai, if I thought there was time, she asked if I wanted to have a ride to Chiang Mai with herself and the abbot who was going on a short vacation. I thought this would be a delight and accepted.

So the next morning, after goodbyes to the wonderful old nuns, I did my last prostrations before the Buddha in the cave temple. I did this both in the Vipassana style with both palms touching the floor, and the way I had been accustomed to at home with palms facing upwards, so as to cover all bases, and carried my pack in the 4:30 am darkness to the jeep, where five of my young friends, including Lek, were waiting.

We set off in the dark. Dawn revealed the flat plains, the water buffaloes grazing along the side of the road, and strings of those strange upright mountains stretching across the plain in random outcroppings.

Then, to my surprise, we drove on to a dirt road, and after half an hour, drove up to a temple.

This was in such different surroundings from the cave temple. It lay on dry hot baked dirt, a wall enclosing the temple buildings which were ornately decorated. It was the head temple where the monks came every two weeks or so to confess. This is a practice in the Hinayana way since there are three hundred vows to keep. The abbot's temple was only a residential community. Official ceremonies took place here. We all went in and prostrated before the abbot, who was, surprisingly, smoking a cigarette.

The nuns took me up the stairs to an inner shrine where, in a large glass case, the body of Achaan Jamnien's teacher was laid out, mummified. At first I didn't see past all the gold leaf square offerings pasted on the glass, but when they pointed the body out to me, I saw the old fine face, brown and parched like an Egyptian mummy.

We prostrated here and went down. A big breakfast was served us. A few other monks gathered, but they looked as dry and crusty as the land they practiced on. We finished eating and then — we waited.

I went back to the jeep expecting to leave, but someone came to me and said, "Come, you take bath". I didn't need a bath, but they insisted and it seemed easier to go along than to continue protesting.

The cement bathrooms with the water tank and dipper were familiar, and I bathed quickly. When I came out, a nun tried to hand me a white skirt saying, "Put this on". I then began to realize what was happening.

In alarm, I declined the skirt and hurried back to the jeep to find Lek. "Are they planning to ordain me?", I asked. "Yes." "But I can't take vows." I found myself protesting. "I can't understand what I'm saying and though I truly feel like a nun, I can't take vows.! I know I must go on. I can't stay here now. Help!" Then she went to explain to Maechi Im, and the abbot.

Suddenly the "vacation" trip to Chiang Mai disappeared, and they prepared to return to the cave temple. I began to realize it had all been a clever attempt to get me ordained. But the time wasn't right for me. I couldn't agree to it then. I felt a great need to keep moving, though there was also a great pang of regret at leaving everyone I'd come to love.

They drove me to the railroad station and one of the young nuns stayed with me to wait for the train. It was at this time I learned she had taken vows for only one month as a nun, leaving her family of two children and a fine husband to practice as a nun for that time period. This way she felt she was gaining "merit". The vows were not permanent, then. But too late.

The abbot had bidden me goodbye with his usual twinkling good humor, amused at my predicament but accepting it. He told me I was welcome to return any time, which was a great honor, I felt, and I wondered as I watched them drive away if, in leaving, I'd done the stupidest thing in my life!

Chapter 29 - Bangkok

Thai trains are comfortable. I had a soft seat by the window. I observed other experienced travelers spreading newspapers or cloth over the seats before they sat down, to avoid vermin. I neglected to think of this possibility.

We all watched the sun setting as the train pushed into darkness. Food and small closed drinking canteens came out of bags, and people offered food to others in the seats close by. All politely refused. I saw again the working of Thai consideration. No one ate his food while ignoring others.

Then came darkness, and everyone crammed themselves into comfortable positions in the upright seats to doze and wake with the joggling of the train.

I was on the move again, after that wonderful time of silence and relationship. I already missed the nuns. The evening chants rang in my ears, but I knew I was right in going on, though I felt as if I was leaving a whole lifetime behind. In the dark, I wondered if I had dipped into an alternative reality that seemed to be going on simultaneously with the life I was familiar with; but dreamlike, I had only caught a glimpse of it.

In a way, that's what traveling became to me; a passage through states of mind that were all my own.

A golden red sun rose across a flat plain of rice fields. Water buffaloes walked out to the fields behind children who looked to be only five or six years old. In the distance were the same unearthly upright mountains of the seashore. Odd that I should feel so recognizably at home here, when just a year ago this place was beyond my imagination.

Gradually, the progressive shabbiness of the outskirts of any large city appeared as we approached the industrial outskirts of Bangkok.

We arrived at the main railway station. I grabbed the pack that I hadn't carried in a month, and faced the usual onslaught of offers to help me find a hotel, drive me in a rickshaw, give me a lift in a taxi.

In Malaysia, a student had torn from his guidebook the pages on Bangkok and Chang Mai for me. They indicated reasonable accommodations close to the railroad station. I decided to settle in immediately and begin to explore Bangkok.

The station building was an enormous vaulted Quonset hut that reminded me of the railroad station in Washington DC some forty years ago when, during the war, I arrived, twelve years old and alone, to meet my father who was working there. Vintage railroad bustle greeted me. "Red caps" were pulling old trollies that might have been the very ones the United States had long since discarded. The tawdry information counters, the jail-like barred ticket windows took me back forty years under that great echo chamber. Curiously, for some instants, I could have been twelve years old in a strange city with the expectations of a new adventure!

However, sign boards, enormous wall murals, newspapers, displayed that beautiful Thai script which seems more art work than a means of communication, and made me realize quickly it was another reality. Except for the eager transportation people, everyone brushed by in the hustle of big city anonymity. I stepped out through the main front entrance. The oval plaza resembled the Washington, D.C. entry. Here however, the place was crowded with barbecue salesmen offering chicken and beef, sizzling over charcoal from small wheeled carts. In a daze, I passed fruit sales-men, crowds of people socializing on the worn grassy center. Across the street were slums along the sidewalk with signboards in Thai I couldn't read. I walked on, feeling the weight of my pack, a little dazed by the sweltering heat. I was surprised that the blast of heat which greeted us on arrival affected me less than it would have if I had not acclimatized in the monastery. Nearly everyone revealed big dark sweat streaks on shirt backs but out-wardly ignored the heat. There was no alternative for them.

I had given a large donation to the monastery, and was nearing the end of my money supply, so I had to wire for money and survive as cheaply as I could until it arrived. Therefore, I had no grand ideas. I wanted the cheapest place available. I went to the hotel recommended in the guide book, but it seemed too expensive, so I walked on.

Just as you get used to bright light after coming out of a dark room, I began to see some signs in English and after walking back and forth checking prices in several "hotels", I settled on the cheapest.

The front entrance of this building was wide open to the street. A small "cage" for the proprietor was back against the wall. Several tables were spread out on the filthiest linoleum floor I've ever seen. They had marble tops with pedestals of what once must have been beautiful oak carved claws. In some distant elegant past those tables must have graced a dining room, polished and gleaming with pressed white cloths. Now they had mop splashes on their faded grain. Funny what your eye catches when you first enter a room.

The price was right. I followed an old Chinese clerk in his undershirt upstairs to a second floor, which was filthier than the first. We walked along a dingy hall with striped grooved wood walls. The collection of soot, fingerprints and grime amazed me. I was getting accustomed to the squalid environment where people looked personally neat, well groomed and clean, and gathered in restaurants with walls that hadn't been washed in centuries.

My guide unlocked a padlock and showed me a room with one bed, clean sheets, one chair, a dresser, a sink, no fan. Well, it was a shelter, it had a lock, and a window. I was exhausted, so I took it. He disappeared to leave me contemplating the grubby walls. I noticed several holes drilled in the wood of the walls, and proceeded to stuff Kleenex in them, assuring myself of at least some privacy.

Chapter 30 - Sleeping by a Buddha's Tooth

Chiang Mai was a tourist town, but to my relief, prices were on an affordable scale. I had no trouble finding a place, since I shared a cab with some travelers who knew of a beautiful place overlooking the river. Lodging cost the same as at my dingy hotel in Bangkok, and was clean and lighted. I had a fan, and could step out on a raised wooden deck that overlooked the river.

It was a Western haven, but I had decided to take a "vacation" and enjoy the company of fellow travelers for a change. I took the "tours" offered since they were fairly reasonable, and thus visited the "Hill tribes", or at least a very tour-jaded village where residents still lived in bamboo huts and permitted tourists to inundate their town, so they could sell handicrafts. They did beautiful embroidery, weaving, hand carving. Other thrills were offered. One leering old man approached me to see if I wanted to see people smoking opium.

The people of Chiang Mai are becoming prosperous. The tourist trade has boosted the whole economy of Chiang Mai. I visited lacquer ware "factories'", orchid growers, wood carvers - all producing for tourist consumption. Wood carvers were carving hundreds of bar cabinets which apparently were gobbled up at $300 apiece by French, German, and Dutch visitors. These visitors thought nothing of flying in to Chiang Mai for a week's vacation and returning with all sorts of booty.

A salesroom the size of a city block displayed bar cabinets, tables around which were chairs carved like elephant heads, whole wooden couches carved with ornate scenes of historically opulent kings riding on decorated elephants. None of the furniture permitted relaxation. If anyone leaned back in a chair, the elbow of a man or a branch of a tree would poke sharply into the muscles of his back. Conspicuous consumption exuded from the useless enormous items which apparently millionaires purchased eagerly to fill up spacious living rooms with exotic possessions. After coming from Bangkok where so many people were sleeping in the streets, the contrast appalled me.

There was a display of "cheaper" items; small wood-carved water buffaloes at exorbitant prices. I commented at the high price and the clerk lowered the price twice as I just "considered". Perhaps the bargaining skills I'd developed in Indonesia were paying off. Apparently they posted the prices for the inexperienced traveler who was used to paying and who thought he was getting a bargain at what was an outlandish price to the local people.

At the craft factories, artisans were turning out mass produced art, working in what I'd call primitive conditions and I'm sure not getting much pay. Sweat shop conditions were coming even to the artisans. The acquisitive habits of tourists were encouraging a whole class of acquisitive Thai millionaires at the expense of the working people. I've never been interested in economics before, but the creation of poverty was right in front of my eyes. Thailand is one of the few Buddhist countries in the world. One of Buddha's steps to an enlightened path was "right livelihood"; to make a living that doesn't exploit other people. Yet the greed of the West is encouraging a living style which seems to lead to suffering in Eastern nations. I had to look, myself, at how I am, by my presence, also contributing to that development.

Chiang Mai has many temples and stupas. I walked one day to several within reach of my "guest house", and felt comfortable with the monks walking the grounds. In a way I had a nostalgic feeling for Watt Thom Sua. Lek had suggested I stay in a monastery, but I'd found the guest house so convenient, I had decided to stay there.

One afternoon, I took a bus up the hill to Doisetep Temple. Here, the usual restaurants and rows of souvenir salesmen preceded the site of a fantastic temple. Two serpents of yellow ceramic tile flanked a steep staircase in the form of two banisters each a foot in diameter, undulating upward for at least 500 feet. I passed lavender blooming plum trees into the temple gate and wandered around a white stupa which held a Buddha relic. This was bigger than any stupa I'd seen in China. The top, bigger than the dome of Borobudur, gleamed with gold in the late afternoon sun.

My camera had been "lifted" just as I left to go to the airport in Bangkok, so I had no way to capture the brilliance of this place. I wandered into the worship hall dominated by a giant Buddha as big as those in China. I paid my respects by prostrating, as I'd learned in Watt Thorn Sua, and felt the tremendous peace of the place.

I was standing looking at the Buddha, when a monk whom I later learned was the abbot, asked where I was sleeping. I told him. "You will sleep here tonight," he said with such certainty that I agreed. I had no reason to go back, and it was late afternoon already. He told me he would make arrangements and disappeared.

I wandered around with a wonderful feeling of contentment. A photographer who said he could develop a picture of me in an hour took a picture of me standing against the ornate dome. Then the abbot came and led me to a small building next to the stupa. Inside was a lone nun who spoke no English. We were introduced and she pointed to a grass mat where I was to sleep. He reminded me that they don't eat after noon so I would have to go down the hill to eat. Then he left. The nun, a woman perhaps in her 60's, motioned to follow her. We wandered together outside in what I took to be walking meditation. Then she encountered a friend and began to talk. The Thai friend told me I could go down the stairs to find food and return. I assumed she'd translated to the nun that I'd be back.

So back down the stairs between the wavy serpent scales which showed green tiles on the uphill side, I came to the concessions again. In the restaurant, I was the only customer. I talked with the proprietor, a beautiful woman, mother of five daughters who gathered around me. We talked as if we'd been friends forever. Each daughter had a look as if she was from a different part of the world. One looked Mongolian, one Italian, one more European, and another Japanese. The fifth looked like an

American Indian. They spoke pretty good English and we joked about her international family. She said she traveled by meeting the tourists. She had an extremely broad way of looking at things. I felt it was almost a symbolic family with beings of all races of the world living congenially together. They were all her own children, not adopted, but it was hard to believe. I felt I was talking to sisters as we shared food.

Three of the sisters walked back up the stairs with me to the temple enclosure. When I got to the building where I was to sleep, it was locked, and when I knocked, no one answered. I might have given up, but the sunset was so beautiful, we went to a balcony overlooking the valley and watched the golden sun set with the rosy reflection on the fantastic gold of the stupa. We talked a bit, and the girls went down. I was waiting there in the dark wondering what to do. The abbot had been so certain and I, too, felt it would be a very wonderful thing to sleep so near the stupa, but the door remained closed.

There was a platform near the side building, and I decided I would sit up all night on it if nothing else happened. I settled down in the stillness and began my zazen, listening to the playful dogs scampering by, sniffing me, but apparently accepting my presence. Then a cheery voice of a man who had been running a souvenir stand interrupted me. He was surprised to see me and suggested that I "come to his house" I thanked him, but said I felt it was for me to spend the night there. He thought I'd get cold. It was getting chilly, but I'd encountered more difficulties than that, so I could survive.

As our voices traveled, the door to the building opened and the nun looked out. I rose, and she let me in after I left my sandals near the door outside. The room was dark. There were no windows. Only the golden statue of a teacher sat on one end. She spread out the grass mat for me and I lay down. I noticed that she chose to sit in meditation, so I too joined her. We sat in the dark for a long time. I was feeling the strangeness of this adventure, but sure somehow that my being so close to a relic of the Buddha was affecting me. Somehow the energy of this monastery, the feeling to the Buddha hall, the peace of the surrounding stupa felt extraordinarily good, and I just sat.

Finally the nun lay down to sleep. I sat a bit longer, and then lay down myself. I slept a bit. Then, for some reason I woke up and began to sit again. The nun too woke up after a time and sat with me. This companionable being together with someone I couldn't talk to in such a strange situation, was very nice. I kept wondering why she was there alone, and if she had been there just for her own meditation, or whether my wish to sit near the stupa had drawn that whole situation to me. No need to know. We sat through the night on that still mountain top where a tooth of Buddha rested beneath a gold covered dome in Thailand. It seemed very natural at the time.

No world shattering thoughts occurred, no flashes of light. We just sat together. Was the energy of the place becoming part of me? What did happen to the pilgrims who visit holy spots? Was there some accumulation of being that occurred there? Certainly through all time there have been practices of visiting graves, places where saints were born or died. In some sense I wondered whether I was putting Buddha together in some way in myself by touching base with so many of them.

I felt again that odd state of mind wondering whether there's any reality besides the extensions of my own thoughts and intentions. I questioned whether a deeper part of me was magnetically drawing these experiences to me.

So the night passed and the 4:30 morning prayer bell sounded. I went out to find one of my sandals missing. No time to worry, only to find the bathroom and look for the worship hall. One poor nun, and there were now a cluster of other nuns who appeared, was sick and groaning in discomfort as other nuns leaned over her by one of the water drains. There is so much stomach disturbance here that people are used to it and comfort the suffering ones sympathetically.

We gathered in the Buddha hall and repeated the chants that had become familiar to me, and did morning service. Then it was time for me to go. I walked around the stupa three times, and met the abbot who pointed to where I was to have breakfast. No one spoke English, but I waited in the outdoor kitchen and watched lay people cook soup and thick cereal for the nuns and monks who filed by the charcoal stove with small buddha bowls to be filled by a server. Everyone was good natured. No one looked sleepy. The practice seemed to enliven them all.

Then I searched for my lost sandal, which a dog had carried off and deposited in a stairwell. Time to go down. Past the giant serpents down the stairs never to sleep so close to a stupa with a Buddha relic again, or so I thought.

Chapter 31 - Elephants and Butterflies

I went on a tour with four other travelers, driving by car to a beautiful waterfall in a park. The guide had not mentioned there were other falls and quaint bridges so my companions were content to eat barbecued chicken while sitting on a grass mat, spread on the rocks overlooking the first waterfall.

I walked up the trail along the burbling stream past nine shimmering waterfalls, observing a bit of what I did in Malaysia and Maine, that water everywhere behaves the same. I was the only Western face trudging along the slippery mud paths. It was nice to see so many young Thai people enjoying their own park. Here, big butterflies of fantastic blues and yellows flitted in and out of the thick jungle growth. Several small boys were out with butterfly nets stalking them.

In the shops are glass framed pictures displaying stone hard butterflies, their wings stretched to the fullest. Tourists buy these for their decorator possibilities. I wonder how many had seen them for a flashing moment resting on a branch or darting across a shadowy path. Could they still be content with the lifeless shell? If I'd not just wandered off, I'd never have seen the splashing cascades or the brilliant butterflies. Perhaps then I could have bought a stiff one, but I think not.

We try to capture moments and make them stay long past the experiencing of them. Souvenirs are supposed to reawaken the experience. Memories are the hit of the tourist trade, yet I think some tourists become more focused on acquiring the substitute and purchase souvenirs of things not fully experienced. The attempt to capture moments not ever encountered has led to a faded world. Once life itself was full. Native people feel their "poverty" when they see others buying things. Especially the young people don't notice anymore what they have that money can't buy. Then it all shrivels in the rush for progress, added income, the greed for more and more.

I had to be pulled away from the waterfalls that I could have listened to all day. The tour must continue. Again I felt reaffirmed that traveling alone provides an opportunity to complete each experience before moving on. This way I felt cut off in mid-discovery; perhaps that's another reason for the souvenirs.

However, we went to watch the elephants. This was a show cooked up for tourists, but still exciting. Some elephants were submerged in a stream which we crossed. They were standing with water tickling their underbellies. Their riders were pouring buckets of water on their glistening backs and scrubbing them. The great beasts were helping by showering themselves and other riders with trunks full of water. They swirled in the eddies, lifting their giant feet for a scrubbing, blowing water at some gray giant nearby. Flapping ears, shiny bellies, tiny riders, sitting on the necks of those enthusiastic monsters, all got splashed in the joyful spray.

At the approach, a toothless woman squatted by the trail with bunches of high priced bananas. I bought one bunch which I clutched as we passed outreaching elephant trunks like snakes that grabbed bunches from the people ahead of me.

We were shown to a set of seats, where, thanks to our tour guide, the wind was at our backs. The great creatures lumbered in pulling long logs nearly two feet in diameter, dragging on chains behind them. Elephants have served Asia as tractors for ages, and the teamwork of men and animals cooperating excited all the onlookers. The riders were from a special tribe that had been working with elephants for generations. They gently tickled them behind the ear with their bare feet to give signals. The elephants trotted their great bodies with quick strides, pushing and pulling with feet and trunk. Sometimes two elephants worked on a log to stack them in a pile.

Dust rose in clouds as they dragged twenty logs over the dry dirt.

Spectators were engulfed by dust. Each elephant had a wooden "bell" with two clappers on the outside, and the sound of knocking wood was a musical xylophone when they moved. It reminded me of the "Mokugio" or wooden drum sound at Eiheiji temple in Japan.

Then it was over, and we could ride on an elephant if we wanted to.

This was sheer delight. I'm sure that sitting for long in a wide spread-eagle position while they jogged would take some extra stamina, but for a short trip it was incredible! The bodies are enormous, and you can imagine a fat creature plumping along with perhaps jolting smashes as the feet hit the dirt. I was surprised to discover the fantastic grace of movement. There was a rolling from back to front and sideways of smooth coordinated muscles while one foot picked up and the other settled down softly. It was a dance! The swells of motion seemed to circulate like the coordination of the legs of a centipede. You can't tell where the motion begins and ends. I loved it!

The hill people seemed to feel my joy, and became friendly as I got down, helping me save my bananas for the baby who charmed my heart. He gulped the whole bunch of bananas, skins, stem, and all to my astonished gasps. I had held out one banana in my hand, keeping the rest of the bunch in the other. His impudent little trunk waved past the single banana and encircled the whole bunch. Laughter melts differences, and somehow I felt an echo of some distant time when a part of me trained elephants.

The young man who carved the beautiful teakwood "bells" let me examine them all, ringing those he felt best for my hearing. We exchanged money and product, but his grinning face and the gassho (bow) we exchanged was what our interaction was about.

They got the elephants to trumpet goodbye and we returned to the mundane world of the guest house.

It was March by this time, and seven planets were supposed to be lined up in one quadrant of the sky, a phenomenon that hadn't occurred since 700 AD. It was a bright night, and I sat up to watch the stars. A beautiful English woman perhaps ten years older than I who was traveling alone, and starting an import business, talked with me as the full moon rose, casting its silver beam across the river.

We talked while the moon rose higher with its brilliant light blocking out the lesser stars and planets. She was a very kind person aware of the sufferings of others. She had visited the leper colony in Chiang Mai, talking to the doctors in charge, learning of the excellent treatment they gave the patients. She had no religion, only a strong conviction that we're on earth to help each other, to learn and to love. She had been through the difficulties of divorce and had had to face the challenge of self support. Again I noticed that the "catastrophes" in our lives are really like great gifts to wake us up to further growth, independence and compassion for others.

We retired not seeing the whole line of planets, but content at a night's sharing in a strange land. I felt like a sister to her.

I woke up at 4:00 AM, still the habitual rising time for the monastery. Time to sit. It was still dark outside, and I went out on the deck to look up into the hazy sky. All stars were blotted out in the mist, except for the brighter planets which stood alone in a great clear line across the sky. The moon already on the horizon had lost some of its power to outshine those distant lights. Well, there it was. Predictions had been of great earthquakes and outbreaks of war, but on that peaceful night in Thailand, I saw only the dark quiet river, the serene stars, and a silver moon with a rainbow mist around it, beautiful and still.

It felt time to move on from this comfortable vacation spot.

I was refreshed, ready for whatever Burma might provide.

Chapter 32 - Transition

The shock of the clean modern airport this time had less impact on me. I'd been staying in Western lodgings (a Western toilet) and had seen mostly tourist sights. How easy it is to settle into one world!

Since the plane didn't leave till the next morning I had to spend a night in Bangkok. I arrived at six in the evening. It would have taken me two hours by bus to get back to the area where I had stayed. Then it would take two more hours to return, hardly worth checking in for lodgings. So I decided to sleep while sitting in the airport.

The restaurants were expensive, but comfortable, and I managed to drink endless cups of coffee in both the coffee shop and the dining room. It was crowded and people joined me occasionally. I talked to a couple from Indonesia. The wife had been born there, but was Chinese. She had gone back to China recently and had been greatly disillusioned. All her nostalgic dreams melted under the experience of government restrictions and requirements. She had left with no desire to return. Both had traveled widely, even to the United States, and appeared to be enjoying life tremendously. Such a different contrast to the helpless feeling of most poor Indonesians I met.

Wandering through the hallways and waiting rooms of airports has always spurred a feeling of pleasure for me. To be amidst so many people in the process of change rouses you to a readiness for anything. The jangle of the thoughts of everyone in the great waiting room must, if they solidified, become a tangled knot of disparate realities.

Waiting creates passive patience or irritated restlessness. There were Moslem men in fez hats pacing the floors. Women in saris slumping on uncomfortable wooden benches were surrounded by cardboard boxes tied with strings. The Indian travelers usually came in groups, several women, men and at least two or three children. Single Western travelers with knapsacks wearing broad "jungle" hats threaded their way over their stretched out feet.

Drowsy tourists hovered in secure groups, looking vacant, while the alert looking guide negotiated passports and tickets for them. Old, old men and women, with tight sinews showing on bare arms in the hot night, passed through the diverse crowd. Were they travelers or did they have some job they were coming to or going from? The bathrooms were always occupied by women in saris who obviously didn't clean the toilets, just held their hands out for contributions - for what? The right to use dirty toilets? I never knew.

For an hour or so, I sat in a hallway with air conditioning where bustling tour guides collected tourists going in vans to elegant hotels. I could doze frequently for half an hour in this position. I thought again of the abbot at the monastery who was sitting upright for a whole year! It's astounding his patience was so great. Waking up was a deep pain, a jolt out of some restful peace to find my legs were tripping a passerby or to hear some ill tempered tourist haranguing the agents.

The coffee shops closed, the place emptied out, and I was greatly tempted to nestle into a marble corner on the floor and sleep, but somehow a desire not to be "moved on" kept me dozing upright. Finally dawn came, and the call to stand in the line for Burma. Someone had told me that nearly all tourists to Burma purchase duty free liquor and cigarettes to trade on the black market there, but I had resisted, feeling uncomfortable about it. I finally succumbed at the very last minute.

One young traveler I had met in Malaysia reasoned that the people buying the liquor and cigarettes were rich. That way the money was recirculated to the poor. I still didn't take advantage of the last liquor shop before we were sequestered in the waiting room after passport inspection. Even there, there were two duty-free stores just in case one had neglected to buy his quota beforehand. At that very last minute, I decided to purchase the one bottle of liquor, and one carton of cigarettes, feeling some-what sheepish.

As we passed by the X-ray scanner, my purse caught on the moving belt, and I had to pause and wait as other passengers filed by. I could see the X-ray revealing the contents of each bag as it passed. One, sometimes two, transparent, easily identifiable liquor bottle shapes shone white and clear in every container. The attendants ignored this procession. Well, my bag too, showed the telltale bottle, and we were ushered to the plane. How easy that leap into space, flying like some magic carpet over the water! Then Rangoon - and touchdown.

Always the stewards passed out snacks of cheese and crack-ers, rolls and coffee. To the others it was an extra meal. To me, it was my lunch for the next day. I managed to feed myself that way each time I flew. I had time to get accustomed to the exchange rate, the location of reasonable restaurants, find lodgings before hunger drove me to spend unnecessary money.

I was wondering how I'd get rid of this heavy burden on my conscience when we arrived in Rangoon. I'd never participated in such clandestine activities. But a man edged up to me, even while we were in line to get our passports checked, and asked, "Have you anything to sell?" Somehow I found myself saying, "No" and lugged the heavy contraband all the way to the Garden Guest House in central Rangoon.

I shared a taxi with some young travelers who knew of this reasonable place. I'd had a choice between two groups of travel-ers, and had randomly picked the one that chose a guest house situated as close as possible to a large temple or stupa, within easy walking distance of the Burma Airlines and bus stops I would need to frequent.

The Rangoon I saw was the most destitute, impoverished, neglected city I'd seen so far. I got the feeling after walking in the streets for several days that it looked much like a place in the woods where someone picks up a log that's been the shelter and nourishment for thousands of termites, ants, slugs, spiders and invisible microbes that all at once are set scurrying about in vain search of some new cover and provisions.

The British had built what must have once been magnificent marble-faced white "colonial" buildings. These still remained in some decrepit way, decaying at the cracks and crevices, turning a dingy gray like the fading face of some old man or woman who has outlived his or her use and is rotting dismally amidst a family that wishes he or she would die.

The streets were paved but pocked with holes. The tiles on the sidewalks were tipping and buckling in the shifting earth, much like Medan in Sumatra.

It was the dogs that caught my heart at first. I remembered an incident in Bangkok that stood out like a vignette. I was walking somewhere along a back street which was near the shiny shops for tourists only three blocks away. It was more a business district. At curbside, a woman was selling sausages, barbecuing over charcoal, and people were purchasing the savory smelling meal and walking away munching contentedly.

Nearby, a big black Labrador type female dog was sitting, head hung low for lack of energy, her ribs standing out like the ribs depicted of the Starved Buddha. Her eyes were beautiful. I ordered a sausage to be cooked, but it took a while, and the dog got up to wander into the traffic. I'd told her to wait, and she'd looked at me understandingly. Now she carefully but slowly, as if every bone in her body ached, walked to the center island and urinated. Then she painfully avoided cars and buses, and came back to the curb. The sausage was done. I paid for it and to the astonished horror of those standing by, fed it to the dog.

She looked up at me with the most profound gratitude, and we just stared at each other soul to soul. She stood there, not stooping to gobble the first bite, but waiting with it safely between her paws for it to cool. I had to move on, but looking back from across another street I saw her emaciated body straddling her prize, waiting with all the patient acceptance of Asia for her food to cool. There was in that starved countenance a tolerance for her condition; some dignity in suffering that made her a noble being.

Even the dogs in Rangoon were bereft of dignity. They suffered from fleas, scratching incessantly till kicked aside by some passerby. They were, in collection, the most miserable dogs I saw anywhere. Those wretched creatures just seemed to endure from minute to minute, yet there was no one to notice.

I'd learned this in other parts of Asia. In Bali, the dogs flocked around Australian and American tourists who petted them and played with them. In Thailand, I'd learned you never greet a dog in a household before you greet the host and hostess, even if he rushes up to you. It's an insult to pet a dog, then shake someone's hand. Luckily it had happened with someone who understood Western ways and felt free to tell me.

I'd seen in an old Sutra, or teaching of Buddha, a terrible curse laid on those who wouldn't pay attention to the teachings. It cursed them to be reborn a cur, flea bitten, and ulcerated, shunned by people and starving in the gutter for life after life. I couldn't help seeing these miserable beings as the fulfillment of such a curse. Or was it the belief that they were such base beings that prevented any caring person from tending to them?

Chapter 33 - Rangoon

I had arrived on a Saturday, and because offices were closed, had to wait till Monday to arrange a flight to Pegan. Only seven days are permitted to tourists in Burma, so this cut my time short, but did give me unexpected time to explore Rangoon.

My "guest house" was like some of the apartment buildings I'd lived in as a student. Wood frame, it had a narrow stair leading up several flights to floors full of dormitory beds, much like a hospital ward. One great fan on the ceiling circulated the hot air with a continual hum. It was harder for me to ignore this than the hum of the mosquitoes. I'd brought no mosquito netting of my own, and hiding under a cover no matter how thin, was sweltering, so at night, I concentrated my mind on the fan to mesmerize myself to sleep. Luckily, it must have been an off season, because the whole room of twelve beds had only three tenants, all exceedingly individualistic. We read or wrote letters in privacy in the midst of other people. By this time I'd perfected the skill of dressing under my long wrap-around skirt, and since I got up early to sit, I felt I had a great deal of privacy.

The first evening I was there, I went down to explore the enormous sparkling white Stupa which, by some stroke of luck, was only half a block away from my guest house. It was brightly lighted, and at 7:00 PM many Burmese were making their regular visits. I entered with crowds of people through an iron gate between whitewashed walls two feet thick. There was a flight of stairs as wide as a street leading up to the main level of the Stupa some thirty feet higher up.

I left my shoes with the "shoe clerk" and walked barefoot past the groups of women selling flowers for offerings. As I walked up the steps to the higher platform, I was surprised to see the first big Buddha statue. It was six feet tall, of polished bronze, seated peacefully in a samadhi position with three bright neon haloes of red, yellow and green flashing on and off around his serene head.

On this level, people were everywhere, walking along a "lane" around the main dome. Against the wall of the dome sat many small statues of Buddhas surrounded by wire racks holding burning incense. The air was thick with the fragrance and smoke. Men and women were lighting candles and offering incense, chanting prayers aloud, sitting on the edge of the marble "lane" in meditation while people streamed past them. Each seemed intent on his or her own practice. They seemed to be everyday people, stopping after work to carry out their devotions.

There were many small marble chapels placed side by side, framing a hallway around the center core. Many were closed by iron gates, and presumably only the owner of the chapel could offer incense there. Each chapel contained a Buddha figure, mostly in the position of Touching the Earth at the moment of Enlightenment. These chapels, which were reminiscent of small mausoleums or side chapels in a cathedral, had marble floors which were covered with the same type of kitchen linoleum with bright designs I'd seen in the monastery in Thailand. Jumbled on the altars were smaller Buddhas, places to put incense, many vases with flowers in every stage from fresh to wilted brown, and lots of candles.

As I walked around this place of busy worship, I discovered three other central bronze Buddhas. They seemed to face the four directions, and a set of stairs led down to the street level from each. All were crowned by neon haloes or encircled by rows of gaudy "theatre lights" glaring brilliantly around the serene face.

I found one chapel with a floor space about fifteen feet square, where people were sitting in meditation in front of a small pure white Buddha, so I joined them. Each had his own sitting schedule, men and women, and got up singly when they were finished. There was a general hubbub of talk and people walking past, but after a few minutes, all settled in my own mind, and I no longer heard it. It felt very nice to share this "quiet space" with Burmese I'll never see again, but with whom for a while I felt very close.

Small children accompanied their parents here, and when I

got up to go, a lovely little girl who was with her mother, handed me a flower and we gasshoed to each other. What a beautiful gift in a strange place!

Her mother was a doctor, and came each evening as a regular practice to sit. She was pleased to see a Westerner with whom she could practice English. As we walked together round the Stupa many people smiled greetings. At-homeness flooded over me.

The doctor had told me that people sat at the chapels around the Stupa at 6:00 AM, and I wanted to sit with them. I spoke to the proprietor of my guest house about going the next day. However, when I got up in the morning, I wasn't prepared to find the door padlocked. I couldn't get out without rousing the poor sleepy attendant who heard my steps on the creaky stairs.

In the early dawn, the Stupa's golden dome shone above the white stone walls surrounding it. The gates were open, and already the flower salesmen and women were ready with roses, orchids, yellow sunflowers, and bunches of incense.

I took my offering to the chapel where the peaceful white marble Buddha, five feet tall, sat in quiet repose. His eyes were heavily painted with red eye liner and his lips were red, a rather startling effect, but no more so than the neon haloes on the bronze Buddhas. The signs of enlightenment that are said to identify a Buddha were carved in the white soles of his upturned feet, and red paint was rubbed into the grooves of triangles, circles and stars and all the lines so that his feet were full of red designs. I'd seen equally beautiful marble Buddhas in China, and realized they must have come from Burma. There's an unmistakable appearance to the milky white stone, the broad shoulders and the four fingers of equal length touching the earth in unison.

Luckily, my body was still attuned to sitting on the bare floors of the Watt Thorn Sua, and the time sped quickly. There were only a few people there, so it was quieter in contrast to last night's hubbub . As I left about 7:15 still more people were arriving.

I wandered out into the streets of Rangoon with the brilliant morning sun creating golden flashes of light even on the crumbling sidewalks.

On one corner near a church, an old woman sold sunflower seeds to feed the pigeons. Around her crowded children wearing the Asian poverty uniform. I had visions of thousands of inappropriate castoff party dresses with ruffles and frills, collected in Europe or America, floating in one ragged magic carpet to settle down and cover all the destitute children of Asia. With seams unsewn. dresses too big, slipping off narrow shoulders, broken zippers hanging open, children must be growing up with a curious idea of style.

Around them strutted the fat pouter pigeons who swarmed in greedy flocks upon any seeds thrown into their midst. They personified the portly dowagers drawn in Helen Hokinson's cartoons of ladies at bridge parties and charity meetings. Had they too, like the dogs, been condemned to this thoughtless existence for eons?

After passing dumpling salesmen standing on the open sidewalks next to improvised charcoal cooking stoves made out of tin cans or discarded pots, I found a breakfast place in a tiny restaurant. Business people were eating at tables no bigger than a foot and a half in diameter. A young man was baking bread in a huge oven built into the corner much as a pizza cook might operate in the US. It was a huge round brick oven covered with plaster, in which a red hot charcoal fire radiated on this hot day. The boy was skillfully flattening rounds of dough with efficient pats and shoving them with a paddle onto racks inside the open hole of the stove. Quickly, with bare hands, he pulled the cooked bread out and served it to customers. Someone in the back was cooking white rice and meat in dough pouches. I watched children come with empty pots to buy "take out" cooked rice and bread. An occasional beggar turned up to be given a portion of rice, and sent along.

I had no idea what to visit in Rangoon, but a man at a neighboring table told me of the great Shwedegon Temple. I could get to it by using the buses. He gave me his map of bus lines and told me how to decode the Burmese numerals which seemed to consist of circles, lines, dots, and combinations of these.

I caught a bus and got off several blocks later in the midst of tourist crowds almost like a circus. Above their heads rose the enormous dome. There was a long covered wooden staircase leading to the upper platform where the greater Stupa with its gold leaf dome was surrounded by mini-stupas. The whole complex covered as much as three city blocks.

The stairs, which went up for a distance of what seemed to be about a hundred and fifty yards or so, were lined on both sides by small stalls selling jade and wood carvings, flowers, incense, brass bells, T-shirts, umbrellas and back scratchers.

Up I rose, landing after landing. I arrived at the top, facing a larger than life-size bronze seated Buddha. The medley of people, chapels, domes, children, mosaic walks and bright light dazzled me into a stupor. I walked around in the unfamiliar atmosphere grateful for the prior introduction to this architectural plan by the smaller stupa near my guest house. Here everything was magnified ten times. If there had been a swirling jumble of noisy people before, here the confusion was twenty times greater.

I walked around the enormous inner dome once, seeing only from a great psychological distance. Each ornate side temple had its own Buddha; some had several Buddhas, arhats (Enlightened ones) and statues of temple tigers, dragons, decorated columns, marble floors, golden columns. Each temple superseded the next in artistic carving, size, amount of gold, the size of the Buddha. The whole place radiated the intent of each builder to surpass his predecessor in opulence and design, hardly what Buddha had intended. Yet this was Burmese Buddhism 2500 years later.

There were tourists from all around the world here. The conversations I overheard as I walked along the street-wide aisle between the Stupa and the smaller chapels, were in German, French, English and Japanese among those recognizable to me. I circled the Stupa three times as a pilgrim, again finding that all the chaos helped me to keep an inner stillness.

The hot sun shone on the black marble designs till it burned my bare feet, and I raced to the next white slab and onto a shady place where the cool stone drank the pain from my burns. I wanted to just sit down somewhere and absorb the place. I wandered off onto a side court where a few people were sitting on benches among some trees in an open plaza. I found a tree trunk to lean against, shaded from the blazing sun, and just sat, dozing in the heat and feeling the impact of this strange place. It felt a bit like Borobudur in Indonesia. It was as large. Tourists clambered all over that quiet place, yet it retained a sense of stillness.

For several hours I just sat there, moving as the sun moved, to keep in the shade, not thinking, just gazing. Finally I pulled out my guide book to read a bit about it. There was originally one stupa, built around 500 AD. Later, a larger one was erected next to it. The smaller one contained the relic of Buddha. I'd been sitting gazing at the smaller one right next to me, without knowing anything about it. My inner guide seemed to be taking me quite close to Buddha relics, even here.

I finally moved on to discover a photographer who came all the way back with me to the spot where I had been sitting to take a picture of me with the smaller stupa. While the picture was being developed, I waited on a marble platform in front of one of the larger chapels. There were some bright-eyed half-naked children playing there. A small baby was under the charge of an eight year old sister, no parents in sight. I played pantomime games with them, noticing small sores on their legs and arms. They all seemed to take these for granted. All the children had the runny nose which seemed a requirement for growing up in Asia.

As I was playing, a woman I'd seen on the airplane coming from Bangkok came up to me. "I'm so glad to see you. Do you know the way to the cars?" She looked hot and frazzled and was totally confused by the symmetrical layout of the temple.

Like the stupa near my lodgings, this stupa was completely balanced, with four identical sets of stairs leading out to four different streets. Walking all the way around took nearly fifteen minutes, and it was easy to confuse one entrance with another. They all looked alike.

I told her I wasn't sure. When I told her that I'd come by bus, and pointed to the exit I knew, her face dropped in surprise. She realized I wasn't on a tour and backed off away from me. She stood with her back to me fifty feet away even though it was in the hot sun. Apparently she didn't know how to deal with someone who wasn't on a tour, and chose to ignore the whole encounter. She also had looked surprised that I was playing with the children. Finally, her husband, after trying two other stairs, found the right one and came to get her. They both ignored my friendly goodbye. That woman must have felt very ill at ease in that place.

When I finally came down from a nearly six hour stay at the Shwedegon temple, I decided just to ride the buses, and see Rangoon.

I got on, noting clearly the odd semicircular number so as to recognize it again if I got off. I had a map that had helped me to figure out where it was going, but after being in the midst of all those jumbled temples, Buddhas, gold arhats, and milling people I just sat down and gazed out the window at the passing scene.

I felt a bit as if I were riding past the gingerbread houses of the Midwest in the US, when they lined the streets in the early 1900's.

Again came the odd jolt of displaced time perception that Asia seemed to provoke. All the hotels we stayed in in China had been equipped with what looked like the recycled parts of Nineteenth Century American "elegance". The old white octagonal terrazzo floors I used to stare at on bathroom floors fifty years ago now are reassembled in Chinese hotel bathroom floors. The old steam heat radiators that banged and clanked when I was young, now bang and clank in China. Even the strange flat link chain that held the bathtub stopper to the tub and the sink plug to the sink are now in China. I kept experiencing the feeling that I'd stepped into another Time reality.

This was the beginning of unhinging my feelings of Time. The question of "am I dreaming?" came again and again as I encountered different stage sets recalling different places I'd been to before.

Now, the streets of Rangoon that I passed in the bus looked like Columbus, Ohio where I grew up, but much shabbier, as if neglected since the time I'd been there forty years ago. It was as if it had been uncared for by my memory until now when I visited it again. As I "floated" by in the bus, just glancing at the old clapboard houses with picture windows enclosing window seats and attics with half circular window frames, that past was again right now! What in my mind could have made it so tawdry?

We turned towards the river and to my surprise, took a direction I'd not expected from looking at my map. I kept on riding wondering "what next"? Then a man who was standing near me, pointed to a stupa rising up above some old black factory type buildings in the foreground. He smiled, pointed again, and I decided to get off here.

I had to walk along some railroad tracks, past a poor starving calf that was licking the juice from a discarded melon rind near a fruit stand. Children, dressed in poverty garb, were selling peanuts. I bought the peanuts to their delight, and fed them to the poor calf. Again I watched myself feeling the misery of the "dumb animals" in Burma. The children seemed in better physical condition, though they weren't in school, and looked destined to perpetuate this beggar's life style.

It was hot. Later I learned it was 102 degrees. I was thirsty and just by the entrance to the stupa was a small drink stand, consisting of a counter under a burlap canopy with two chairs and a bench at a board table covered with oil cloth. I sank into a chair and gratefully sipped some orange juice.

A young monk, about seven years old came up. He must have been given to a monastery by his parents who couldn't support him. The vendor had some ice cream, so I bought a cone and gave it to the surprised little monk. He sat there licking it, gazing at me in silence.

When he left, a man nearby began to talk to me in English. He said this was a very old and special stupa. There was a hair of Buddha in it. Oddly, the guide book had indicated other stupas, but not this one. It was only identified by a small pictorial symbol on the bus map I had. As I got up to visit the stupa, the man came with me. He had a pleasant, familiar face reminding me of someone I knew, but dream-like, I couldn't identify.

We checked our shoes and entered a chamber glittering with a mosaic of millions of inch-long diamond shaped mirrors all over the walls and inside the dome. In the center, behind an iron latticed fence, in a deep tube like a stair well, was a platform with three buddha bowls resting on it. People were throwing coins into the bowls. If they land in the bowls, the man explained, they will have good luck. The hair of Buddha was encased in a large stone pillar behind them. I bowed, and sat down for a while along with others who paused for a moment to meditate in the small space, and then moved on.

When I got up, the man was still there, and guided me around the other rooms I'd probably not have found if I'd gone alone. He pointed to a pock-marked stone above my head which he said was from the first pagoda erected very shortly after Buddha's death. They had excavated the area, and had placed behind strong iron fences displays of many four to six inch golden Buddhas found when they erected the later stupa. There seemed to be hundreds of stone images of Buddhas and other solid gold images. There was enough gold there to alleviate all suffering of Rangoon if clinics, schools, housing had been erected. But here it lay, tribute to the Buddha who taught the illusion of this existence and how to transcend it.

We crossed a courtyard to another building where a great shiny bronze Buddha sat, six feet tall. The British had taken it to a museum in England. There had been much talk about this desecration. When Burma gained its independence, the British gave it back.

The man was humorous and tolerant, and though we couldn't talk easily in English, I felt comfortable with him. As we left to go out, he picked up his bicycle, looked at me and said "Do not forget me!" Though I don't even have his name, I never will. Nor will I forget that happenstance visit to the most unusual stupa in all my travels!

It was only a few blocks from the Strand Hotel, and I walked back along the railroad tracks, to that once prominent hotel. They were serving cold soda, and since ice is so often contaminated, I drank a cold soda with gratitude. Travelers on middle income tours stay here. It has long since lost its former elegance, like some dust covered and forgotten old piece of furniture. There was a group of fat French tourist women and two oblivious Americans complaining of the heat, the food, the accommodations. They hadn't seen the same Rangoon I had.

After a short rest I walked towards my guest house, and, on the way, miraculously bumped into the unobtrusive museum. The first floor of this old marble British relic displayed the splendor of the Kings of Siam. It was beyond all fairy tales. The clothes were stiff with gold embroidered thread, rubies, diamonds, sapphires. Emeralds studded the drinking cups, boxes, seats made of spun silver and carved wood. What a strange contrast to the pocked-marked children and the starving calf I'd just seen.

Maybe the British weren't so different from the king in their capacity for exploitation. What mind state is it that permits such accumulation of affluence and ostentatious splendor in the midst of starving beggars? It seems to be the state that wars are made of.

The upper floors were devoted to excavations of early stone age man in the regions of Northern Burma. Archeological displays of art like the Caves of Lascaux in France entranced me. Whole rooms showing the splendor of Pegan prepared me for my visit there. The signs were all in Burmese, so I was unable to benefit by the exhibits as much as I could have wished. I lost myself in those rooms of the past of a Burma I'd not encountered in my wanderings through Rangoon.

In the evening, when I went to eat, before returning to my dormitory, I met a young man, a mountain climber who had climbed with the mountaineering club in his university. He told me there was a new Rangoon ten miles further out with modern buildings, banks and expensive hotels. This must have been where the woman I met at Shwedegon was staying. I couldn't even imagine her at the Strand hotel.

As I walked back, gigantic banners fifty feet long depicting the most gory segment of the current movie tempted me to explore the movie row. Long lines of working people wound around the block. They stood for an hour to get in. One movie seemed less blatantly displayed, and I joined that line. An attendant soon came up to me and offered to help me cut ahead in the line so that I could get in. This seemed to be because of my Western face. I declined the privilege, and stayed in line to wait my chances with the rest. It was like any line in the United States, with working people, and office workers waiting for seats. No one was very expensively dressed. There were no rich people here.

Young boys about 10 years old were going up and down the line selling cigarettes, probably the very ones the tourists had brought in that morning. Only they weren't selling them by the pack. They were stacked in cups and people not much better off than their salesmen were buying them one at a time! I realized all those bottles of liquor and cigarettes weren't going to the wealthy. All the marked up prices from the black market transactions were being passed on to these simple people.

I never got into the movie, but while I stood there, and as I walked "home", I had many offers to buy my liquor and cigarettes that still bulged in my pack in the dormitory. I still couldn't bring myself to sell it, though the offers could have made it possible for me to stay in Burma for the entire week on the expense of $13.00 for the liquor and cigarettes. It looked as if the poor people were paying for the tourists to come.

Chapter 34 - A Poor Man's Tour of Rangoon

I walked to the Burma Airlines office located down by the Irrawaddy River to negotiate my air line ticket to Pegan. No reservations could be arranged beforehand, and I was wondering whether I'd have to take a train. The airline office was one of those forgotten British buildings that once elegantly faced the river bank. Now it had a seedy dustiness about it, paint cracking off the doors, the interior full of Burmese, waiting in hunched lines.

Here the power of officialdom prevailed. People stood in one line for hours to be told in the end that they needed to wait in another line. There were surprisingly few Westerners here. Perhaps those I saw were tour guides, representing others who were spared this sardine press of alternately frustrated, patient, humorous, sometimes self-important humanity. No particular approach was consistently successful. Some shoved forward, got what they wanted and left. Others pushed to the front only to be diverted to a different line by importantly indifferent clerks. Nowhere had I seen such a long time expended on misdirecting people. The Burmese who waited seemed to be used to this interminable way of doing things.

I finally got to the counter, after five people had shoved themselves in front of me. The clerk informed me she would have to wire the airlines who originated my ticket to verify that I'd paid for the trip to Pegan. I pointed out that I'd paid for the entire ticket. She said it would take an extra day to verify this. Nothing else to do but to co-operate, so I left my ticket with her. It would cut down my travel in Burma considerably. I was to return in the afternoon.

I wandered out through the barrage of beggars at the door. Children with their dark brown pleading eyes, men in ragged clothes, women mostly in saris all with hands out. There are particular styles to begging: the pathetic, helpless look, the aggressive

approach, the reasoning approach that uses the guilt of the afflu-
ent traveler to persuade him to share his wealth. I realized here
that I could easily "share" my wealth to the point of nothing, and
the lives of these people wouldn't be changed much.

Often I chose to look at begging the way I looked at bargaining. It was a way to make contact with someone whom I might
not otherwise meet. Whenever I was particularly struck by one
among the many faces, I sometimes gave a small bit or talked for
a while since they often had learned English.

There was a woman in this crowd who was "my beggar". She
embodied the same image as my friend Patricia in California, the
woman in Bali who told me her troubles on the beach, and the
beggar woman by Manila Bay. They all were of the same family
of faces: a kind of person who everywhere seems to bob to the
surface of my awareness no matter where I am. This woman, too,
was an essentially beautiful woman, thin bony body, high cheek
bones, hollow cheeks, deep brown eyes in which I somehow saw
myself. I gave her a small amount, struggling in myself against
giving her all I had. The same feeling welled up in me that sur-
faced in Indonesia with the farmer to whom I could have given
my shirt, but didn't. The deep knowledge that all the money in
the universe would not help to change the begging state of mind,
guided me to acknowledge her as a person beyond her need for
money. I felt the familiar unaccountable love rush through me as
I looked at her and passed on.

I noticed the ferry loading at the dock about a block away and
wandered toward it slowly, passing more beggars squatting and
cooking by the curb. For a small sum I boarded the giant boat
along with a farmer carrying rice bags, business men, women with
large baskets of freshly purchased goods and families out for an
excursion. My companions were obviously contented with each
other. The old woman couldn't speak English. She smiled as her
husband talked. The old man seemed to be almost a Confucius
type, content with his life as it was, feeling no particular desire for
anything other than what was. He spoke of his ideas on education: that all children should be helped to know people across the

world, to respect other cultures, and thus have peace.

He admired the United States which was more a symbol to him than an actuality. It stood for courage to object to Colonialism, to establish independence. He felt we had started the whole world on a new track of establishing individual responsibility and affirming freedom.

In American history I had read the word "Colonialism" many times but suddenly it took on the fullest meaning. It had been ripening during my time in Indonesia, where I experienced the shadows of the Dutch rule on the people who felt that to have white skin meant supremacy, to have industrial technology meant the only admired progress, where everywhere people struggled under a psychological inferiority that prompted veneration of anything made in the USA no matter how tawdry.

Now on a river in Burma from which the crumbling remains of the British buildings could be viewed along the shore, I could recognize the ultimate devastation of foreign rule and the results of exploitation. The people of Burma were still scattering, looking for shelter after such a long dependence upon the British.

I stayed on the ferry and rode back across the river again musing at how many famous rivers I'd crossed on this journey: The Yangtze in China, the Chao Phrya in Bangkok, the Irrawaddy, the Rhine I'd ridden on in Switzerland just the fall before. Each carried literally the commercial life blood of the country. Barges floated on them with food, fuel, lumber, but the civilizations they supported were as different as the very attitudes that created the commerce. These rivers were also like crossings of barriers in my own mind, each reflecting an attitudinal rearrangement.

I had decided to let go of the air flight, to take the night train to Pegan so I wouldn't waste so much time in Burmese Red Tape. When I went back to collect my ticket at the Burmese Airlines, the 'official' woman who had first presented me with the frustrating news of the time delay, had kindly reserved my flight for the next morning. All the red tape was brushed aside. She even told me how to duck out of the bureaucratic snafus on the Pegan end as well. What had happened to change her mind? Was it my attitude of acceptance? It felt a bit as if she'd been there as a test to check my state of mind, as so many situations potentially frustrating had presented themselves head on, and then faded away under my "watching mind".

As I left with my transportation taken care of, I saw my beggar woman again. She came up to me, not begging, this time, just to greet me. She began to tell me how hard it was to live in Rangoon. She'd come from Bangladesh the year before, had become ill, or so she said, and was finding it difficult to make a living. She spoke excellent English, and I asked her if she had tried to get a job doing translation.

As we continued talking, she suddenly asked if she could show me something. I had no other plans, so we set off down a back street. She had a Hindu temple she wanted me to see. We walked for about five blocks in the hot sun. The sad countenance she'd shown me. She greeted her beggar friends with a happy grin, and I wondered how many others she'd fooled as we walked, taken on this "tour". We were seeing bedraggled and dirty streets I would not have chosen to walk alone. I was glad it was daylight, because they had an aspect of darkness even in the afternoon.

At a gate to a large iron fenced area were three kid goats tied up. They were precious. Remembering my days of caring for the goats in my mountain life, I petted their soft fur as they nuzzled me affectionately.

We went through the gate, ducking because of the low lintel, and we were in a courtyard to her temple. Perhaps the low entrance was to induce a humble bearing on entering.

We came to a large room with a strange black object, obviously the altar, in the center. It looked like an upright cylinder with three white horizontal stripes painted on it. She couldn't explain but said it was a Shiva temple.

I gazed at the altar, curiously feeling it had some connection with African design, but completely ignorant of its significance. Around the outside rim of the platform the cylinder rested on was a kind of channel with a lip like a pitcher. Then suddenly I remembered the sweet goats and realized this was a place of sacrifice.

The twinge of surprise that went through me only provoked the sudden awareness that I was being shown a place sacred to the Hindus. I felt I was just continuing my education from temple visits in China, Japan, Philippines, Bali, Thailand, and now here in Buddhist Burma, I was getting a feeling for the ritual of the Hindus.

She showed me two subsidiary chapels with doll-like figures in them. In a side room were several men counting the offerings for the day. Pennies were strewn all over the tiled marble floor which a ragged man was busy mopping.

We moved on through more side streets to a second Hindu temple, again stooping through a low entrance. This one had the same cylindrical altar, but a towel was draped around it. There was a two-foot red sculptured bull lying in front. As with the other temple, there were Tibetan thankas on the walls, and stone Buddhas. The Burmese seem to love make up. Each Buddha was painted with red eye liner, red hands and feet.

We sat down on a bench in the large room which reminded me more of a large union meeting hall than a temple of worship. There were two ragged beggars beside us. I wondered what she wanted me to see, but as I sat there, I distinctly felt little bugs transfer their allegiance from the beggar beside me to my legs and neck. Was this truly the beggar's tour? Was she hoping I'd get some sympathetic experience from feeling for a time the beggar's bane - fleas and lice which seem to accompany the usual condition of dysentery? I chuckled inside at this subtle touch, thanking all beings that I could go back to my guest house no matter how shabby it was and take a shower, wash my clothes and hair, and be free of these invading vermin. I did truly, for a short time, catch a glimpse of what it must be like not to be able to take a bath for long periods. This was a deeper look into the condition of poverty than in the Bangkok hotel which only showed me the veneer.

I mused as I sat there that filth, disorder, poverty and illness so often keep the same company. Here in Rangoon it seemed that the last vestige of hope for the human condition had drained through the chinks of the cracking floors, leaving behind the dregs of misery like a slime.

In some strange way those little beings in the fleas knew where to congregate to aggravate the already wretched existence of their hosts.

The dogs who'd worn through their fur to bare skin from nipping in a frenzy at the persistent fleas, only too well depicted the terrible irritation of biting bugs.

The "Confucius" on the ferry boat had said I must have led a very good life in my last incarnation because I was so healthy in this one. Again I thanked the state of mind that helped me not get caught up in the torment of biting fleas. I'd been able to notice the bites but not to become so concentrated on them.

Perhaps that was a benefit of practicing zazen, where sometimes the pain in my knees was so great I couldn't experience anything else. I'd learned to accept the pain, acknowledge its reality, and then it strangely melted away. So, thank heavens, it was with the fleas. After that trip I experienced no further agitation. Still I'm very grateful for that brief encounter which stretched my awareness of what the experience of true poverty was—if even for a moment.

I shared with my guide that she reminded me of others I knew, and asked her name. To my amazement it was Patricia! She had protested she was Catholic, crossed her self to prove it, began to say the Lord's Prayer, as if expecting that's what I wanted to hear. Yet when I said I felt she was still Hindu, she smiled and relaxed. I wondered how many people felt forced to profess a religion not native to them because of outside pressure.

It was late in the afternoon. I had no idea where I was, and she led me back to the stupa near which I lived. We said goodbye, a feeling of sisterhood between us both.

That evening I sat again before the peaceful, translucent white marble Buddha in the chapel at the large stupa near the guest house. There were people all around me fingering their prayer beads, offering incense and flowers. The overall feeling of cheery loving of life as it is, was much more comfortable to me than the bedraggled hopeless feeling in those Hindu temples. In both places I witnessed the strange way people of different cultures take the true teachings of spirit and dress them up so that, in time, the teachings are hidden underneath a whole pile of tradition and ritual which obscures the original light.

Note from my diary.

As I walk down a side street, past old dirty marble faced office buildings looking like Washington DC would after years of neglect, I come across a sidewalk market.

Men and women in torn vests and dresses ragged and rumpled, sit with their wares spread out in neat rows before them.

Each has a neat square on which piles of jeans or tee shirts, combs and hairbrushes are neatly laid out in lines. There are other squares with pencils, soap dishes and articles of daily necessity. I spot a plastic razor and pull out my money to purchase it.

Suddenly there's a whistle and everything around me turns to one quick flash of activity. The wares I see are spread out on squares of burlap, and each vender grabs the four corners. All things tumble into the "sack". Then in another instant I am the only person on the street, numbed by the fast action, puzzled at the disappearance of a whole market in seconds.

Then the salesman with whom I negotiated for the razor appears with it in his hand. "Government" he says.

Obviously these sidewalk merchants have arranged for the most efficient and effective illegal practice. How wide awake they have to be! It seems many things in Burma are illegal !

Chapter 35 - Pegan (now named Bagan)

From the Rangoon airport, the flight in a twenty passenger plane to Pegan was only an hour. As usual when we got off the plane we were deluged by opportunities to sell our contraband. Still I said "no", wondering what I was going to do with the liquor. Five of us shared a jeep ride to the small village. We drove out through a flat countryside of tawny dry earth covered with tawny thistles. No trees. Only occasional bushes. A desolate place.

I'd never heard of Pegan, but the young travel agent who had already contributed to my adventures by inadvertently leading me to the Sisters of St. Francis in the Philippines, had said that Pegan was a "must" to anyone interested in Buddhism. So here I was, ignorant but ready, for what, I had no idea.

The jeep dropped us off at one end of the tiny village. Nearly all of my fellow travelers headed for the small guest house only a few steps away which was mentioned in the book, Southeast Asia on a Shoestring.

I went with them, but not particularly eagerly. I needed to get the feel of this place. So I got permission to stack my heavy pack there while I went for a walk.

Just next door, I stopped by the Burma Travel Bureau, a tiny "office" where I found two men in shirt sleeves sitting with an enormous book in front of them. They had the look of St. Peter himself as I asked to make a reservation on the plane in four days. They importantly said I'd have to wait. They "had to contact the Burmese Airlines by wire", which they said would take several days. But as I walked further down the road, I passed the only other official building, a small store-front building made of cement blocks where the Burma Airlines had offices. Here they took my ticket, and immediately made a reservation with no waiting, no trouble. I'd forgotten that the woman in the Rangoon office had told me to go directly to the Burma Airlines. If I'd not walked down the road, I'd not have noticed this obscure office. Later I learned that my fellow travelers had waited in uncertainty until the very last day they were to leave before being told they had reservations on the plane. Even in a village of temples, officials were playing games with power.

I walked alone past bamboo houses and wooden shacks along the main street. Drivers with horse-drawn carriages waited under the shade of some spindly trees. All offered me a ride, but I wanted to walk.

Gradually, beyond the yards behind the houses I caught glimpses of the temples. Two, three, and five tiered pyramidal buildings stretched in every direction into the distance like a peaked forest jutting up from the flat plain. Most were built of red brick, but one brilliant white temple at the end of the road caught my eye as I walked. It was undergoing reconstruction and bamboo scaffolding obscured its top stories.

I wandered towards this white structure gleaming in the near noon day sun. I could have stopped for lunch or a cup of tea in one of several small open "restaurants" I had passed earlier, but something pulled me to that temple. I walked around it examining beautifully carved designs, flowers, and vines on the white walls.

The whole temple rested on a square fifty foot base above which rose tiers of gradually smaller square stories to the top where a spire pierced the sky. It seemed as if I'd always known the workmen who smiled as I came by. They were digging out the last layers of dirt that still piled around the base from the last earthquake.

The workmen showed me where I could enter the building and find passages inside the walls which led to the top. Feeling strangely familiar, I took off my shoes and entered. As I got used to the darker interior, I found some people seated together, possibly a family. They appeared to be caretakers, and approached me for a contribution to help them buy gold leaf to encrust the Buddha statue. They were very plainly dressed, their clothes having the familiar brownish tone of clothes washed in muddy water. They seemed to care little for their own appearance, and showed great delight at each small gift to gild their Buddha.

I left a contribution with them and they gave me a very official looking receipt. They seemed contented, humorous people, friendly and warm with none of the Rangoon flavor of helplessness about them, or the bravado of the Burmese tourist people with their big book.

I climbed the dark stairs which got progressively narrower till I had to turn sideways to come out on a second balcony. On I climbed up steep outside stairs which led to a narrow walkway around the top. I stood with my back to the wall as if I were on a cliff of a mountain, and gazed out in three directions over the flat plain. It was dotted with the ornate pyramids receding into the noon haze of dust. Cattle were grazing on the thistles. An occasional horse and carriage squeaked along the dirt road one hundred fifty feet below, and the calls of the workmen floated up. Noon silence spread its peace around me.

I edged around to overlook the Irrawaddy River and the barren mountain range on the far side. Everything was in a dull haze like the indistinctness of memory or half perceived dreams. As I gazed at the slow muddy expanse of water, and the similarly mud toned mountains, my eye caught the spire of a stupa on the ridge of one of the mountains. It shone with clarity and, almost like a spotlight, beamed me its brilliance.

I was in an odd state of mind, receptive, quiet, not thinking really, and just gazed at that brilliance across the river in a reverie. Not knowing anything, not having anything pressing for me to do, I just gazed, feeling an uncertain echo of something recognized and then forgotten, slipping out of conscious touch. Yet I was content to stare and feel the peace of this expansive place.

Inside, I discovered an inner hall that went around the building where, facing the four directions, sat great twenty-foot-high Buddhas. They were still being repaired and were covered with a dull black tar-like coating so only the features of the peaceful face were clear. I liked very much these simple undercoated black Buddhas, even in preference to the great gilded shining Buddha at the entrance, but it was clear they intended to gild these too.

I hadn't found a place to stay, and meandered back along the dirt road that I had come. It was hot, but I hadn't noticed till now. I wandered into the open yard of a small restaurant and guest house. I was the only customer. The family that owned the house handled everything. The wife took my order as I pointed to the menu which was in English. She couldn't speak but understood what I wanted.

As I sat drinking tea (real tea without the Thailand condensed milk) and waiting while they cooked the meal, the son of the proprietor, who spoke English well, came to talk with me. He showed me a small book in English which told a bit of the history of Pegan.

As early as 180 AD, when there were only bamboo huts for the villagers, kings had begun building temples here. Through the centuries many temples spread across the plain, and in the 12th Century, it became the site for one of the great universities of Asia. It was for a while the capitol of the kingdom. A king in 1057 AD brought together Theravadan scriptures written in Pali. He brought together Buddhist monks and large numbers of artists to begin a great period when most of the temples were constructed.

As the proprietor's son talked with me, his face looked startlingly like the faces of Mayans sculpted on walls in Chichen Itza in Mexico. The young man from Borneo whom I met in Bali had also looked extraordinarily Mayan. That same nagging fascination that tickled my awareness came again. Everywhere the same people appear as if we have been all together through Time like a cast in a repertory theatre, taking different parts in plays of different cultures and eras.

He was interested to hear I'd been on a sort of undirected pilgrimage, that I'd come to Pegan without knowing why. I spoke of the beauty of the Gawdawpalin temple (the one I'd just climbed) and that my eye had caught the sparkling temple across the river.

"Would you like to go there? I can arrange for you to go there if you would like."' I explained I had allowed myself very little money for this trip. "It won't cost you anything, I have a cousin who can take you." He protested that he understood this was a pilgrimage for me, and that there would be no cost except the food to take as offering to the yogi, the ferry across and that was all. The idea startled me, but why not? Out of my four days' stay, the trip would take two, but I felt clearly it was the thing for me to do.

"There's a very powerful Yogi up there, but you may not be able to see him, he's only available if he wants to be. He used to be a Colonel in the Burmese Army, but quit his post to meditate in a cave on that mountain for the past twenty years."

I went back to the guest house where I'd left my pack and brought it back to settle into one of the three rooms they had in this small place. There was a rudimentary outhouse in the back and a "shower" room where the familiar large tank of water held the bathing water to be splashed on with a dipper. It was all I needed and I was used to this.

There was a metal cot out in the yard under a tree and I sank into it thinking I'd take a short nap, but found I slept for four hours! I woke to delighted shouts of children playing with a pet rabbit that was scurrying in and out, daring them to catch him. A woman's voice singing a very beautiful song drifted past the tall hedge from the house next door.

I had wanted to see Shwezegon temple listed in the guide as having a Buddha relic. It was a pilgrimage spot for travelers all round the world, but as I hired a horse and buggy and began to plod along the dirt road, I realized it was much further away than I had judged. I'd only get there in time to turn around and come back. So I asked the driver to take me to some temples I couldn't walk to that were not so far away.

It was late afternoon, and the same brilliant gold light I noticed in Chang Mai, Thailand, was already catching on the dust in the air turning everything to a dreamy brilliance.

Very few people were about. It was not the usual tourist place. Only an occasional farmer, guiding his cattle back home, stirred up the dust among the thistles and cactus. The light tinted the old white bulls till they glowed a creamy yellow, and the white flowers of the thistles gleamed saffron. Even the dusty gray grass shivered in that slanting light and whispered gold.

We passed smaller crumbling brick structures glowing against the sky, and drove up through a red brick wall to an enormous silent temple. There was no one around besides my driver, his horse, and me.

He waited outside while his horse cropped the grass, and I entered into the great dark hallway that led around a solid square inner core.

From my Diary

My bare feet pad along the wide corridor and echo along the dark walls and mosaic floor. There are openings every so often to give enough light to catch the murals as my eye adjusts to see them. Clear paintings of thousands of monks in brown robes sitting in rows on rows are visible, and on one wall a reclining Buddha stretches fifty feet.

There are beautiful intricate designs in fading color on the smooth stucco surface painted by workmen who have long since crumbled into oblivion, leaving their masterpieces behind to crumble at a slower rate.

When I stop walking to examine the walls, everything echoes silence. Then I walk again and come to a giant Buddha, serene, secret, silent, sitting there through the centuries. The length of his great hand, in the "touching the earth" posture, is one foot long. He wears painted brown robes. I stand before this giant, feeling its majestic peace, the solidity of Time. That crossed legged posture, the tripod structure of stasis, balance, stability, exudes its quiescence into the air around us. That Buddha and I merge for a moment. I gassho.

Then I move on. On the four corners are the stairways leading to the second floor, wider than the Gawdawpalin temple. Instead of white, the passageways are dark red brick.

I come out into a chamber where an even more enormous Buddha of at least forty feet sits. As I enter, great bats, the size of pigeons, flutter out of place, shriek, and the walls reverberate with echoes in the stillness. My heart is startled into beating rapidly, and I can hear its dull thump knocking against the wall of the chamber as if that were the walls of my body.

Downstairs I'd felt impelled to sit, but had dismissed the urge because of the waiting carriage driver. Here the imposing figure sits as if there were no Time, no one waiting, nothing to hurry for. I sink into sitting position, that posture I have assumed for years, the "Burmese" posture, where my legs are parallel against each other, my knees resting on the floor. How comfortable this posture is, and I've always called it the Burmese posture. Only now do I realize the meaning. Here I am in Burma feeling at home!

We sit together, that great Buddha and this tiny gray haired lady at its feet, together in an empty, long neglected temple in Burma. We both just sit. I could sit on here forever. Stillness becomes nothing, everything ceases to exist. Profound silence, reverence, an unforgettable instant. Then time slips back into place. I rise, leaving a piece of myself still sitting there, like a misty shadow and move on.

I go down, wishing I could return and spend a day here at least, but taking an impression keen enough to last a lifetime.

We drive on to what my guide says is the biggest temple in Pegan. Its red brick inner corridors also wind around a central core like the others I've seen. Large Buddhas sit here, back to the wall, each facing in a cardinal direction. There's a double hall here, but the entryways to some inner center are bricked up mysteriously.

I have a strong wish to stay, even think I could sleep here all night. But an eerie feeling leads me to think it might be creepy there all alone in pitch black. It's already getting dark. With my bare feet padding, echoing against the thick brick walls, I climb to the top. Now I see the ornate Ananda Temple where, in the morning just before sunrise, I have agreed to sit with the proprietor of my guest house who meditates there daily. Prickling with spires, it gleams white and yellow gold in the late afternoon rays of the sun.

I go down along the empty corridors, back to the carriage. In the twilight, we hurry to a temple where a thirty foot long Buddha reclines, tightly enclosed by a long, Quonset type of shelter, like Alice in Wonderland, too cramped to move. The stupa that rests beside this beautiful Buddha is a step pyramid, clearly like the Aztec or Mayan temples in Mexico. I climb rapidly up the steep stairs, and, right shoulder to the center, walk three times around a Buddha relic deep inside the core. How many times I've encircled Buddha!

I crawl carefully back down the steep steps with grass sprouting in the cracks between the bricks, take a hurried look again at that beautiful reclining Buddha - the once in a lifetime look. I pay respect to the inspiration that created it and has kept it restored through centuries.

I felt that what I was doing was the thing to do, yet I certainly would never have planned this section of the trip!

The proprietor of my guest house told me that villagers usually went to the Ananda Temple, the most impressive temple in Pegan, at 5:30 A.M. In the pre-dawn light, I set out walking past the thistles and cactus on worn, dirt paths used by the villagers who went to the temple. It stood white against the lightening Eastern sky and frosted with ornate carvings. Many subsidiary spires framed the great central spire. It looked reminiscent of the cathedrals which were being built about the same time (1100 AD) in Europe.

I approached the great wooden door of the main entry just as other figures emerged from the dark shadows, coming like rays to the center.

When I entered, the grinning proprietor appeared out of the dark to guide me to a rack where we left our shoes. He guided me to a chapel where a slim standing Buddha shone golden in the light of many rows of flickering votive candles.

The other people who entered with me disappeared to the left, and I moved up to the flat square rugs laid out for sitting right in front of the Buddha. People were already sitting cross legged in meditation. At first I could not settle down. I just looked at this great Buddha. The smooth lines of drapery carved with delicate skill were like the thin folds carved on statues of Egyptian Pharaohs or the most classical Greek sculpture. One hand was raised upward as if showering rays of light towards all onlookers.

I fell into a deep quiet while the echoes of chanting came from another hall to my left. The people who had been sitting around me gradually rose and left, and when I rose there was no one around.

Then I wandered along the four hallways surrounding the square central core. Against each wall stood a tall Buddha, each facing in one of the four directions. Each seemed at least thirty feet high and each displayed a different mudra or position of the hands. They were gold in the semi- darkness and towered above me with grace and majesty. They were the only standing Buddhas I saw in all of Pegan.

This temple is usually the most frequented by tourists, and I was so glad to see it in the flickering light of early morning candles. I was sharing the time of devotion, seeing the temple not with the eyes of a tourist but as a participant. I rounded the fourth side, and returned to the place where I had sat. The proprietor, who had been waiting for me, invited me into a small compartment set aside by waist-high shelves where he had tea poured and four men, who seemed to be temple elders, were sitting around a small makeshift table. We couldn't talk much, but the warmth of the tea, the smiling wrinkled faces of those kindly men made me feel at ease. We sat together in the dark corner while the brilliance of the Buddhas radiated off to my right. Our silent company crossed the boundaries of nationalities and religions, of cultures and language. There in the silence of a temple five people drank tea together, recognizing a communion in morning devotion, a richness of being.

It was time for me to get back, and we all left together. As we returned to the quiet guest house, the proprietor was curious about my sitting practice. He pried me with questions while I waited for his wife to cook breakfast of rice and eggs. As I answered, I had the feeling that I was being tested for my understanding of Buddhism as I'd experienced it. It was an opportunity to verbalize all that had been happening to me. One question was a challenge. "What do you think is the difference between Buddhism and Christianity"?

Ever since the conference on Buddhist and Christian Meditation I'd been seeing the commonality. Now here was this question compelling me to see a difference.

After some hesitation and with a hopeful trust that what I said would do justice to both traditions, I answered. "It seems to me that Christians believe that it's through Christ that they will be saved or brought into the Eternal way. Buddha taught not to rely on anyone outside for salvation, but to rely on one's inner self which would lead to universal understanding of the Eternal."

Over and over again the Christian words "the Kingdom of God is within you" seemed to say to me that Christ was also pointing in that direction. But I'd just been to Malaysia where the Buddhists were praying to their Buddha statues for riches, fame, and health. It was clear that no matter what the teachers taught, the spirit of the teachings can be bent through the centuries into the view most congenial for 'followers'. True living of the spiritual path of honesty, compassion, simplicity is exceedingly difficult.

I could see little difference in the way of life between the Sisters of St. Francis and the early Zen monks whose lives were sparse. The Sisters trusted for their guidance in prayer. Zen masters perceived clarity in meditation. The compassion of both Buddha and Christ originated from their understanding.

The proprietor seemed to feel, however, that the way to salvation through the intermediary of Christ was the crux of the difference between the two religions and was pleased I'd mentioned it. At least I passed his test.

Chapter 36 - Pilgrimage

Then Aung Mueng, whom they pronounced "Ah Mo", a six-teen-year- old boy, arrived. He was to be my guide for the trip. He spoke monosyllabic English. His face was clear, and he had a delightful smile. I felt glad that he would be my guide.

We set out immediately, carrying offerings for the yogi of rice and prepared food in a plastic shopping bag with broken handles. Carrying required an iron grip on the slippery sharp edged bands. I took my sweater, a flask of boiled water and my sleeping sheet in my small day pack. It was too warm for the sleeping bag.

We left the main dirt road and walked along a side road towards the river, past the Maha Bodhi Temple, an exact replica of a temple in Bodh Gaya in India near where Buddha experienced enlightenment. The street was bordered by small bamboo houses where the people greeted us warmly as we passed.

Ah Mo cut into a courtyard walking directly towards a ceramic cistern sitting on a shelf in the shade of the large bamboo house. With the dipper resting on the top, he drew out cool water. I had my own boiled water, had been warned about the danger of unboiled water, but the friendly way he offered the dipper to me made me unwilling to reject it. Taking the dipper with a quiet prayer that the little parasites in it lie dormant, I drank it grate-fully. He filled the dipper again for himself, drank, and put the dipper back for the next thirsty passerby.

Along the dirt road, there were the ruts of carriage wheels and pocks from the hooves of cattle and horses, but the dust of the dry season leveled the uneven holes with velvet powder.

As we passed some trees with wide trunks and broken branches leaning wearily to the side, Ah Mo said, "Sal." And I understood, the sal tree was the source of the black lacquer that they painted on the Buddhas. How many centuries these trees had supplied this black protection that glazed the stucco surface rubbed over the brick Buddhas I couldn't learn, but sensed their long lived contribution in their decrepit look.

We passed some crumbled and neglected temples where the weeds grew shoulder high. In one, a brick Buddha sat unperturbed within walls that were powdering, and the bricks of what was once the roof stuck up like bumpy elbows from the earth around it.

As we neared the river, the brilliant white of a Pagoda that I had seen the first night at sunset from the top of the Thub Nyu Temple, blasted my eyes.

Ah Mo pointed to the pagoda then to his teeth and said, "Buddha."

I gathered this was the "Tooth Pagoda". I'd heard the son of the proprietor talk of a tooth of Buddha that is supposed to be encased within it. As we passed, I made a gassho to that part of Buddha, which along with the other parts, hairs, bones, I'd happened to encounter in my wanderings seemed to symbolize the "Buddha nature that pervades the whole universe" as familiar chants implied.

We walked around it in the usual pilgrim pattern. There were two-foot-tall bells hanging in rows on racks. Ah Mo took a large wooden club and struck them, motioning me to do the same. I've long felt that each person striking a bell has a different sound. The peal from Ah Mo's strike rippled out clearly into the air with a sweet open vibration. I couldn't talk with him, but the sound of that bell ringing opened my heart to him. I too struck the bells, but they sounded like dull thuds in comparison with the sound evoked by my young guide.

As we rounded the pagoda we came up to a balcony overlooking the Irrawaddy River. We could see the temple at our destination high on the mountain across from us. Those mountains, threadbare, sharp and sparsely speckled with vegetation, seemed stark and uninviting. They also looked like the holy mountains in China near the place where Bodhi Dharma, one of the early founders of Zen practice, sat in a cave in silence for nine years. What kind of energy is it that draws contemplative beings to such bare places defying survival in their ruggedness?

We walked down to the river's edge where a boatman with a small boat quoted a high price for crossing. The son of the proprietor had been very firm in saying I should not pay more than a certain sum, so I refused to go higher, wondering "now what" when we were unable to settle on a price. Ah Mo merely turned and walked quickly along the bank up river.

We walked and walked along the sandy shore and I could see no sign of a boat anywhere. The temple across the river fell behind us, and I began to groan at the thought of having to walk all the way back down on the other side. But I had placed my trust in Ah Mo. I could have 'chickened out' and turned back to the certain crossing at the higher price, but I felt that was not for me to do. Perhaps this too was to be a hard earned pilgrimage like the strangely difficult time I'd had in Thailand getting to the monastery. I was content to walk, slipping in the sand, farther and farther from the temple.

We passed a group of teenagers carrying buckets of water to a big hole in the sand near the shore. Others were working on a wooden ramp, shoveling wet sand onto it. "Gold", said Ah Mo in his brief and direct communication, pointing to the temple tops from whose domes gold leaf had peeled through the centuries, apparently settling in the shore of the river.

Ah Mo's young stride kept me pacing on. We finally came in sight of a dock ahead still a long distance away. "Ferry," said Ah Mo. And we trudged slipping in the shifting sand, till finally we reached it. It felt as if we were about two miles above the temple, and I contemplated the other side where I would have to walk two more miles back before even starting up the mountain, which looked very steep.

A boat holding perhaps twenty people came into view and all those waiting on the shore came to attention, watching it pull up, spill out the people, sacks, packages and bundles. I couldn't see any signs of civilization across the river, and wondered at the amount of baggage. Then it was our turn to walk the unsteady center of the boat, sit on a bench and watch the pilot shove off again from shore.

It was wonderful to sit down, to feel the rocking, see the water swirling, feel the air and notice the shining light of the sun catch on the ripples. The boat thankfully headed down stream so we had a longer ride to enjoy and the distance of our walk became shorter.

As we pulled into the main current of the river, which was about a quarter of a mile wide, I fell into a peaceful mood. I could see the flat plain on the left side with all the man-made 'hills' of the temples rising like a vast collection of stalagmites into the mist. It was a bit like the overwhelming feeling of Kweilin in China, seeing all the mountains that pop vertically from the flat plain stretching as far as you can see. There was a general brownness to the sight. The dusty brown earth, the brick tone of the temples, the haze, yet on the shore the Tooth Pagoda radiated its whiteness.

As I looked with the relaxed, dreamy unfocused gaze prompted by the floating feeling of the boat, I saw from the Tooth Pagoda arching upward, a purple haze, a sort of aura hanging above it, enveloping its whiteness in a purple gauze, transparent and elusive. It startled my heart. I could look away and back and still it remained. I stared at it for a long time as we floated further and further from it, until at last I turned my gaze towards the sparkling temple on the mountain above and to the right of us.

We neared the shore, slid into the sandy beach and stepped against the rounded ribs of the boat to brace, and jump to land. It was a small port; a lemonade stand supplied barefoot children with refreshing drink. I was tempted to buy some, but Ah Mo firmly set out with his pacing stride up the dirt road, round the bend and towards the sharply rising mountains.

We were alone again, passing more prickly bushes, dry creek beds, dusty trees. Everything looked parched, stiff with that enduring wait for the next rains which were still months away. The dust was one inch thick.

We rose steadily slowly until I could look back and see the river and Pegan beyond it. Then we came to a watering place. A wizened old man tended a collection of three foot-high earthenware water jars. The dipper rested on the red ceramic plate that covered each. All three were under a small roof providing shade to keep the jars cool from the already warm morning sun. It was 9:00 A M. "Rupees," Ah Mo announced, holding up two fingers. So I paid, and Ah Mo handed me the dipper full of water which had already surely serviced many pilgrims before me. Again I said my prayer for immunity and drank, smiling my thanks at the old man who seemed pleased.

Then, up stone steps we rose, slab after slab, fitted into the crusty earth. There were markers along the way, carved with the enigmatic ancient Burmese script.

We continued rising through the scanty underbrush of thorny bushes. I saw some caves in ledges of limestone off in the distance and had a sudden wondering moment when I couldn't place myself either in Burma or China, where I had walked an identical trail through the same kind of mountains to the cave of Bodhi Dharma. I'd walked that trail in November. This was March. One was in China, this one in Burma. Time smashed in like a wave receding on itself, and for an instant I was nowhere.

But still Ah Mo climbed in front of me, turning to smile encouragement. At one point he stopped to show me a resting stone, but I felt as if I were not even stepping on the stones I felt so light, and to his surprise, wanted to keep on walking. I tried to carry that awkward plastic shopping bag he gripped so tenaciously. He only offered to carry my pack too. I at least refused to let him take more of a load even if he refused to let me share his. By this time sweat was pouring off us and the smiles we exchanged of exerting together were warm and full of a shared delight to be doing this with each other. I was amazed I was not more tired.

The sharp knife edges of the hills began to show below us,

and we arrived at a covered 'hallway' of stairs. A corrugated metal roof sheltered us from the sun, supported only by posts at intervals. I could look out at the beautiful expanse of range after range of barren knife-edged mountains on either side, cut by deep drainage gullies joining the river.

Finally the endless rising stopped. We reached the first small pagoda which I had seen sparkling like a star as we crossed the river. The larger stupa was beyond another rise out of sight.

While Ah Mo shouted to someone, I found a tiny yellow flower and offered it at the stupa. There was a convenient vase where wilting flowers from some other pilgrim drooped. This process of offering flowers to a place or to a friend, taught to me by the Balinese, seemed by now a very natural act. It felt a wonderful way to recognize and pay respect to the special things that come into our lives.

A shout answered Ah Mo who brightened. "He's here!"

We went down a set of steep stone steps and arrived at an entrance to a cave in the side of the mountain, under the stupa on top. Here the yogi came to greet us, with kind sparkling eyes, round face, amazingly like, in body type and face, the abbot in Thailand. He spoke English well enough for me to understand. He wore the simple skirt worn all over Asia, which Ah Mo too was wearing. "You are very lucky." he said. "I'm not available to everyone."

With him was a tall thin bony friend with an ancient, kind hollow-cheeked face. He reminded me of Hirano Roshi at Eiheiji Temple in Japan and the old Japanese Tai Chi Master teaching Tai Chi to many Chinese in a park in Shanghai.

The yogi asked us into his cave. Part of the cave was natural, but a door had been constructed at the entrance, and it had been enlarged to about twenty feet square, leaving three foot wide columns to support the natural stone ceiling six feet above us. On the left there were two beds, or rather low wood platforms, with goat skin rugs stretched on them for "softening". The columns created areas, and we sat down in the central area in front of a Buddha carved in bas relief into the rock at the back of the cave. The yogi served us tea.

I'd never really (not consciously anyway) thought about encountering a yogi on my travels. If I had, perhaps I would have been nervous and self- conscious. But here I was, seated in his cave talking very comfortably with him. I told him I'd like very much to meditate. After tea, which was full of laughter, though I can't remember what we talked about, he set me before the stone Buddha on a small rug.

He seemed joyfully delighted to have a "student". He suggested that I picture the moon in my heart, focus on the breath at the tip of my nose.

I'd practiced zazen, or 'just sitting', for seven years and had not been particularly interested in seeking other ways. But in Japan, just before I left for the Philippines, a friend, Elliott, who was studying Zen practice, blurted out, "If I were traveling in all those countries, I'd want at least to experience the way they practiced!"

So I sat here with the Vipassana mudra, holding my right hand in my left, closing my eyes, and felt the silver full moon expand the ribs of my body. The yogi was breathing loudly, rhythmically. He'd suggested with every out breath that I think "death", with every in breath I think "life".

So I sat for a while. Somehow, no matter what method I use, the Quaker 'sitting with the light' the 'just sitting' or this way of thinking of the moon, I fall into a quiet state where my busy mind no longer focuses on ideas, where silence stretches time and where awareness of the outside world takes on a quality of detachment.

I could hear the buzzing of mosquitoes around me, yet they were no disturbance. Some time later I was aware that both Ah Mo and the yogi were fanning me to keep them off. But I sat there, I don't know how long, until the yogi said, "Time to stop".

He entered his "kitchen" area and began preparing an offering tray.

There were five small bowls of rice and one of water. The rice was a symbol of the five senses. I forget what most of the symbolism was.

He handed me the tray which I held above my nose so as not to breathe on it, and Ah Mo led me up the stairs to the large stupa. From a colored marble mosaic floor like those around the stupas in Rangoon, rose this large white circular mound maybe seventy-five feet across with the top gleaming gold. It was flanked by four smaller stupas. Tiny bells hung from spires around the base, tinkling in the strong mountain wind.

A five-foot-high bronze Buddha was placed with its back to the stupa. We stopped to give our offering. I prayed as I "felt disposed" as the yogi had suggested. I found myself praying for further understanding of the deeper part of my life and self, and for a way to truly be with others. Then we walked three times around this shining stupa 3,500 feet above the river, wind playing a chime on the bells. There was only one other person there, an older Burmese man.

We struck the many sonorous bells hanging at shoulder level from big racks. They were nearly three feet high and ornately decorated with bronze dragons and leaves winding round the circumference. They rang again at Ah Mo's bidding in a clear beautiful sound. My bells, as I learned to ring them sounded better, but not as clear as his. We laughed as I made faces at the tinny sound.

From this place on the top of the mountain, we could look down on Pegan below us across the river, and see as far as the Shwezegon temple up river from the village. We surveyed that immense stretch of pyramids rising in the haze, a fantastic tribute to the inner reaching of men.

I was struck again that expression of inner reaching took the form of building great and beautiful buildings rather than some social out-turning toward the condition of mankind. Those enormous buildings of brick and stone were intended to inspire the hearts of people. But they were standing now, stretched out across the plain, unused and empty, echoing the time of splendor of past intentions. It was the skeleton of a past era drying in the afternoon sun.

We came down the stairs again to the cave, and I had another opportunity to 'sit' while the yogi organized dinner. I wasn't very hungry, but he and Ah Mo, his friend, all watched as I ate, without eating themselves. I felt comfortable with him, as if I'd known him as a friend forever. Then it was time for them to eat and I took a short nap under the tent of mosquito netting. When I woke up, they'd finished eating, and Ah Mo was deeply asleep. So I sat again until Ah Mo woke up.

Then the yogi took us for a walk all over the mountain top. There was a monastery on a shoulder of the mountain, but the yogi seemed to prefer his isolated place. A young monk with a beautiful face came up to talk with Ah Mo. When he left, Ah Mo said "Brother". So that was why he came with so much food. The yogi said all the monks appreciated our offering.

We passed another cluster of buildings, a convent for nuns. Under an open roof were some nuns, dressed in peach colored robes, their heads showing just an inch of hair. All gave me warm wrinkled smiles. We exchanged gasshos in greeting and passed down some steep steps headed for a dazzling mini-stupa on a promontory below us.

As we walked down I felt a rush of well being, a rich feeling of the fortune of this experience. It helped me float down the trail till we reached the pagoda which the yogi said he'd repaired himself. He'd taken hundreds of bits of broken mirrors, many of them cut in diamonds and triangle shapes, and had embedded them in the white stucco till the whole thing sparkled with the innumerable facets. It was an amateur's job when examined closely, but had a wonderful effect.

"Do you feel anything?" the yogi asked, looking at me closely.

I could only own up to the pleasant sensation of well being. "You had to come here! You had to come across the ocean to this place. You were a prince once in Pegan. Then you helped build this place. You promised you'd return in another life to pray here." Well, I had no confirmation of all of that, so I politely took it with a grain of salt. However I did continue experiencing a wonderful elation. I felt apologetically dense. It was a wonderful place to be, and indeed I felt as much at home as I had in so many other places in Asia.

We stood there together looking out at Pegan which was disappearing in afternoon haze.

We climbed back up to the main stupa, going round the side to a large room with glass windows. Here in the center was a twenty-foot high standing gold Buddha made in the same style and grace matching the four Buddhas in the Ananda temple that I'd sat in early that same morning. This Buddha was holding his arm straight out pointing with his index finger at Pegan. "Buddha stood here. He came to this mountain with Ananda and looked across the river at the plain before him. He pointed and said "The *ogre* of this temple will be born a great ruler in a future life and will establish a great center of culture and university of Buddhist Studies which will become as famous as Nalanda is in India'."

There were two stone slabs about two feet long in front of the Buddha. They were shaped like feet. On them were carved all the eighty-six marks which Buddha had on the bottom of his feet. They indicated that Buddha had once stood here. I'd never heard of Buddha getting as far as Burma, but perhaps he had come up the Irrawaddy River centuries before. This mountain already had a temple on it in 600 BC and it certainly felt extremely wonderful.

We looked at the beautiful statue, standing on that mountain top, the only time in my life I would be here. Then we walked back, passing by a locked gate to a cave where the yogi said he had also sat for five years. We returned to the yogi's cave from the opposite direction from that from which Ah Mo and I had come. From this side we came on two entrances to two dark hall-like tunnels carved deeply into the rock of the mountain. The tunnel we entered led back to two large chambers where an upraised platform twelve feet long by six feet wide was carved into a truly king-sized bed with a stone "pillow" stretching along one end.

As I looked at the straight walls, the square room, the yogi said, "The Aryans carved this." I'd no idea about the Aryans except from the distortion Hitler made of them. They had practiced meditation from 6,000 to 3,000 BC.

He pointed to the bed and said, " The Super Buddhas slept here." It was a gigantic bed. I was in such a dazed state at the unbelievable nature of my being there at all that I never thought of asking who the Super Buddha were. I had a sort of vision of a Prometheus-like giant actually dwelling on the earth. I had been brought up on the myths of the Greeks, and had read of the American Indian giants that preceded man and helped him in his early development.

While I stood in those hollowed recesses of that mountain, those myths became reality for a moment. I was too amazed to think, too unclear to understand the rapid speech of my guide. Perhaps it wasn't my reasoning self that came here. I'd come here by some amazing accident and was standing inside the dark stone of a mountain like burrowing through my unconscious thought. It was not for my mind to fathom. I could only be there.

There was another chamber beside the first with a hole in the floor. This too had a gigantic bed. The yogi said once a prince and princess had practiced here. The prince was upstairs in this room, she in a cave below. He lowered food to her through the chink in the floor. He looked at me as if waiting for some reaction from me. But too bad, I was very interested, indeed, stirred by strange feelings, but felt no understanding.

Outside the corridor at the entrance were carved a peacock, and a rabbit. He said the peacock represented the sun, the rabbit the moon. "If you sit long enough, you will understand the meaning of this temple."

My guts were stirring strangely as we walked along two parallel corridors flanked on both sides by rows of sitting Buddhas with the "Touch the Earth" positions. They were painted silver. Nowhere else in my travels did I see silver Buddhas. Their headdresses seemed like ornate crowns similar to those carved in Egyptian tombs and there were wing-like projections behind the neck. When I called these to his attention he just said, "Yes".

Then we returned to his cave. He pointed to the hole in the ceiling. It was directly below the room with the hole in the floor. We ate again. I wasn't hungry, and decided to "sit" again. "Where do you want ?"

I chose the hallway cave which had a small room at one end where the yogi had sat for 6 years. He seemed pleased, but said "It will be very dark". To my surprise I wasn't feeling afraid. He gave me a small candle, an quarter of an inch in diameter, some matches and five pieces of incense. It was 7:00 PM. I figured I could sit till midnight.

He guided me to the entrance and left to return to his cave. I lighted the candle to see my way to the room. I had to cross one hallway stretching out on both sides, which gave me a bit of disquiet as the faint flickering caught the rows of seated silver Buddhas receding into blackness. I continued down the hall flanked by four seated silver Buddhas until I faced a larger Buddha at the end. To my right was the small cell about four feet long and six feet wide.

I spread my rug on the floor, lighted the incense which I could just wedge in a crack in the rock and sat down to face the wall. Then I blew out the candle. If I'd let it burn it would have burned out in one hour, and I'd have had no light to find my way outside. I preferred to sit in darkness with the faint glow of the burning incense behind me.

Time passed, and I fell into deep quiet. No magnificent thoughts, no "visions", just quiet. My legs hurt for awhile; it felt a bit chilly since I'd brought in no warm clothes except for my sweater which served better as a cushion for my ankles against the hard uneven rock.

Time passed. I looked around, the incense had burned out. It was pitch black. Incense burns about 50 minutes so I felt it was time for me to stretch my legs. I felt around for the matches and candle, lighted it and walked down the dark corridor across the open intersection of hallways where I could feel a cool draft, and a few feet further to the opening. There was the clearing, a stretch of rock ledge about 40 feet wide before dropping over the steep slope.

There were faint shadows coming from some dim electric lights in the monastery down the hill off to my left. I could hear the yogi laughing and talking to his friend and Ah Mo out of sight in the cave off to my right. I could imagine the friend smoking the foot-long cigars of rolled leaves he'd been smoking ever since I'd met him. Their reassuring voices drifted up to me. I could hear nothing when I was inside the cave.

The stars were out and I walked in my usual "kin hin" or slow walking pace for ten minutes between each sitting period. Then I turned, lighted my candle and passed again into the dark caves. I felt the creepy feeling at the intersection of hallways, and a little bit amazed at my courage, proceeded to my recessed sitting spot.

Again I lighted incense, stuck it in a crack in the rock, turned around, sat down, blew out the candle and sat in dark silence. I had decided to sit most of the periods in zazen style with open eyes. Usually, objects or the wall fade in definition and only an unfocused light or darkness remains. Here in the pitch black, the same thing happened, not necessarily light, not necessarily darkness. Only my breathing sounded down the corridors. Then that too faded from my notice. Again my feet got numb and I looked around to see that the incense had again burned out.

From my diary

I go again outside to walk under the bright stars. I see the line of planets in the sky as I saw them in Thailand. Then time to sit again.

I sit, walk, sit, walk, each time passing along that spooky row of Buddhas in and out. I don't know why I am doing this, I just am.

Towards midnight my knees are aching, the incense is all burned up and I feel drowsy. So I decide to go back to the yogi's cave to sleep for a while. As I come down the hill the yogi greets me.

"Very good" he says. I tell him that maybe I'll sit some more after a short nap. I fall asleep instantly on the hard wood platform.

I am waked up at 3:00 AM by the yogi's friend hacking and coughing in loud spasms. He's outside. I've been used to Asian coughing. Everyone seems to have fits of coughing and spitting, but after the long sitting this coughing reaches my own throat and lungs. It's time to get up. I have to step over the yogi who's sound asleep and snoring, to get to the door which I find locked. I finally find the way to slip the bar and step out into the dark. The friend greets me, points to my watch. I hold up three fingers. He nods and proceeds to light the charcoal stove.

This time I've forgotten to bring my rug or sweater though I'm gripping my candle and matches. I go again into the dark reaches of the mountain as if I've done this all my life. This time there's no glowing incense, I sit in black silence. At some time, I feel the yogi has crept down one hall to check on me, and I slip into the breathing he taught me. Hard in, hard out, but this fades, and I'm unaware even of my breath.

There is a flapping sound down the corridor, a rat or bat, I can't tell. I'm too still to wonder at it. Time seems nonexistent.

Finally Ah Mo comes down the side corridor with a candle to tell me it's time for us to go down the mountain. I rise and as I get my legs to stand, he catches what appears to be a bird. Had it gotten caught inside or did he bring it in with him?

The yogi greets us very pleased at my long sitting. As we come out into the bright light, Ah Mo hands the bird to me. "You let it go", says the yogi. "You are very lucky". I open my hands and the startled yellow bird sits in my hands, then takes off flapping its black wings in the morning air. It feels good to let him go, but I wonder if he's been captured for just that purpose. What bird would get trapped in that dark cave?

We eat breakfast, rice and tea. This time the yogi joins me. I still feel comfortable with him. During our talks, I comment on how much I love the beauty of this earth, how hard it will be to leave it behind.

"Now you're talking like an ordinary person. You're changing. Your mind is changing", he says. I feel that's true, that as I have traveled and sat, I've changed some, but can't tell how. I do feel as if this unusual night of stillness, sitting under a Buddha relic inside a mountain hollowed since the time of the Aryans, has changed me, but how?

The cheerful yogi walks us to the steps where the descent of the mountain begins. "I'll come to see you in America to check on your sitting", he tells me as we say goodbye. I may never figure out what happened at this meeting, but I'm truly grateful for it.

It's early dawn, and the light of the sun gilds all the dry shrubbery. I take Ah Mo up again to the great white stupa above for one last circling, and ringing of the bells. Then we start our descent.

Just at the beginning of the stairs is a scaly outcropping of cracking lava rock only about a yard long. One end juts out of the earth. Ah Mo stops and points. "Serpent" he says, "Tail." as he motions a waving underground and surfacing. Then he points across the river at Shwezegon. "Head." I gather there's a belief this vein of lava snakes under the earth and surfaces at Shwezegon.

I decide we'll see that together this afternoon when we get back. It's a fitting end to this incredible pilgrimage. He understands and grins warmly. Then points to me and says "mother" to himself "son". I feel that too. Without talking we've formed a loving relationship that will last for ages. Perhaps it already has.

Despite only three hours sleep, I'm full of fresh energy and we go down, easily passing the familiar landmarks. The valley stretches out below us coming closer as we go down in the golden morning light. Children are already out grazing scrawny water buffaloes.

We reach the river where an enormous ferry boat is docked. Many people are waiting for this once-a day landing, and we stand with them. Shy children peek from behind mother's skirts; one smiling girl plays with me with some stones in the sand. At first the adults look quizzically at me, then smile in a friendly way. I get the feeling not many Westerners come here.

When I get back across the river we walk to the Shining Tooth Pagoda and ring the bells on this side of the river. There's a building with open doors where inside, a painting of the Tooth Pagoda is framed and hangs on the wall with pictures of many monks around it. Around the Tooth Pagoda the artist has painted the purple aura I saw when I was on the river! So at least it wasn't just my hallucination. Others see it too.

I look across at that high mountain stupa shining gold. Its subsidiary mirrored pagoda sparkles flashes of light, and I wonder how I ever got there. I even wondered if I had only been there in a dream.

We walked back through the bamboo village past the ruined temple with the uncovered brick Buddhas. This time I plowed through the underbrush to stand before that peaceful face oblivious of the crumbling ruins around him. Even here in this tumbledown temple someone had brought offerings of flowers and there were the remains of burned incense.

It reminded me of the foundations cut in bare rock along the beach in Bali where long ago a temple must have stood and where people continued to leave offerings of flowers in bamboo boxes that floated in the pools washed up by the waves. Pegan had been a flourishing community, but only the brick temple skeletons remain. The people lived in bamboo houses much like the ones we walked beside in the morning light. Only a spirit of caretaking remained. The villagers couldn't rebuild, but they continue to show their respect with offerings.

I myself have continued to "pay respect" in a sense to past experiences or memories that my life has long since outdistanced. To see that tendency depicted outward symbolically in at least two places, (Pegan and Bali) and find my mind perceiving it as a somewhat empty act, was like looking inward at my own life patterns. I kept a chair used by my father for many years after he died. One leg was beyond repair and no one could comfortably sit on it. I kept it out of memory for him, yet nothing about him was in that chair, except that he'd sat in it.

Do we pay homage to the energy invested in an object by people with any benefit to ourselves? What does it mean when material things begin to crumble? Are they sinking into the forgetfulness of the unreality they came from? Why was I standing on these sites invested with the vitality 9000 years before and feeling stirred?

I had no answer.

Ah Mo and I walked back to my guest house. I needed to "take a shower" with dipper, rest in the shade for a while. Then we would go together to Shwezegon Pagoda to finish our pilgrimage.

Chapter 37 - Shwezegon

We set off for the Shwezegon temple in afternoon light. The horse pulling our carriage had the benefit of a ludicrous looking diaper, a canvas arrangement tied under his tail to catch any droppings which might dirty the unpaved street.

We drove beyond the greater concentration of temples, passed through an ancient gate and trotted along the dusty road. We passed a wide dirt road bordered by huge carved stone lions reminding me of the row of carved animals that flank the road to the Ming Tombs in China. This must have been the road taken by kings in ancient times. No one used it now.

Finally the magnificent golden dome of Shwezegon came into view. The bell shaped spire hung in the sky as large as the Schwedegon temple in Rangoon, but here it dominated comparative wilderness. I pictured how Pegan must have been centuries ago as a thriving metropolis and wondered if it served as a prophesy of a future Rangoon. Do we always build our own memorials in the shape of cathedrals and temples to witness our existence when all else has crumbled? Perhaps that glimpse of its graceful grandeur would have been better to keep in memory than what followed.

We drove to a parking lot, and immediately from every direction swarms of vendors shoved everything at us from shoes to incense. As we entered a hall, the stalls selling flowers and Buddha statues were all that caught my eye. Everyone pushed to catch our attention.

The peace and stillness I'd had experienced in the past twenty-four hours still rested inside me, and I managed to cut a path through the confusing crowds. I really don't remember much of that temple except that it was beautiful and that most of the crowds there were either tourists who had come to "see" it or vendors who were eager to make money off the tourists.

With some difficulty Ah Mo and I discovered the other end of the "serpent" or outcropping of rock which was supposed to stretch between the temple on the mountain and this temple where a Buddha relic was enshrined. Off in a side court, it was painted with garish colors and not truly recognizable, but then the atmosphere of profiteering was covering the inner temple like a garish paint job as well.

Ah Mo and I walked three times around the central gilded stupa to complete our pilgrimage and left, glad to be free of all those grasping hands.

I returned "home" too tired to go on another trip to see any more of those magnificent temples. I rested and read the small leaflet given me by the landlord on Vipassana meditation, discussing breathing, from the Rangoon Center for Meditation. "The tip of the nose is the center of sensation. While concentrating there, it becomes impossible to allow all the fits of thought that come into being. We are therefore free from Karma while sitting."

Maybe that's what happened while I sat in that dark hallway on the mountain. The little coils of reality that uncoil as I think stopped their dreamlike creations and all things stopped being as I sat.

The brochure also said there were three things essential to being a Buddhist. The first one was "Absolute Morality". My eye stopped at that idea. I don't remember the rest.

Ever since arriving in Burma I had carried that heavy load of liquor and cigarettes. Sideways, I'd hoped I could do what everybody else was doing - sell it on the black market. I hadn't brought myself to do it yet. Still the temptation played in my mind. I would be the only traveler in Burma who didn't take advantage of that opportunity. I could pay for my whole stay with one exchange. It didn't feel right, but still the idea of having extra money tingled my imagination.

Absolute morality is hard to maintain in a world where everyone else is doing something slightly less moral. The memory of all those greedy hands reaching towards me at Shwezegon, or more broadly all over Indonesia, tumbled in my thoughts as if they were the embodiment of my own greed. I felt if I cashed in on that liquor now, I'd merely create a host of greedy hands to confront me further on. I couldn't do it. I played with the thought of carrying it with me all the way to Nepal, and eventually finding someone who wanted to drink it. I knew I wasn't going to sell it.

The hard climb of the day before, the all night sitting, the hot day plummeted me into sleep. I didn't wake up till 5:00 AM the next day. It was my last day in Pegan. I went to the Ananda Temple to sit again as completion of the whole experience. I walked along the dirt road in the semi-dark and came to the great wooden door at the entrance. This time, I was familiar with procedure and left my shoes with a smiling clerk.

I settled down on one of the rugs in front of the great golden standing Buddha whose graceful drapery glistened in the sub-dued light. His upraised hand was like a sermon speaking of that Absolute Morality each one must hold inside himself. The stillness I'd experienced on the mountain hung about me as I sat wondering at the whole adventure. Then I rose, walked along the inner corridor. The four standing Buddhas facing the four directions down here were identical with the golden Buddhas on the mountain pointing to the plain of Pegan. As I circled the four directions, I knew what I was going to do with the liquor and cigarettes.

I walked back marveling at all the golden spires of the nearby temples catching the clear light of the still rising sun. I looked back once at the white marble Ananda Temple gleaming like a cathedral in its magnificence with all its ornate carvings.

I was just in time for breakfast. The 'landlord' who had loaned me the leaflet on Meditation and his son were there. I told them about the liquor. I wanted to give it to them with the hope that they could share the profit with Ah Mo's family of seven broth-ers and sisters. They were delighted. The son immediately said they'd give the cigarettes to the yogi ! When Ah Mo came to say goodbye, I asked the son to explain that this gift of the liquor wasn't in payment for his guidance on our pilgrimage. I knew Ah Mo had been a companion on that trip and that he had wanted no compensation for it. We'd shared a beautiful time of close affection and I treasured that. Rather, as a result of my experiences, I had considered the effect of my own greed and wanted to relieve myself of the liquor. I wanted his family to share in what came from the liquor as a partner to my insights.

Very shortly I received an invitation to come next door to visit with Ah Mo's family. His mother, whose happy voice I'd heard singing over the fence, was beautiful. I recognized his step-father as one of the temple elders I'd had tea with on my first visit to the Ananda Temple. He was a quiet man who asked me to offer incense before his altar with a picture of his Vipassana teacher on it. We shared tea and the company of people from different worlds who respected and appreciated each other.

It was time to leave. I gave a big loving hug to Ah Mo and warmly took leave of two families I'd come to hold with warm affection, knowing we'd probably never see each other again.

At the airport I met again all the foreign tourists I'd lost sight of since I came. They'd stayed in a more Western atmosphere, had eaten in the one Western style restaurant and had seen a different Pegan.

The small plane took off and below us stretched the tiny pyramids across the sandy earth. The river seemed to slice the flat plain off from the area of jagged mountains stretching beyond view. My eye caught one flash of light from the temple on the ridge and we turned towards Rangoon.

Chapter 38 - On to Nepal

I was told that the free limousine to the Airport left from the Burma Airways office on the river front at 4:30 AM. I got up at 3:30, got the sleepy clerk who slept on a cot in the hall, to unlock the padlock and let me out the front door. I walked in the dark down to the old decaying Burma Airways building along the empty streets of Rangoon.

When I got to the road along the river, I could see small camp fires. People clustered around them talking and laughing as if they had never been to sleep. I was the only one waiting, and I was a half an hour early.

As I sat on the steps watching the stars above the river, a man left a large campfire across the street and came towards me. When he got close enough, I could feel his relaxed curiosity about this person waiting so early for the bus.

I asked him why the group of people were up so early around the campfires. "They live there", he said. They were men without families who had very little money. They slept under the trees, though none of them slept for long. During the day they repaired the roads and begged. At night they kept warm by the fires. His attitude towards this sparse life of his was cheerful and accepting. He liked it.

The humor and good nature of this man were delightful. As he observed the hardships of his life, it was with an amused broad tolerance for the lives of everyone rich and poor. Everything he said was in the simplest of language because he spoke broken English, but I had the feeling I was talking to a very profound philosopher. He asked about my life and why I traveled alone, seeming to understand the freedom of adventure, yet he'd never left Rangoon.

On that roadside in the early dawn, I felt a very warm tie to this simple contented man. The sense of kinship leaps the barriers of economic class and nationalities. I know that for those moments in Rangoon I'd talked to someone I was related to whether in some other time or only in similar mental attitude. There were times as I waited that we didn't talk at all, just sat there hearing the laughter from the campfires, and the sounds of activity on the boats by the dock. I felt that in a way he was protecting me in the dark shadows of the steps. He never asked for anything.

When the limousine drove up, I shook his hand "Like an American" and then we gasshoed to each other like the Burmese. It was as if I were saying goodbye to a brother. His eyes were so gentle despite the hardships of life. Then I climbed into the shiny limousine, sat on the fine upholstery and rode in comfort from the chilling winds to the airport.

That peculiar juxtaposition of life on the cold Rangoon streets with nothing but a campfire and a cooking wok, and the comfort of the upholstered seats of the airplane, the uniformed stewards bringing sweet rolls and coffee while I soared above the earth, overwhelmed me again.

We flew towards the Himalayas that looked like white snow-capped teeth biting the blue air along the horizon. Then slowly the plane descended as we looked down on the green steps of terraced rice and corn fields carved into steep mountains, and we were in the Kathmandu Valley in Nepal.

I'd been wanting to go on a back-packing trek in Nepal, and had been worried that the trekking season was almost over. In fact I'd tried to bypass Burma in order to make it to Nepal in time. Again, it seemed that the events of this trip were happening not from my planning. I had to stop in Burma because the airline ticket couldn't be changed. It felt as if the whole magic adventure in Pegan had to happen. I couldn't have avoided it.

I found the Western quarter of Kathmandu and crashed head on into tourists from all over the world. It was nice to be near a real shower again, and I found a single room in a modest hotel with a bed and electric light, access to hot boiled water, and an Asian toilet. I sank down on the bed and slept. When I woke up, I was woozy, nauseated and wanted only to sleep some more. For several days any thought of back-packing was impossible. I'd been traveling since August. It was now March, seven months of shifting, being in new places, seeing new things. It was time for a rest.

There were book shops and restaurants. I purchased The Snow Leopard and settled down to sleep and read for the next week. As I opened The Snow Leopard, there was a dedication to Eido Shimano Roshi, the Zen Master I'd first seen in August in Boulder and with whom I'd gone on the pilgrimage through China. In a way I'd felt as if most of my pilgrimage was over when I left Burma. I couldn't believe any more experiences would just happen to me. This just reminded me not to expect anything.

I learned to my relief that there was still snow on the passes, and there was time before the monsoons to trek. I realized however, I was too weary to try hiking, and needed just to recuperate.

I began wandering the streets of Kathmandu, getting lost in the winding streets and almost by accident coming out at some familiar landmark. Here for the first time I saw the sacred cows I'd heard of so much. They meandered down the main streets, and lay placidly waiting for the traffic to go around them.

The whole city was an experience of visually beautiful colorful vignettes. I'd felt the experience of touch with the wind and air of the Philippines, the moisture of tornado humidity, the feel of gentle breezes and warm sun. In Indonesia, I'd encountered the impact of sound, the noises of sweeping, the calls to Muslim prayers. In Thailand and Burma, I'd felt the impact of light - the golden light of dawn or sunset shining on the gold topped stupas or the gold carved roofs of the temples, and the silver river ribbon of the moonlight on the river. Here I saw the color, form, and imagery of Nepal. Everywhere there was a picture, from the clusters of sometimes nine dogs sleeping on the street, to the ornately carved window frames, to gatherings of women and children around the water fountains washing their great brass water jugs, and talking in the early morning. Everything was a visual feast.

Down by the garbage-strewn river, pigs, ducks, water buffaloes and people alike bathed, washed vegetables, and drank the water together.

The wrinkled, high-cheeked, jolly faces of old men peered out from tobacco stalls, seed stores, hardware shops. Old bent-over women walked with offerings to the giant Kali statue, a big black demon-like deity of creation and destruction which dominated one square.

Hindu Shiva shrines seemed embedded in the brick sidewalks. The bull appeared on many streets. Women in colorful saris walked with baskets and shopping bags, many Tibetan-dressed women sold vegetables in an array of bright orange carrots, purple beets, green chard, white garlic, and unidentifiable Asian greens and brown roots that appeared in the morning market and were gone by midday. Sometimes I couldn't recognize the same street at different times of the day. The character and usage changed so much.

It was approaching April, when my friends back in California would be convening for a week-long sesshin or meditation period which usually went from April 1st to the 8th. I wondered where I could find a quiet place myself. I was sitting in a restaurant drinking fruit juice when a young woman sat at my booth because the restaurant was full. As we talked, I realized she was active with the groups studying Tibetan Buddhism in Kathmandu. I asked if she knew any place where I could go on retreat. She drew me a map of a "good place" telling me how to catch the bus and hike three hours to get there. It seemed just my speed.

Leaving the larger part of my pack in a storeroom of my hotel, I took a day pack with only the things I needed - a camera I'd gotten second hand, a change of clothes, and a sweater.

I took the local buses which collected in a large paved lot, strewn with lettuce and cabbage leaves being munched on by wandering cattle. The buses were the most rickety looking I'd seen in all of Asia, but people piled in, confident they would get them to their destination. I found my bus and sat down next to a window and waited as people crowded in. A mother with a tiny baby sleeping in her arms sat next to me. She was struggling with her shopping bags, and to her surprise, I offered to hold the baby. We smiled and the baby continued to sleep in my lap. The mother seemed greatly relieved of her burden for a while and let the baby stay there. I realized not many tourists used these buses, and I'd already gotten feelings from the country natives that tourists who brought needed money were otherwise a big bother. With the baby in my arms, everyone grinned and accepted me, smiling goodbye as they got off.

Enormous bags of rice and baskets of greens were unloaded from the roof at small villages along the way. Each village center had its great banyan tree. Nearly all other trees had been cut down for firewood, but these great wide-trunked sacred trees remained and served as the only shade for people who were almost always clustered around the base. They were perfect for bus stops.

Finally, after about three hours, we arrived at Dulikel where I found the Lodge, the only hotel for Westerners. I slept the night since I wanted to see the sunrise come over the mountains from a Hindu shrine on a hill above the village.

I took a walk in the late afternoon through the brick constructed town. I smiled and talked in a friendly way for awhile with some women and their teenage daughters in a central square, but after I left them, a group of children followed me, appearing amazingly unfriendly. One girl offered me popcorn, thrusting it aggressively in my pockets when I refused. I'd seen the approving eyes of elders who obviously approved of this form of begging on the part of the children. Apparently French travelers who come often to this spot gave small coins to the children, and they'd come to demand it.

I tried ignoring the troop of about 15 who followed me until I came to a Shiva temple. It was on a little hill, and a gateway separated it from the street. I hesitated, since I wasn't sure whether a foreigner would be allowed to enter, but two young women above beckoned me up the stairs to the top. I could see in the three directions into tiers of hills towards the setting sun beyond. I examined the carvings on the corners of the small shrine. Lions with paws extended reminded me of carvings on temples in both Nikko in Japan and Bali in Indonesia.

I walked to the end of the town with the children trooping after me. I'd tried to be friendly, but when I didn't give them money they badgered me. One little girl tried to pull up my skirt, two others threw some small tomato fruit at me. I walked on quietly ignoring them but they wouldn't go away. When I sat down near a peaceful banyan tree, pointed to the setting sun so we could watch together, two boys stood in front of me in audacious challenge. I couldn't figure out what was the cause of their obvious hostility that wouldn't melt under any approach. I finally turned and walked back to the lodge. Still some followed me. The teenage boys tried to stop me, and finally I said in quick anger "That's enough, go away"! It was the only time in all my travels where I felt unwelcome and unable to cross the bounds of fear and suspicion.

Fortunately they left, but I returned ruffled and uncomfortable. There was a young German couple staying for the night and as we talked, I learned they too had experienced the hostile aggression from the people. They had walked down the streets where dogs were sleeping. (As far as I could tell dogs barked all night and slept all day everywhere in Nepal.) Children had prodded the dogs and sicced them on the couple.

This couple also felt that the habit of travelers, who thinking they were being benevolent gave coins to the children, had begun to change the character of the countries visited. Instead of enjoying what was given, children had begun to demand more and to develop ways to extort money from the tourists.

In the morning, an hour and a half before sunrise, I packed the sandwich they'd made for me the night before and started up the hill towards a temple outside the town. I didn't have to go through the town this time and with relief walked away from it. Quite a few people were awake, even at 4:30 AM. There were women bringing offerings of flowers and jars of water. They took some short cuts, but I wasn't sure they were going the same way until one of them waved to me to follow her. On up to the top of the rise we climbed and made our offerings at a small temple at the very top. I'd picked a flower from the road and offered it as the women smiled and approved.

Their braided hair and high cheeks reminded me of American Indian women. We sat in silence waiting for the sun. I wondered for an instant whether I was on a hilltop in New Mexico sitting with some Navajo Indians waiting for the sun to rise.

It was cloudy, and I wasn't sure we'd even see the sun. I looked in the same direction the others were looking at what I thought was the horizon. Suddenly, the first orange light appeared high off the 'ground' with an obvious nick in it where an invisible mountain peak revealed only its negative silhouette. I had a momentary sense of the true height of the Himalayas, since the great gap between the visible horizon and that toothy profile in front of the enlarging sun was like a wide band of dark sky with pointy ridges. We shared that dawning and then it was time to go on. A boy who had been standing by asked where I was going. When I said Namo Buddha, he offered to guide me.

The proprietor had tried to arrange a guide for me in Dulikel, but I'd felt I'd rather go alone. But this young boy of maybe twelve years old, I liked. He spoke more English than Ah Mo, seemed polite and eager. So I accepted.

Chapter 39 - Namo Buddha

First Victor, as he introduced himself, wanted to tell his father where he was going. So we descended a side of the mountain I would have to climb again, and went along a ridge bordered by terraces of knee-high corn. He pointed to one field. "I planted that. It's my field," he said with pride.

Just when I was afraid we were going to descend all the way deep into the valley below, we came to a set of stone houses where a water buffalo, pigs and chickens filled the tiny yard. Victor's slender father came out to greet me and ask me in for tea. He spoke English well and guided me through the dark room where his wife was heating water on a charcoal stove. The whole house was made of stone with mud smeared like stucco all over the inside walls to cut the drafts. The ceiling was black from the cooking smoke.

We climbed a set of steep wooden steps to a sort of loft where beds lay on the floor. Here we sat and drank tea and talked. The father wanted me to stay with his family, and I'd have loved it but was eager to get to Namo Buddha. I could see that Victor made a good contribution to the family income by guiding people. His father had taught him English, was teaching him the Hindu Scriptures in Sanskrit, and even offered to teach me if I chose to take the time. It was a fine family to be with, so different in feeling from Dulikel.

After perhaps an hour, we started back up the same hill we'd just descended, then took a side trail through more flat terraces on the steeply sloped mountain. Everyone seemed to be growing wheat and corn. The people we met on the trails were carrying hundred and forty pound bags of grain along the hilly trails to Dulikel where they caught the bus to Kathmandu. There they would exchange it for rice. That explained the heavy sacks of rice I'd seen on the bus coming up. It was too dry on the hills to grow rice.

At the top of one hill Victor pointed to a distant banyan tree many miles away. "Namo Buddha", he said. Then looking back, we could see the banyan tree on the hill top where we'd watched the sunrise. Those were the only trees visible on the barren mountain landscape, trees too sacred to be used as firewood.

We walked for three hours along a road flanked by the terraces of plots only twenty feet across. An occasional stone house was perched along the unpaved dirt road. We could see out over long valleys to the horizon where hanging in a faint veil were the white, high Himalayas. Then after passing through a tiny village we came to a whitewashed stupa about fifty feet across. On the other side was the trail that led to the very top of the mountain. We had arrived at Namo Buddha.

I was tired, thirsty and still didn't know if they would let me stay on the hilltop retreat. The girl who had drawn me a map had said there was a small hotel where I could sleep on the lower level near the stupa if there wasn't room for me on the top of the mountain.

As we walked up, there were several Tibetan monks seated on the ground in the sun along a grassy walkway that paralleled a rectangular cement building with seven small cubicles. Luckily, among the monks was a young English monk with whom I could talk about the odd way I'd learned of this place and my wish to meditate for a few days if it was possible. "You're lucky," he said, "There are only two places for people staying a short time. I've got one, and the other one became vacant just today because the person who had it became sick and left this morning".

He translated what I wanted to one of the five monks who were there sitting in the sun. I was immediately shown to a small room with a bed and desk and the remains of a half burned candle for light. The cost of staying was reasonable, and I could eat my meals with them. There it was. I said an affectionate goodbye to Victor, stuck some rupees in his pocket and gave him the sandwiches which were left. I'd come to feel almost as close to him as I had to Ah Mo.

It was almost noon, and I talked with Phillip, the English monk. He said the monks were practicing to become lamas. They had to stay on the hilltop without leaving for three years, three months, three weeks and three days. They woke up at 3:00 AM and chanted in their own rooms, then meditated till breakfast at 7:00. Then they held a Puja, or chanting ceremony, together after breakfast to which I could come if I wanted.

I was free to sit where I wanted. They would ring a bell for dinner. I walked around the main building which had the Buddha Hall at the end, and the rows of seven rooms each about nine or ten feet square. The kitchen was a tiny hut at the end of the long set of rooms. A huge pile of wood was stacked against the outside wall. There was no electricity. I discovered a stupa, smaller than the one I'd seen down by the village. This one was at the very peak of a hill above the meditation cells and was almost hidden by the lines of prayer flags stretching from the top like clothes lines. It cast the only shade in the area.

When I looked around for a place to sit zazen, I found a small stupa about five feet across and about eight feet high located on a promontory away from the complex of rooms. There was a flat grassy space there which felt like a very good place to meditate. I could see down the hills on three sides over terraces and winding paths that led to the valleys far below. It felt so good to sit quietly after the clatter of Kathmandu. The atmosphere here was one of stillness.

So I settled easily into a routine. At three a.m. each morning, when the monks began their chanting and clashing of bells, I sat zazen in my small room with lighted candle and incense. As dawn light came, I moved down to my open area beyond a banyan tree by the small stupa. I sat on the open hilltop every morning until the meal bell rang at seven, and after breakfast until it was too hot at about ten. Usually, then I moved up under the prayer flags for shade and sat. Every afternoon, the monks did a second Puja, which I attended. The clanging of bells, blowing of horns and chanting mixed in with my memories of the chants of the nuns in the Philippines, the Muslim call to prayer, the

Thailand monastery, and the monks chanting at Eiheiji in Japan. All of them used sound to establish a state of mind.

For the five days I stayed there, we ate the same food at each meal. Breakfast consisted of a dumpling with peanut butter inside it, lunch was cooked cabbage and cauliflower in a soup, dinner was rice with lentil sauce. There was no variation. That was what was available. We had a tea which really startled me the first day. It was salty. Apparently the Tibetans mix salt in their tea as we use sugar. The monks laughed at my surprise as I tasted it. I was able to drink one cup with them daily, but I did sneak into the small shack where the young male cook offered me plain tea to quench my thirst.

I discovered the cook's wife carrying water uphill from the spring in a brass jar. There was no ready water on the top of the mountain. When, after several days, I wanted to take a bath, Phillip pointed down the hill along a steep dirt path. It was the first time I had left the top, and it seemed like going into another world. When I got to the watering spot, half way down the mountainside, some of the neighboring farmers' wives were washing their clothes. Not wanting to interrupt, I sat down and waited. I watched them use a dipper to pour water over the clothes which rested on a rock. They kneaded the soapy clothes, like bread, rinsing them by pouring more water over them.

Phillip, the English monk, had told me that animals take precedence at the spring. As the women finished, a teenage boy came with his herd of cows. They sucked the sweet water each in turn since there was only a small puddle. Then he just stood and stared at me as I proceeded awkwardly to wash my slacks and shirt. It was obvious he had no intention of leaving. So I negotiated my bath under the canopy of my skirt while he looked on. I imagined the hilarious laughter that must have accompanied his story of this to his family.

I noticed here what even several days of quiet sitting did in helping me. I proceeded with what I'd come to do, having seen the women also bathe topless. He could do what he wanted. As

I finished, and left, I saw him turn his cows down the path. The show was over.

I had only my wet clothes to carry, but climbing back up the steep path in the dust generated enough sweat and dust for me to feel as if I'd never taken a bath when I got to the top of the hill twenty minutes later. My respect for the young woman daily carrying water (about sixty gallons in the brass jar) for the monks swelled to admiration.

One day there was great commotion. I'd come up the hill after my morning sitting in the open, when a clanging of bells and blowing of horns announced the arrival of a whole retinue of lamas and Rinpoches, old and young. These were members, as I gathered, of a different sect from the monks here on the mountain. They'd come to chant around the stupa and erect fresh prayer flags.

They collected on the grassy walkway and began printing. They rolled ink on wood blocks about ten by sixteen inches in size which they pressed on a gauzy material they had brought with them. I had seen a fresh pile of green bamboo poles arrive a few days before, and now monks industriously erected these poles adding to the older yellow ones already covering the stupa. They hung the prayer flags on ropes so they looked like a wash hanging out to dry. I had wondered why they had let the old flags get to looking so ragged and faded. Apparently they erected new ones every year, adding to the worn out ones which they didn't remove.

They gathered under the fluttering lines and began a Puja in front of a row of at least thirty lighted butter lamps, tiny brass squares holding a wick which burned in yak butter. Under the shaded canopy of prayer flags, they began a rhythmic chant which hung like a veil in that open cloister round the stupa.

There was a young monk, maybe ten years old, who someone said was a reincarnated lama. He chanted without the use of a sutra book, though most of his older companions held these in front of them. His high voice mingled with the low rumble of the older men. There were three venerable monks who directed the changes from one chant to another.

I was standing on the side, watching, when a monk motioned for me to sit down, took my camera, and took a picture of me. He commented that I might want a photograph of them. I had wanted one, but was reticent to take a picture until given permission. They seemed so casual in the midst of all this high ceremony, so full of laughter. It was a contrast to the quiet sitting I'd been doing. When they left, it felt like an even greater silence.

Much of the time there was just quiet. I watched beautiful black and white butterflies that looked, when their wings spread out, like skeletons. The interplay of life and death for so big and small, "important and unimportant", on this planet seemed to stretch in an endless pageant passing through my watching eye impersonally. For a while on that mountain top nothing seemed particularly surprising. Everything seemed to just breathe out and in, in an on-goingness, and I sat there and observed it, or was a part of it, or just breathed. The quiet settled in my bones.

It was around this time I began noticing the ravens. These sleek black birds perched and squawked near me like some shadow of the black robed monks in Japan. They came quite close while I sat. They sat with me as the spider did in Thailand. A deep feeling of serenity settled around me.

So far, I'd been sitting the "sesshin" or week-long sitting which we do in April around the time set by the Japanese as Buddha's birthday, April 8th. It suddenly occurred to me I could visit Lumbini on the 8th. What a nice way to end this sitting time. I felt immediately that it was time to go. I had already been sitting five days. As I prepared to go, the monks with whom I'd sat posed for pictures, each gave me a warm goodbye. One even gave me a silk scarf to take with me.

Chapter 40 - Lumbini

It was the sixth day of April. In the early morning I started down the narrow path from Namo Buddha, my small pack on my back. On a level shoulder below the hilltop was the large stupa where the fingernails and teeth of Buddha in a previous life were enshrined. It was surrounded by pilgrims who had walked long distances to give offerings. They were Hindus as far as I could tell. Each had a bright red paint spot on the forehead between the eyes. It seemed to be the badge of recognition for having visited a holy place. They too were celebrating Buddha's birthday. I made an offering of a few coins along with flowers picked from the path. A man standing next to the small niche where the offerings were made reached out quickly and dabbed red paint on my forehead too.

Most visitors only stayed long enough to make their offerings and circle the stupa before turning back down the hill again, so I was accompanied by whole families carrying heavy baskets of food, their goats trotting freely beside them. The path led through terraced hillsides of corn and wheat down to a flat fertile valley where irrigation ditches divided rice fields. Young boys were washing big black water buffaloes in the algae-green water of one ditch. Occasional villages of mud brick houses flanked the fairly wide dirt road. Chickens and pigs wandered in and out between children and dogs.

After three hours, we came to a bus stop I'd noticed on my way up the week before. I had, by using a different path, completed a wide circle around the mountain. Here all the heavy-laden farmers heaved their wheat sacks into the rickety bus, and we all found seats, even if most of the wood slats were slanting or broken.

My seat was tilted where the wood had slipped through the support, so I balanced uncomfortably for two hours. I caught one beautiful view of the white Himalayas as we descended the windy road into the enormous Kathmandu valley. Everything looked green. New crops were sprouting.

We passed an area which must have supplied most of the bricks in Kathmandu. There were deep square cuttings in the yellow clay by which stood piles of newly formed bricks. The old mounds where kilns hid under piles of earth, sprouted tall brown smokestacks. They were surrounded by piles of red baked bricks. There were so few trees, no wonder the need for bricks in construction. But I wondered what they used as fuel to bake the bricks.

Then we entered the chaotic suburbs of Kathmandu and drove into the garbage-littered bus station. I decided to walk back to the central bus station many blocks away. After the clean silence of Namo Buddh with its green countryside, the shabby street fronts, garbage heaps, and people everywhere met me with a newer confusion.

The bus to Lumbini didn't leave until dawn the next day, so I walked back to the hotel I'd stayed in before I left. It was full, but the attendant showed me an unfinished cement room they were constructing where I could sleep on the floor, so I spread out my sleeping bag and rested. It seemed the tourist season was just beginning.

Next morning I walked to the bus station through the quiet streets.

All the open stalls were closed with wooden doors which gave the impression of permanent walls. The garbage of the day before had been swept away, and the only people I met were the early-rising women bringing flower and rice offerings to the Shiva shrines and Buddhist stupas scattered around the city. What a pleasant peace.

The bus ride was an eight hour speed race in a rattling bus that should have gone five miles an hour, and I imagined it leaving vital screws, nuts and bolts all along the bumpy dirt road that wound along a canyon above a river raging in torrents, far below.

We could have been riding along the approach to Yosemite park, the terrain seemed so similar, and only the children, cows, and dogs, scurrying to the side of the road as the bus blasted through the tiny towns, brought me back to the reality of Nepal.

As we went south the land got progressively more parched. The occurrence of trees diminished till there were only a few dusty stumps to show there once had been large trees growing.

We reached a village by the river that we'd been following along the canyon. It marked a flat muddy expanse between barren sandy shores. We drove the big bus onto the most inadequate looking ferry I'd seen. There were two large row boats with planks across them, and we straddled the two boats. Everyone seemed confident that this would make it across the river, and it did, though we all stood on the planking outside the bus as we half floated and half rowed across. I saw the structure of a new bridge downstream against the setting sun - a promise of a more secure crossing in years to come.

In the late afternoon sun the dust on the road, stirred up by the cattle and some few cars, rose in a beautiful golden haze to cover the barrenness of the earth. Yet I could still see the stubby growth choked with dust and the caked clay earth.

Through the dark we rode, bumped into numbness. Then up on a hillside I spotted a line of bonfires. At first I thought it was a fire out of control, yet all along the way I saw more and more fires set in a row and burning with no sign of people to tend them. I'd seen the burning of rice hulls in Bali and wondered if they were some seasonal part of farming here. Yet the fires appeared through the trunks of trees in a forested place, on hillsides, and on open fields. Finally someone got on the bus who spoke English enough to say "Buddha - Birthday".

A full moon had risen through the still golden haze and now answered back from the sky with its bright light. It seemed as if this trip was a continuing celebration. In Thailand, I'd celebrated Buddha's birth, death, and Enlightenment. Now it appeared I could share Buddha's birthday with all those fire builders in the dark all the way to Lumbini.

I felt suddenly truly like a pilgrim, seeing the lights that Buddha's teaching had kindled over 25 centuries ago still burning, a tribute in the dark. We stopped at a village one hour short of Lumbini. A bus would leave for Lumbini in the morning, and I had to sleep in a "hotel" there.

Fortunately I was up early and on a bus which waited until it was so full that not another being could fit inside. Many people were headed for Lumbini. As we waited, a beautiful Hindu woman with a light blue sari sat down opposite me. She had a tiny baby wrapped inside the folds of the sari, and a portion looped over her head like a soft blue shawl. She sat serenely watching the child. I felt that Jesus' mother, Mary, must have looked exactly like that.

In fact, it was my first recognition of that costume common to all women in the East. As I watched her soft beautiful face and gentle patience, my mind saw the "Hindu" garment which had cloaked a Jewish mother who had a son that began the Christian religion. Buddha's mother was a Hindu who bore a son that started the Buddhist religion. All the differences melted with that loving mother on her way to pay devotion to Buddha. He was one of the great beings that arrive on this earth periodically to remind us of what we all have in common beneath our apparent differences - a brotherhood of compassion.

We drove through dry flat land with hovels made of twigs on the side of the road. An elephant, bearing loads of grain bags, paced by in the opposite direction, and no one even craned his neck as I did in astonishment. Elephants were common here, though I couldn't see how, in this neglected land, they could produce enough food to keep them.

Finally the bus stopped. We were in Lumbini. I remembered the question someone asked me - "Why do you want to go to Lumbini? there's nothing there?"

There were no visible buildings, but there were wagons and

carts parked along the roadway into the distance. People were milling everywhere. Canopies and tents housed eating areas, and salesmen sat at the roadside barking in Hindu about the wind-mills, stuffed toys, candied cakes and an infinite number of plastic toys, and cooking hardware.

I stepped down into this chaos and in an incredibly peaceful state, wandered in the direction others were going. All the still-ness I'd felt on the hilltop in Namo Buddha seemed to encase me in some wonderful bubble. I floated among the darting children, families dressed in costumes from all over Nepal and India, sou-venir stands and picnickers, as if there was no one there at all. It was almost as if the jumble of sounds had been turned off and people moved by me in a dreamlike other world like ghosts, while I walked alone in my own world.

There was a circular marble monument which had marble benches around it in a wide open grassy field. I sat down there to get my bearings, watch the crowd, and feel the overwhelming stillness.

From where I sat, I could watch a sea of people with bright col-ored saris and shirts swarming towards a square marble mauso-leum-like structure in the distance. There was a giant banyan tree surrounded by a massive crowd. On the left was a small steep pyramidal hill of dirt. People were climbing on it and there were rows of people gravitating towards it.

In my daze, I got up and walked towards the rectangular building, passing people spread out on the grass eating picnics of rice and cakes. Cloths were spread out and people walked around talking between the long strips of as if with some brightly colored maze.

I'd read that King Ashoka, the first king to spread Buddhism throughout his empire, had erected a pillar in 200 BC which still stood here. As I walked towards the concentration of people, I saw it enclosed by an iron fence. Slowly I edged through the peo-ple to stand for a moment before this pillar, now broken and lean-ing, but still bearing his script commemorating the spot where

Buddha was born. People were tossing bright colored paper offerings and boxes over the fence and the pillar was half buried in purple, red, blue, and yellow paper decorations.

The chaos of pressing people caught me in its current. We flowed like thick lava in the only direction physically possible, towards the white marble building just beyond the pillar. There was a stairway leading to a walkway around the white rectangular wall. The whole building must not have been bigger than fifty feet long. People were swarming towards the stairs, and officials were standing with clubs beating off the excess crowds as they came up the stairs like clusters of insects. There was a group of women in brilliant red and fuchsia saris being helped up the stairs while the more scruffy populace was being beaten back.

I was still in my euphoric stillness, and felt little desire to stay in that urgent crush of people. With some effort I plowed against the stream and found myself walking near the edge of an enormous tank or bathing pool filled with water.

Nearly every stopping place was filled with people, but I managed to come close to a great banyan tree at the edge of the tank. Here people were squatting under the enormous branches at the trunk, and it seemed as if hundreds of beggars thrust open hands at me. Some had make-up like Indian war paint with white and yellow stripes across their foreheads and cheeks. They were dressed like holy men, but the aggressive way they demanded "baksheesh" persuaded me they were charlatans. The peaceful feeling inside me helped me brush by them undisturbed. I realized I was the only Westerner in all this sea of dark faces.

I finally pushed into the open areas farther from the marble building to the steep pyramidal mound, which I climbed. From this point I could see the bright colored crowd scattering and swarming like an enormous sea. It was the biggest crowd I've ever been in. Thank goodness for that inner peaceful feeling or I might have panicked. It was very hot and dusty. I'd brought no water, and made my way towards the outer edge of the crowds where the canopied food stands were. I walked along a road that led to a group of buildings. There was a sign that said in English as well as Nepali "Lumbini Improvement Association'".

For some reason I walked up this walkway towards the porch where a small group of people were seated comfortably in the shade. An official greeted me with some surprise that I'd arrived on this day. He looked like many of the carved faces of Buddha I'd seen in China. He showed me a seat which I accepted gratefully. I'd been up since dawn and wandering through the chaos of people since 8:00 AM. It was 11:00 AM.

He told me that it was the full moon in April that the Hindus chose as the birth of Buddha, and that, though there were more than 40,000 people gathered here, by evening the place would be deserted. I had found the only day in the whole year when crowds ever came. He explained that pilgrims came to bathe in the tank (the large one by the banyan tree) where Buddha's mother had bathed before he was born.

She'd been on her way from Kapilovastu towards her parents' home to have her baby there, according to custom. However, labor began, and she stopped in the Lumbini gardens, where he was born. She'd washed him in a spring, and his father had taken him to the Shiva temple about a mile away to bless him. Now people come, bathe in the tank, change to clean clothes and make their offerings at the white memorial and the Ashoka Pillar. After a day's celebrating, they disappear.

There were several well dressed men there. The Chairman of the Lumbini Improvement Association, who first greeted me, introduced me to the government archeologist. He spoke a smattering of English.

I had mentioned my interest in Kapilovastu, which I had thought was in India, but which he assured me was only thirty miles away in Nepal.

"I can arrange for you to go to Kapilovastu if you wish to go this afternoon. There are no buses that go from here." It was being served to me on a platter!

The chief engineer, who was working on a new road between Lumbini and Kapilovastu, lived in the nearest town. He would be leaving in the late afternoon and I could ride in his jeep. The chairman asked if I would like to take a shower. I was indeed hot and sweaty and looked a bit rumpled from the crowds. With deep gratitude I went upstairs to a clean tiled bath where I washed myself, my clothes, and like a true pilgrim emerged clean and fresh. I spread my Tibetan dress out on the grass to dry and then went to explore the area further.

There was a stupa at a Theravadan monastery further along the road, and I walked toward it. The crowds were thinner here, and I noticed an excavated area with foundations indicating a series of small rooms. The archeologist had said that there had been a monastery here where Buddha's father and son had practiced. For centuries this site had been neglected. It was only recently that someone had rediscovered the Ashoka pillar and the government began to develop it. I had the feeling that the mounded hill I climbed might have once have been a stupa which had been buried under dirt for centuries.

I wondered if that deep peace would have occurred to me if I'd been there before anyone knew about the meaning of Lumbini.

I went into the temple of the monastery which looked like all the ones I visited in Thailand. Since I couldn't get close to the "mausoleum" building, I gave an offering here. I squeezed through the people at the door, past the beggars aggressively demanding "baksheesh". On my way back to the main house, I passed what the archeologist had spoken of as the spring at which Buddha's mother bathed him after birth. It was now a faucet with an arched enclosure and people were lining up to fill jars of water. The more confident were pushing past the more polite, patient women, so that as I watched, seven people pushed in front of one gentle woman waiting for her turn. I'd noticed that people from India seemed not to hold the concept of standing in line or taking a turn. They all pushed and shoved in ticket lines, buses and even here, where water continually flowed and there was enough for all.

I waited on the cool porch until the engineer was ready to go home, which was nearly two hours after the chairman said he'd be ready. But still I could watch the torrents of people surging round the tank and memorial building, climbing the hill, and flowing towards the food canopies. I had planned to stay another day at Lumbini, but I'd done what I needed to here. Then I squeezed into the jeep along with five engineers and began the trip to Kapilovastu.

Chapter 41 - Kapilovastu

There has always been a walking trail between Lumbini and Kapilovastu. The government of Nepal had just begun in the past year to build a roadbed through the villages in between. On this dirt road, which dipped down across rice paddies, through villages of mud houses, we rode in the late afternoon sun.

The dust stirred up from medieval V-shaped wagons with wood wheels, drawn by great white bulls, hung in golden particles in the air. It was harvest time for wheat here, and teams of six white bulls or cows were lashed to long poles connected to a grindstone. They walked in the same patient plodding way, round and round, as I'd seen those bulls do in the Indonesian rice paddies. The dust of the grain rose in the afternoon air and contributed to the golden aura that seemed to glaze even the yellow mud huts in a gold more splendid than all the gilt on the temples in Thailand.

There was another contribution to this magic golden haze. It was mealtime, and the cooking fires from the cow dung raised a smoke above each house that glowed in the almost setting sun.

Because of the bumps in the road, we had to go not more than fifteen miles an hour, so I had time to look into this "untouched" world. There were no trees for miles between the villages of perhaps fifteen or twenty houses at the most. There was a fountain, common to everyone, and there seemed to be many well cared for cows. It must have seemed an incredible anachronism for those simple people to watch the jeep "race" by when any evidence of mechanical help was restricted to wooden wheels and grinding stones.

At an irrigation ditch, two teenage girls were lifting water from one level to another. Their skirts tied up, they each held a rope tied to the handles of a very large iron wok. They dipped it into the lower ditch and pulled the ropes taut. This swung the saucer up and splashed the water into the higher ditch in one big pull, then it fell like a pendulum back to the lower ditch again.

Here in the golden light I saw many "white" cattle glowing yellow. There were very few water buffaloes and these had light brown fur. Perhaps it was too dry for them.

It was too noisy with the bumping jeep to hold a conversation, and I thankfully watched this medieval world pass by. I wondered what the construction of the road would do to and for these simple people.

We arrived in the town where the engineer lived. It was barely more complex than the villages we passed through. Here many roadside stalls were made of crooked twigs bound together to make walls. Roofs were made of thatched rice stems. At the far end of town were more modern houses of stucco, some with two stories. The engineers drove into a government complex. One of them commented that there was a Buddhist family in the area that made their house available to pilgrims, and he sent someone down to see if there was room available for me. He then drove me back perhaps a quarter of a mile to a large house where a family welcomed me, showed me a comfortable room and brought me a dinner of rice and lentil sauce.

For the first time I was alone with time to wonder at the happenings of the day. I had been wandering in my peaceful state in the midst of Lumbini, had an opportunity to come over an inaccessible road to Kapilovatsu, and more unbelievably, had comfortable accommodations and warm hospitality! As the still nearly full moon rose, I fell deeply asleep.

In the morning I got up at dawn and went to the small temple my host had in the rear field of his house. Inside was a beautiful white marble seated Buddha about four feet high with the red eye makeup lining the eyes that I'd seen in Burma. On both sides were smaller marble Buddhas. The whole temple was just like the small temples surrounding Shwedegon Pagoda in Rangoon. There was an iron gate across the front but there was room to sit on a platform outside. Here I did my sitting in the gentle morning air until a nun dressed in peach robes, like those in Burma, came to make offerings. I wandered through the back courtyard where two great white bulls rested on straw. There was a central fountain, and a pump which produced water to wash in.

No one spoke English, so I had a bit of difficulty locating the outhouses, but eventually discovered them. The engineers who drove me here had located a guide to take me to the site of Buddha's palace at Kapilovastu, so I waited until he showed up. The host brought me breakfast of soup and rice and sat with me while I ate. Then finally my guide arrived, a short Hindu who had been trained at a government complex as a guide. He spoke broken English in rapid staccato bursts and was obviously very dubious about taking this lone woman anywhere. He wanted to hire a rickshaw at an exorbitant price. I said I'd come with limited money and couldn't afford to ride but was willing to walk.

We settled for the bus which rode a half mile along the main road and dropped us off. We walked along a dirt road and came to the West Gate in the wall of the estate where Buddha had lived 25,000 years ago. The brick wall was being uncovered and rebuilt by archeologists. Two red brick mounds on either side of us was all there was to indicate the gate as we entered the grounds. The only structure visible was a tiny temple about 12 feet square which we walked to first. It was crumbling, the roof had fallen in, but on one side a big banyan tree had intertwined its wandering roots in such a way that it entwined itself into the wall and was holding it up. Though I could barely understand my guide, I grasped that Buddha's father had erected the temple in honor of his mother, who died just one week after he was born. It was an odd feeling to be walking on the "Palace grounds" where Buddha walked and where he spent the first 29 years of life. My guide, a rather argumentative person who felt contempt for my lack of knowledge, and who made no effort to hide it, walked towards the excavated ruins of Buddha's father's "palace".

With all the stories of Buddha's princely life, I'd imagined a palace the size of some maharaja's vast lodgings. Here the foundations showed a modest enclosure about the size of an average house in the United States. It seemed divided into three rooms at the back with an open room onto a veranda much like the far smaller dwellings in the villages I'd passed. There were additional buildings for cooking, storage of grain, and houses for servants, but all were on a very modest scale as far as I could see. Perhaps the euphoria I'd experienced the day before in Lumbini had worn off, perhaps the rather obnoxious arrogance of the guide affected me. But I just stood on the spot where Buddha lived, and looked calmly around.

There were some beautiful old oaks allowed to live by reason of respect for this spot, that stretched through open pasture land. The river flowed through a frame of oaks some distance away. An enemy clan had crossed this to invade Buddha's father's home and destroyed the whole Shakia clan.

We walked across the grassy field to the East Gate, the one Buddha had ridden out of on his hunting party. His father, fearing the prophesy that Gautama would leave home if he saw sickness, death or old age had sheltered him the way the king in the fairy tale had sheltered Sleeping Beauty. All old people were kept from the palace, all sick not allowed to enter, and there was no mention of death.

On that first sortie, the father had taken great trouble to hide all evidence of these dreary sides of life when Buddha rode out through the East Gate of the palace. Somehow, like the old witch with the spinning wheel, no matter what care was taken, a sick man was left lying by the road side. Buddha's first encounter with the painful realities of life ended the hunting trip, and he reentered the gate to brood on this disturbing discovery. Two more times he tried to leave his idyllic palace, which surrounded him with beautiful dancing girls and a loving wife and child. The next time, he encountered a dying man, and the third time, an old man. The shock of these inevitable realities of life disturbed him profoundly.

I stood at that gate gazing out over an open countryside perhaps not much changed from the time of Buddha. An odd numbness settled over me. We walked across some more open land to the ruins of an ancient stupa built shortly after Buddha's death, now only a flat raised brick disk sitting in a field by the river.

The oddity of ancient remains flooded through me. All temples in Pegan, the ruins of emperors' tombs in China, the dilapidated broken Hindu temples in Java on the Dieng Plateau, and the cracking moss-covered stones of Borobudur merged with the Aztec temples in Mexico now being "restored". Like aspects of ourselves we try to forget, but which push up through our awareness even if in a crumbling state, they haunt us like ghosts until we acknowledge them.

We wound our way back on a path past a hut where cucumber vines grew on the thatched roof. An old woman living there came out and conversed with the guide for awhile. Then we walked back to catch the bus. It had passed while we were still walking, so we walked back to the town, the guide wiping sweat from his brow. He was somewhat surprised that I was not exhausted.

There was just a short time left for me to wash with water from the fountain and settle into my room before the host brought dinner. From the small amount of English he could speak, I learned he was a landlord, owning the mill to which the farmers came from across all the fields to grind their corn and wheat. A group of very poor men were busy at his "paper factory" on the front porch, spreading the mush made from the bark of trees and rice stalks in a thin paste over the stone slabs of his entryway. When they dried in the heat, and it was hot, they could peel off the sheets which then hung together like crude paper. Later in Kathmandu I saw this paper used to wrap valuable objects.

I was left alone again to rest and read the guest book. There were comments of other visitors who had come as pilgrims and received such kind hospitality. The internal churning that had started while I looked out the East Gate of Kapilovastu continued. I couldn't exactly understand why, but I was disturbed. I finally fell asleep to wake up at dawn again and sit by that beautiful marble Buddha in the side field.

A young mother and her son were sleeping on the floor out-side the iron fence as I came up. She got up and moved to a neigh-boring building. Was this her bed? All of the sculptured fineness of the pure white marble Buddha contrasted with her rumpled cloak. I sat there with the richness before me and poverty at my back, and the disturbance of my stomach continued.

The guide was late in coming that morning. He was going to show me the "museum" of excavated objects. He guided me into a cramped shed where stone statues, beheaded sculptures and objects were laid out on dusty shelves. He showed me its objects rather indifferently I thought, and when I asked him about them he said "What kind of a Buddhist are you?" I told him that in America I had learned to sit and meditate as Buddha taught, but that I knew few facts of Buddha's life or even his organized teach-ings. I wasn't sure he really knew what the objects were himself, and he used his arrogance to intimidate me. He was supposed to take me out to a site where a Buddha prior to Shakamuni Buddha had been born, but his arrogance and his high prices for the guid-ance were too much for me.

I left to go on my own to discover what I could. I had brought along a little brochure about Lumbini, written by the Nepal Tourist information agency. It included a short description of Kapilovastu and the nearby locations of two other birthplaces of Buddhas before Shakyamuni. So I followed the directions myself, walking along the dry rice paddies to a clump of trees in the dis-tance.

I came upon the ruins of a complex of temples, pyramidal in shape, rising in crumbled mounds. I walked up the paths between the stones and discovered an altar cylinder like the ones Patricia had shown me in Rangoon. I gathered this had been a Hindu Shiva temple. People were still making offerings here. Just as at the ocean-washed carved lava foundation of the temple in Bali, remains of incense and dried flowers mingled with fresher offer-ings, even though it was halfway sunk in the clay on the crumbled mound of earth.

Young children were playing in and out of the trees and ran when I came up, but a young man walking his cattle home pointed to the direction I should have gone. It was too far to go since the sun was already near setting, so I started "home". I was glad to see this site which I would have missed otherwise. Again I felt gratitude to whatever led me to march out on my own without a guide.

I walked back along the dirt road. It was much easier and more direct than walking along the levees of the rice paddies zigzagging along farmers' boundaries. Farmers were on their way home from the mill with huge sacks of grain piled in medieval carts made like triangular wedges with huge wooden wheels creaking on wooden axles. We greeted each other. Without a camera I was free of the temptation to photograph everything. I truly felt a part of the scene. The great bulls that pulled the carts eyed me with their patient eyes and plodded by.

On the edge of town was a small tea hut made of twigs. I sat on a wooden shelf, and a beautiful but exhausted woman surrounded by babies and young children served me tea. She had just finished serving tea to another customer when I arrived. We couldn't talk, only smile. I couldn't play with the children who openly stared at me as I waited for the water to boil. An old man was resting on a bed just outside the hut-shelter, which was without doors. The beds here were made of two-by-fours or one-by-ones. It was just a frame across which a rope web was woven. Since all the beds were outside at this time of year, I had noticed people sleeping on a stuffed, thin mattress, but here the man slept on the bare ropes.

The thin woman reminded me again of Patricia, my friend in California, and for some unexplainable reason a feeling of love flooded through me as we looked at each other. I wished I could order hundreds of teas to aid this proud woman in raising her family. She seemed accepting of her lot, not even noticing it was a "lot". She tended the tiny fire with crusty hands using only enough fuel to bring water to a boil. Her four year old daughter playfully hung on her and she patiently accepted the distraction. The daughter was beautiful with large eyes and soft skin. I wondered how old her mother was as I watched what this hard life had done to her finely shaped face.

Two small boys around five years old came racing through, and she sternly reprimanded them. They quieted quickly. An older girl, maybe eleven, was teasing a younger sister, and the mother gently diverted her to a more useful occupation of washing cups. The cups were enameled metal, and the washing process apparently included dipping them in slightly soapy water, rubbing them with the fingers and setting them stacked on a stone to dry.

I gazed at the crooked twigs tied together to make this hut, wondering how cold it must be in the rainy season even though the rice thatch must keep it from leaking. While I sat there watching the capable mother, the churning feeling I'd experienced at Kapilovastu returned again. Buddha had been sheltered from sickness, old age, and death, inevitable realities that stirred him deeply when he saw them. Somehow the stark poverty of this family, apart from all the beggars or other sparsely clothed barefoot people I'd seen, stirred my deepest concern.

This woman wanted nothing more than the price she set for tea. The hardship of her state didn't bother her; it bothered me. Or was it the opulence of my state? I felt an incredible tie to her, almost as if we were sisters. She did not want my pity. She welcomed my warm love which we both acknowledged with our eyes. I sat there watching the interplay of the family, feeling oddly that I was looking at myself in some other time, in a way like watching a play, but deeply involved with my heart. I couldn't separate my self from the experience of it.

I was rested, there were more customers and I got up to leave. She rose, and we bowed to each other with the gassho or "Namaste" gesture. "I salute the God within you".

When I got back to my lodgings, the young engineer who had

driven me down to the house came to invite me to dinner, and I went to his house on the other end of the village from where my tea lady lived.

There was obviously a good and a poor part of town. Here, trees and landscaping surrounded large stucco houses with lots of space between. He had a cook who had prepared a very delicious meal of four different courses and plenty of tea and fruit juice to drink.

He had finished school only three years before, and expected to be working on the road project for three years. He commented that there was very little to do in the town, and few people he felt comfortable with, none who were interested in his "ideas". His glasses, his serious expression reminded me of any student in America who took his education seriously. He was curious to hear of my adventures, since he'd had few opportunities to travel, and was amazed I traveled alone, as nearly all Asians have been. He'd read widely in American literature, as had David in Thailand, showing great curiosity for the ideas of the Western World.

So after sharing tea in the twig hut with my poor friend, in the same village I shared dinner sitting on the breezy roof top of the engineer, and another day of enormous contrasts swept by. I felt a warm affection for this young man, as we talked of ideas and travels. I felt as if we were all experimenting with the ways of living - poor, rich, educated and illiterate, as adventurers of life on this amazing planet. l It was almost like a dream, this seeing myself in everyone I met.

Chapter 42 - Birthplaces of other Buddhas

At dawn the next day, I was sitting by the white marble Buddha when the nun I'd seen the first morning joined me. She opened the gate and sat inside the entrance. We sat there together as the sun rose, casting a yellow light on the Buddha. A very nice way to begin the day.

The brother of my host, who spoke a bit more English, told me in which direction to go to find the village where an Ashoka pillar commemorates the birthplace of a Buddha born before Shakyamuni. Apparently Nepal boasts of having five Buddhas born within its boundaries, three within about a thirty mile radius of each other near Kapilovastu.

I set out on the lumpy, raised levees that framed the dry plowed rice paddies. I didn't want to press down the earth so carefully loosened by the rice farmers or I would have cut across the fields. It was an interminable stumble along the narrow walkways around square plots, each offset from the other, forming a zigzag path.

There was no one in sight. It was getting hot, and I'd forgotten to carry water. A group of trees became my focus. As I came near, I could see a young girl concentrating on chopping some green weeds and putting them in a large basket, perhaps for sheep or cows she kept at home. When I got near enough to ask the way to the village, she stood up suddenly, stared at me in wide eyed fright, and ran towards some houses just over the hill. I suspect she thought I was a "witch woman" though I've no way of knowing.

I walked to the village, hoping it was the right one, though no one seemed inclined to talk to me, even to repeat the name of the village. I wandered on past some very well kept and neatly swept mud huts framed by high fences made of tied bunches of rice stalks. Nearly every family kept a pair of white bulls under a shelter adjacent to the house rather than in a separate 'barn'. The bulls or cows were round and well fed, contentedly chewing their cud. This was a prosperous village.

Finally, I found a young man who could speak English. He pointed beyond a rise where six cows harnessed to the spokes of a large horizontal wheel were walking around the radius of a circle, stepping on piles of wheat. I presumed they were loosening the seeds of wheat from the stalks. In China, I'd seen the villagers lay wheat or flax on the road for cars to crush or thresh. Some children joined me. They were smiling and friendly, and I suspect a little curious why this old woman had walked way out just to see their Ashoka pillar. I saw carriage wheels in the hard mud of the road, and realized most pilgrims took rickshaws out here. I'd taken a short cut through the fields.

At the far end of the village, there it was. A broken stone column set in a deep tank or bathing pool half filled with algae-green water. I sat down. I'd never heard that there were other Buddhas besides the one of historical fame, but since the teachings say enlightenment is available to everyone, it seemed reasonable. It felt good to be there, to sit on a spot recognized in 200 BC as a place where an Enlightened one had chosen to land on this earth.

A crowd of curious villagers peered over the wall above me talking to themselves. The Ashoka pillar was half broken, jutting out from the fragmented bathing tank which was obviously no longer in use, as the slimy algae painted a rim where it met the green water. Just what <u>was</u> I doing here?

I wondered what it is about a spot where a famous person is born or lived that evokes commemoration. Like the great trees in Bali or the old temple ruins, these places world wide are marked and celebrated though they are covered with weeds and seem half forgotten. Maybe the spot itself is sacred, and like fertile soil nurtures great beings. So I sat there, not in the same state I felt in Lumbini, just quiet contentment. Was this because I'd never heard of this Buddha before? Just to be there for a while seemed the right thing to do.

It was already after 2:00 PM. I was thirsty, hungry, and realized I still had about five miles to get back to the town where I stayed. So I got up, turned away from that ancient stone marker, and started walking back through the village. By now, I guess everyone had decided I was harmless and smiled as I passed.

At one of the more impressive homesteads where the great white cows were under shelter, an old woman waved me in to sit on her bench. Two motorcycles rested against the wall and two fine looking young men in their early twenties came out to talk. They both spoke English well. As we sat, they insisted on feeding me dinner and tea, and some shy women peered around the corners as we visited. The mother was proud of her boys and was very pleased when I commented how fine the were. They were curious about me and my two sons.

The "old" woman asked my age. It was the same as hers, though she looked old enough to be my mother. I'm used to people always asking how old I am. In Asia it's important to know someone's age in order to know how to address them. Older people are respected highly. I told them that in America people showed respect for what you accomplished, always asking "What do you do?" They laughed. They really want to be like people in the United States.

We compared lives. My two boys were the same age as hers. My work with children, her work with the villagers expressed concern for others' well being. I showed a picture of a class at the school I'd worked in with children of all the races. They pointed to the darker skinned children with approval, but were truly charmed by a bright blue-eyed blond girl. Even here, the attraction for white skin had penetrated. That legacy of imperial rule may take centuries to overcome. Both boys were going to school, were home just to help with the harvest.

I felt again that I was visiting a replica of myself. The bond between me and the mother was strong. It was getting late.

I'd finished the fine meal of rice and sauce, smiled at all the women shyly watching me. I bowed deeply to the wonderful mother I'd never see again but whose warm way and pride in her children warmed my heart.

On my way back, I found a more direct road. A woman carrying a bundle of wheat in a kerchief on her head walked beside me. Her husband was carrying a basket of vegetables. After some time of each of us smiling at the other, I offered to try to carry her bundle. She gaily placed it on my head, and laughed as I felt the weight crunch my neck bones. I carried it none the less, though I couldn't do it hands-off style, and we laughed too much for it to balance easily. After about fifteen minutes, she took it back to my great relief, since I was going too slowly. I couldn't see my feet or the bumps in the road without tipping my head and letting the bundle slip. I mentally played with the theory that the reason all Asians were shorter than Westerners was that they'd all had their back and neck bones collapsed like a folding telescope from carrying burdens on their heads. I indicated that I much preferred the back pack method. It was a happy walk together, and they waved goodbye to me when we reached the main road into town.

It was already time to start the fires for the evening meal when I passed my tea woman. Again she served me tea, and we just looked affectionately into each other's eyes. I already felt as if I'd known her for years. Then, I left her tiny twig hut and walked on towards home.

In wandering along some side streets, I discovered the place where the rickshaw drivers gathered, and asked how much one would charge for a day trip to the other Ashoka pillar. It was an all day trip, and I was depleted by this last walk which felt as if it were at least ten miles in the hot sun. The price was surprisingly little compared to the price my arrogant guide had quoted, so I agreed to meet the driver the next day.

I was hot, dusty and tired from my walk, but triumphant that I'd found the way. The brother of my host who had offered me the use of his bicycle was amazed I had walked the whole way.

When I walked through the streets early the next morning, people were still sleeping on the rope and frame beds outside their shops. Women were carrying offerings to the Shiva temple. I met the rickshaw driver who asked me if I'd like to visit their temple.

He led me to the center of town where a small vaulted stone building housed their reclining bull and the by-now-familiar cylinder stone. Though no one knew how old it was, the stonework looked as old as that in Pegan. It must have been many centuries old. He told me that when they discovered the ruins, the altar was sunk deep in the dirt. They had excavated to a protruding rim around the upright column. Then the man in charge had had a dream in which he was told not to dig further, so all work was stopped. A building was constructed around it and no one has dug any deeper, though there are supposed to be six such rims or circular rings around it. Fragrant jasmine flowers were scattered around the altar and floor, fresh offerings made early this morning. I felt lucky to have a glimpse of this.

Chapter 43 - A Third Ashoka tower

Our rickshaw ride took us way out past Kapilovastu again and along a raised dirt road between rice fields. Along the way there we saw the most beautiful blue birds, the size of magpies but with radiant blue feathers, which kept flying along with us. In contrast to the drab dry tawny earth and gray-green leaves of some sparse weeds, they stood out like flowers.

Then we had to get out of the rickshaw and walk, the road was so bumpy. The guide pointed to the Ashoka pillar standing by a lake in the distance. I started walking across the fields toward it while he waited. Here in the midst of nowhere, surrounded by just the rice paddies, stood the remains of a tall pillar bearing inscriptions still readable on it. The broken top piece lay to one side.

So here I stood alone in a rice field in Nepal by a place King Ashoka had chosen to commemorate for all time as the birthplace of an early Buddha. Now nothing visible was left but the pillar. Whatever echoed there in nonexistent houses and of people long passed away was left for visitors to recognize in their bones.

I had noticed a village across the fields a half mile off with a gleaming white dome of a Shiva temple. I wanted to visit this. My guide was delighted that I wanted to walk and we set off together, stumbling on the lumpy, caked earth. We arrived at another neat village with swept paths, smooth mud houses, and well fed cows. The villagers gathered to watch me as we came to the Shiva temple. There was a bush right at the entrance with fragrant white flowers. One man, perhaps a leader of the village, said "Jasmine". He went to the bush and picked several blossoms for me, and demonstrated how I was to offer them inside the temple. It reminded me of the old Balinese temple codgers.

I accepted the fragrant blossoms, and shoes off, we entered. There was the familiar column with three stripes, the reclining bull facing it, which I'd also seen in little uncovered temples all around Kathmandu. The whole temple was sparkling white and new in this ancient mud and dust village. The villagers had recently renovated it and were delighted I'd taken the trouble to visit them.

The leader brought us tea as we came out. We sat by the fragrant jasmine bush and drank together. A woman came up and sat next to us and smiled though she said nothing. Later, she got up and left. Many other people gathered and smiled at us. I wondered if she had been the psychic of the village who had come to check out the spirit in which I'd come, had found me acceptable and left.

Then in late afternoon sun, we walked back another half mile to the rickshaw, and I gratefully accepted the long ride back. The farmers were herding their ducks, keeping the scurrying birds together with long sticks. Many young people had bicycles and were coming home from work in town. I'd not seen any signs of what work they could have been doing requiring city clothes, but most were well dressed and wore shoes.

Both villages where the Ashoka pillars were, were prosperous. It was only the miserable town I stayed in that showed the signs of poverty - the ragged clothing, the huts made of twigs, by people too weary to bother smoothing the jagged branches.

We entered the village as the cooking fires were starting. There was still time for me to visit the bank, a shabby building with paint peeling off the doors. I wanted to cash a travelers check, but for some reason they wouldn't do it for me.

I thought I had enough money to get me by bus to a more prosperous city so I wasn't worried. I visited my tea mother again, for one last cup of tea together. As we sat there, unable to exchange any words, tears came to my eyes. I was so aware of the hardships of her life, and the differences in our life styles, and yet was unable realistically to change a thing. A man who'd seen me come from the bank saw my tears and asked. "Do you need money? I'll give you some if you need it". He was drinking tea also.

I tried to put into words the swelling that was coming out my eyes, the feeling of the inequity of existence, my awareness of having so much more than I needed for myself while she had so little. I finally said "Buddha Sadness." It was, as if I was just coming out of the gate of Kapilovastu myself, protected from the realities of poverty and being swept into a deep pain at seeing this comparatively poor life. It was not as hopeless as those hovels in the Philippines made out of corrugated cardboard, or the back city streets of Bangkok where people slept on the cement, but it brought tears.

Buddha had been protected from the suffering of old age, death and sickness, things which we must all experience in this life. He'd been protected from experiencing poverty and the disparity between rich and poor which it seems to me should be avoidable. It seemed so sad, in all the time since Buddha who taught compassion, that conditions even near his own home had not changed.

The man talked to the woman for a minute, then turned to me. "She loves you", he said. I told him I too felt great love for her and that I would remember her all my life. I tried again to leave more money than the cost of the tea, but she corrected my counting, held my hand, and we said goodbye with our eyes, bowed "Namaste", and I left.

My pilgrimage was over. It was time to return to Kathmandu.

My host fed me breakfast, and helped me find the waiting spot where the daily bus passed each morning. I waved goodbye and climbed into the bus. We passed the excavations of the palace of Kapilovastu, the "forest" of the few sparse trees which remained only because it was a park, and crossed the river used by the Shakia clan and their attackers.

Then we drove through the most abjectly overused and depleted land I'd seen. No trees, dry road, dry paddies, barren fields, not providing anything for the skinny goats grazing there. Fresh from this unexpected adventure, I gazed passively out the window as the depleted world raced by.

I had to change buses in a larger town two hours later. I felt I was seeing the kind of life lived in India. Nearly everyone was Hindu, women wearing saris, the men wearing the draped loincloth, the uniform of the poor .

From my diary April 11, 1982

I write this from an open air restaurant between buses on "Main Street" in Boteva on the way back to Kathmandu.

I look out on a dusty stone road intersection. There's a beggar in a "white" loincloth which has become the color of the brown earth he squats on. He's in the middle of the intersection and I see his black back all caked and clogged with the dust raised by passing vehicles. He sifts the sand with his fingers and occasionally seems to eat something he finds. A grain of rice?

Shaggy white cows and calves stand by the roadside in the hot shade where they find it. Radios blare wailing Asian songs, bus horns scream, rickshaws blow horns in pathetic beep, beep, beep insistence.

I watch men in woven Nepali hats, which indicate the region they come from, give warm greetings to each other. Their grinning teeth sparkle through the dust that blows all around them. A bus labeled "Buddha Bus" passes. Shabby paint splotches, dented metal sides, cracked window panes and a broken baggage rack on top contribute to its dilapidated appearance. All the buses that pass have the irascible roar of a motor driven to extremes. There are squeaks of tired springs. Bells, jangling from the street venders under sagging burlap shelters, announce oranges, bananas, cucumbers, and Coca Cola.

Vendors keep large crock vases of drinking water open to the street dust. A dipper stands ready to pour this dusty water into glasses "washed" in a pan of soapy water, and "dried" with a corner of a sweaty tee shirt or with a cheesecloth washed so often in muddy water it is the color of the earth.

Women pass, dressed in clean radiantly colored saris, wearing a jewel in the left nostril, a red spot on the forehead. Other women, eyes on the ground, carry big bags held on their backs with the rope band across their heads. They dress in wrinkled, tired cotton cloth draped "Virgin Mary" style over their heads. The sari is a useful garment: many hold the cloth over their noses as a filter from the odors and the dust.

Women here wear a thick waist cloth: a long twisted belt of cotton cheese cloth. There are babies everywhere with dusty bare bottoms. They squat and cry in a habitual whimper. Others with serene baby Buddha faces, casually entertain themselves by playing with stones. Bigger boys play "Karate chop". They must break a stick held by another boy between his fists.

Always there are the gray-haired wrinkled women bearing shopping bags and an umbrella. Behind their gold dangling earrings and snarled hair, a long braid extends down their backs. A wool fringe adorns the end.

Sikhs in colored turbans, with trimmed beards and a white skirt drawn between the legs to make baggy pants, walk through the milling crowds. I see some carrying enormous oil drums or bales of hay balanced on their heads as they walk.

Men go hand in hand, arm in arm, affectionately leading each other. Skirts are more prevalent than the more Western pants. Many men wear a dirty towel balanced on their heads, draping one end down the side to protect them from the sun. Some have draped the towel around their neck in "temple scarf" style over the shoulder. They use the end to dry sweaty hands and foreheads. It looks as if everyone spits. They spit after hacking coughs, aiming carefully so the wind doesn't carry it. They spit out windows in the bus, into the road, anywhere. They spit in many styles, through the teeth, through pursed lips, sideways.

The houses I see are dusty with their steps crumbling. Burlap canopies stretch out over ropes or corrugated metal bends out to shelter the windows from the sun. One whole wooden structure *looks as if it will blow over in the next wind. Square cement houses, with stucco and paint chipping like some ancient fresco, compose a chaotic mosaic of neglect.*

Clean laundry, but already dull with dust, hangs out on rooftops. There are many yard goods shops. At each one, someone stands ready with a treadle sewing machine. They sew clothes from the purchased cloth to order on the spot.

Dogs look threadbare. There are sores from fleas and infected wounds from dog fights. People kick them as they pass. The "trees" in the forests we passed on the way looked as threadbare as the dogs - they had no leaves, no limbs (which had been cut off for firewood). Their roots clutched at the earth with gnarled "fingers" in a dying grasp.

Always there are the scrawny water buffaloes with sharp pelvic bones stretching leathery skin, backbones traceable by a lumpy line down the black back, ribs corrugating the dusty sides.

Chapter 44 - Swayambhu Temple

After the long bus ride and the walk across Kathmandu, all the cheaper lodgings I knew of were full. Rooms seemed more highly priced than I remembered. I spent one night in a more expensive hotel, but decided I'd better look for a cheaper one next day.

Tourist season was in full swing. Phillip, at Namo Buddha, had told me of a Lama in Kathmandu with whom some Westerners stayed. Except for the group of monks practicing to be Lamas at Namo Buddha with whom I'd come to feel very comfortable, I'd preferred not to look up the Lamas so far, being somewhat intimidated by them. But now, with no available lodging, I decided to look up Thangha Rinpoche near Swayambhu Temple on the outskirts of Kathmandu.

As so many fortunate coincidences had helped me before, I met a young American woman at the door of the house when I had finally gotten up enough courage to approach it. The house was full, she said, but she wanted to go over to the other side of Kathmandu to see another Rinpoche for a few days. She was delighted that I could keep her room for her. She showed me up and left. It was a comfortable large room with lots of light. I gratefully unloaded my pack.

Later Thangha Rinpoche arrived with his translator and when I asked if I had his permission to stay there, he smiled and said "If Monica has already given you permission to use her room, you have it." He was solidly built, oddly reminiscent of Achaan Jamnien in Thailand and the yogi in Burma with a charming smile. I wondered for a moment if I were just seeing the same man again and again in different countries and costumes.

With a roof over my head and a Western toilet, a line to hang my clothes when I'd scrubbed the dust off them, I slept well and deeply.

The other tenants, who were all studying the Tibetan Religion, were German, English, French, American and Danish. They all flitted in and out on their own business. Thangha Rinpoche was preparing to leave for a trip to Europe in two days, and I was surprised he had time to talk with me at all, but I had had a strong feeling of wanting to talk with him. To my astonishment I persisted in arranging a time to see him. It was to be afternoon of the next day. Since I had time, I began to wander around Swayambhu Monastery which was only a 10-minute walk away.

Tourists call it the "Monkey" temple because all around the lower grounds are colonies of the same kind of monkey I'd seen in Bali that had stolen my hat at the "Monkey" temple there. Family groups sat preening each other in comfortable clusters and watched as I passed.

At the beginning of the climb, a set of stairs led to a gateway where twenty foot high Buddhas sat flanking the path. The stairs rose at nearly a 45-degree angle up to the temple on the top of the mountain. It was almost as steep as Kulkulkan temple in Mexico. Colored ceramic figures of peacocks, rabbits, elephants and lions marked the landings. Tile decorated the steps. I remembered the enormous undulating serpents that flanked the steps of Doisotep Temple in Chiang Mai where I spent the night sitting with the nun. The yogi in Burma had told me the peacock symbolized the sun, the rabbit the moon.

People were resting at every landing. A very large Hindu woman was clutching a steep banister that ended abruptly before the last steep ascent to the top. From here on there was no support. You had to go up those dizzying steps unaided. Perhaps that is symbolic of the way of spiritual life, the further along the way, the less support is given. One has to rely on one's own inner resources.

When I finally reached the top, the great white stupa with gilded dome rose in the center of an open courtyard around which gathered a whole world of people. Monks, old and very young, were everywhere in their bright maroon and orange robes. Beggars sat on the sides against old stone walls, salesmen spread their wares on cloths and barked out in Nepali invitations to come buy.

Perhaps I was still dizzy from the steep climb, but I again experienced that strange floating sensation, and aloofness from the crowds.

Here were travelers from everywhere going around with their right shoulder towards the stupa, spinning big metal prayer wheels which made a beaded circle around the base. They casually slapped each foot-high cylinder carved with prayers and started it spinning. There were tiny niche-like alters set around the base with figures inside to which people were bringing rice offerings. Almost as soon as the rice was deposited, large aggressive monkeys would move in and gobble it. At points around this stupa were places for lighting butter lamps. Tiny wicks flickered in lines of saucers filled with melted yak butter.

I walked slowly around this complex structure three times. Lamas having audiences with Tibetan women paced faster than I while their companions slapped the already spinning prayer wheels. Each time I circled it, I saw new things in the carvings. Brass animals in bas relief were placed beneath the eight altars. A series of ancient sculptures off to the side, weathered by what appeared to be centuries of rain, caught my eye. A strange feeling of being in the presence of things way beyond my comprehension, but of feeling natural walking among them, swept over me. Time seemed nonexistent. I realized I'd repeated this dazed wandering behavior before - at Borobadur in Indonesia, at Swezegon Pagoda in Burma, especially. I just sat down allowing that state of mind to be, just quietly observing everything that seemed to race around me.

I watched the stream of people. There seemed to be some sort of festival which brought people from all over Nepal, who then made a pilgrimage to Swayambhu before going home. There were groups of "mini- monks", children under 10 years old. A monk in charge of them was gathering them together, perhaps for lunch. Sensing I would like to leave an offering somewhere, I gave the monk a small sum for the young monks. He couldn't speak English, but said "Cha"? which I interpreted as an invitation to tea. He led me into a back section of the monastery which opened up on several levels at the back of the stupa .

I found myself in a room with a Lama and a group of Tibetan women. He welcomed me and told me the women had all walked from the Kumbhu region in four days' time. At that time I wasn't aware of how far that was. Later, when I hiked there, I realized they'd done a remarkable feat to walk nearly one hundred fifty miles in four days! I'd done less distance in ten. He asked me what I wanted, and I told him I was puzzled at being there at all, since the young man had plunked me there. He seemed perfectly used to this type of intrusion and was pleased by my reactions to Swayambhu. We shared tea, and he then began to speak in Nepali to the women and I excused myself. It was all a bit embarrassing, though the Lama seemed to know what was happening.

I continued my wandering around that strange and wonderful stupa until the afternoon sun began to glint off the gigantic gold Dorje, or symbol of wisdom, placed right at the head of the steep stairs. It was time to go. All the way down the hill I met beggars, mostly Hindu mothers reaching for money for their children. All looked amazingly fat so I gave nothing.

Then lower down, past the gate of the four sitting Buddhas, there was a woman with a small cobra in a basket. She would let it out, snap at it with her fingers to startle it into spreading its hood. I stopped to watch since this was my first chance to really see a cobra close up after the startling experience in Thailand. The cobra began to slide towards me, she picked it up and handed it to me. I sat there petting the tiny white body about an inch in diameter, feeling sorry that such a wild thing was kept in such a small basket. A Lama came down the steps and watched me, and commented to his friends to tell me I'd better put the snake back, it still had poison. I immediately handed it back, thankful that my ignorance had protected me and smiled my thanks at the Lama.

At the base there were "restaurants" and I bought my dinner before going back to the house.

Chapter 45 - Healing Chant

I Bump into my Son, Mike

It came time for me to speak with Thangha Rinpoche. For some reason I'd had the strong impulse to ask to talk with him, but really had no idea what to ask him. What do you talk to a Lama about?

I came into the room where Rinpoche sat on a couch. His translator, a smiling good natured short man in his thirties, sat on the floor. I presented the nice silk scarf given me by the monk-Lama at Namo Buddha, and Rinpoche took it and draped it round my neck and asked me to sit. I told him I'd been traveling for 8 months, having visited the origins of Zen Buddhism in China and Japan, and that I'd just come from Lumbini. I said that I was just wandering and wondered if such a pilgrimage made any sense.

He commented, "You have a Teacher."

I smiled, admitting that was true, but I'd not seen him for a long time, and was curious if my odd wanderings were "off the track" in some way.

"You're going the right direction. You're collecting energy. Just keep following your intuition."

Kobun had also told me to follow my intuition. Sometimes this lack of direction had seemed senseless to me but I'd ended up in many places I'd never have gone if I'd planned the trip.

I laughed, "You mean I'm going around like a bee gathering pollen unknowingly as I visit these Buddha spots and when I get home I can kind of shake my elbows and share that energy?" He, too, smiled. "That's right".

He told me of another place to go, Parpang, which I'd heard of and wanted to see.

All the time we'd talked, he was working with a dark clay,

~295~

pressing it into tiny molds and forming little dark cakes with bas relief sculptures on them. Alan in Thailand had given me a similar protection amulet like that worn by most Thai people. It was made of monk's hair and herbs and pressed into a tiny cake. With his hands still gray from the clay, he placed his palms to my cheeks in a warm goodbye and I left.

The following day, my friend Philip from Namo Buddha arrived, as did many people who'd come to see Rinpoche before he left for Europe.

I was glad to talk to Philip because I felt a bit out of place. Philip said that Rinpoche had decided suddenly to give a "Medicine Initiation" and that the people were coming to attend that. I felt I had better get out of everyone's way, and since Philip had already attended such a gathering before, he suggested we go out to breakfast.

We ate breakfast and then walked all the way around the base of Swayambhu, a walk of 45 minutes. He showed me some stone slabs laid along the walkway, said to be mysteriously growing images of Buddhas. They were created by the energy of people coming to pray before them, and were becoming more distinct each year.

There were stones I'd heard of in China that "grew" a face shape, and in Thailand, Jampa had shown me a cave where a stone had grown almost across a dark recess in the past six years. The abbot had said it was not to be explored yet. It was distinctly fresh stone which couldn't have been molded by man or set in place there. I had come to that credulous state where, given the way of thinking of Asia, any changes of the physical world were possible, since the belief was that all substance was a manifestation of mind anyway.

On the way back around the enormous stupa, we came to a "house" where there was a gigantic prayer wheel placed upright on a wheel of spokes. People would enter between the spokes and push, keeping the fifteen foot cylinder rotating, and thus activating the prayers written on it.

We had been gone an hour and a half. When we returned, the people were still gathered around Thangha's house. The ceremony had not yet started. So somehow I found myself sitting in the middle of the small room in which I'd earlier talked to Rinpoche. It was crushed with people. There were Tibetan women mixed in with many Westerners. He began chanting and ringing bells and waving a bell shaped object in his hand which held what I later learned was the picture of the Medicine Buddha. I'd watched the monks in Namo Buddha ringing their small bells shaped like cymbals which resonated with each other and continued their sound for more than a minute. There was also a hand drum which when rotated caused two balls at the end of strings to strike the drum.

Thangha Rinpoche ably struck these instruments in turn, waved the bell and chanted. Then he began to chant something that the others repeated after him. Still feeling I was not so much a participant as an observer, I sat listening. Then I realized he was repeating smaller and smaller sections which I recognized, and began to chant along with the rest. Over and over we repeated it until I'd learned it. Then he stopped and began touching the head and hands of each participant with the bell, and the ceremony was over.

Outside, I asked Philip what had happened. He told me we'd been given the chant which could help heal people. He wrote it out for me in phonetics suggesting I practice it myself.

Among the group that had come to the ceremony was a tall blond young German named Mike. I talked with him for a while, and said I'd waked up that morning with the idea that I might trek to Thangboche, one of the highest monasteries in the world. My own son, Mike, had wanted to go to Thangboche when he'd been in the Himalayas two years before and had suffered from cerebral edema at 21,000 feet, luckily coming out alive but seriously affected by blood clots. He'd been unable to continue the climb. This young Mike said spontaneously, he'd possibly go with me and that we should meet the next day at Bhodinath, the other great stupa, across Kathmandu, to talk about the possibility.

I was planning to leave Thangha Rinpoche's house that following morning. I woke up chanting the medicine chant half in my sleep, half awake. It was solidly in my mind. I began to pack and somehow noticed how dirty the room was. In Nepal, someone had said "dirt is dirt, we don't mind it much."

Thangha Rinpoche's house had just recently been rebuilt with beautiful Western toilets, shiny linoleum floors and painted walls. The Western students staying there had just let it slide into the Nepalese state. So I began mopping the hallway. Then the bathroom looked less clean, and I scrubbed it. I dawdled this way for about two hours, somewhat surprised at my delay at leaving the house. If I'd wanted to catch a bus I'd have had a much easier time earlier, yet continued cleaning.

Then just as I was going down the stairs to leave, I met a monk who spoke English. I wanted to leave a contribution for my stay and gave it to him. We began to talk, and again I wondered at my delaying. Suddenly the young monk blurted out "You're American, aren't you? I thought you were German !" When I asked about his surprise, he said "There's an American boy looking for his mother . " Immediately I knew it was my son Mike, even though he was supposed to be in the U.S. "I'll bet it's Mike!" I showed him a picture of Mike and the monk recognized him.

"When did you see him?" "Yesterday. He was at Swayambhu asking if anyone had seen his mother. I told him to try Kopan Gompa near Bhodinath. A lot of Westerners stay there. I never thought of you."

So I was a day behind. Without stopping to marvel at the fact that I ever even heard he was in the same city, I dashed across Kathmandu in a taxi, spending more in that half hour than I'd spent all week.

I stopped at Bhodinath, glancing quickly at the restaurant where I was supposed to meet the other Mike, later. I began to walk around the stupa, which was brilliant white with the lines of colored prayer flags flapping from the top down to the base of the dome like a Maypole.

Most stupas in Nepal have a square base under the top dome with a great pair of eyes staring out of each of the four sides, representing all-seeingness. I stood in the shelter of a shop on one side of the stupa to let a rain shower pass and wondered if those eyes could see Mike who might very well be on the other side right then. I was highly tempted to go all the way around the stupa, but it was so big it would have taken another half hour, so I discounted my hunch he was just on the other side and continued on up into the hills. I was already a day behind him.

So up through rice plots in the hills, I passed water buffaloes and their farmers working rice paddies, people bringing wares to market, and school children out for recess. For two hours I walked and finally reached the gompa or monastery on the top of the hill. I arrived at a time when no one was in sight. It was deserted. There was a lovely garden at the front of the building I gathered was the Buddha Hall, but the doors were closed. I sat down on the steps to admire a beautiful banyan tree, ancient with the wandering roots which had fascinated me before, especially in Lumbini where they had intertwined to hold up a wall.

I sat there alone for nearly half an hour wondering "what next?".. There seemed to be nothing to do. Then a monk came across the open garden, and I asked him if there had been an young American man here recently. "Wait." he said, and disappeared. I wasn't sure if he understood me, and was looking for someone who spoke English, or what. So I waited. I waited fifteen minutes longer in that still garden under the shade of the banyan tree, praying that somehow Mike and I could be connected with each other. Then the young monk appeared again. This time he had with him a gray-haired nun my age who told me she was from Bloomington, Illinois. "You're two hours behind him!" was her first greeting. Then she showed me a letter Mike had scratched out hurriedly on notebook paper and had left with her.

I'd been traveling for eight months, had never known where I was going to be or how long I would be there, so I had been without mail for all that time. It had been all right with me. My thoughts were so much with where I was, and what was happening, I'd had little time to let my thoughts dwell on family and friends or even home.

In Namo Buddha, I'd found a quote from Tilopa, a Tibetan poet and hermit, who had said "Wandering and wandering through other people's lands, it's hard to remember my homeland".

Now suddenly, here in my hand was a note from Mike not more than two hours old ! His "Hi Mom." was a delight. He was planning to set up a trek and would be at Himalayan Rover Trek in two hours! It sounded as if he had given up looking for me, but wished me luck in my travels.

I exchanged a few words with this smiling nun who was delighted to help us get together. I hoped I'd meet her again, and dashed back down through the fields around the Buddhist stupa on the other side, caught another taxi, and rushed to Himalayan Rover trek.

Chapter 46 - The Everest Trek Begins

At Himalayan Rover Trek, an organization which arranges treks to the mountainous regions near Mt. Everest, I met the owner, Dawa Norbu, who was waiting to see Mike in two hours.

Mike had known Dawa from two years before when Dawa had helped his climbing team to organize their trip to Makalu II. On the ascent of this peak situated near one of the ten highest mountains in the world, Mike had developed cerebral edema (swelling of the brain cells due to water retention), a usually lethal form of altitude sickness. Mike had been unconscious for five days, and had developed a blood clot which rendered the valves in the veins of his leg nearly useless. He had been carried out one hundred miles on a litter, and had spent two weeks in the hospital in Kathmandu. Dawa had brought Mike fruit and supplements to the rice fare in the hospital and they had become friends. I had heard Mike speak of Dawa, and was grateful for this wonderful opportunity to share with him my deep appreciation.

Dawa was a sherpa, possessing the firm character developed from life in the mountains, and was devoted to a simple way of life. He had been to the United States and was appalled at the number of choices of food available. He was used to eating whatever the season provided and it truly was appreciated that way. He was hoping that his son would marry a Kumbhu (High country) woman whose ways were simple.

As we were talking, Mike breezed in with joy and surprise at seeing me. He'd given up hope of our meeting after three days of fruitless search. How strangely ordinary it seemed that we would connect and talk together this way in the middle of Katmandu ! How perfectly natural that I would spontaneously agree to walk with him to Mount Everest starting in two days! The Russian climbers presently making an official ascent of an unclimbed route on Mt. Everest were friends of Mike's, and he wanted to walk to the base to congratulate them.

With Dawa's help, we arranged for a porter, studied maps, and left to pull together the rest of the gear needed for the trek.

I had carried a pair of heavy hiking boots in my pack all the way through China, Japan, Philippines, to Indonesia before I used them. On the jungle hike at Lake Toba, I'd gotten such terrible blisters I had been afraid to use them again. I'd carried them nonetheless all the way through Thailand and Burma. Now I decided to rent a pair of truly comfortable ones. Here in Kathmandu there were many equipment rental shops. I had my sleeping bag which I had not used so far, as well as sweaters, winter underwear, and heavy socks. Nearly all the weight in my pack was from clothes for my trek in Nepal, and I discovered I could have rented it all very reasonably right here in Katmandu.

We bought ropes, baskets, and umbrellas since it was raining daily now in pre-monsoon weather.

Those two days of preparation, full of visiting and catching up, were also two days of getting to know each other again. Mike had been mountain climbing since he was twelve. During three years in college in Berkeley, he had climbed in Alaska, Peru, British Columbia. He'd climbed El Capitan in Yosemite with the same Russians who were now climbing Mt. Everest. He'd also climbed with them seven years earlier in the mountains of Russia as a part of an Alpine Club exchange.

Occasionally he had returned for brief visits to share his adventures with me. In fact it was Mike who, with his enthusiasm for traveling with a lean wallet had said, " Mom, you can do it, too". He'd sparked an old desire of my own for foreign travel and encouraged me to entertain the possibility.

But visits are not like living together. So here was a real opportunity to get to know each other again on a day to day basis. Mike had to be very careful not to gain altitude too rapidly to avoid altitude sickness because of his recent experience with cerebral edema. When we met he joked that I was the only one who could keep him going slowly enough to acclimatize safely. I'd already said, "Better not count on that; you've got to make yourself go slowly." I felt his keen eagerness to get going, and sympathized with his impatience when I got sick with dysentery and we were held up for two days.

News had reached the embassy that the Russians were already high on Everest and seemed to be ascending rapidly. He was afraid he was going to miss them. At one point I spent a sleepless night worrying, and in the morning told him I couldn't go with him. If he was goal directed towards reaching the Russians, any delay would frustrate and anger him. I didn't want to get in his way. He too had debated through the night, and told me that he had been hoping he would meet and trek with me, that if we reached the Russians in time he would consider it an extra bonus. There seemed to be a clearer cast to the air after that.

So armed with Steve Bzruschka's "Trekking in Nepal" and a porter who was going to carry our packs for the first one hundred miles to Thangboche at 12,000 ft., we set off by bus.

Dawa had suggested that we walk all the way to Lukla. Many people begin the climb by flying to this precarious air strip at nearly 10,000 ft. in altitude. That way they skipped the eighty mile approach across a series of mountain ranges. If either of us had looked carefully at the mileage we'd be walking perhaps both of us might not have begun. But the number of "ifs" were already accumulating. What if we hadn't met at all? What if Mike had not seen the tiny three-line mention in the Berkeley newspaper that his friends were climbing Mt. Everest? There was no time to be wasted on if's.

Here we were riding on one of Nepal's more rickety buses. Osselman, our porter, sat on the top with many other passengers and our packs. After a three hour ride, we reached Lomosangu, where the bus dropped us off. But there was no visible way to go on. Apparently people chartered trucks here. Osselman said if we waited perhaps we could hitch a ride with another group. So we sat and waited, and after two hours a truck carrying a group of Australian trekkers came along and we were able to negotiate a ride with them. There was just room for us on the top of their two story truck along with their baggage.

We began a ride up a winding gravel road which tipped the bus at a scary slant over steep canyons. At several rock slides we had to get out to move rocks blocking the road, and I prayed that no more would roll over the high cliff onto our bus.

It started to rain and the group of six of us on the top held a billowing canvas tarp over us while water dropped in rivulets at the folds onto our shivering legs and wet gear. I was glad for the year's preparation for this ride which seemed really normal travel for Asia. I must admit I was sure the bus would topple over the steep slopes.

When we reached a small group of houses it was dark and the Australians unloaded tents and set them up in a muddy field. It was pouring rain, and a Nepalese man who had been traveling with us "arranged" for us to sleep in a nearby house. I was shown a wooden shelf where one of the teen-age daughters of the family was already sound asleep. He motioned for me to climb up beside her.

The next morning we discovered that the family upon whom we had intruded had no idea what had happened. The man had told us where to sleep without waking up the family! After receiving some glowering looks, we respectfully apologized through our porter and showed our appreciation for their "sharing" much needed shelter with a contribution. All was cleared and the wife smiled as she cooked us hot tea and potatoes.

Apparently many travelers come to these parts expecting hotel accommodations, but these simple people have only their homes to share. We didn't know the man was not a member of the family until the next day. That's one of the drawbacks of not knowing the language. Thank heavens everyone's good nature cut across the initial irritation.

The sun was out and the bus drove for another hour up a steep mountain and down another. That second day we covered a full day's "walk" by bus, as one of our Australian companions pointed out. The road had been extended since he had walked the trail the year before.

I was grateful for a day's reprieve as we left the bus at Chirontichop, the last cluster of houses on the road. The driver had refused to go farther without another "contribution", though he could have saved us another day's walk on the newly constructed road. The Nepalese were learning to demand more money the same way as they had in Indonesia. Not wanting to meet their exorbitant price, we just stepped out and began our walk. The gravel road stretched out on a fairly gradual incline, but Osselman darted up on a "short cut" which led us up what seemed like a forty-five degree slope. I stumbled along, climbing steps that had been cut in the mud.

Nepalese people passed us in bunches. One group of young men were each carrying enormous coils of cable wire which must have weighed a hundred and fifty pounds each. They stepped around me and rose up the steep slope as if they were on an escalator. I felt as if I were walking up a "down" escalator as I strained to keep up with Mike and Osselman.

Osselman was a Newari, from a tribe of Nepalese people who settled around Kathmandu. He'd been climbing these mountains all of his twenty years. He was carrying both our packs in an awkward off-balance hump on his back and didn't seem to notice the weight, which centered on the head band draped across the crown of his head.

We rose straight up over one mountain ridge and dove directly down the other side, descending into a magic rain forest full of ferns and deciduous trees and the sweet smell of molding earth, mushrooms and roots. If I'd been exhausted from the climb up, the trail down allowed me to breathe again. But as we hit the stream-bed that cut the steep V in the mountain, we headed right back up again through progressively drier country out of the shade of trees to grazing lands for cattle. Around every bend I was praying for the end, but another zig or zag was always beyond, until finally we came upon a group of stone houses with

"Tea House-Lodging" written in English on several.

The Australians had already erected their tents. They were surprised that we'd taken so little time to get there. I felt then that I must still be in pretty good shape. But perhaps my pride might have driven me harder than I should have gone. I slept like a rock. We were up early and on the trail while everyone was gradually getting up in the Australian camp.

The exertion of the first day had rendered my legs too weary to move. Only strong will power got them operating again. Of course we had to walk down, hopelessly down, into a canyon across which I could see the steep ascent on the other side reclaiming the altitude we were so easily losing.

When someone had told me the Everest trek was all "up and down, up and down", I had smiled thinking I knew what they were speaking of. Only now my body knew.

But it was beautiful. The open grassy slopes where new green wheat waved reminded me of Switzerland, as did the tiny villages of only three or four houses. Even the water buffaloes grazing along the edges of the wheat fields seemed like displaced dairy cattle. We ate lunch by a clear rushing stream. I could have sat for a whole day, savoring the sound of the water, and the sparkling of the granite stones on the shore. But we soon began again. The upward steep grade wound in and out of rhododendron trees with petals from the recent blooms scattered all red and white along the trail.

Then it began to hail. I had my poncho which let the hail stones bounce off and settle on the whitening trail. Osselman and Mike opted for the umbrellas. Somehow the idiocy of that symbol of civilized city living; the English Gentleman picture, sheltering two scruffy climbing men burdened with weight, made me giggle uncontrollably.

Then the rain began and the water spilling down the stone staircase built by sherpas long before made a stream bed of our path. I felt exhausted. Water slopped in my boots with every step. About this time I began to chant inwardly my healing chant, taking a step with each syllable. The rhythm helped me take the interminable steps upward. The sounds of the chant alternated in my mind with complaints that I'd ever begun this endless trip. But I stoically marched on. There was no other choice. The joy of the mountains was fast disappearing in this dogged attempt to hurry on.

My whole trip so far had been full of the freedom of spontaneity, the true benefit of independence. Now I was locked into Mike's goal. I was continually grateful when we stopped so he could rest his leg, sloping it upward so the circulation could clear.

The gray trunks of the rhododendron trees twisted in the rainy mist, and glimpses of the terrain caught my eyes as I wiped the drenching rain from my cheeks. Now that I'm writing this, I realize those glimpses had equal time duration with all the other illusory time experiences I'd had. Now I remember those branches fading into the distance as clearly as if I'd sat and stared at them for hours.

We plodded on. The pass we reached as light was fading was revealed by flashes of lightning. The rain was coming down in that wet intensity that makes you grateful for the intervals of air. I was a soggy mess from sweating under the poncho, and from wading through the waterfalls that cascaded down the steps. We had reached a test point on the trail. The dreaded pass at 9,000 feet was our highest point so far, and we were going to sleep here. A small stupa surrounded by many mani stones proclaiming the "Om mani padme hum" chant marked the highest point.

Two houses rested here. In the rain the Australians had arrived and already had set up their tents. Luckily, we found shelter in one tiny house where the whole front room leaked waterfalls of water in several places.

We were concerned about how Mike would weather this night at the pass, but it was I who was exhausted. I let the men hang up our ponchos and a tent fly to divert the rivulets away from enough space on the floor so we could curl up in our sleeping bags and be comparatively dry. They draped our wet clothes near the fire in the next room where our hosts slept.

We had an opportunity to discover how the altitude was affecting us. I had borrowed Mike's water bottle while we climbed. I'd been fairly certain I'd given it back to him, but had searched all my things when Mike thought I still had it. The emotional feeling of having lost a vital piece of equipment and that Mike thought I'd been careless, had led me to suggest someone must have taken it, which exasperated him.

Mike was coping with the tension of uncertainty of how high he could reasonably go. We had completed a very long walk, perhaps ten miles, and he was determined to make it to base camp. He was beginning to realize I couldn't walk as fast as he wanted us to, and the impatience mixing with the worry about altitude peeled the guards from his anger.

I was surprised that I had been so calm. Perhaps it was tiredness which required too much energy to respond, but perhaps the effects of my sitting were still with me. Any solicitous motherly attempts to ameliorate had only angered him still more.

I realized there was going to be a new relationship between us. Perhaps we were more friends than mother-son. At least the old relationship of older-younger was gone. We were equals and had to deal with each other from that intimate level of genetic closeness on a plane of common respect. Thankfully affection and genuine respect pulled us through rather well. Perhaps the altitude was a help in forcing straight interaction. One gets too tired to cover up. Despite the thunder I slept deeply.

At about one o'clock there was a loud knocking on the door. The storm had knocked all the Australians' tents down or flooded them. They were looking for dry places to sleep. There was no dry space left on our floor.

At two a.m. I got up to go outside to the bathroom. White hail spread a half inch thick over the land, which sparkled like crystallized sugar in the clear light of the moon. My appreciation of what brought me here in spite of the discomfort flooded over me as I gazed at this wonderland and the crystal stupa in the silver light.

Next day we got into the clothes that had fortunately dried. Then Mike found the canteen with his gear in the morning and we realized how unsure memory becomes at high altitude. I felt very sheepish when I realized we still had it. Mike's exaggerated anger, and my own loss of accurate memory, were signs that both of us were being affected by the altitude.

Mike had commented with amazement the day before when we were resting with his leg raised, that he'd noticed no pain or swelling in the leg where the blood clot had damaged the valves in his veins. He had been used to a constant discomfort, and had expected swelling because of the exertion and altitude. I told him then, somewhat cautiously, that I'd received the healing chant from Thangha Rinpoche and was chanting it silently as we walked. "Keep it up " he said, " It seems to be working. I've never walked this long before without resting for two or three days afterwards. There's no redness at all"!

As we were preparing to leave, the very nice woman who had shared her own house with us, told us she had a very bad toothache. She had asked the Australians if their doctor would pull it out and he had refused. At first I was surprised, and a little embarrassed that he should refuse help when he might be able to give it, but I suspect this dilemma comes to all the doctors who pass through this area. They might treat something but they're moving on, and the effect might be to make the matter worse. People in this area have lived without doctors for centuries, carrying their sick if possible three days' walk down to the bus and to Kathmandu. Otherwise they have just borne the ailment until it healed, or killed them.

This was a very strong Buddhist area. On the walls of the tea houses where we had stopped, I had seen the pictures of Padma Sambava or Guru Rinpoche, the founder of Tibetan Buddhism, and the special deity of this area. In this house, placed out of reach of the dripping roof, were thankas, or pictures of deities printed on rice paper, pasted on the dark wood walls.

I felt very warmly towards this woman who had kindly but dubiously fried the fiddle heads of the bracken fern I'd picked as we walked the day before. I had had difficulty getting her to cook them for us since she felt they were inedible. She'd watched curiously as I ate them and finally tried a taste herself. It wasn't an area where vegetables would grow very well, and she had been delighted.

So I told her as simply as I could that I would chant the healing chant Thangha Rinpoche had taught me. She agreed, and I held her jaws in my hands and chanted. There is so much we don't know about healing. I hoped that at the very least the concern I had for her pain, the touching of one being to another, might ease her discomfort. This was the first time I chanted out loud, and was amazed at the feel of the sound in my hands. Then we bowed to each other and Mike and I set off again.

The Australian group were drying their tents since they had been completely flooded out in the night. When we left, only the last piles of hailstones lay against the stupa and in the shadows of the mani stones. It was all that was left from that beautiful magic of the night before.

From this point, we descended into the next steep valley, passing wheat fields on the upper regions, down to the lush rain forest growth in the canyon by the stream. Despite my weariness, I delighted in this fantastic contrast between the dry upper mountain peaks and the soft deciduous growth 4,000 feet below. There were forests of blooming rhododendron trees. The red blossoms against the green leaves looked like Christmas, then a sprinkling of white blossoms created valentines among those brilliant red flowers!

In the early morning as we descended, it wasn't raining, thank heavens. As we went down the clay path I wondered how the sherpas managed these slopes without slipping. Osselman had on the costume of the area, plastic zoris with only the big toe through a plastic thong. He managed to trudge along with the enormous weight of our packs without slipping or losing his shoes. We'd given him money to buy a pair of tennis shoes, but he'd chosen to spend it on something else.

The mist from the wet ground rose in a soft fog which veiled the pink flowers and the green wheat. Then we walked into a bower of sheltering maple leaves where orchids bloomed in the branches of tall trees and blue primroses dotted the path. There were oaks and hemlocks covered with lush green moss. Even the light looked green. Then I found my first Jack-in-the-Pulpit hiding by a stream. The plants here were just like those on our East Coast in the woodlands. I could have been walking along the Appalachian Trail. The familiar plant life lifted me continents away.

On the other side of the river, we began trudging along up the endlessly steep trail where rhododendrons grew more sparsely. As the "mist" got heavier and turned to rain, we rose through a ghostlike terrain. Twisted trees stood dark against the gray mist. A flock of snow cocks big as ptarmigans darted across the trail and down the steep slope, fading in the foggy distance. The other-worldliness of fog enveloped us. Even the leaves were soggy and made no sound as we walked. We couldn't see beyond ten feet on either side of the trail. We walked in vaporous moisture. The twisted dark trunks of trees looked like wobbling columns on either side.

We reached the second pass, at 11,000 feet. The wind carried the mist in clouds across a saddle of upheaved rocks. There were the remains of three bleak looking stone houses with the roof gone from each, standing like ships parting the almost solid fog as it blew by. The mani stones stacked in long hillocks reflected the feeling of grateful prayer in coming along this ghostlike plateau.

On the other side, the cheerful sun dried the terraces of wav-ing wheat and we started down again. We could look at the next impossible mountainous earth-wave rising across the white rag-ing stream far below us. Oh for the wings of a crow! My feet and legs went into automatic as weariness stepped time with me. I began to want to sit longer at each rest spot and enjoy the scenery.

We passed occasional hikers who had news of how high the Russians were getting on the mountain. Mike, looking at my impossibly slow pace, feared they would be finished before we even made it to Lukla, and would already have flown back to Kathmandu.

For one more day we walked along more gradual slopes. There was a small group of people who became familiar as we walked. We left early in the morning each day, and later they would catch up and pass us. I recognized the man who helped us find lodging that first rainy night in Chirontichop. He was walking to his home in Bandar. "All the way is up and down, up and down. For you not so good", he smiled.

Actually I was doing at least as well as other trekkers. But this group passed us and later as we came slowly over a rise, there they were resting and cooking breakfast. This time we sat with them. Mike spoke a little Nepali. "Ama", he said pointing to me, "Choro" pointing to himself. Mother and son. They all looked at us and began rolling with laughter. Finally the man told us they'd figured we were lovers!

From then on they walked a bit slower and with us for portions of the way. But they were used to skipping over these mountains. They walked once a week to the market, a three day walk for them. When they went to Kathmandu they walked. It was the only way to travel, and they enjoyed it. Actually Osselman was planning to walk back from Thangboche in five days when we had planned to take eleven days to get there.

The trail went from 9,000 feet down to the stream bed below at 4,000 feet then up again to Sete at 8,450 feet. On the map it looked like four miles, but it was closer to six by the time we zigged and zagged.

In the rain again, we arrived thoroughly sopped at the pass where there were two stupas. A monastery was above. The tea house was full, and as we looked around, a young boy invited us to his house. Thankfully we entered an open room where a warm fire glowed. I could scarcely see the faces of the family sitting around it, everything beyond was in shadow. The mother was cooking tea over flames with a large pan set to one side for chapatis, the big pancake-like wheat bread. Above the fire near the soot covered ceiling hung a three foot diameter tray-shaped basket on which wheat grains were spread out drying.

There had been so much rain recently that the wheat was in danger of rotting before harvest. The potatoes were actually beginning to spoil. The only two crops in this region were wheat and potatoes. There was danger of a hard time of shortage.

I slept in the daughter's bed at her insistence. My clothes were drying by the fire.

In the morning the father showed me a very bad open sore on his foot where he had burned himself. Mike had some antibiotic salve we could leave with him, and again I chanted, since that was all I could do. A six year old son, who was learning English, caught the sound of the chant. I wrote it out in English phonetics hoping he could continue to chant it after we moved on. I felt as if I were carrying messages to all these devout Buddhists from Thangha Rinpoche: strong feelings of good will.

Mike commented as we left that he'd felt good to do something for these people, that somehow the chant seemed to give encouragement if nothing else. It seemed to bring us closer to the people of the area.

Chapter 47 - On to Namche

Since the sun was blazing on the green wheat under a clear blue sky, we began our interminable walk again in good spirits. We still had to climb up over a 10,000 foot pass draped with prayer flags, and down into another unbelievable rain forest of moss, ferns, trees and rhododendrons.

I was getting sick again. Perhaps it was a bit of pride that had kept me going so far with all the people being surprised at how I was doing. But perhaps it was also for Mike with his eagerness to get to base camp before the Russians left, that I had urged myself on a bit beyond my own energy level. He'd been very good about not pushing me, had gone slowly like "a herd of turtles" as he said. In fact he was aware that the slow pace was really to his advantage because he acclimatized more slowly. We were both holding the worry about what higher altitude would do. He'd come through the 11,000 foot bleak pass with no apparent effects, but this was still child's play in view of base camp's nearly 18,000 foot level.

At each rest stop I fell asleep. Usually I could drag on after a while. But finally it became clear I needed to take a day to rest. We stumbled into a tea house in Junbesi after coming down the hill from one of our first views of the snow capped Himalayas. The enormity of our walk was dawning on me. I slept all night, all day and the next night, grateful for the hard bench where I could spread my sleeping bag. I guess the proprietors were a bit surprised that we didn't go the next day, but seemed to tolerate this weakness. It was good to have Osselman along to translate and explain, to locate places and teach us how to cope in this terrain. I think, in a way, Mike was secretly grateful for the rest despite his hurry.

I had suggested he just go on and let me go back by myself. Since I had traveled alone for so many months this was no difficulty. But he chose to stay. He had decided this was a trip the two of us were taking together, and if the Russians were still there it would be a big bonus. He was beginning to see the enormity of the trip himself and appreciate that what he'd done so far was a real accomplishment. Previously he had not been able to walk more than three miles before the leg began to hurt.

Memories of the next day are faded with step after step up or down, not seeing, just progressing doggedly on. I had wanted very much to rest by the stream but made it up another steep hillside.

All the joy of walking in the mountains, the experience of foreign ways, the energy to meet people had drained out of me until I was just a crumpling body slogging along. Occasionally a very beautiful vista, stretching out along the endless valleys we'd trudged, would come into my awareness and fill me with energy I didn't know I had. I began to view this trip as a necessary ordeal, a trip I had to take to surmount the sense of my limits, that it really wasn't a trip to see the beauty.

Mike walked behind me so I could set my own pace, but I knew how much terrain people usually covered each day. This egged me on. What a crazy way to travel. I was promising myself that if I got to Lukla where the airport was I'd stay there and let Mike go on alone.

We'd just reached the top of one high climb, and were on our way down, which was always like a deep sigh of relief for me, when we met a young woman pushing up the steep path, sweating and exhausted. She looked at me and said, "YOU climbed this"?!, in surprise, and staggered past. I had made it so far, and the discovery gave me courage. My feet got lighter.

It wasn't all dragging. Sometimes I was lifted by a sweet breeze blowing across the green wheat, or the sight of the thundering stream below. I could step faster, forget the gravity pulling at me or the struggle to breathe. I just walked, and the mountain light, glistening on leaves or shining through the grasses, sparkled around me. Rather, my feet walked themselves and I seemed to float along for periods without knowing. Then again my movements would slip back into the reality of weariness and every step was pain. There was no reason for this flicker between states, but when I was in one phase, it seemed the other was non-existent. Heavy trudging made no room for floating - only dust and rising stairs prevailed. But while I was floating, the struggle of moments before was out of my awareness.

We crossed the streams on wooden bridges, some swinging on cables over the white water. They bounced with their own rhythm. It felt a little like walking on waves. The possibility of being catapulted over the side onto rocks and cold rushing water kept me concentrating on holding my balance when the waves set by Mike's steps joggled with my own.

We took eight days getting to the Dudh Kosi River, made of the melt water off the Khumbu Glacier near Mt. Everest. The map showed a trail paralleling the river. As we turned to walk along it I felt we'd finished the hard part. However, when Osselman turned uphill, away from the river and the level trail in an illogical direction, I grumbled to Mike, "It looks as if he doesn't know the way".

We had earlier crisscrossed a "road" being constructed which would make it easier for future trekkers. Many workers chipping granite rock by hand, scooping dirt with shovels, had greeted us as we passed. Now that roadbed wound off to our left at a much lower altitude and I wondered why we didn't keep to it. Insanely we rose sharply up to a pass at 10,000 feet while all the good nature drained out of me. Osselman spoke in monosyllables maintaining this was the only way.

When we got to a high vantage point, Osselman pointed. I could look down 3,000 feet to where the road had crumbled and fallen another 2,000 feet to the river below. Only the steep V-shaped slope remained. The road was wiped out. Indeed the way we'd come was the only way. A young boy walked with us for a while carrying a huge basket of eggs on his back suspended by the carrying strap across his head. He was cheerful and obviously loved the job of walking these long distances.

We kept to a level contour, walking around canyons, rather than sharply down and up, but the walking seemed to stretch out into senselessly endless zigzags. We walked half a day, and had only gone about 4 miles of distance forward. This Alice in Wonderland treadmill effect did not help my sense of accomplishment. Finally when we came on a house in the woods I was greatly relieved to go in for tea. Thankfully, we decided to stay the night.

There was a leathery woman who was obviously the head of the family. She cooked the meals and negotiated for our overnight stay. A very old woman was sitting in a dark corner grinding wheat with two round three-inch thick disks of stone. She turned the heavy stones around against each other with a stick placed in a hole in the top stone. The flour slid out the fine grooves between the stones onto a yak hide spread out with the skin side up to catch it.

A carpenter, (her husband?) was busy making repairs on some cylindrical storage bins she had, cutting wood collars that fitted with an ingenious buckle around the barrel shaped boards. All the time the man worked, the woman spewed a stream of invectives at him in a loud voice.

When the boy came in she warmed up with delight and charm. He had obviously taken some grain for her to grind into flour and brought some eggs for her. While I sat, stupefied with weariness, I watched her pull out a huge roll of rupees and pay him. She was doing a good business of lodging travelers and feeding them chapatis. We were her only guests and she seemed pleased to have us. Later, as my energy returned, I tried to grind some of the wheat the way the old woman was doing it. My arm began aching after two minutes. We all laughed together at my weakness.

I wished I could have photographed the dark interior of that house. She had been cooking on her mud stove for so long that the rafters were shiny black with soot and long lumpy stalactites of soot hung above the fire. She had shelves with great brass bowls three feet across, some to store wheat, some to bathe in that were even bigger. Cylindrical storage bins lined one side of the room like butter churns. There were the usual wooden benches near the fire. We all slept in the one open room. The woman unfolded big woven yak wool blankets for herself and the carpenter on the floor.

We ate in semi-darkness with the firelight casting Rembrandt-like illumination on shadowy figures.

Next day we set off early and, despite the idiotic directions our climb took us, I didn't complain.

Then there it was, as we rounded a curve and looked through the trees from a high pass. Lukla air strip sloped from the flat plateau, breaking off sharply into space above the deep V-shaped canyon of the raging Dudh Kosi. At last we'd reached it. We hadn't seen any airplanes fly overhead because of all the rain and fog which closed down this rather dangerous air strip until the weather cleared. Now as we stood on the hill, three planes took off one after the other, and Mike felt sure it was the Russians. Helplessly we watched them leap out into space from that slanting runway that just stopped abruptly at the mountain's edge. I felt terrible. My slow pace had prevented Mike from doing what he most wanted to do.

But Mike had already worked through his ordeal. When he had been on Makalu II, Mike had been unconscious for three days at 21,000 feet while his partners tried to figure out what to do with him. It was not easy, since nearly everyone with cerebral edema dies if they are not taken down to a lower altitude quickly. There had been a good climber who was making an ascent of a nearby mountain. He probably could have managed to get Mike down in a shorter time to an altitude conducive to recovery. He had chosen to continue his climb for which he had been preparing for several years rather than fail at his own attempt in order to rescue a group who had not taken the time to acclimatize slowly to the high altitude.

Mike had experienced a great deal of anger about this. He felt that if he had been taken down in time he might not have suffered the blood clot that injured the valves in his leg. For the last two years, with all the determination he could summon, he'd gradually worked himself so he could walk for brief interludes.

As we walked, he talked of understanding his kinship with the climber who had gone on to do his own climb. "We're the same", he said. "We both have one-pointed goal direction." He had already seen his own impatience as he kept to my slow pace. Yet given the choice, he had decided to stay with me, to complete one human interaction rather than miss that and possibly miss the other as well.

I felt that all the energy wasted on anger at what might have been was useless. He was miraculously alive and that was enough for me. Still it's not easy to let go of wanting something to have been a different way, to just accept what is and make the best of it.

Finally, after two years of struggle, the anger subsided as we helplessly watched those three planes leap into the air. Mike did not indulge in even one "what if"! The trek itself had become enough. Even walking with this exhausted slow poke of a mother became a joy in itself. After all, it was a miracle we'd ever connected in the first place.

Eleven days it had taken us to get to Lukla, not too bad really, since average time was 7 or 8 days. We came out of the marvelously "untouched" region into a world of trekkers milling about the air strip, sleeping in dormitories, talking English, and carrying the stamp of Western civilization wherever they went.

From the impact of this blast of trekkers, I looked back at all the peaceful days spent among blooming rhododendrons, high passes decorated with prayer flags, tiny bazaars and Tibetan monasteries, wild torrents of water, steep mountain stairs and silence. Only now that I was in the vicinity of airplanes did I recognize how quiet that vehicle-less walk had been. Even in what had seemed to me to be a mad dash there had been unforgettable moments of beauty and a sense of accomplishment.

Now I was at Lukla it seemed I could go on, even though I'd

kept promising myself I would stop there. It was becoming a wonderful opportunity to share with Mike — a time we couldn't duplicate in any other way.

And to top it all the Russians were still climbing Everest. They'd gotten some climbers to the top but were doing their best to get the whole team up before the monsoons came in. So the race was on again. Suddenly, however, I was aware I was acclimatized, and hardier than in those aching first days.

We walked through Lukla and along a level trail by the river till we came to Ghat. As we entered this tiny town a calf walked beside us. The skin around its eyes, legs, and underbelly were ulcerated. Strange growths protruded everywhere. It was a terrible sight. We walked along a mani wall of prayer stones with this miserable calf and my heart ached for it. The whole feeling of Ghat was strange, yet I could go no further.

Across the river was what seemed to be a deserted village hung with decaying prayer flags and with a ghostly air about it. Ghat was situated in a bog, the water turning putrid in the soggy earth. I 've never seen such a depressing atmosphere. I felt that perhaps the village on the other side had experienced an epidemic or something, and that they'd moved to let the old site rest. But that was only feeling.

The tiny house we stayed in had a compartment for the family, and an open area for travelers with the usual two foot wide board bench to sleep on. At the back of the house the old man of the family sat counting his prayer beads and chanting endlessly. He was in the room where they stored the chang, the local fermented rice drink which people in Ghat seemed to imbibe in quantities enough to still any anxiety! They all seemed acutely jolly.

A whole troop of women went into the family section of the house and gathered around a pewter pitcher full of chang which they poured to overflowing in each cup, and drank, refilled and drank until they giddily trooped out, well stocked. I wondered if they would have the balance enough to cook the night's' dinner. But apparently everyone in Ghat was tipsy so it didn't matter.

Perhaps it was a festival, or the time of successful fermentation — I wondered if they continued with this congenial practice all year. The chang didn't seem to affect the old man's chanting "Om Mani Padme Hum" over and over till I finally fell asleep.

Next morning was May Day. I woke early and walked outside. Wild flowers were growing everywhere in the boggy peat-mossy earth, and I gathered a few to make a May basket for our hostess, who I'm sure could not make sense of it. But while I was returning, I watched our hostess collect water. I'd assumed they collected water from the river about 3 blocks distant, or from some stream. But the woman went out in a boggy cow pasture and where water collected in the foot tracks of the cows, she dipped enough to fill her jar. Then she came in and poured it in the collection barrel. I vowed I'd not drink another sip of water here and urged Mike to come to a less sickly looking town for breakfast. The ulcerated calf had been somehow a warning to me of the state of the tiny village. I must have been very tired. Not in all my travels so far had I balked at people's ways.

The walk became splendid. The valley was fertile and warm. For the first time, the white peaks of the mountains were continually visible poking the blue sky. It felt a bit like the trails in Colorado in the Rockies. Wild flowers clustered among the rocks. Dairy cattle and goats wandered the steep grassy hills. The people we passed smiled cheerfully.

We crossed a new cable construction bridge where a group of very concentrated Britishers were so busy working they didn't look up at us. Later, we learned one of them was Hillary, the first to climb Mt. Everest, who had devoted his later years to helping to make life more comfortable in the Khumbu region in Nepal.

[Editor's Note: Hillary and Tenzing Norgay, the Sherpa, climbed Mt. Everest together. According to Tenzing Norgay, "When we got close to the summit, we joined hands and walked together to the summit." (oral personal communication from interview with Tenzing on May 3, 1981)]

When we got to the wide bridge crossing near Namche, we

began to meet villagers dressed in their most festive costumes coming home from the bazaar which was held once a week there. It was late in the afternoon when we began to climb the 2000-foot mountain to the biggest town in the Khumbu area. As we wound up the zigzaggy path, we suddenly caught a glimpse of Mt. Everest, whose steep dark triangle peak poked above the white mountains in front.

The Russians might be up there right now! We gazed for a while at the snowy banner blowing in a horizontal line off the peak, signs of high winds. I'd finally gotten used to gauging distances by foot. Visually, it seemed impossible to cover such an expanse. Then, step by step, there would be a miraculous diminution of the space between ourselves and our destination. It began to feel possible to cover a stretch of endless trail by meandering down one steep slope, up and out of sight on another. But this felt a bit like watching the moon where astronauts walked far from this planet.

At Namche we would have walked nearly 100 miles! The tiny triangle peak of Everest emerged from the clouds. This was only the second sight of Everest. We had seen it first in the far distance on our third day at the Everest View Hotel. There, a consumptive child coughed and coughed, leaning helplessly over a barrel in exhaustion, waiting patiently, hands folded gracefully in her lap for the next depleting volley of coughing. The child had wiped out my memory of the mountain. From that distance we'd seen more of the massive pyramid than we were seeing here. We were getting closer. We turned the bend and again it was out of sight like some mirage that lured us on but continually receded as we walked.

About the time when weariness would have enveloped me, sight of the sharp green V-shaped valley we had risen above and waterfalls from ice fields pouring off the high mountain opposite us, lifted my feet. Then we came to the miniature purple iris, whole stretches of them only three inches high along the trail, catching the sun in their velvet petals. How easy it is to climb with such enticements!

The later in the day it became, the more full of jollity and chang were the villagers descending. One old man was swaying so much I wondered if he might take the shortcut over the cliff as he sang and staggered down towards us. Most of the women we met wore the Tibetan dress common to the Khumbu region. It was a wrap-around tunic. Married women wore an apron of cloth hand woven in bright rainbow colors. All of them were giddy with good spirits and not a little chang.

Then there was Namche. Gray stone houses were arranged so steeply on the slope they looked like the seats in the highest balcony of an opera house; long rows of identical gray rectangles against a barren hill, but what a welcome sight. Suddenly trekkers were everywhere. Small stores displayed chocolate (at exorbitant prices), canned fruit, hiking socks, and items which had been out of our reach for days.

Scattered on the stony path where we walked were discarded shoes of every kind, sandals, tennis shoes, boots — as if the weary thankful travelers were making an offering of the exhausted shoes to the spirits of the mountain for a safe journey. It was a reminder that things hold up just as long as they're needed (and not a moment longer sometimes).

We'd reached the point where the up and down nature of the hike changes to a gradual ascent, so we had planned to stay two nights. The 11,000 foot altitude didn't seem to bother me, but the minute we found our trekkers' lodge, I sank onto the wooden bench as if it were the softest down.

Namche showed signs of civilization not so frequent on the trail. Pictures of the New York subway system colorfully covered the cracks in a wall of one of the tea houses. Posters of the New York city skyline, Tokyo at night and many models of modern cars were preferred as decoration. On my bench was a piece of foam rubber, probably a piece of booty left when mountain climbing expeditions simplified their loads before returning to Lukla.

The rustic town was full of international flavor. Many of the porters and restaurant people spoke French, Japanese and English interchangeably. I remembered Indonesian children who quickly picked up the language of the people handing out money.

Mike set out to discover the people in the UNICEF program working on alternative energy solutions. He found a friend working on a hydraulic system which would bring electricity to Namche. We were still using oil lamps in the dark rooms, or the light of the tiny cooking fire inside the clay stove where holes provided the "burners" for the pots.

He also discovered the women's climbing group that had just successfully climbed Ama Dablam, the beautiful mountain near Thangboche a day's hike ahead.

Though we both had an undercurrent of concern for his reaction to this high altitude, Mike seemed to be doing extremely well, and he jauntily set out on his explorations.

For two days we basked in "luxury" - varying our usual potato diet with beans, yak meat and an occasional pan fried "cake" with chocolate sauce that jogged our taste buds into existence again. Only now did I recognize that with the invariably identical meals, the anticipation of taste had dropped out. We ate for nourishment no matter how monotonous the taste. But we kept hearing from travelers along the trail about the cake, and we fell subject to its lure in Namche, paying more for the cake than we did for four nights' lodgings! Indulgence seemed to be acceptable, we rationalized, since we were in the midst of comparative plenty after a week's deprivation. But the prices were on a scale with the privilege of traveling. Outlandish!

When I felt rested a bit, I wandered along the winding dirt alleys around the nearly seventy houses, carefully avoiding the great horned yaks wandering the streets with small boys occasionally prodding them on. These gentle eyed creatures suddenly were everywhere with their horns spreading clear across the narrow passageways, so I often deferentially found another way to go.

I rested for two days while Mike connected with and helped

people working on various projects for alternative energy, visited with his friends among the women climbers, and generally delighted in the atmosphere of social exchange. Everywhere in the mountains people of all nationalities shared the joy and challenge with mutual appreciation.

Time came for us to move on. Though my bones felt as if we could have rested more, Namche was too full of people to feel the silence of the giant mountains that overlooked it. On the morning we set out, a fresh snow had caught on the steep sides of the mountainous wall across the valley. While we walked past purple irises, we could gaze up at the snow etched cliffs.

From 11,000 to 12,000 feet is only one increment of 1,000, but the apparently gradual ascent seemed endless. Here the village people, mostly women, walked with bundles as we'd walk down the block to the grocery store. They were nearly all my age, and somehow it helped me pull from myself my most energetic exertion as we cheerfully greeted each other in passing. Then again came the familiar V cut of the stream where some 1000 feet of descent to the raging level of the white water just promised that across the bridge were 2000 more feet to climb up again. But here the rhododendrons bloomed in pinks, speckling the pale green of new spring leaves with pastel clumps. Again the joy of beauty lifted my feet. The last climb of 1000 feet began to weigh on me when I met a jaunty monk with crinkly face and his bright orange and maroon robes coming down the hill. His surprise and respect for my attempt again roused me to my best effort.

During this part of the hike Mike and I walked separately, lost in the pink and green splendor and our own efforts. Now as we stepped up the last turn and saw the stupa, mani wall and square buildings of Thangboche a strange surge of tears came to me — of familiarity, of at-homeness, of unknown emotion. Mike had wanted to see this monastery, when he was last in the Himalayas, but he had been carried on a stretcher in another direction over equally up and down terrain. We gazed at this - one of the highest monasteries in the world. Kontega mountain, and Ama Dablam, shaped like a Tibetan hat, hung above it on one side, the deep chasm of the Dudh Kosi River cut downward on the other.

The buildings of stacked rectangles were painted brightly, and monks in orange and maroon were washing clothes in the "fountain", in the center of a wide open area. It seemed like a communal park where trekkers, travelers who had come across from Tibet with yak teams, and mountaineers could meet in common with the "mini monks", young boys six to fifteen years old, and other personnel of the monastery.

We found a small, comfortable dormitory with six bunk beds with foam rubber mattresses and we settled in for the evening.

Osselman, our porter, was planning to walk back to Kathmandu in five days. He was leaving in the morning with no rest. We had taken eleven days, and I felt exhausted. I was so truly grateful for the patient acceptance of our burdens. He had carried both our packs for one hundred miles, always with reserve energy, but patience at my slowness!

He'd done the whole walk in the rubber zoris with the thong between his toes.

We were staying for 2 days and I wanted to do my laundry, which I'd been too tired to do before. Next morning after bidding goodbye to Osselman, I went down to the spring where ice water froze my hands in one minute. I'd borrowed a bowl from the Sherpa landlord but could scarcely squeeze the water out, it was so icy. I draped the pants and shirt on the bushes to dry in the wind and found a soft place to rest. I later learned why everyone was washing at the fountain in the afternoon when we arrived. There was a long black pipe leading from way above the valley which collected the sunlight and warmed the water by the time it reached the fountain. This had been erected by Hillary some years back.

At one time, I had thought I would stay at Thangboche and meditate, till I realized it was not set up for visiting practitioners. At the site of the convent, I sat among the trees with the roaring water of the Dudh Kosi far below the steep cliff and felt satisfied just to be still. I could have spent weeks there, but something made me feel I was to go with Mike all the way to the base of Everest.

Chapter 48 - Into Yak Country

I'd never been above 12,000 feet before. Perhaps my curiosity about how I would hold out kept me going. Perhaps it was the beauty of the mountains which only now were sharing their presence with us continually. They were like great tolerant beings whose motion was so slow that the dust of a hundred snows had accumulated on their enormous shoulders.

We were on our own now. Our packs were lighter, but were on our backs for the rest of the climb.

We had gone half way down the mountain when we met two young women I'd gotten to know in Khatmandu. They'd been out three weeks already. One of them was feeling the effects of altitude and was struggling along with a painful headache. Our visit pepped them up and me too. They'd been up to base camp and had enjoyed an overnight visit with the Russians. They brought us news that teams were still busy climbing as far as they knew.

We walked on perhaps three miles further when we came to the camp of a group guided by Dawa, Mike's friend from Himalayan Rover Trek. A woman about my age from San Francisco had organized a Sierra Club expedition along lesser traveled back trails. They invited us to stay the night with them. What luxury! After the meager diet we'd been used to, we savored salmon cakes and custard dessert - all courtesy of the yaks who carried great bundles on their backs to supply every imaginable desire! In the evening, after a game of frisbee, we talked together in the dining tent.

Ginger, the leader, and I began to share thoughts. I told her of Mike's experience two years before, of his determination to overcome his handicap and of our amazing meeting in Kathmandu. Mike told of his fall when climbing with the same Russians who were on Everest, which was, perhaps, the cause of his susceptibility to cerebral edema.

I'd been at the American Alpine Club meeting at which slide

talks of both the Nanda Devi climb and the Joint Russian and American climbing expedition were given. I had seen a picture of Mike being carried down out of the mountain on a stretcher, his face glazed with unconsciousness. Then Willie Unsoeld had told his story of the last climb he and his daughter took together, how she had delighted in the intensity of being alive. She had commented with joy about feeling the crunch of the snow beneath her feet. He'd been so shaken by her death (she just didn't wake up the next day) that his story gripped the hearts of everyone listening.

Now, Ginger, reacting with the practical judgment of hindsight, voiced her feeling that Willie Unsoeld had been foolish in allowing his daughter to go on further up that mountain when she was showing signs of discomfort that she thought were reactions to the food. Ginger felt it was Unsoeld's sentimental attachment to the mountains that encouraged her to become a climber in the beginning.

This was a heavy consideration for me at this point. Here I was, accompanying Mike on this crazy hike into high altitude when he'd just recovered from the effects of a similar climb. Was I sentimental and foolish? Was it somehow my unconscious wish which drove Mike on? I had to examine deeply what thoughts I had.

I certainly had taken great vicarious pleasure in Mike's adventures through the years of his climbing in Alaska, Peru, British Columbia, as well as the Himalayas when he got the edema. I'd had a strange calm trust that he was doing what he loved most to do, that even though there was much danger involved, he was climbing with skilled people who also took that keen pleasure in the mountains. His friendships gained from sharing those experiences were life-long and spanned three continents. I felt I was supporting what he wanted to do rather than driving him to do it. I suspect that Unsoeld's daughter also had that same drive within herself. If it had not been there, all the ambition or dreams of Willie Unsoeld could not have budged her from the safer regions of existence.

We left the next morning after a sherpa served us hot tea in our tent! It's a luxury which people on organized treks indulge in. How easy it would be to sink into that comfort! We parted warmly feeling it had been a fine chance to sample a whole different way of travel.

Now we began the walk along the steep gorge of the Dudh Kosi where even bushes became sparse. The trail was only a narrow winding light brown ribbon on the edge of the stony river bank which dropped off 1,000 feet to the river below. On the other side, the barren, grassy slope of Towoche rose like a wall. It felt as if we were walking endlessly along its side. At one point, we looked up on the cliffs above to see wild sheep scampering across rocks as if dancing on air. Their graceful feet slipped into invisible footholds as they raced out of sight.

We'd had three days at the 12,000-foot level and were rising to 14,000 at Pheruche. Here we'd crossed to a trail winding over the rubble of a recent landslide to reach a sweeping plain of brown grasses and stubbly bushes. On both sides rose gritty mountainsides whose peaks were out of sight beyond massive shoulders. Pheruche seemed deserted. It was a cluster of gray stone houses with turf roofs. Curving stone walls surrounded private yards in amoeba shapes, full of brittle brown alpine grass. We had to stay two nights here, though Mike was tempted to move on because he felt so well. I persuaded him that a longer time would serve to maintain that well-being. Besides, I needed the rest. There was not much to do in Pheruche. It snowed the first night, and the morning light displayed a white world rather than barren brown. Against it, the grazing yaks stood out like dark wooly lumps across the plain. We slept, sat by the fire to keep warm, and explored a bit of the meadowlands around us.

When we left, the young woman who ran our tea house referred us to their mother, my age, who tended a shelter at Loboche, further up on our way.

Notes from my diary May 6.

Sherpa stew cooks over a hole in the mud stove with thin twigs poking partway into a small fire beneath. The woman pushes them in as they burn, adding pieces of yak dung to keep a red heat.

She and her children stay here in summer to graze the yaks, then go back to Katmandu for the cold winters.

We sit in the dim light coming from the door. There are no windows. Everything is in semi-darkness like Rembrandt's paintings. Warm yellow light strikes the faces and the gleaming brass pots on the shelves. The rest is shadow.

Snow falls softly on the roof with occasional sounds of thunder.

At night I get up to go to the bathroom. Bright nearly full moonlight glows on the silver meadows. Towoche stands like an enormous dark hump in the crystal clear black air.

I can't sleep on my stomach, my weight presses my lungs so I can't get enough air. Otherwise, I feel fine.

I was glad we had rested so long. When we set out again, I felt fresh, and the pack on my back felt lighter. A wonderful giddy light-headedness was with me.

Mike laughed at my free associations which seemed completely sensible to me at the time, but which must have been hilarious to him, since he sat down frequently to record my idiocies in his diary. He called the area between 14,000 and 16,000 feet the "whacko belt" since everything made me giggle with delight. I couldn't remember the name of the mountain (Towoche) that flanked our whole day's walk.

The enormous yaks were grazing on the infinitesimal blades of grass which seemed as incongruous as whales living off of plankton, but when I spoke of it, Mike assumed I'd gone a bit crazy. Perhaps I had, but the mumbling, however senseless, kept my feet stepping one ahead of the other, through that endless valley. It did come to an end at a steep moraine, the deposits of a glacier which, after pushing rock along from the crumbling mountain sides, had long since melted and dropped its load like a giant bulldozer backing away. Up this we wound past great granite boulders that had looked like gravel from a distance.

All sense of proportion left me here. Everything was on such a massive scale that my eyes tended to minimize things to fit my comprehension. Only our feet which stepped on endlessly could gauge the enormity accurately. After this point, I realized we would walk for several days with the same mountains walling our way, and they only grew more massive as we rose. Now we could catch sight of the snow-capped peaks that had been blocked out by the closer shoulders.

There was Ama Dablam rising behind us, the clear sun casting shadows on its great white glacier. Two dark buttresses stretched like jagged knives. Next to it was Kontega, different in shape, with its flat cap of snow which seemed to change form as we walked above it.

The dusty rose-colored trail wound like a long rope visible in the landscape of treeless rock for miles, continually rising and falling as if we were walking on dry waves. Each time we reached a crest, we could see how far we'd come and gaze into the barren distance at how much further we had to go. Dugla, at 15,000 feet, was a welcome rest. Two or three stone houses overlooking the white roaring Dudh Kosi appeared from the wasteland. We had to climb down and cross on a newly constructed bridge, and climb up again to the houses.

We stopped for tea, and incongruously, bought some crackers which had been left behind by a Japanese excursion. A pretty, rosy-cheeked young woman in a Tibetan dress served us with smiles. We ate inside the dark windowless house blackened by soot while outside the brilliant sun glinted off the peaks of Towoche. We could still see Ama Dablam stretching its white peaked cap into the blue sky.

More news of the Russians' progress came with an adventurous New Zealander who'd been to base camp just two days earlier and slept in one of the tents of a climber still on the mountain. "They're great people" he commented, a bit in surprise. Funny how our expectations are built up by the barriers of political attitudes, and how simply people straddle the gaps created when they meet. The Russians were still on the mountain but preparing to leave shortly.

By evening we'd be at Loboche, but that was at 16,000 feet. We would have to stay two nights there to ready ourselves for the last step at 17,000 feet before base camp. We couldn't go any faster. All the advice of Dawa, who helped us plan this trip, was to go slowly. But Mike's mind and heart were already at base camp. If he'd been alone, he'd have raced on, I'm sure.

He had to wait for my steady plodding feet. Women from the Ama Dablam climbing team raced by us on their way to congratulate the Russians. They danced past us and out of sight as we stepped slowly on. Mike admitted he was glad he was with me, because all the manliness in him would have challenged him to keep up with them. Physically he could have, but he was consciously forcing himself to keep my slower pace by walking behind me. This, in a way, egged me on to the fastest I could muster. But if he'd risen any faster up that slope, it would have been dangerous.

Already we'd received one warning. The New Zealander had news of an Australian expedition that had been climbing Chuoyo, in the Gokyo area, one of the side valleys. The doctor on that trip had developed cerebral edema, and before they could get him down to lower altitude had died at 12,000 feet. It was a sober encouragement to keep going slowly.

It was exactly two years ago, May 7th, that Mike had climbed Makalu and gotten the cerebral edema which caused him to be carried out on a stretcher for 100 miles of up and down terrain. We had been crossing the same type of swinging bridges that I'd seen in pictures of the sherpas crossing carrying the stretcher above their heads. These bridges undulated, swayed, and bounced unpredictably and I was again grateful for the devout way the sherpas had flags at both ends of each bridge, chanting for half an hour before braving that balancing act.

We walked on tundra with tiny purple flowers clustering along the stream which stretched and meandered through rocks.

From my diary

Gigantic snow peaks are all around us, though heavy clouds are coming in. Will we get to Loboche before the snow begins? Finally the stone houses and grazing yaks appear. We find the "Promised Land" Hotel and tea house, like all the others. A group of young people sitting by the stone wall ask "Ama? Choro?" as if they already expected us, but how? The woman at Pheruche had said her mother ran this hut.

This was the last place people usually stayed, and walked to base camp and back the same day. I was full of admiration for the vigorous Swiss couple we met who spoke nonchalantly of doing this.

I felt joyful for having made the climb so far - to be greeted by "Ama strong" comments, but after a dinner of boiled potatoes, I gratefully slipped, shivering, into my sleeping bag while snow flurries blew in the open door. In the night I went out shivering under the clear stars which were more brilliant than I've ever seen.

The holiness of these mountains pressed on me, glittering as the sharp brilliance of the rising moon burst with a radiant beam around the side of Nuptse. Silver light on blue white crystals in the cold air. As I stared at the planets, still in a line across the sky, I felt the meaning of purity. If it hadn't been so cold, I'd have stayed up all night staring.

We were at 17,000 feet. My hands were swollen slightly, my head ached when I coughed, but still no real sign of altitude discomfort appeared. I could understand Mike's feeling that we could press on tomorrow, no need to wait.

Nearly all night the "old" woman, who was my age, and nearly toothless, chanted her Buddha beads "Om, mani padme hum - Che!". She ended each incantation with the burst only to begin again.

In the morning, thank heavens, Mike agreed to spending one more night here, but suggested we walk down to Dugla, one thousand feet below, to get some pancakes. We'd heard of these fabulous creations from ecstatic hikers who cherished eggs. Most pancakes up this high were more like richer chapatis on which we could spread jam. What a wearying thought - to go down so far over what we'd gained so slowly. Yet it was a wise decision for Mike. It's a good way to acclimatize slowly. If it had been anyone else but Mike, I believe I'd just have let him go down alone. But some lingering mother instinct in me spurred my tired bones down with him.

Actually it was magnificent. We had climbed the day before in cloudy weather which covered Kontega, Toweche and Ama Dablam. Now in the fresh morning they gleamed white against the blue sky. Those unbelievable peaks which I would probably never set my eyes on again in my life etched their way into my memory. Going down we faced them, had the benefit of gravity, and all the joy of mountaineering helped me bounce along the stony path.

A crazy descent just for delicious pancakes, but worth the walk. In half an hour, we turned around and again ascended the rising waves — up over the pass where yak herders probably stayed under the shelter of some broken stone huts. There were mani stones and stupas and the magnificent view of Kontega, Ama Dablam and Towoche, fast going under the billowing white clouds.

Night at Loboche again with nearly full moon, frosting the barren tundra, the sparkling planets Jupiter, Saturn, Mars and Venus all in that fantastic line across the heavens. That stillness and the brilliant clarity of the stars in the pure black sky encompassed all eternity until I was nowhere. No wonder all the yogis and monks sought such clear spots to practice, unblemished by evidences of mankind, only the sharp cold that makes the mind crackle with awareness.

We were at 16,000 feet, aiming still higher for the 17,600 foot base camp, an increase in altitude enough to cause concern, despite our efforts at acclimatization. It was a scary thing to know that if anything should trigger the reactions of altitude sickness, it would not be possible to get Mike down quickly. We had risen steadily since Thangboche at 12,000 feet and taken 5 days.

I wondered if the woman who ran this hut felt any concern. She chanted incessantly on her beads. She was a very humorous woman, could speak only a few words of English, but was full of good natured laughter. There were four little yellow breasted towhees that popped in and out of the hut during the day like little friends pecking at invisible seeds and crumbs. We shared our delight in their flitting. In the morning, she left ahead of us striding across the tundra like a mountain goat, at home in this land of long distances.

We had to pass several placid-eyed yaks grazing in the open. I couldn't get over their similarity in some primordial way to the American buffalo. They had a great hump on their shoulders and their fur fell in wooly fringes. There was one poor shivering soul that had been recently shorn of all fur, probably to make one of the wonderful, if raspy blankets which the women wove by hand.

We passed the dark body of a yak that died that day on the trail just after we'd passed the day before. It was carefully draped with tarps to claim it for its meat. The Buddhists up here eat yak meat if they don't have to kill the beast. This great creature that had obviously carried loads up and down these rocky trails for years, had just laid down and died. Whenever we passed the laboring caravans I had taken comfort in the fact that they too heaved laboriously for breath as I was doing. This one was a reminder that even those accustomed to the terrain and thin air did not last forever.

We walked along a flat valley between ancient moraines, with snow cocks calling from hiding spots among the sparse clumps of grasses. Then we reached a giant boulder where names of sherpas and famous mountain climbers who had died on Mount Everest were carved in bold letters.

As we rose up the rock and crumbling gravel trail, I could actually feel the air getting thinner. I developed a theory that on the down slopes I could breathe better because I went faster and so could scoop up more oxygen. It felt as if I were literally breathing in the tiny life-giving particles like sending a net into the sea to gather swarms of little fish into one large collection. Odd how the mind perceives reality on different occasions. Despite the hard breathing, which could also be attributed to the continuously steep slope, I felt well and stepped along through the now rather drab surroundings. Clouds covered up the large mountains. Only the immediate rocky trail was visible.

At Gorakshep, a lonely stone hut with several orange plastic tarps drawn across for a roof, there was our friend, the woman who had tended the hut below. She'd walked ahead to open it since it was already closed for the season. The monsoons were expected momentarily. Thank heavens we had such a chance - a shelter from the snow, a chance for our usual fried potatoes dinner and chapati breakfast, and hot tea. Other people had already found this last outpost deserted and had to walk back to Loboche.

The woman spent her free time chanting her Buddha beads. She taught me how to chant, and showed me her little makeshift altar where a rice paper "thanka" picture of Guru Rinpoche sat before two tiny candles and a small glass of water, her daily offering. I gasshoed in respect before this, and she chuckled at my odd way. She showed me how she bowed to her altar, thumbs tucked into her cupped hands holding them to her forehead, throat and heart.

Strange, again, to see these gestures and be "taught" the way the old codgers demonstrated for me in Bali. But here we were, nearly at the top of the world in a place sparsely used by people. Again the similarity of the ways of devotion everywhere struck me. It created a bond that crossed our language barrier. She was exactly my age but her face was aged and weathered, and like so many women my age in this Khumbu region, she was without her two front teeth. Her mirthful sparkle, comradely slaps on my shoulder helped me feel I'd found a kindred spirit.

I shivered all night despite the heavy sleeping bag supplemented by a yak blanket she had given me. The cold helped me wake up to take a trip out to see the stars. All the houses were securely locked by great beams leaning against sliding doors, and in the pitch black of night it was always a great challenge to open them. I had to step over a young daughter who had come in later in the evening. She was curled up on the floor with just her jacket on. I stood for a while to make sure she was warm enough; there was no shivering. So I decided to keep the blanket under which I was shivering myself.

I came out into the night again - one of those precious nights of silence I'll keep with me all my life. The moon made the white boulders even more enormous and eerie. There was the little black dog who'd followed us all the way from Loboche curled in a tight ball and shivering as if that was its normal state. The terrain was a silky creamy tone of rocks, blue black metallic shadows and gleaming ice against a black sky. Then out of the quiet came the thundering as ice walls cracked and cascaded down the hill in silver clouds. Shivering drove me back to cuddle in my sleeping bag and finish the fervent prayers that on this last push upward Mike's good health would continue.

I woke to the "Om mani padme hum - Che", the vigorous chanting of my friend at dawn.

Many people had been to Loboche and said they thought it wasn't worth the effort to struggle up the glacier. Now looking back I'm so glad I did that last climb. It was like walking in a totally different world from any I'd ever seen.

We walked over what seemed to be gravel and huge hills and

valleys of loose rock. Yet underneath we would hear the deep hollow cracking sounds of ice. It was like a giant ice cube powdered in bread crumbs. The awareness of the ice came only rarely. We clambered down steep slopes and up another, following cairns which appeared on the horizon each time we thought we'd lost the trail. We were on the massive Khumbu Glacier which stretched from the foot of Everest cascading in the wonderful ice fall and in slow motion rippling along as a frozen river for miles.

As we progressed, huge torrents of rocks would break from the bare walls of Nuptse and slide thundering to the edge of the glacier. Then we came to what looked like a cemetery. Small shoots of ice two feet wide by five inches thick would press up as high as two feet in clusters like white tombstones. These were obviously ephemeral as some were already melting in the hot sun.

Then we came to the streams. They were wide, rushing, clear, freezing cold water - sometimes 15 feet across with occasional narrow places where one could jump from rock to rock and pass over eight-foot channels. Mike strode across these with the assurance of a mountain climber. I was really stumped. His joking at my hesitation gave me courage as I sometimes perused different passageways for five or ten minutes before crossing. Some rocks were so small I had to put one foot on one and leap across to the next. There wasn't space to poise two feet on one sure place before going on.

Mike still was in fine fettle, full of laughter, though we both found going slowly comfortable.

The gigantic, glassy "ice ships" or knife blades of ice pressing up through the rocks, sometimes 50 to 75 feet tall, made glistening blue walls to our left with jagged ridges cutting the blue sky. Then came the "mushrooms" - the narrow three-foot high-columns of ice supporting boulders sometimes four feet across. They dotted the rocky slopes in an incongruous fairyland of rock trees. These jutting ice blades were the only reminders of what lay beneath the buff colored, brilliantly shining rocks around us.

Each time we climbed another slope there was the next beyond.

But all around us towered the great snow and glacier covered walls of Nuptse and other mountains. We felt as if we were in a great cauldron standing on slowly churning ice which, if time speeded up a bit, would have swirled us in a violent turbulence. Because the time was so miniscule in movement we could "ride" the ripples and stay afloat. The crevasses gurgling underneath us kept this in our awareness.

Then Mike began to feel pain. His leg was swelling and he sensed a blood clot stopping circulation in his leg.

When we'd been at Thangboche Mike had met a doctor, one of the experts on altitude sickness who'd heard of Mike's surprising recovery. While talking to him, Mike had mentioned the anticoagulants he'd brought with him in case of an emergency. The doctor had commented that if Mike were to give himself a shot of anticoagulant, it might cause his brain to hemorrhage. So Mike had left all his medication back at Thangboche when we lightened our packs for the final climb.

So here we were, sitting on a hillock of stones and boulders just like all the others around us for as far as I could see. We were perhaps an hour away from base camp. I'd walked so slowly we were four hours from Gorakshep. If I left Mike alone to get help I probably couldn't find him again. Cairns were all over the place, I couldn't lift him, let alone cross all those streams I'd only dared to cross myself. There was nothing to do but use the healing chant Thangha Rinpoche had taught me, and pray with all the concentration we were capable of.

I put my hands on his leg, and looking up to the crystal mountaintops so clear against the brilliant blue sky, began to chant.

Never in my life have I offered such a concentrated prayer. That circle of mountains surrounding us placed us in the center of a gigantic bowl as if all thoughts echoed off the rocks and bent back, in some highly focused way. The mountain peaks themselves bore the names of Tibetan deities in recognition of their purity. As I chanted there, I knew what drew yogis like Milarepa to sit in the cold mountains where everything in existence is distilled in strength and silence. I called on the help of all holy men who had practiced here, on the spirit of the Power which shines in us all and in the whole universe, and chanted that chant.

Something shook through Mike and I took my hands off, fearful that something was wrong. "Keep it up", he said. Both of us felt the power of that moment as the sound of an ancient chant poured out into the stillness and his leg pulsated. Then Mike said he felt the circulation return to his leg and I stopped, full of intense gratitude and empty of everything else. We both just sat there in tears of thankfulness and awe, mute in the presence of such enormity.

All the way up the difficult ascent into that pure place I'd fussed and been amazed that I pressed on so persistently. Now it seemed so clear what brought the two of us together in the hub-bub of Kathmandu and why I'd managed to surmount weariness and sickness.

That moment brought us together nearly at the top of the world.

Chapter 49 - The Russians at Base Camp

The stop energized me. We got up and began to walk again along the rocky trail, crossed a small crevasse, and rising up the last slope caught sight of a cluster of green and yellow tents perched incongruously among the rocks - the Russian base camp. The scale of the mountains readjusted to those tiny man-made shelters. The enormous Kumbhu Ice Fall, white and cracking endlessly up to the snow capped lower shoulders of Nuptse. We'd made it.

There was a sign on a large rock in English stating the Russian Expedition of 1982 was camped here, "Please don't proceed beyond this point without authorization". Mike, elated, strode on ahead while I waited. He returned with a young man in a red windbreaker who invited us to the "Hospitality Tent" where we were offered hot tea and a dried yogurt spread on crackers. It tasted delicious.

The young man was the TASS News representative for Nepal and had come up from Lukla in four astonishing days without acclimatizing to report on occurrences as the successful climbers came off the mountain.

They'd not only managed to climb Mt. Everest by a new route in difficult weather, but they had gotten eleven men to the top, four of them in the dark, one without oxygen. They'd had no serious mishaps and they were jubilant.

Had we come any earlier, we'd have interrupted the concentration of the climb, but they were winding down, in a mood for celebrating.

Serge and Slava, the two friends with whom Mike climbed in Yosemite, were both away from camp. Slava was up on Mt. Everest at Camp 5 arranging the dismantling of the equipment there. Serge was up another slope demonstrating for photographers the techniques that they used while climbing. Another Nordic climber in shorts and one shirt (!) showed us to Slava's tent where we were invited to spend the night.

I was so grateful for the reprieve. I had wondered whether we were going to have to hike back to Gorakshep again that day.

While Mike visited with another Serge, whom he'd also met in Yosemite, I rested until a loud gong announced dinner. Everyone filed into a large round tent where makeshift tables ringed the outer edge of a circle. What a friendly bunch of happy men! They all smiled at us, though few could talk English. The food, cooked by sherpas in another tent, was delicious. There had been one person assigned to planning the food for the expedition who had been working for two years on the project. There were different types of food for each gradation of altitude, and on the high reaches of Everest, the men were eating cosmonaut food.

Without being hampered by the talk in another language, I watched the men around the tables. They looked much like any group of Americans whose features reflect the wide range of national heritage. The leader of the group, a man of great kindness and dignity, had a Slavic sharpness to his jaw, high forehead, clear blue eyes, as did a good number of the men. Then there were the more rounded faces with dark hair and eyes of so many sportsmen in the United States. They commented how Russian we looked.

After dinner a newsman, reputed to be the "Walter Cronkite" counterpart in Russia, and Serge sang Russian folk songs full of the sweet beguiling melodies of love and jaunty bouncy story telling rhythms. It was the first music I'd heard since Kathmandu. Here in the rocky wasteland by a glacier nearly at the top of the world, we were all celebrating together our common joy in being human, full of the sweetness of love, the buoyancy of laughter, and subject to sweeping sadness and tears.

It had been an extremely long day since we left Gorakshep, rose through the magic forest of ice "mushrooms', jumped across melting ice, and experienced the anxiety of Mike's coagulating blood, the concentration of the chant and the last climb to base camp. With those melodies dancing in our minds, Mike and I stumbled up the rocky trail to "our" tent. Mike slept soundly. I, on the other hand, full of the alertness to the effects of altitude, kept monitoring his breathing, trying to distinguish regular snoring from the gurgles we'd been warned against as signs of altitude sickness.

Next morning I got up to discover two inches of snow had smoothed out the sharp rocks into a brilliantly rolling landscape where it was hard to distinguish anything. I sat outside in my down jacket, mittens, and hat feeling the purity of colorlessness. There was only the occasional sound of the ice pouring down the mountains and the great cracklings as the glacier shifted. The prayer flags the sherpas erected on a clothesline flapped in the wind. The caw of the ever- present crows sailed out to greet the ice flow across the wide expanse.

The sky was pure blue, and the sharp line of the mountains nearly cracked the air with its keenness. I was empty. It looked as if Mike was going to be OK, though he'd not been able to mention his condition. Slava, the doctor, was still up on the mountain. I'd made it all the way with Mike. That was done. Now I just sat on that cold rock, not wishing to move or think, or even see. All was well. That was all.

Mike rose rested and joyful. After breakfast, the TASS newsman representative (whose name was also Serge) was planning to interview Mike for an article in a sports paper in Russia. He was intrigued with the idea that Mike had walked all the way up to greet his friends whom he'd not seen since he'd fallen while climbing with them in the Caucasus nearly seven years before. He'd been able to keep contact through letters, but the delight and drama of surprising them by congratulating them at the return from their successful climb had sparked his adventure. After a delicious breakfast of scrambled eggs brought up by someone returning from Namche, Mike and the two Serge's went off to have their interview.

Mike had told me he'd coughed up a clot of blood that morning, so hopefully it was out of his system.

I went back to the tent high on the mound above the drop-off to the crumbling boulders of ice. They cracked and heaved as the great ice river coming from the Kumbhu Ice Fall turned in a giant quarter-mile curve to slide slowly in one enormous pseudopod of ice inching down the wide valley.

I could sleep now. So here, in the midst of crystal beauty of the highest mountains on earth which would otherwise have riveted my complete attention, I went unseeing to sleep, the most restful sleep I'd had since Mike had started climbing. I slept all day. At lunch, I rose to eat, and cheerfully assured the surprised leader that I had no effect from the altitude, but was just tired. Those stretches of magnificent mountains which I could have gazed at just leaned their peaceful energy on me. I had perhaps a more healing sleep than in all my life.

While we were eating dinner that second evening, there were shouts outside, and the whole group of men went outside to greet the last four climbers who'd come back from the top of Everest.

As they climbed up the last slope of rocky ice to base camp from the glacier, the warm affectionate greeting of comrades' acclaim echoed out into that giant stillness. Four men emerged, were greeted with hugs and were ushered into the tent to share their experience as the reporters listened.

I was so conscious of the clarity of their eyes. I've seen this before with mountain climbers, but here were men who'd just been to the highest place on earth and their eyes shone like beautiful crystals. They didn't need to say a thing, and as I couldn't understand their words, that sparkle which shone from their eyes spoke everything. It's the same deep beam of light that comes from the eyes of people who've meditated for a long time. There seems to be a sifting out of all the extraneous elements of our existence by sharp focus on a single point. I had the feeling then that the people drawn to climb the highest peak touch that same deep place in themselves as those who meditate.

These men climbed in teams, men from the same area of Russia bound by friendship and common culture, but each man standing on that high peak must have experienced that centering alone. A little bit of what inspired the natives to call this peak by the name of a deity came down with those four men and still gleamed in their clear eyes.

The genuine affection Mike shared with both Serge and Slava leaped the years between their being together. During their first encounters, Mike couldn't talk much Russian. Now they were able to talk together, laugh and share experiences, since Mike had learned more of the language.

Mike was seven years older, no longer the "foolish boy" they teased him about. Serge and Slava were seven years more mature, more deeply affected by the restrictions of their political world. Even at this outpost in the wilderness there were restraints on speaking of freedom. Perhaps these mountaineers experienced more freedom than most Russians, but still there was a consciousness that what they did was for their nation as a whole. They chided Mike for speaking his thoughts so freely. Here were people so extremely like us with a whole different political view of life. And yet the affection of human mutual respect was drawing them together with us through a common meeting place, the mountains of the earth.

Americans are so tenaciously committed to individual freedom and the right to free speech. The Russians' way was that of interdependent cooperation where they felt the barriers of social control even in the mountains. The individual always was conscious of the group he belonged to.

It's so odd that thoughts of politics should reach this place at a time when political tensions were high. All the way up on our climb we had heard snatches of news about the Falkland Island dispute. We'd wondered, since the views of Russia and America were different on this matter, what would be our welcome when we came. Friendship overrode all matters but the love of mountaineering; the friendship of fellow climbers as we greeted each other. But the undercurrent of caution was ever in awareness.

We talked after dinner with the TASS news agent who felt

most American parents were so separated from their children that we must be an exception. To have a son want to share such a long trek with his mother was a big surprise for him. We talked of ways of child rearing where a parent could give a child the full respect and responsibility for his own life. I commented that the mothers of all these climbers must have been full of adventure in their hearts to be able to watch their sons go off into dangerous unknown areas and scale cliffs and glaciers. I felt a common bond with all mothers who let their children do what their spirits draw them to without surrounding them with anxiety for their safety. I think perhaps we survive more as psychological bolsters, supporters for that leap into untried circumstances.

The next day we were planning to leave after breakfast when Slava offered me a chance to take a shower. They had a tiny "moon module" where ice water was thankfully converted into warm water. I'd been washing with snow which was effective, but less luxurious, and I was delighted to take the first shower since we left twenty days before!

There were warm goodbyes. I was so glad to meet personally the men who'd helped save Mike's life when he fell in the Caucasus. He'd spoken so warmly of them ever since, and what a privilege to greet them after a successful climb up Mt. Everest! I have always been grateful to the circumstances that draw kindred sprits together all over the world.

We'd taken so long to leave that the sun was high and melting the snow, which made the rushing streams deeper on our return. I was so grateful that Mike was apparently well, that I negotiated the streams jumping from rock to rock with more confidence than on the upward stretch. Also I was well rested, which aided me. Even so, there was one place where I stood for five minutes mustering the courage to cross the slippery stones.

Always the way back seems shorter, and we sped down past the now melting "ice ships" that showed a granular consistency of soft ice, past the boulders heaved up on the ice stems, past the "tombstones", and reached Gorakshep in late afternoon.

There was our friend, the mother, chanting her beads in front of the shelter and greeting us with her broad toothless grin.

Chapter 50 - More Above 12,000 Feet

I had the feeling she'd been there chanting her "Om Mani Padme Hum - Che" ever since we left. Perhaps that's what brought us through safely! Anyway we had a comfortable night's sleep with no snow.

The next morning I was expecting we'd head directly down-hill to lower altitude, but Mike wanted to climb to Kalapitar's viewing spot where we could see the tip of the otherwise invisible Mt. Everest. That meant going to nearly 19,000 feet. "We'll only go a little way," he protested.

Feeling this was as crazy as the rest of the trip, I followed after the now striding Mike. He'd come to his full vigor, and it did look as if he could stride straight up Mt. Everest! I fell farther behind him on the steep slope. I couldn't keep up enough to remind him he was going too fast.

Finally I hopelessly called out, "Mike, what are you trying to do?"

The impatient energy which ignores all possible danger was in full swing. I felt nothing could stop it. Then somehow a fleeting bit of sense captured Mike's runaway enthusiasm, and he exerted the wisdom I'd seen he had from childhood. He was only 24 years old; he had the rest of his life to do this again. No need to push his luck foolishly.

We had luckily climbed high enough to see the dark pyramid of Everest peeking above snow capped shoulders of Nuptse in front of it. There it stood, the highest point in the world. Cold. Sharp. Still. I'd always thought this tallest peak was made of granite, from the molten rock of the inner core of the earth. Yet here it was, dark gray limestone with streaks of calcite dikes running across its face. It was evidence that this part of the earth was once under the ocean and was heaved up newborn, a mountain, in some cataclysmic way to heights probably greater than its present 29,000 feet.

Rocks had shaken from that summit to strew the Kumbhu Glacier with what looked like ash from our high spot. Still hiding behind the white icy peaks of Nuptse, this little black pyramid held up the sky. No wonder the sherpa people living near it felt its holiness. A time capsule of all earthly existence, a witness to the apparent changeability and solidity of matter. So we had seen Mt. Everest (Sargarmeths as the natives call it). We could go down.

I was deeply relieved, not only for myself, I could feel my heart pounding, and the efforts of this added altitude slowed my steps. But Mike had no apparent signs of any further effect of altitude. I'm sure there was that wonderful feeling of "why not go further?", the impetus behind all exploration and adventure, but it had been only two years since the cerebral edema. He'd shown himself he could go higher if he went slowly. Perhaps it was time to stop while all was well. So we turned and went back down. For Mike I'm sure he'll catch other close glimpses of that peak. For me, I suspect that will be the only time in my life I'll get so close, but it was worth all the effort.

I said goodbye and left our thanks with that wonderful woman for whom I'd developed a high regard. She had come all the way up to Gorakshep to open it for us, had stayed there while we were at base camp and now was going down again to Loboche.

The monsoons were near. Clouds hid the mountain peaks every afternoon. Trekking season was basically over till fall.

Serge and Slava had given us some of the canned hiking food used on the expedition. They had enigmatic Russian characters so it could be a surprise, but we were now free of our dependence on potatoes for a while. We went down a great deal faster than we came up.

Then Mike wanted to go up the next valley behind Nuptse.

I was getting tired, but this was probably my only time up here in my life, so why not? It was all lower than the 17,000-foot

Gorakshep. Perhaps there was no further danger. So we walked through Pheruche, now a totally deserted village. The houses were all locked up. It began to snow as we rose over a pass and descended into the next valley. We had no idea what lay in front of us. We came through the flurries to a cluster of stone houses though it looked as empty as Pheruche. Luckily someone came outside and waved us in.

We entered the dark open rectangle of a door. There was hardly any light. A woman and an eight year old girl were tending the fire. A very old man was bent over next to a small window chanting softly, and turning the pages of what I recognized from my trip to China as an old Sutra Book. It was good to have shelter. Mike and I cuddled, shivering in our sleeping bags while snow blew in the open door.

I watched as the young woman of the house prepared dinner. She'd boiled potatoes and after peeling them, took out a large slab of granite rock with parallel grooves in it. With a stick rounded on one side, flat on the other, she mashed the potatoes with a skillful flick of her wrist as she rolled them across the grooves. It looked easy, and miraculously the potatoes didn't stick. She left one small potato for her daughter to mash. She had the results I figured I would have had if I had tried it. The potatoes got all mashed and ground into uneven grains of the stone till they were hopelessly smeared. But the daughter was well occupied for a long time, was learning the skills of housekeeping she would need later.

The mother, who spoke only a few words of English, then rolled the smooth potatoes in the palm of her hand till she had one long "noodle" about a half inch thick which piled up on a plate into a mound like spaghetti. All this time mutton grease was melting in a deep brass pot over the fire. I was anticipating deep fried potatoes. But she poured this fat into some water to make a greasy soup and put the noodle in to cook like a dumpling. The flavor of the mutton grease was something I wasn't used to, but the meal was certainly an unusual way to fix potatoes. Mike called it "interesting".

The Swiss had introduced potatoes to the Nepalese only a hundred years ago as a good crop to grow in these high altitudes. They had apparently converted their diet to include mostly potatoes and onions with a minimum of spinach.

The small girl tried to teach me a game she played by tangling her fingers together and singing a song as she touched fingertips in different ways. We both laughed at my ineptness. She showed me her book on English with pictures of words and we practiced. She taught me the Nepali word and I taught her the English. Then Mike took over, and I slept.

All this time the old man chanted and turned the pages of his Sutra book. Mike was writing in his diary, and only a faint light penetrated the thickly falling snow through the still open door. I couldn't help thinking of Rembrandt's pictures where nearly everything is in lost in shadow.

The eaves of the house were hanging with long stalactites of black soot that looked like straight spider webs, dangling like two foot long "icicles" to which soot clung in quarter of an inch clusters. The cooking fire in the floor was the only heat, but everyone was dressed in several layers of clothes and no one seemed to notice the cold. As evening came, a woman with a baby dropped by to visit, and to feed the potato paste noodles to her child. They huddled near the fire enjoying each other.

The next day, I woke and looked out the window to see the side of a mountain rising into the sky all white with the new snow Everything was brilliant.

The little girl was gazing at me and sticking her tongue out at me. Mike reminded me that in Tibet this was a sign of respect. I hoped it was here!

We left our packs to walk up that magic Chukung Valley in the shining sun. The old man had moved his chair out to the front of the house, and continued to chant in the warmth of the sun.

This was another fantastic day of walking up to the great black wall of Lhotse along a trail flanked by azalea bushes not yet in bloom. Junipers spread up the sides of the valley, and we saw one woman collecting the branches for fuel since there were no trees here. The juniper branches burn hot and fast and seem excellent for cooking, but were being used more rapidly than they could grow again. This was gradually denuding the mountain sides. Blue flowers peeked through the melting snow along a stream bed. It was a beautiful day. I was glad to be wearing my sunglasses since the brilliance of the snow would have been blinding.

We were trudging up to 17,000 feet again and I remember going "into automatic" in an effort of endurance.

The rocks and stream sparkled with clarity and crispness. The long shoulder of the mountain beside us was etched with trails which appeared as tiny black lines along the white mass. They gave the true scale of the wall since they looked like tiny strings against the enormous white mass.

We were walking to Chukung, but I had given up ever seeing the sign of a house again in this gradually rising valley. It was so extremely different from the rocky barren glaciers on the other side. Here, if there had been a glacier once that carved the valley, it had melted into this green flat grassy rise dotted with azalea bushes just leafing out. The reddish junipers were scattered up the sides. This was closer to Shangri La, more habitable. Yet at the end there were only three stone houses, two of them tea rooms for trekking expeditions. We drank our tea and headed back down to sleep again in our friend's house.

That evening a woman carrying a huge roll of foam rubber, probably from the Russian camp, came in. Her eyes were swollen and she lay down to rest on the floor, obviously in pain. As we prepared to leave the next day, I could see her face all swollen around the eyes, and red with the pain of snow blindness. Her eyes watered continuously. She had not bothered to wear the goggles she wore around her neck.

While I walked I chanted quietly to myself for that woman's eyes, praying she could experience some ease. I think that chant was also for me, since I was beginning to feel very tired indeed.

The fact of Mike's eagerness, the beauty, and the realization that this would be my only time here, kept me going when I would probably otherwise have been willing to go back down.

But there was another valley yet to wander in.

We descended to the Dudh Kosi river again, watching the wide buttresses of Ama Dablam change, the giant lizard-like profile of Towoche shorten again into a more pyramid shape. We'd walked all this distance, but still the same mountains just showed other sides to us. There was a point where we could look over ranges below us to a set of peaks way off a hundred miles in the distance, to the first peaks we'd seen when we started our trek a month before.

Only a month! Yet in that time we'd settled into the way of walking, traveling with only a pack and being surrounded always by snow capped peaks. Any other view of life was out of conception. The night-time light was starlight. Time was infinitesimal. I'd lost all track of time. It would be easy to grow old here, and never even notice.

The snow had all melted, yet when we crossed the river on the now familiar swinging bridge, we found a young sherpa teenager lying face down, who when I touched him, turned to show us his eyes all puffed and draining with snow blindness. He too was wearing snow goggles around his neck!

Mike and I walked along a trail nearly a mile, above the Dudh Kosi to Pangboche where the famous Yeti Skull was kept in a monastery there. There was a trail leading off the main trail which I followed through a grove of tall cedar trees untouched by the people searching for firewood who had cut down every other tree for miles. The odor of cedars and their flaking bark brought a sudden discovery. I had seen cedar trees around almost every monastery I visited in China. 400-year-old cedars surround Eiheiji in Japan. Here in Nepal, where trees in general were nearly non-existent except on very steep slopes, I'd not seen a cedar tree before. But here was a whole forest. Was there some old tradition or was there a recognition of the nature of cedar trees that associated them with places of meditation? Fortunately for the political power of the lama in the monastery who had guardianship of the trees, they still existed.

We walked into a deserted cluster of buildings. The monastery, the usual stack of rectangles with bright red paint decorating the mud colored walls, was in the middle. As we got ready to walk on through, a woman appeared who spoke a little English. The Lama was not here, but we could see the Yeti skull for a few Rupees. She took us into the entrance of the monastery which had the same feelings of the old monasteries in China. There were frescoes all over the walls in the room outside the Buddha Hall. On one end was the gigantic figure I'd seen often - a ferocious dark bear-like figure grasping the world in clawed paws. All the realms of the universe were depicted; the world of the Titans, the human world, the world of hungry ghosts, and others making the six realms of the Buddhist religion which I'd seen depicted on the friezes of Borobudur in Indonesia. They were more graphically and dramatically presented in these Tibetan temples. The walls were covered with deities, some of whose faces I thought I recognized. One was Padma Sambava or Guru Rinpoche, founder of Tibetan Buddhism and a seasoned hermit who'd meditated for many years in the Himalayan mountains on the Tibet side.

Philip, the young monk at Namo Buddha, had explained these deities as aspects of ourselves both good and evil. There is this wonderful all inclusive acceptance of everything human, no brushing away of what might seem less desirable sides of ourselves, just awareness of our capacity for both, a feeling that everything is the same at the point of origination.

We entered the dark Buddha Hall where the same benches with cushions for sitting and chanting that I'd seen in monasteries in China, dating back to 500 AD, were lined up in the center of the room.

Our guide lighted some oil lamps so we could see into the corners where the sutra books, the sacred writings, were kept, and the altar where all the offerings of rice, water and fruit were piled.

While we gazed about in the semi-darkness, the woman casually dumped the water out of the offering bowls and tidied them up. Tomorrow new offerings would be presented in their early morning chanting time.

Then she prepared to take us out. We reminded her we'd come to see the famous Yeti skull. For some more rupees, she said, we could see it. Curiosity prompted the outlay of more rupees. Mike was getting irked at the way so many Lamas expected donations, but I saw the revenue here was not enormous since life depended on offerings from the surrounding natives who were themselves extremely poor as far as money was concerned.

She brought out a package wrapped in several shawls and finally revealed a rather strange skull with red hair on a shape that looked like a pointed helmet. Then showed a hand all mummified and not particularly long. That was it. We looked and then she wrapped it up again in all the layers of leather and cloth. Time for us to go and have tea.

We went upstairs in a building of stone like all the oblong houses in Namche. The yaks were kept underneath and steep stairs came out through a square hole in the floor above. The kitchen area was arranged around the stove on the floor, and the shelves along the walls showed the usual collection of gigantic brass pots. Tea took an interminable time, but we'd walked a good half day and I was glad to sit. She cooked us some chapatis and eggs for fewer rupees than the cost of seeing the Yeti skull.

As we were getting ready to leave she said the Lama was in, and we could see him. I wasn't sure I wanted to see the Lama. I had nothing to say. But as she led us around to another building I looked up the canyon above to see a deep set of caves. I wondered if perhaps Guru Rinpoche had sat here. We entered through the kitchen, and there was a young man sitting by the kitchen fire identical to the one in the room we'd been in before. He ushered us in to see the Lama. As we entered, I bowed as was the custom in Thailand, Burma, China and Japan. Mike stood, and watched, making me feel a bit silly.

Prescribed behavior seems fitting and expressive in any group. But seen from the view of a stranger, it appears incomprehensible, and perhaps weird. I was aware that these "in group" rituals apparently set people apart rather than join them together.

Then the Lama served us tea (the Tibetan salty tea I became used to at Namo Buddha.) The slim faced monk watched with amusement as Mike sipped it. Then he took the cups and offered us our more familiar tea. He brought some papers with him which he proceeded to fold in an intricate fashion, which he said was for our protection, and gave them to us. They were the rice paper pictures of Guru Rinpoche which I'd seen tacked to nearly every house we'd been in. It was an essential part of the house. People tacked them up on the thick supporting posts next to their wedding pictures from which they stared stiffly with the firm seriousness of early daguerreotypes .

We left the Lama and walked up the canyon to the caves following a stream bed. In all our walks up these steep valleys, we'd not seen anything like this rock formation. This was on the Towoche mountain we'd looked at as we'd walked from Thangboche up around into the valley of the Kumbhu Glacier, and which we'd seen all day as we walked up to Chukung. A gigantic crack slit the mountain with a stream falling in waterfalls down the shelves of rock. As we approached, a wonderful silence settled over us. There were several recesses where sitting was possible and I sat facing outward. There in front of me was the magnificent shape of Ama Dablam like a pointed Tibetan hat all crystal white, also a small brown village-sized stupa was silhouetted against the white mountain.

Mike also sat, and somehow we let an hour pass in the sweet stillness of this place. I wondered, as I did in China, whether it was the energy of men who practiced in these places that imbued them with such strong serenity, or whether the rock itself drew people who recognized its properties. Whatever it was, the deep stillness of those rocks, the power of silence rippled through us both. We then explored a bit, finding some seemingly inaccessible caves that were hung with prayer flags hanging wash day style. How they got up to put them there was a mystery, but they seemed to indicate a holy place.

Reluctantly, we moved on, having felt for a moment the impetus which prompts men to seek these retreats from the chaos of talk and interaction - to experience the stillness of no-time.

Chapter 51 - The Last Valley

We went single file along a narrow trail against the cliffs on the mountain. The drop-off to the river 2,000 feet below was so steep there was nothing to stop us if we lost our balance. We were the only ones on the trail, but even if we had met someone, it would have been hard to pass in places. We saw droppings of yaks, and as we stepped up steps and down precarious rocky ledges, we both prayed we'd not meet any of these enormous beasts. Then, at the only wide place in the trail so far, we confronted a man with five yaks. Thankfully the yaks chose to walk around us on the outside edge. Their gentle eyes greeted us as they passed. Their long sharp horns didn't look so gentle.

As we walked along this high trail, I spotted pink clusters of rhododendrons nestled in niches below us brightening up the brown rock and sparse green grass.

On a high ledge above us, dancing from rock to rock, were some wild sheep that didn't seem to know the difference between horizontal and vertical, or the strength of gravity either. Their secure and confident prancing was a reminder of how much our actions are guided by our states of mind. If they had hesitated they would have plummeted down the steep rock without a thing to stop them. I've often thought how easy it is to step along the edge of a two-by-four on flat land. But that same two-by-four, lifted up 1,000 feet, would present an awesome obstacle to strad-dle. Even the narrow log bridges had challenged my confidence.

We could look across the steep V-shaped canyon at the Thangboche Monastery buildings below us. They rested on the top of a pointed promontory at the foot of Ama Dablam. On both sides there was a steep drop-off to the river. We could look over nearly the whole distance we had walked along the Dudh Kosi, which sliced the high mountain ridges.

As late afternoon came, we walked on a schist-like rock that glistened rainbows in the slanted light. Some rocks were purple, others beautiful green-blue. When I picked them up and turned them, I realized the color was from the light catching them. I wanted to take one with me, but my pack was already all I could carry. So I walked on these shimmering rainbow rocks which still linger in my mind as one of the delights of my life.

It was late afternoon when we arrived at Phortse, a village situated on a point across from Thangboche. It overlooks the tributary of meltwater from the Gokyo glacier at the head of the third valley we wanted to walk. The terraced fields were brown from fresh plowing, rimmed by gray rock walls reminiscent of New England stone walls. Most of the stone houses were grouped towards the top of a flat slope that dropped off sharply to meet the river nearly a mile below. The sound of children's voices greeted us from a school yard way off below us as we rounded the curve that led to the village. They were playing ball, their tiny figures crossing the green field. There was no other sign of life, no smoke from cooking fires, no one outside.

The young man at the monastery had told us his house was at the far end of the village, but we couldn't distinguish it. We wandered along the trail seeing no sign for tearooms. I was tired. The altitude was 12,000 feet. What to do? I told Mike what I'd done in my travels each time I got to an apparent dead end. I sat down and waited. We walked to a point where I could see out to the beautiful white current of the river below while I sat under a grove of what seemed to be trees. When I came close, I saw the gigantic rhododendron buds on them. I sat down too tired to think.

Then out of one of the houses a cheerful young sherpa, perhaps in his thirties, invited us into his house. He cooked an excellent sherpa stew for us and chatted about the times he carried loads to the foot of Mt. Everest with his father when he was ten years old. He spoke of the travelers who'd become his friends and, because he couldn't write in English, asked us to write a letter for him to a friend who'd sent him a letter three years earlier. He told us that letters coming from Kathmandu by the porters were always opened and read by them. Everyone knew everyone else's business up here.

He showed us pictures of his parents' wedding. The stately couple stared solemnly from behind their stiffly ornate Tibetan costumes. The bride wore all kinds of beautiful turquoise, coral, and silver jewelry that reminded me of Navajo Indian jewelry made of exactly the same materials. These Kumbhu people looked a lot like Navajos as well. No matter where I am on the earth I am reminded of people in other parts of it.

The young sherpa explained that his name meant Tuesday. Nearly everyone was named for the day on which they were born. I had wondered why there were so many people with the same name.

The picture of the King and Queen of Nepal stared out seriously from one of the pillars holding up the roof. It was amazing how far these same pictures reached into the back country. I had a sudden vision of helicopters dropping pictures of the royal family all over the area. It was always of the same cold, lifeless dolls, staring straight ahead. I couldn't figure how this picture of the King and Queen could endear them in the hearts of the people. Up here they were far away from the political rule of anyone.

There was also the same series of white dots spread in rows and triangular clusters all along the gray wood rafters that we had seen in other houses. They had been put there by a lama during the Tibetan New Year. The local lama dips his thumb in white paint and prints these blessings on the wood to keep them safe until the following year.

There was the familiar rice paper picture of Guru Rinpoche, Padma Sambava, the founder of Tibetan Buddhism. He had come from Tibet in 700 AD, had vanquished all the local deities and unified them into one religion. There were stories of his miraculous encounters with the spirits of the area. He had meditated in several areas in the region.

I gratefully slept on the bench allotted me, thankful for my warm sleeping bag in the bitter cold.

In the morning we were served a wonderful mashed potato pancake with green onion slivers and chili peppers. We melted yak butter on them, spreading it around with a small piece torn off the pancake. No dishes to wash and a nourishing meal.

He told us that because of the monsoons the people up the Gokyo Valley had already left their houses. Everyone moves out of the higher regions where snow fills the valleys. He showed us how to get to the only village where people still remained. He knew that the bridge to the other side of the river had already been taken down. We said goodbye and set out. The way led steeply up along the back side of Towoche which we had walked around all the day before. I could look across the steep canyon and see an apparently level trail on the other side paralleling ours. But we were on this one, nothing to do but continue. Maybe it just looked less steep. My pack seemed to get heavier with each step.

Mike was alive with delight. He strode on ahead of me, waiting at points for me to catch up, collapse, and rest awhile. Again I was thankful for the sparks of beauty that energized me. At one point I turned a corner to surprise a beautiful bird with what appeared at first sight to be a rainbow-colored tail. It was as large as our magpie and the rest of his body was bright blue. At several spots along the way we found flocks of crows or ravens, some with red beaks and feet, startlingly handsome on the cracked gray rocks. Occasionally, a curious crow would follow us for several of the switchbacks that continually lengthened the trail by winding in and out along fresh water streams that cut smaller valleys into the larger one.

We watched a beautiful stupa on a high point in the trail come closer in an infinitesimal way as we walked. It marked the highest point before the trail took a downward slope. Its dome stood brown against the white peaks of Cho Oyu, the enormous mountain rising at the end of the valley. This was the mountain that had claimed the life of the Australian doctor before we got to Everest Base Camp. I was getting slower and slower as we walked. We sat at this stupa for nearly half an hour.

I marveled at the ingenuity of the lama who must have managed to inspire the people to collect so many rocks from the desolate landscape in order to build this stupa. It was at least ten feet high and fifteen feet across, made of rock and well shaped into a curved dome. It was constructed using the classical shapes. The square base symbolized earth. The cylinder symbolized air and heavens, the triangle, fire. Here at 12,000 feet, the spiritual side of mankind found expression in this beautiful stupa. Perhaps the higher you rise above the earth's pull toward the center, the stronger is the impetus for spiritual perception.

We continued to walk this endless, lifeless trail, going through a gray stone village with doors locked, no sign of life. As we neared the glacier that Mike wanted to climb on, I began to realize my reserves were gone. He could see a "village" of several houses at the foot of the glacier, but when we arrived, it, too, was closed for the monsoons. He had used another trail from the one our sherpa friend had indicated because I knew I couldn't make it up the steeper trail.

It was already evening. Then we spotted a yak hut, a tiny shelter just the size of a yak with an opening big enough to crawl through. I decided immediately I could go no further. It was clean, and big enough to lay our two sleeping bags down in. While it was still light, I roused what energy I had left to collect some broken twigs and chips lying along the loud rushing river, which must have been spilled from loads of wood collectors. I found enough to make a small fire. While Mike collected water, I found some yak dung by one house, and to my surprise it was indeed a neatly compacted nugget of fuel which had no odor. It was getting cold, and as the sun set, Mike hung a tarp across the opening to cut the whipping wind and I built the small fire. Luckily the smoke escaped through the chinks in the rock and we thawed out a bit.

Mike and I ate the last of the mysterious cans with enigmatic Russian labels that Serge had given us. This time it was ham and cheese; a delicious reward for the day's hard climb.

This whole valley had been so totally different from the other two.

The Kumbhu Glacier had been bordered by the snow capped peaks, and the rocky granular glacier had produced those odd ice "ships" and "mushrooms". The Chukung valley had been grassy with the brook winding through junipers and azaleas. This one was a steep sharp V along which we'd walked to a stony, barren flat land leading up to the edge of the glacier. On this, willow plants clustered around the stream. There was no sign of life. A dismal gray feeling pervaded everything – the rocks, the gray brown walls of Towoche, the gray moraine. Probably it was the reflection of my exhaustion. We slept deeply, except Mike kept expecting a yak to stick its horned head in and demand his shelter back.

Somewhat rested in the morning, I decided to stay along the side of the river, do my laundry and let Mike explore the glacier alone. I'd had dreams of him spinning off into space, slipping while jumping crevasses and other such horrors. However, I was too exhausted to go with him.

I warned him to be sensible and waved him good by with the hope that some frail element of self-preservation would protect him. I washed my slacks in the pure icy stream, spread them on the willow branches, and went to sleep.

Near the end of the day, Mike turned up just at the point when I was most anxious, and we began the walk back down the valley. He was jubilant with that time of wandering alone on the glacier. I was still exhausted. We were finally turning back. All the resources I'd had to carry myself forward seemed to have diluted into this thin air, and I was left with two solid feet to step on in an almost automatic weary way. Odd, how our body goes on working even when we don't think we can operate it.

We trudged back along the trail which had seemed all uphill the day before, but which was still oddly uphill going back. We'd come again to the deserted village and were sitting on a rock resting when way up the hill I saw the figure of a woman in the Tibetan long dress walking rapidly along the trail. We watched as she hurried and realized she was coming towards us. She asked if she could carry my pack. At that moment, if I'd had $1,000 I'd have given it to her. Ten rupees seemed ample to her.

Gratefully I transferred the weight which periodically changed from 90 pounds to the 25 pounds it actually was with the state of my exhaustion or exhilaration! What a difference. I could at last move my own body again and walked easily.

I must say I was actually proud of having carried that pack myself up these unbelievable heights, but was equally as grateful that there was a willing helper at this point.

We walked a comparatively short distance, perhaps for an hour, until we reached the shelter where we'd stopped the previous day to have tea. A capable young girl of perhaps fifteen and her six-year-old sister were tending three yaks in a walled-in yard. They had what appeared to be a barn stuffed full of grass and a small room with space for a fire on the floor and room to sleep. Here, over the open fire, the young woman boiled us some potatoes and tea using only one pot in which she cooked the food in succession. The younger sister squatted with incredible patience by the fire, which came to life whenever a new bunch of sticks or yak dung was needed. Then she would scamper outside and return with needed fuel.

The woman who had carried my pack left us and walked back to Phortse where she lived. She told our new hostess to guide us back.

I was so tired I couldn't think of moving. So we spent the night. A young newborn yak calf was let in with us for the night and we slept on the hard earth floor which felt like the most wonderful bed to my weary body.

In the early dawn I watched a cute little gray pika, a round-eared guinea-pig sized member of the rabbit family, scamper through a hole in the barn and steal twigs of grass and run out. When I got up to go outside, I saw him on the roof, munching his grass in a nervous way.

Up the valley in the clear light of morning the magic white mountain of Cho Oyu filled the end of the valley. The air was crisp like fall, and some wild flowers bobbed in the wind. What a different green feeling after yesterday's bleak gray desolation! It felt as if the world around me took the form of my feelings .

I watched the young woman milk the patient yaks and put the milk in a jar. She made a pack out of a shawl for the tiny six-year-old girl who was told to guide us to Phortse. This tiny child cheerfully bounded ahead of us along what felt like four miles, resting rather impatiently when I got tired. She played games in the dirt with a stick, sort of like tic-tac-toe, but I was too weary to learn them. What seemed uppermost in my mind was just moving my body.

I had been traveling for eight months before this trek, eating rice the last six months. I'd probably used up all the fuel stored in my body from the foods I was used to. Potatoes didn't quite do the trick to build up energy. I began to dream of the lasagna and fruit pies back in Kathmandu. I didn't know then that I was feeling the first symptoms of hepatitis.

Still, the impressive sight of the stupa on the highest point in the trail caught my heart, and the schist, glittering rainbows in the sunshine, helped each foot move forward.

Around one of the last deep bends into a subsidiary valley, we met the young sherpa friend we'd stayed with two nights before. He was clearing a tangle of branches from a garden where new sprouts were coming up. He said that they protected it from the sheep until the plants were big enough. This was the first place in all of Nepal where I'd seen domesticated sheep. Most of the people traded for wool across the Himalayas in Tibet, where the wide flat plains were suited to sheep. I thought again of their light footed wild relatives that danced on the cliffs, but perhaps they were too free to be domesticated.

The woman who carried my pack was this young man's sister. They'd heard (I wonder how?) that we didn't get to the last village and she'd come hoping to guide me to her house. When I could go no further than the barn with the yaks, she'd come home. We walked into the village following our six-year-old guide who turned us over to one of several women at the village fountain, where she had been washing berries they'd gathered from the trees. The fountain was surrounded by pink blossoming rhododendrons. These trees became thicker and more beautiful as we came into the village. They bordered the whole group of houses, rosy clumps tinted with pale green spring leaves against the darker green of their own leaves. It was a frothy wonderland. They had obviously been transplanted from other areas perhaps thirty years before.

This time the town that had been completely deserted when we came through before, was teeming with life. People were out working in garden plots, walking from one house to another, visiting at the "fountain", a place where water dripped from a long pipe in the same fashion as that at Thangboche. Perhaps Hillary had engineered these waterworks too.

I ate, and fell asleep quickly. The next morning we decided to take the direct way to Thangboche, which lay just across the canyon. It led steeply down to the river thousands of feet below, and then just as sharply up again the other side of the V-cut of the river, but it cut off a distance of about four miles. As we walked carefully along the stony, dusty trail with many switchbacks, we met some men carrying firewood in baskets using the head band across the crown of their heads. They were all panting from hauling the huge loads of wood, but they cheerfully greeted us, surprised we took the "hard" way.

It was so beautiful. We could look out across the steep trail we'd traveled the day before and in the other direction along the miles and miles of the endlessly long Kosi Valley. I had that familiar temptation to disbelieve that I'd actually traversed the impossible looking distances.

We ate our lunch, (some halvah left from the Russian supply), on a bridge over the torrents of cold water fresh from the melting Kumbhu Glacier we'd just walked on days before. I could see the knife-cutting power of the water sawing on the bright white granite rocks. Everything gives way in time to such a persistent onslaught, but it looked like a knife cutting butter. We'd come down a barren rocky bank, but the other side of the river was a forested woodland. The earth smelled of ferns and fungus. The trees, which were brightened by clumps of yellow rhododendrons, were pine and deciduous maples.

That transformation gave me the added energy to climb up the last steep slope to Thangboche. Another burst of beauty rewarded the effort. Pink rhododendrons scattered over the whole flat top of the mountain on which Thangboche was perched, a fantastic frosting on a cake with the white iced Ama Dablam rising high above.

We slept two nights here. Then we picked up the rest of the packs we'd left behind, books and other items. I was thankful we'd not carried them up to Mt. Everest. But the added weight now compounded my weariness. Down the trail was not difficult, but once the steep trail on the other side began, I was resting every ten minutes. Mike, in better shape than he'd been in years, loaded my pack on his. So we managed to get up that last overwhelming climb, and I could stagger on with my own pack again.

We somehow covered the fairly level trail to Namche. Forgetfulness comes at this point. I was so weary that just lifting my feet was my whole concentration. I do remember a beautiful grove of delicate lavender rhododendrons that arched above our path and dripped the sweet gentle rain into puddles that reflected the lavender above.

I was not aware that I was beginning to develop hepatitis. Perhaps if I had known, I would never have made it further. When we were in Namche three weeks before, the young three-year-old boy at the lodge we had stayed in had been extremely fussy and the parents had indulged him amazingly. I'd heard after we'd stayed two days that he'd been sick with hepatitis. Well, by then it was too late to do anything. I had let the time lapse between hepatitis shots because the clinic I had visited in Bangkok had been out of serum. Then I had forgotten about the need since I had been so healthy so far.

Now we came back to the same lodge and he was up and bouncing. While we waited for our meals to be cooked, he put his mother's apron over his head and danced a circular swaying dance that the lamas do on Mani Rimdhu, a festival which happens once a year at Thangboche. He had a talent for imitating a dance he'd seen only once the year before. It seemed impossible that he could remember.

The lamas speak of Tolkus. These are lamas who in very early life, usually three years old, show signs of remembering a past life in which they were an outstanding lama. The ten-year-old monk at Namo Buddha, who knew all the chants better than the old monks and led the chanting, was a Tolku. The Karmapa, the head of one sect of the Tibetan Buddhists on the same level as the Dalai Lama, had shown signs at three years old that he was the reborn Karmapa who had died several years before. They had tested him by showing him some seventy-five articles, only five of which belonged to the previous Karmapa. He'd successfully picked out these five articles, showing he was the reincarnated Karmapa.

This little clown, dancing before us full of the warmth of a great personality, seemed to make all this thinking possible to me. He breached the barriers of language, charmed and enchanted everyone who watched him. The skill and variety which he called on in his dance was far beyond the level of a three year old. There was an obvious danger here. He was like any normal three year old. He loved attention, and I could see it would take very great skill not to rear a talented "show off" with all the admiration he was getting. That's probably why all the training of these talented and knowledgeable Tolkus is so extremely strict. It evidently takes the discipline of this life to encourage humility.

Thank goodness Mike was busy learning what was being

done to reforest this now threadbare area. I slept while he went to a village meeting at Khumjung where they decided who was to benefit by a solar water heater which had been installed.

I felt as if I could sleep forever. But the monsoons were imminent. Already it rained regularly every afternoon. Soon the airplane at Lukla would not run, and the idea of walking out that arduous way we came was overwhelming. We left Namche three weeks after we'd arrived there. The tiny purple iris had all finished blooming. The mountains were lost in clouds. It was time to leave.

Usually it takes a day to walk to Lukla. I was so tired that I was not even embarrassed when we decided to stay the night after coming half way and finding a tiny tea house in a canyon near a wide rushing stream.

The surroundings, the snow peaks, deciduous trees, willows growing among granite boulders, looked like Colorado. After a short nap, I walked up the stream to soak my feet and wash some clothes in the icy water. The babble of that stream, the birds chirping nearby, replenished my exhausted body. The healing power of water refreshed me.

The pretty young woman who ran the tea house was pregnant and carried on her back a darling round-cheeked cherub girl whose laughter and sparkling eyes enchanted me. She couldn't speak English, but understood as I pointed to my "choro", Mike. In the evening, her young husband came up from a house below, and they visited around the fire in a separate room, while Mike and I rolled out sleeping bags and slept.

Next morning after paying for our lodging, I wanted to give a small gift to the baby, and asked the mother to purchase something she needed at Namche Bazaar. She took a necklace from around her neck of coral and turquoise and gave it to me. Obviously not many people came to stay overnight. I was touched. I'd left money, and I went away with a gift which I will keep. The safety pins I left with her seemed such a strange exchange.

We set out again for Lukla. As we walked we met a middle aged nun in the long maroon skirt and yellow blouse walking without a pack in the opposite direction. She was either British or American and I broke out into a delighted smile as we passed. She floated by in regal style not looking at me. She was followed, five or six feet behind, by an old man saying his prayer beads out loud. It was an odd procession.

At last we reached Lukla, the end of our walking. The airplanes were still running, to my relief, but there was a long waiting list. They had not run for several days because of the rain.

We found a dormitory where a hodgepodge of Western travelers stayed. There were several Swiss, a Danish couple, an Israeli girl, a young British man, and two Australians. Again we were in the world of modern conveniences. There was chocolate in the small store as well as canned fruit (canned in India): two items we'd dreamed of for weeks. But I was so weary, I just lay down on my shelf (with a foam mattress probably acquired from an expedition) and slept while others played cards and chatted.

We waited three days in that limbo between the quiet mountains and Kathmandu. Lukla was basically an air strip, a sloping meadow that dropped off sharply at the lip of the deep canyon of the Dudh Kosi river. Some "hotels" clustered around this and some houses had been made into dormitories. It was to me a rather colorless place.

Then I found the stream. Just beyond the houses there was a mountain stream. A short walk led to cascades, small pools and a waterfall dripping down moss and ferns. This was my retreat. I washed my clothes in a small pool in the same way I had watched a mother and her small son do their laundry. The young boy struggled with kneading and soaping his own socks, shirt and pants. They spread them on the warm granite rocks and waited while they dried. I too, spread my clothes on the rocks, propped my feet up and dozed in the warm sun. I found a little niche which few people frequented and lay listening to the sound of the water.

Finally there was room for us on a small plane carrying 12 passengers. In forty-five minutes we traversed the canyons and mountains we'd taken eleven days to walk and one day by bus. I could see the denuded mountains, the sandy tributaries, sparse planting on once fertile terraces. The high peaks were in the clouds of approaching monsoons. We arrived in hot Kathmandu on May 27th, after being away for five weeks and walking nearly 200 miles.

Chapter 52 - Kathmandu

Back in the jumble of honking horns and traffic on narrow streets, I could rest. We found a room in the Kathmandu Guest House, at a reasonable cost.

I slept for a week. Mike, too, was tired, but still exhilarated by seeing the Russians who had all arrived in Kathmandu two days after we did. There was a big celebration at the Russian Embassy to which he was invited, and also several parties among other travelers we had met on the trail. He had a delightful rendezvous with part of the Canadian climbing team that was preparing to climb Mt. Everest in the fall.

He was still making connections with people involved in alternative energy projects to help prevent any further denuding of the "forests" in the high country. Carried on by the impetus of these he lasted a week longer, then he too slept for a week.

There was a farewell breakfast to which I dragged myself, though I'd had no appetite since returning. We posed for one last goodbye picture. It was then that one of the girls commented while looking through the viewer of the camera that I looked yellow. They were all sure I had hepatitis. We bade goodbye and I returned to the hotel. There in the lobby was another young woman I'd gotten to know before I met Mike. She'd lived in Nepal for a year and a half. She took one look at me and suggested I go to a doctor whom she knew had worked with hepatitis patients successfully.

Knowing nothing else to do, I went. I was still under the impression that I could walk, and so set out through the streets, passing the vendors with bananas and roasting corn squatting along the curb, and the enormous cows that complacently lay in the middle of traffic on the streets while buses, carts, bicycles sped around them. I reached one of the smaller white stupas in the city, turned up a back street and plowed my way through a gang of children playing ball in a small courtyard.

Here was a tiny office where people were waiting to see the doctor. Westerners and Nepali men and women of all ages waited. The doctor sat with each on a bench side by side, questioning them astutely, prescribing, and examining them on a small table in the same room with a curtain drawn around it.

Dr. Bajra Bajracharia was a most compelling man. A warm concern emanated from him. It came my turn. I noticed as I passed over to the bench, a picture of Lumbini hanging on the wall and commented that I'd been there just a while before. He told me he was a Buddhist priest versed in the art of Ayurvedic medicine, an ancient practice from the early Hindu religion. He examined me, quickly questioned about my liver area and found it tender, saw my jaundiced skin and eyes, and in five minutes had started a messenger to obtain an herbal medicine for me. He agreed I had hepatitis. Very rapidly, as Indians speak, he ticked off all the foods I should not eat, which left only potatoes and rice, it seemed. I must rest, do nothing, and read the booklet he'd written on hepatitis and anemia. I had to drink his herbs two times a day before breakfast and dinner.

I returned in a rickshaw, since I was too exhausted to walk back the quarter of a mile distance to my guest house.

For another week I did nothing but rest and drink the herbs religiously, though they tasted much like the bitter drink my friend in Indonesia drank daily. I had no appetite. After all my dreams in the upper country of apple pies, lasagna, salads and hamburger, I had not the slightest inclination to drink or eat anything but water. For the first time in my healthy life I was beginning to experience the state of mind of a finicky eater. Food tasted unappealing and sometimes repelling. I will for the rest of my life bear the picture of unappealing food, and understand more completely how so many older people feel about food. It was in that way a gift for me to experience this.

In one week all the yellow cleared from my skin and the itching stopped. I had wondered if in our travels I'd picked up some invisible vermin, but apparently, when the liver doesn't work, the pores of the skin expel the wastes collected. That explained the yellow tint and the itching.

I was still weak and felt I'd found a good place to recuperate. After all, by this time it was June. I'd been traveling since September of the year before. Time for a rest.

Mike had found an opportunity to trek into the Pokhara area to help set up a windmill that a friend was constructing with UNICEF funds. He'd rested two weeks and was ready for another 200 mile hike!

I continued to lie in bed and read when I didn't sleep. Twice a week I slowly walked through the streets to the bank. I had wired for some money as soon as we had returned from our trek, but it was very slow to arrive. I'd forgotten a warning from some traveler who had said, "Don't try to get money in Nepal. It takes forever". Having gotten some money in Bangkok in four days, I felt sure it would work the same way here.

The first week after the money sent me didn't come, I accepted the stories of broken computers, time delay between East and West. The second week there seemed to be a "mistake" in the "code system". My money had been sent, but they needed the correct code to release it to me. They would wire to verify the correct number immediately. Finally, even my trusting nature began to realize something else was happening.

It was a curious time. I began to become acquainted with other travelers checking regularly about their money. Some had waited a month when they'd hoped to leave Kathmandu in a week. They had gotten into debt to the hotel proprietors and restaurants, and now couldn't leave until their money came. Though I had never done anything like it before, I made efforts to see the higher bank officials, and even to talk to the U.S. Embassy.

Apparently many people were aware of the situation. About three months before, thirty Americans had been in this same limbo waiting for money for over a month. The Embassy officials had talked to the Bank officers and things had improved for a while, but everything reverted to the old practice in six months.

I verified by telephone that my bank had sent the money the day my friend had deposited it. The officials at the Bank of Nepal were sure I couldn't do this since bank hours in the US coincided with night in Nepal when the public telephone center was closed. I suspected people staying in the better hotels used Visa Cards, American Express, or some experienced travel agent who knew how to by-pass the difficulty.

One day as I walked to the bank on my usual errand, I was congratulating myself on my "clear-headedness" in this situation.

Suddenly I heard a voice inside me say clearly, "Don't get proud!". It was a startling experience. But after all my meditation, traveling to Buddhist places, and opening my mind to Buddhist teachings, here I was, embroiled in the matters of the world of illusion - and falling into all the traps of this existence. I was down to nearly my last dollar. I'd not paid our hotel bill for which Mike had left money. That money paid for the food which I was beginning to eat. I was experiencing the feeling of helplessness and frustration of being in a strange land with no way to leave or exist, since money is independence to a traveler.

To some extent, the anxiety was alleviated by the fact that Mike could bail me out if my money never came, but I identified with other travelers in my situation who were not so lucky. I could cancel the request for the money, but it had been deposited in the Bank of Nepal account in New York. Who knew when I'd ever get it back? I'd gone to the bottom of my funds, so I could not afford to be without this amount. So I was worried.

Then when I managed to unsettle the officials, I must admit there was a flavor of pride at my persistence. I'd obviously learned nothing. It may have been good for me to pursue the problem which was causing inconvenience to some travelers and great difficulty to others, but there was no need to allow my own self-pride to get into the act.

I suddenly realized the meaning of a Japanese Zen poem: "The moonlight shines on the water and leaves no trace".

I was exuding traces of my self involvement everywhere! It was perhaps the most profound teaching in all my travels. I thanked whatever that voice was - my inner deepest self? - for that startling awareness.

I had been wondering if my "pilgrimage" had stopped, if I'd let myself be sidetracked by Mike and that wonderful trek. Yet I'd felt strongly the rightness of that climb on the high point on the glacier where I had chanted after he developed the blood clot. I'd learned through the extreme effort pulled out of me at points of "impossibility" that we can transcend our limits when we must. And now I was truly learning that "each step of the way is a practice place" as Kobun had told me when I set out. Nothing in our going or staying is not a place for practice.

So I simmered down to a less ego-involved checking on the possible arrival of my money.

During this period I contracted Giardia in my weakened state, the workings of a little organism on intestines which results in diarrhea and vomiting. I could eat nothing for a week and a half and became totally depleted. What weight I'd not lost before, I lost now, finding ankle bones and ribs my portly body had hidden for most of my life.

I entered another period of learning. I experienced the total despair that weakness brings on, the hopelessness of never getting better which was devastating to a healthy person like me. I was so sick for a week that I couldn't walk more than to the bathroom which was thankfully close by.

During the second week, I intentionally dragged myself to sit in the sun in the garden for an hour or so a day, moving back exhausted to sleep and read the rest of the time.

While I was resting, a charming girl from Israel came to visit me several times. I'd met her in Lukla when we were all waiting for a flight back to Kathmandu. She had been struggling with the conflict of duty which called her back to take her place in the Israeli Army in the war which had broken out in her absence. She had her own deep wish to expand her life by travel. I'd already been attracted to her tolerance of others, and her naturally peaceful way.

While mingling with other travelers in the garden of the guest house and sitting in the Western style restaurants, I met many diverse people, among them a young Arab living in Israel. While he was visiting me one day, my friend the Israeli girl walked in. I introduced them and he commented he too was from Israel. She had seen him before, and realized suddenly he was an Arab. She hesitated at the door, and then her own open nature overcame whatever prejudice she was wrestling with. "Well, if we can't talk together here where and when can we talk?"

She came in and sat down. Here the two began to talk together about their treks, about further travel, about the shoes they wore, like two young people anywhere. They had many common interests and as long as they steered clear of politics, they managed beautifully.

He was a great dreamer full of hope for the world; she too, could see the possibilities of peace for the fulfillment of everyone's lives. She had a free attitude about what was happening in Israel, not caught up by the history of suspicion and fear of centuries. He had a curious mind, eager to understand the thinking of others. But both where caught in the stiffness of nationalistic disputes. At least for an instant, even while the Arabs and Jews were shooting each other in Israel, a truce between these young people, joyfully alive in the world, existed in that room.

Chapter 53 - Recuperating in Nepal

As the weeks passed, I gained enough strength to take short walks around Kathmandu. I had, through a series of astounding coincidences, discovered a friend who was a student of Kobun's who was living here. We began sitting zazen together before she went off to work in the morning.

I would walk through the streets during the time before sunrise, which gave me a whole new view of life here. In Kathmandu, dawn was the time of offering. I was the only Westerner on the streets. Many Hindu women in beautiful saris were carrying brass water jugs on their heads and offerings of incense and flowers to the small open "temples" which were set back off the sidewalks. There was almost always a statue of a reclining bull, and nearby a carved stone stela depicting a deity. These were daily rubbed with a red paint until the form was obliterated by red.

Everywhere, the traffic of devotion filled the quiet streets. The stalls which were open during the day were all boarded up, and the dogs were finally clustered in twos or threes, sleeping after a good all-night's conscientious barking. Women and children were out with brooms of bound rice stalks sweeping all the debris of the day before.

The bustle around the fountains was beautiful. The colorful saris of the graceful women who went to wash and fill the water jugs, the scrambling small children who took turns rubbing ashes on the jars to shine them to a brilliant yellow, the tawny dogs milling around the fountain, lying on the multicolored bricks, was all a picture out of medieval times. Yet, I didn't photograph it. It was so personal and private. The laughter among the women was free of the restraint that occurred later in the day.

I passed the familiar Durbar Square where the fruit merchants were already setting up the pyramids of bright oranges. The green cabbages were being unpacked from two-wheeled carts and bicycles. Many times I wandered along side by side with one of the many placid cows that made sudden darts at delicious looking cucumbers or bunches of leafy lettuce, causing a flurry among the merchants who tried to divert the serene cow, who walked on munching her prize while the unfortunate merchant gazed at his pile of vegetables left in shambles. Some more experienced merchants pulled the outside leaves off their wares and stacked them in the street for the cows that passed, hoping they would leave the more precious commodities alone.

As I walked further towards the river, down the cobbled streets, I couldn't help noticing the ornately carved windows. They would have been the pride of the richest of men, with the carved designs of flowers, animals and lattices, but they seemed to belong to the poorer people of Kathmandu. They served as watch towers. I could usually see a face peeking from one or two of them. Once I looked up and saw the small bare bottom of an infant seated on the window sill. They also served as convenient "drains". I had to be careful to walk well in the center of the street because a sudden tossing of used wash water would jet out from above and splash on the street.

The river served for everything. It was lined with innumerable temples where swarms of people making daily offerings gathered. They always took time to bathe in the "tanks", which looked like empty swimming pools, where spurts of water came from sculptured fountains. Here in public, everyone modestly still dressed in underthings, washed themselves and their clothes which they spread out along the walls to dry. Then they'd proceed, clean and freshly dressed, to the temples. The sacred stones of the temple were shiny where hundreds of greasy hands had touched them daily.

There was one temple with a large pagoda roof right by a bridge over the river where a giant Bodhi Tree filled the whole square. People gathered under this huge trunk for shade all day, and sat on the snaking roots to talk together. In the branches on top of this were clusters of the most gigantic buzzards I've ever seen. Their wing span was nearly eight feet long when stretched. Their big black bodies perched on the branches like harpies in ancient mythology. These must have been the models for the carvings of harpies on the temples near Borobudor in Indonesia - the great black buzzard body with a human female head. Occasionally there was a great mass of flying chaos as these huge birds took off out of the trees and soared over to the garbage.

I soon became aware of why they clustered there. Across the river was the "grazing ground" for the forlorn water buffaloes marked for slaughter. One early morning in the crowd, I 'followed' - because I couldn't get around - a man with two large baskets on the ends of a pole he carried on his shoulder. In them were the cleaned bones of one of those scrawny black buffaloes waiting on the other side. The hoofs were sticking out at odd angles, the still bloody rib bones mingled with other unidentifiable anatomy. These were to be dumped in the heap of garbage on a small shoal in the river. I followed this abject carcass like some sad bereaved relative on the last march to the grave, paying tribute to those patient long-laboring beasts that seemed to fill the needs of people with everything they could provide, living or dead.

Downstream and upstream were people washing vegetables to get ready for market. Others were bathing children in these waters, and still others were defecating along semi-private paths right by the edge of the river.

As I crossed the bridge it was usually sunrise, and I'd pause to look up river to the Swayambhu temple high on a hill catching the first golden rays of dawn.

One morning, a blind beggar boy, full of smiles and talking to fellow beggars, burst into song while the sun rose. It was a combination of song and chant reminiscent of the melodious chants of Ajahn Jamnien in Thailand. The bustle of the bridge fell silent to listen to this burst of joy and devotion coming from that radiant face. Amid the debris of discarded onion greens, papers and dirt surrounding this boy who sat on a burlap bag, drumming on a drum a rhythm that should have awakened all the world, the incredible light of dawn broke fully - golden in its brilliance and pulsating to the melody and rhythm. The bridge itself became a temple for all of us standing there - people in business suits and rags, some with vegetables tied to bicycles, some carrying baskets on poles. We all listened and joined in that greeting to the sunrise together.

Then up past the dirty, disintegrating boarder dwellings, I walked carefully to avoid the remains of predawn defecation which were being swept away by women.

On the other side of the bridge were the more prosperous houses of those better off in the Kathmandu population. Here gardens full of roses flourished and the brick houses were equipped with running water, toilets and sewers. I walked into the serene garden of my friend to sit in silence with her for a period in the midst of a foreign land. I had not sat in meditation for awhile. When I began again, it was difficult to settle my mind, which was full of all the visual pictures I'd walked past only minutes before. But the silence of my friend pulled me into deeper silence than I'd found for a long time.

Walking back to my section of Kathmandu, I came across another time zone in the life of the city. Just outside the garden, a troop of excited boys were chasing after some dogs. Several large dogs were snapping viciously at a small terrified dog. It must have been like the cock fights they have in South America for those boys. They appeared out for blood. Already there were two seeping wounds on the retreating dog, but the boys, yelling, egged the tormentors on.

There was nothing I could do to prevent this. I just stopped, still feeling the silence of sitting, and watched, looking in the eyes of each boy who passed me. They raced on by, screaming as I just stood in quiet and watched. To my relief, they almost suddenly had enough and gave up the chase. The dogs, as if actually propelled by the intent of the boys, trotted off in different directions.

I went to see what happened to the fleeing dog, who had stopped to lick his wounds in relief that the chase was over for a while. So many times I've rushed to interfere in such scenes, to rescue the victim. This time, perhaps, the stillness from my sitting was catching even for those bloodthirsty boys, or maybe they caught the sadness in my eyes, I'll never know. At least I didn't have to witness a cruel bullying.

By now it was nearly eight in the morning and the sun was gleaming golden through the dusty haze of June. The water buffaloes were being herded into the river up stream for a bath. Their bony rib cages and stark hip bones poked through the tired old black skin which gleamed on their wet bodies emphasizing their gauntness. They'd outlived their use in plowing fields, and now with red stained horns or flanks, they waited their time to be slaughtered.

The buzzards were still perched on the Bodhi tree waiting the last pickings. But the swarms of the devoted bringing offerings had been exchanged for a swarm of beggars standing about near the temple square.

The doors of the shop stalls were open now, and the tiny ten by six rooms where the shopkeepers and their family slept by night were converted into stores selling brooms, tobacco, dried beans, colorful displays of clothes, hardware, the endless supply of plastic zoris which were everywhere and which everyone wore. Shoppers, Nepali shoppers, were picking out merchandise. It wasn't yet the time zone for the tourists who were still safe in their hotels eating breakfast or sleeping.

On the steps of a pyramid close to the Durbar Square, a pair of barbers had set up shop. Their old wizened faces intently fixed on the hair and beards of other ancient men who sat placidly amid the noisy bustle of calls and chatter in the street just six feet below them. I had chosen to be here in this chaos, not to set myself apart to photograph it, but the visual experience of this bazaar was an incredible impact of color, pattern, movement and interaction with sparkly eyes of people long used to a difficult pleasant life.

The part of town I walked in was near the palace of former kings of Nepal, where decorated elephants once waited to parade through the city with the golden throne of seven-headed serpents sheltering like a hood the King and Queen riding on the gigantic backs. It was now transformed into a bustling place of commerce intermingled around the decaying temples. The numerous brown sacred cows and herds of goats meandered in and out of the crowd of people who stepped over their droppings out of long accustomed habit. Everyone had baskets filled with the cabbage and cauliflower which I never saw in the restaurants. Oranges and bananas spread their colors among the greens of onions and celery, whites of garlic, and browns of the dried tea and beans.

Inside the dark stalls, sitting like Rembrandt figures in the shades of darkness, were old men and women with withered hands and toothless smiles, talking with customers and friends who sat on the "counter", a shelf about three feet off the ground that stretched across the tiny six foot wide stall. Big baskets of rice or many unidentifiable commodities made great circular designs behind the counter. All evidence that people slept along the sides of the streets was gone. A new day was in command.

The men all wore Nepali hats, woven with different colors to indicate the different tribes they came from. The Indian women were enormously fat. The Nepali and Tibetan women in their aprons of rainbow colors were thin.

I gained my strength daily, and spent much of my energy wandering. I rented a bicycle occasionally and took bumpy buses to the more distant sights. Before I went on the trek with Mike, in early April, the streets were very different. Before the rains, enormous heaps of garbage clogged the intersections, and when it rained it took a good deal of concentration not to slip on the slimy stones. Much was changed now.

It was almost as if everything was changed by several degrees. Great dumpsters were at convenient places and much of the accumulated junk had been hauled away. The streets were cleaner. In Tame, where many of the old brick buildings had been crumbling before I left, there were new many-storied hotels rising out of the old rubble.

Along streets where I had seen piles of bricks as if things had been cleaned from an earthquake, new efforts at building were apparent. The tiny temples were just visible under the rubble, enough to reveal a stela of a deity or a bull resting on his haunches. I had wondered how long the rubble had lain there from some earthquake that toppled all those heaps of bricks. There seemed to be an air of modernization everywhere.

Along with the reconstruction of the city, my health was improving and my strength was returning. Every evening for several weeks, I had sat in the back garden of the guest house and watched the black river of enormous bats streaming across the peach and salmon sunset, going out for their evening meal. It was an awesome sight, which lasted for twenty minutes, and I could have set my clock with their regularity. This had been my favorite evening habit. But suddenly one evening, I felt as if I too could have fluttered my black wings and ridden along with them. I realized it was time to move on.

My money became "miraculously" available after exactly one month.

We both began to get ready to go to India.

We discarded all extra clothing to the benefit of all the eager hotel people who would recycle it to their advantage. We said goodbye to all our new friends and rode to the airport in a taxi. I wondered if my pilgrimage was over.

We left Nepal flying high enough to look back at the snow-capped Himalayas where we'd put our feet so recently. The terraced mountains, the white-tipped peaks, shrank with distance, and I wondered if we had ever really been among those proud and joyful people on that long walk. They receded in the haze as rapidly as a dream slips from memory. As we flew out of touch with the ground, all the time I'd spent traveling seemed to implode and appear to be only an instant. Perhaps it had all been nothing but a dream.

Chapter 54 - Going Home

It was time to go home. I wondered if my pilgrimage was over.

I'd been a little afraid of India because of all the stories I'd heard from travelers. It seemed the very last test of strength, attention, judgment. There were reports of stolen backpacks, passports, money, while the unwary traveler rested a minute and placed something down for just a second. "You have to be eternally awake in India," someone told me.

So here I was still weak from hepatitis, still serene from the familiarity of two months in Kathmandu. Mike was tired from 400 miles of backpacking and a short stint with Giardia just before we left.

We'd spent three months together, which was the greatest gift of my whole trip. We'd been together as adult friends sharing dreams and adventures.

As in other places I had been, it was clear there was one rate for tourists and another rate for natives. And there was the same continual puzzle of poverty. One could give and give to "help" until one's own supply was exhausted, and still there was more demand and people's lives were not much better off. After two weeks of rest in a rather comfortable hill station and escape from the blasting heat of New Delhi, the desire to travel further in India diminished. Mike wanted badly to see the Taj Mahal, and so we decided to go straight to Agra by train.

The approach to the Taj Mahal is no different from all the temples I'd seen in Indonesia, Thailand, Burma. It was crowded with street vendors selling souvenirs (miniature marble Taj Mahals, tee-shirts, inlaid marble coasters), and rickshaw drivers. We walked, after paying admission, through a giant archway and caught our first view of this famous building...At the end was the white, silent Taj Mahal. The sky was turning pink, and grey clouds made a spectacular backdrop. Everyone had come to see the sunset. Even with all the people around the inside was exquisite.

I knew I had to come back again when there weren't any people around. The next morning at dawn, I set off on my own to find the Taj Mahal to watch the sunrise there. I was alone as I walked through the gate with only 5 people. Then the perfection of the building struck me.

I just stood at the gate looking down the long reflecting pool to the exquisite simple white domed octagon. There was only the dripping rain for sound and the subdued light of dawn on the cold stone. Every grain of the marble stood out in the wet making the color of the dome a silver gray. It was so perfect it hurt. So I just stood and gazed.

I allowed the perfection of that place to seep into me like the rain soaking into the grain of the marble. There must not be many spirits in the universe that can conceive of such simplicity and grace. The same nature that designed the Parthenon for Greece created this for India.

Mike was going directly on to Europe, and we waited in the Delhi Airport for his plane. Finally I found a flight out—the soonest one in two days.

I felt I should see something else in India. At a loss, I picked up a tourist map and just glanced at possible spots. Out of all the listed places, Gandhi's cremation place popped into my vision. Of course – that's where I'd go.

I walked up alone to the enclosed open space that once had been covered by the mourning people of India when Gandhi's body had turned into flames and ashes. It was incredibly still. In the center of the enormous circle of grass, with flowering trees creating small spots of shade, was a black flat polished marble slab. At the head of it a flame fluttered in the quiet air.....I felt again that sense that I was still on my pilgrimage, though I'd been a bit afraid I'd lost that spirit while I was sick in Nepal.

I had been reading Freedom At Midnight – the story of the

painful struggle at the time of India's obtaining independence, of the violence, and deep sadness in Gandhi in his last days. Was that what brought me, unplanned, to this spot to pay tribute to this man? My own confusion about what to do about the poverty I'd been traveling with ever since my trip began welled up again with gratitude and respect for this man who, without reservation devoted his life towards bringing the condition of the poor to the awareness of the privileged and rich.

I felt that same sense of heady awareness I'd felt elsewhere in temples, places of meditation or spots of pilgrimage. The energy of those who came to pay tribute seems to hover there afterward and mingle like a cloud with the memory of what they came to honor.

People began coming, families, and groups of tourists. My time alone was over. I went out to read the quote written on the entrance.

"I will give you a talisman. Whenever you are in doubt, or when the self becomes too much with you, try the following experiment.

Recall the face of the poorest and the most helpless man whom you have seen and ask yourself if the step you contemplate is going to be of any use to him. Will he be able to gain anything by it? Will it restore him to control over his own life and destiny? In other words, will it lead to Swaraj, or self rule, for the hungry and also spiritually starved millions of our countrymen? Then you will find your doubts and your self melting away."
— *Mahatma Gandhi*

Because of my illness and the heat, the end of my money and time, I didn't go to Varanesi and the place of Buddha's enlightenment. Perhaps it wasn't time for me yet – perhaps I'd never make it there but I had to go on.

Suddenly the weariness of the travel in crowded buses, the press of people who could never do what I was doing, could never rest or find comfort or enough food or even proper clothes, was too much for me. I felt the time of my travels coming to an end – and I'd not even seen Europe yet. It was the end of July. I'd been in Asia since October of the year before, nine months.

It's expensive to travel in Europe. I was out of money and out of time – and impatient to get home.

I flew to Paris and spent four days there. It was August, the time when Frenchmen flee the city and leave it to the tourists. Thank heaven I had the rudiments of French still with me, but I felt I was more in a foreign land than anywhere!

One last experience. I went to Notre Dame. Again a surprise for me. There was the square rectangular base representing the earthly life and the great round rose window depicting the heavenly existence. The same forms as the Buddhist Borobudur and the stupas used to depict the same concepts!

I went out and decided to climb the tower, remembering Victor Hugo's Quasimodo. Up past the ugly mysterious reptilian gargoyles, no more puzzling than the strange phantom creatures carved on temples in India and Thailand, I walked to the balconies overlooking Paris.

Then we climbed the cramped stairway to the bell tower where, from among all the 25 people there, I was selected to hit the great hanging bell. I was requested to strike out the tune "Frere Jacques" so everyone could sing along. This I did - but inside me I was Quasimodo swinging on the giant rope proclaiming sanctuary, I was the priest ringing the sadness of death, the toller of declarations of war, rebellion, peace and weddings. I stood there striking while that deep rolling brass sound thundered round us all vibrating with all the times it had sounded before in resonance drawing all time together.

Epilogue

Ellen originally prepared a typed copy of her account of her travels, intending to publish it, presumably relying on her diaries. My friend, Marie, borrowed the still unpublished manuscript from Ellen, felt it should be published, but lacked the expertise to do it alone. When I read it 5 years ago, I was also captivated by Ellen's unique way of experiencing the world, and felt that her story should be made available to a wider audience. At that time, publication did not seem possible. But after our intermittent work transferring it to the computer, collaboration in pruning where we could, and thorough editing during the past 2 years, we finally completed the text of the book.

Unfortunately, Ellen died in 2012, too soon to see it come to fruition.

Her son, Mike, with whom she shared the Himalayan trek, lives in Berkeley, as does the granddaughter to whom the book is dedicated.

CPSIA information can be obtained
at www.ICGtesting.com
Printed in the USA
FSOW01n0203160117
29593FS

9 781611 702217